More praise for *The Search For Meaning*

"Ski bums, cowboys, cooks and scientists all think about it, but they rarely talk about it. Their secret subject is the ultimate mystery: the meaning of life. But all of them open up in a collection of 100 inspiring, terrifying and sometimes downright hilarious profiles."

Detroit Free Press

"Remarkable . . . Gripping . . . Amazing . . . *The Search for Meaning* really does tell what Americans believe. It also tells who they are. Read it if you dare."

The Kansas City Star

"Fascinating . . . An impressive and inspiring collection . . . well worth reading for the insights it offers into human nature."

Sacramento Bee

"An inner history of contemporary American psyche—probing and valuable."

Norman Cousins

"Phillip Berman has given us an enlightening and accessible compilation full of the wisdom and foolishness of Americans."

Rabbi Harold Kushner

"A gripping large-souled book that pulls the reader along as if it were fiction . . . Monumental in scope, rich in anecdote."

Malcolm Muggeridge

The SEARCH for MEANING

Americans Talk About
What They Believe
And Why

Phillip L. Berman

BALLANTINE BOOKS · NEW YORK

AUTHOR'S NOTE

The names of some of those featured in this book have been changed.

The identifying characteristics of certain people mentioned in these interviews have been changed to protect them.

The interviews in this book were tape-recorded and transcribed in their entirety. While every effort was made to preserve the original language and content of these interviews, nearly all of them have been condensed and edited for clarity.

References to God were capitalized unless the interviewee requested otherwise.

When efforts to determine the source of a biblical quotation were unsuccessful, I turned to *The New Oxford Annotated Bible*, Revised Standard Version, Oxford University Press, 1977.

Copyright © 1990 by Phillip L. Berman

All rights reserved under International and Pan-American Copyright Conventions. Published in the United States by Ballantine Books, a division of Random House, Inc., New York, and simultaneously in Canada by Random House of Canada Limited, Toronto.

Library of Congress Catalog Card Number: 91-90652

ISBN 0-345-37777-X

Text design by Holly Johnson
Cover design by James R. Harris
Cover photo: Ben Simmons/The Stock Market

Manufactured in the United States of America

First paperback edition: January 1993

10 9 8 7 6 5 4 3 2 1

To Anne
for the deeper meaning she brings me

You know of the disease in Central Africa called sleeping sickness. . . . There also exists a sleeping sickness of the soul. Its most dangerous aspect is that one is unaware of its coming. That is why you have to be careful. As soon as you notice the slightest sign of indifference, the moment you become aware of the loss of a certain seriousness, of longing, of enthusiasm and zest, take it as a warning. You should realize that your soul suffers if you live superficially. People need times in which to concentrate, when they can search their inmost selves. It is tragic that most men have not achieved this feeling of self-awareness. And finally, when they hear the inner voice they do not want to listen anymore. They carry on as before so as not to be constantly reminded of what they have lost. But as for you, resolve to keep a quiet time both in your homes and here within these peaceful walls when the bells ring on Sundays. Then your souls can speak to you without being drowned out by the hustle and bustle of everyday life.

—Albert Schweitzer

Contents

x · CONTENTS

Acknowledgments

During the four years it took to create this book, I received huge doses of advice, assistance, support, and encouragement.

Working without the aid of grants or fellowships (save a small but nevertheless much appreciated gift from the Eulah Laucks Foundation), I relied heavily on the encouragement and financial support of my wife, Anne Gordon. Her unflagging faith in the worth of this project was a constant source of inspiration. She quelled my doubts, raised my hopes, and proved herself an invaluable critic in the long process of editing.

My editors at Ballantine Books—Michelle Russell and Lynn Rosen—deserve special thanks for the intelligence and care they lavished on this project. Michelle's three years of complete commitment improved the manuscript immeasurably, while Lynn did an Olympian job carrying the baton to the finish. I would also like to thank Elisabeth Saksteder for bringing me to Ballantine.

For collectively transcribing nearly two million words, Corda Conkey, Susan Smith, and Vicki McVey deserve much more than thanks. Each deftly pulled words from cassettes and provided me with brimming transcriptions from which I could prune to my heart's content. Bravo!

Several people were kind enough to read portions of this book and provide me with suggestions for its improvement. They were: Steve Bassett, Dr. Douglas Brooks, Dr. Walter Capps, Jim Carrier, Dr. David Eckel, Charles Egan, Steven Gilbar, Dr. R. C. Gordon-McCutchan, Chris Merrill, Jerry Ruhl, and Eric Swenson. Although I was unable to heed all the advice these insightful critics offered, I benefited enormously from their comments.

Upon returning to southern California in 1987 Steven Murray loaned me his rusty but trusty VW squareback. Thank you, Steve.

To my gracious hosts along the road, I tip my hat. Your warm beds, hot morning coffee, and cheerful smiles made my time away from home much easier to bear. In alphabetical order, I thank you all: William and Lynn Bagliebter (New York, New York), Mitch and Chris Berman (San Francisco, California), Dr. Douglas Brooks (Cambridge, Massachusetts), Jeff Canepa (Santa Cruz, California), Carlos Castro (Austin, Texas), Mark and Barbara Clinton (Little Rock, Arkansas), Linda Dubroof and Tom McGinnis (Washington, D.C.), David and Leslie Eckel (Boston, Massachusetts), Mike and Tammy Gordon (Salt Lake City, Utah), Dr. R. C. Gordon-McCutchan (Taos, New Mexico), Steve and Mary Ellen Hoetzer (Bismarck, North Dakota), the Keeling family (San Diego, California), Nina Little (Fort Worth, Texas), Fred Means and family (Shawnee, Oklahoma), Dr. Alfred and Anita Painter (Costa Mesa, California), Gregory Peterson (Minneapolis, Minnesota), Art and Barbara Storeide (Virginia Beach, Virginia), Barry Todd (Sacramento, California), Clarence and Joan Walters (Tulsa, Oklahoma).

Friends, acquaintances, and scores of total strangers led me to the people who appear in this book. Without their hunches and tips this book would not be. I toast you all: Winnie Ainslee, Saul Ash, Lola Blum, Sandy Bond, Douglas Booth, Erica Bouza, Rodney Bowers, Andrew Jackson Brent, David Bryson, Kathy Bullock, Jeff Canepa, Walter Capps, Jim Carrier, Rev. Forrest Church, James Coates, Dana Cooper, John Court, Harvey Cox, Virginia Culver, Rev. Karl Davis, Gloria Dickinson, Daryl Dorgan, Henry Dubroof, Jim East, Peter Eckel, Carl Edward Erickson, Rhonda Fears, Annie Flanders, Jim Flynn, Ben Franck, Denise Franklin, Jim Franklin, Paul Gaer, Brad Gooch, Max Green, Larry Hatteburg, Steve and Mary Ellen Hoetzer, Tony James, Steve Jess, Larry Johnson, Francey Jones, Drew Kampion, Mark Karnopis, Emily Keeling, Will Knofke, Ed Lamont, Trish Lenihan, Rev. Al Lewis, Don Low, Kit Lynch, David McMillan, John McConnell, Barrett McGurn, Patrick McMullen, Rev. William P. Mahedy, Clark Morfu, Mike Murphy, Robert Muse, Michael Musto, Rich Myers, Arlan Nelhaus, Judith Newman, Robert Oermann, Ted Quanrud, Tandy Rice, Francis Samsotha, Steven Savin, Lynn Scarlett, Fanny Schlomowitz, Governor George Sinner, Fred Smith, Homer Smith, Mrs. Billy Speed, Pam Strickland, Don Stull, Eric Swenson, Charles T. Tart, Barry Todd, Michael Toms, David Vann, Vu Duc Vong, Earl Weirich, Jim West, Cheryl Woodruff, James Yee, Michael York.

Not included in this book are about four hundred people I interviewed. To each of you I express my apologies and gratitude. The exigencies of my mission simply made it impossible for me to include you all.

The SEARCH for
MEANING

Introduction

☐

This is a book of stories by Americans from nearly every walk of life who told me about their lives and the meaning they found within them. Most of these accounts are highly personal and confessional by nature, and each addresses the ultimate question of philosophy and religion: How should I live my life?

Many of the men and women I met with concluded (although often with great reluctance) that we are less the arbiter of our own destiny than self-help gurus would have us believe. Our destinies, in other words, are as much the product of caprice as they are of planning. Just when we feel "in control" of our lives the universe has a nasty habit of unfolding in a most inscrutable manner, stepping in either to bless us or bedevil us with some significant and totally unexpected event. How we deal with these pivotal events, and the lessons we draw from them, invariably alters our beliefs—and therefore also our lives.

The pivotal event that altered my life and eventually led me to compile this book was my father's death of colon cancer during my senior year of high school in 1974. In the six-month period during which I watched my father wither I was forced to accept the reality of death. But at seventeen, ready to embark on a life of my own, an acceptance of death was hardly enough. I was convinced that a career decision would have to be postponed until I answered to my satisfaction the same question I posed to those who appear in this book.

Initially, I felt an unsettling urgency for answers. But as I worked my way through college, majoring in philosophy and comparative religions, urgency gradually gave way to a growing, quiet joy in the study of life's mysteries. By discarding the notion that I needed to be certain about what I believed, I decided that William James's advice to "steer safely between the opposite dangers of believing too little or of believing too much" was the best and most difficult advice to follow. It wasn't long before I realized that the meaning of life might well be found in the search for meaning itself.

Part of my own search took me to the Harvard Divinity School in 1980, where my classmates jokingly referred to me as "The Jew studying Buddhism at a Divinity School." My graduate studies in comparative religion were pleasurable enough, but the minutiae of academic research soon left me dry and empty. An activist by temperament, it wasn't long before I yearned to leave those dusty libraries and musty theologies behind. Aware that it was possible to get "all A's and flunk ordinary living," as Walker Percy so keenly put it, I impatiently awaited the day when I could do a bit of learning in the "real world." In the back of my mind a dream gestated that I might one day travel America and learn from the stories of, as Oklahoman Fred Means puts it here, "ordinary people like you and me who, by dint of sheer effort, awake in the morning and go to their work, and do it and come home to their families."

Some four years after completing my studies, on February 1, 1986, I would get my chance. Armed with a contract from my publisher, I packed my car with the essentials for a long journey, added a camera, a couple of tape recorders and dozens of blank cassettes, and headed out from my home in Santa Barbara, California. Over the next three-and-a-half years I would log more than 35,000 miles and visit twenty-two states, zigzagging across the country in an effort to chronicle the diversity of the American moral imagination.

In compiling these interviews I did not intend to provide a social-scientific study of American beliefs with a "4 percent margin for error." Instead I sought to produce a challenging, inspiring, and by turns alarming chronicle of the diversity of our moral and spiritual beliefs. In other words, I set out not so much to undertake a study, but to provide a tool for study. By presenting my readers with an opportunity to peer into the spirit of America, I hoped to provide them with an opportunity to peer into themselves.

Since this is a book about American moral and spiritual beliefs, it is, largely speaking, a book about American religion. Yet it does include a significant number of interviews with men and women who are decidedly nonreligious or even irreligious. I chose to include these not only because I know it is possible to live a meaningful life without a specific religious affiliation, but because I realize (as much, I'm afraid, from observing myself as others) that our professions of belief, however lofty, often exert little influence on our day-to-day lives. We have all met the churchgoing Christian who professes to love Jesus but is full of hate, just as we have met the warm and compassionate atheist. I therefore felt it important to present a sizable sampling of beliefs between the covers of this book, from the passionate, reverence-filled confessions of undoubting believers to the reserved, cautious deliveries of intellectual skeptics. You will even find a nihilist here, Los Angeles performance artist Elisha Shapiro, who believes "there isn't any significance to life, none whatsoever."

Still, whether we call ourselves nihilist or theist, mystic or hedonist, we each must contend with the primary task all theologians face, which is to determine how we ought to live on this tiny planet in this immense and incomprehensible universe. And while it is fashionable in our "postmodern world" to deride those who hope to ferret some meaning from the mystery of being human, no one can deny that mystery. We arrive here, after all, with few clues as to where we came from, and with even fewer clues as to where we are headed. Here on earth, between time and eternity, ours is but a fleeting little stopover, the only certainty before us being death. It therefore matters little whether we claim to be religious or nonreligious. What matters, I believe, is the extent to which we have reflected upon our lives and acted upon the fruits of those reflections with sincerity, commitment, and courage. The meaning of our lives will be found in our efforts to grow.

Somewhere along the way it occurred to me that this book, dealing with religious and philosophical issues as it does, focuses directly on what may be the last taboo of American life. For what you will find discussed within these pages is seldom a topic of conversation at the typical American dinner party, or even in intimate talks among friends, where people focus more often upon work, family problems, and the political and economic issues of the day. Discussions about personal moral and spiritual beliefs are seldom encouraged. And if you bring them up, you run the risk of offending your hosts.

This American aversion to spiritual and existential matters can be traced, in part, to our nineteenth-century heritage of pragmatism. We are, after all, a practical people. We want answers, not problems. And I think we realize, if perhaps only subconsciously, that when dealing with moral and spiritual matters we do deal with mysteries—the insolubility of which we find deeply discomforting. Much of what we call American life is about this discomfort, and the manifold ways we seek to deny it or avoid it. The problem is further magnified by the fact that our capital-driven society discourages reflection in order to encourage consumption. As Roger Walsh, a psychiatry professor I met in San Francisco, put it,

> . . . you can see that basically our lives are, to a large extent, spent in avoiding a confrontation with ourselves. And then you can begin to make sense of the enormous amount of our culture's daily activities, which attempt to distract us from ourselves, from deep reflection, from deep thinking,

from existential confrontation. There's a wonderful phrase by the philosopher Kierkegaard, "tranquilization by the trivial." And I think American culture has mastered that better than any culture in history, simply because we have the wealth and means to do so.

Our national antipathy to deep spiritual reflection can also be traced to the fact that our country was founded at a crucial turning point in history, when the Old World ideas of religion were forced to compete with the New World ideas of the Enlightenment and the scientific inquiry it encouraged. America is therefore unique among the countries of the developed world in that, as University of Chicago religion professor Martin Marty points out, we are "all-pervaded by religion," and yet, at the same time, a "secular, nonreligious culture." As such, we tend to remain sufficiently antireligious or "scientific" to do justice to our modern, pluralistic Enlightenment heritage. But we also tend to hold on to our belief in God (however infrequently we may think about the Diety) as an expression of fidelity to our Old World religious heritage. While some of us lean more toward the secular view, others lean more toward the religious. But the vast majority of us lie somewhere, uncomfortably, in between.

As an oral historian, dealing with this last taboo of American life proved trying. In seeking out a significant diversity of Americans, from the exotic to the ordinary, it was often difficult to find people willing to talk openly about their beliefs. Others simply found it hard to express themselves on the subject. This was especially so among the middle- to upper-middle-class Americans I encountered, young and old alike. Unless they were ardent churchgoers, or had been forced to undergo a painful experience which caused them to reflect on their lives, most thought very little about moral or spiritual matters. When religion did come up, more often than not it was a subject for jokes, not serious consideration. Religion was about Jimmy Swaggart, Jim and Tammy Bakker, or the hokum of faith-healing hucksters.

Midway through this journey I came to liken my job to that of a baseball batter: You head to the plate with your bat (tape recorder), choose your pitch, and swing—hoping for a hit. Typically I would drive into a town, bed down at a roadside hotel, and spend the first two days on the phone picking up tips and setting up interviews. I would call newspaper reporters, radio DJs, local scholars, politicians, various churches, etc., looking for leads to men and women who could talk about their beliefs in a compelling manner. During the evenings I prowled nearby coffee shops in search of additional leads. More often than not, these leads led to nothing.

Inevitably the best interviews, like that rare, out-of-the-park home run, took me by surprise. Take Thelma Black and Joanne Baker, who begin this book. I was passing through Wichita, Kansas, en route to Tulsa, and I decided to stop at a gas station to make a call to Larry Hatteburg, a local TV newscaster who traveled the state in search of colorful Kansans to interview. "Well," said Larry, "you might want to drive over and see the Bakers. They run this little kitchen over on the east side of town." It was early morning at the time and I was anxious to get to Tulsa, but I decided to give it a try. What I found was the Soul Sisters Café, and two of the wisest women I've ever met. Thelma had the human animal figured: "Sex and money has the nuthouses full. *(Laughs.)* That's what people go for—sex and money. That's the downfall of human nature."

Many times I headed for the plate with a tremendous sense of apprehension. I think now of the time I drove north on Highway 95 en route from New York City to Shelton, Connecticut, the home of James Farrands, Grand Wizard of the Knights of the Ku Klux Klan. When I arrived, his first words were these: "Are you here to interview me or kill me?" Apparently, he too was apprehensive. After a few uncomfortable minutes standing at the door, he escorted me inside and told me what he thought of Jews: "Ben Franklin, or who was it that said, 'Good God, if we take in the Jews in this country, we're in for it.'* He was makin' a big old statement on that. Don't take em' in because they're the parasites of the world. Everywhere they've gone there's been trouble. Not that I overly love him, but Adolf said it: 'If ever there was a dirty deed done, there was at least one Jew involved.' " Sitting there before this man, hearing him speak, I was surprised to find that I felt no anger toward him, nor any fear, but only sadness and pity, for what a burden it must be to live with the kind of sickness that spawns such hate. Tommy Wrenn, a black civil rights activist I would later meet in Birmingham, Alabama, captured my own thoughts precisely: "I used to be scared, really afraid of Bull Connor.** But when I discovered Bull was ill, my whole at-

---

* He is referring to a speech that was forged and maliciously ascribed to Franklin in 1934.

** T. Eugene (Bull) Connor, who served as Safety Commissioner of Birmingham, Alabama, during the early 1960s. A rabid segregationist, he unwittingly aided the civil rights movement by turning fire hoses and police dogs on Martin Luther King, Jr., and his defenseless marchers. When Dr. King was awarded the Nobel Peace Prize in 1964, Connor reacted as follows: "They're scraping the bottom of the barrel when they pick him. He's caused more strife and trouble in this country than anyone I can think of."

titude changed. I pitied Bull. And now when I see Bull, and all them little Bulls, I pity them, because I don't have that fear, and they do."

While there were moments of sadness on my journey, there were many more moments of joy and discovery—and also moments of comedy. I'll never forget the interview I lined up over the phone in Fort Worth, Texas, with a senile old cowgirl. I drove about thirty miles south of town through a vicious hailstorm to reach her home, but by the time I arrived at her door she forgot who I was. She then decided it would be prudent to sick her donkey on me. I turned, slipped in the mud, dropped my umbrella, and ran back to my car with her donkey in hot pursuit. When I hopped inside my car and dried off I made the mistake of deciding to rest there until the hail subsided. Ten minutes later I was standing in the rain beside a police car trying to explain that I was doing a book of interviews on American beliefs. "You're what, son?" I finally got out of there, but not before that sheriff and I laughed until it hurt.

My experiences at the New York Stock Exchange were equally comedic, although tainted, too, by a sense of failure and disappointment. Time and again I convinced Italian-suited Wall Street stock traders to sit down and talk with me, and time and again they told me they cared about the agonies of the downtrodden and would turn their efforts to a social service profession just as soon as they made enough money. "How much is enough?" I'd ask. Alexander Curry responded much as they all did: "I'd say that for an individual to live a fair, comfortable life-style you need $100,000 in interest income a year. But I don't think that would be enough for me probably." For many of them, it seemed, theirs was really the philosophy of get yours, get it now, get it quick. They just couldn't 'fess up to it. It would take a chance meeting with Tad Devlin, an honest young college student in Marin County, California, before I finally met a materialist who didn't believe in softening his convictions with false words of compassion. Tad's father had recently bought him a BMW sports car for a high school graduation present and I asked him what it represented:

It's status, to be totally honest with you—it's total status ... It represents to me power, you know. And it's gonna sound kinda corny, but one of my favorite movies is *Wall Street*, 'cause Gordon Gekko, this guy Michael Douglas plays, he's just the epitome of power ... what he controls is just so awesome ... I really enjoy my car, and all my little toys. I like that thing, 'The Man With The Most Toys Wins.' Yeah, I really do.

How Tad came to believe as he does would be difficult if not impossible to determine, for there were countless factors that contributed to the development of his credo. How he was reared, the influence of his peers, the ideas he acquired from his teachers, the type of religious indoctrination he received, the degree of success, luck, or lack of luck he had while weathering the challenges of youth—these all played a part. Yet amidst the uncertainty surrounding the process that shaped his beliefs there is one thing of which we can be certain: Tad's beliefs will change. What will cause them to change? How will they change? How much will they change? The answers to these questions are equally impossible to predict. Perhaps Tad will become the financial wizard he now longs to be. Or perhaps he will roll out of bed one day, sense an emptiness within himself, and sign up for a course in Hindu meditation at a Bay Area ashram. God only knows.

This book reflects my fascination with the unpredictability and malleability of people, and with the ways their beliefs are shaped or confirmed by the countless influences in their lives. Of all the many questions I posed to elicit detailed replies from those I met, none yielded more interesting and surprising responses than this one: What were the pivotal experiences in your life that significantly changed or confirmed your beliefs? The answers were wide ranging: Drug experiences, war experiences, out-of-body experiences, books read, people met, therapy undergone, loved ones lost, imprisonment—these were just a few of the events that dramatically altered or confirmed the beliefs of those featured in these pages.

For many here, the transformative experience was rather quiet and undramatic. Unitarian pastor Forrester Church, for example, had his perspective altered when his father, the late Senator Frank Church, was elected to the U.S. Senate. Upon his arrival in Washington, Senator Church was given Thomas Jefferson's personal Bible. Jefferson, during his term of office, took the gospels and excerpted from them those passages he found most worthy and most compelling and cut out the rest. It was the first Bible the young Forrester would actually sit down to read, and he found himself "gripped by the human Jesus. My father said to me after I read that Bible that for him religion could best be summed up in Jefferson's own words, that 'It is in our lives and not our words that our religion must be read.' In other words, deeds, not creeds."

Others here would have their beliefs transformed by painful and inescapable experiences; experiences which forced them to contend with the problem of evil, first formulated in the West by the Roman philosopher Anicus Boethius around 500 B.C.E.: "If there is a God, whence proceed so many evils? If there is no God, whence cometh any good?" I think now, for example, of Elizabeth Jaranyi, a Hungarian-born Jew who spent time in the Auschwitz Concentration Camp during World War II: "In Auschwitz, everybody pray, everybody pray and pray and pray. I lost my husband. I lost my child. I saw my sister shot to death before my eyes. I was beaten. And when I saw the crematorium, I didn't pray anymore. I was so angry! And when I came home, I'm absolutely not a God-believer again."

Kathryn Morton, a Virginia Beach housewife who spent the first thirty-seven years of her life as a self-described "secular nothingist," dealt with the problem of evil quite differently. Shortly before her thirty-eighth birthday she lost her father to an incurable illness. A few months after that, her eight-year-old son, Kenny, contracted the terminal disease lupus, which caused her to ask some questions: Why this to my son? Why this to a good person like me? What is the meaning of this? After several meetings with a local rabbi, she decided to convert to Judaism, because she was attracted to its "moral beauty . . . that it is a human responsibility to finish creation."

Before departing Santa Barbara I realized that millions of Americans were uncomfortable with the religious fundamentalism of the right and the secular humanism of the left (the two poles between which most of us swing), but I was anxious to gain insights into the many alternative beliefs popular in America.

For many I met, and particularly those between the ages of seventeen and twenty-five (many of whose moral instruction appeared to have been left to the daily prattlings of their TV sets), the buzz words were *fun, sex, money*, and *drugs*. For ex–Aspen ski instructor Scott Salinski it was about "living to ski, basically," whereas for Huntington Beach high school student Debbie Richards it was about "partying, laying out on the beach. Drink till you drop and then quit—that's my philosophy." In New York City, James St. James moved along a similar path: "I'd like to be a heavy metal star. I think as soon as my chest hair grows in I want to start pursuing that a little more . . . I want to do that for a couple of years because the life-style really appeals to me. Just the traveling, the being on stage, the dressing up in funny outfits, the groupies, the drugs—just the whole mad whirl."

One of the most fascinating and burgeoning areas of American spirituality is the New Age movement. Yet the central concept at the heart of this movement—that inner exploration can unlock the secrets of the spiritual universe and produce a positive and radical transformation of consciousness—is anything but new. New Age ideas have a long-standing tradition in America and can be traced, in part, to the transcendental philosophy of Ralph Waldo Emerson and the healing practices of Mary Baker Eddy. Yet, unlike most religious movements, the New Age is considerably more difficult to grasp in that the religious ideas and practices of the movement have been drawn from a wide variety of sources, including Eastern religions, American transcendentalism and pragmatism, science, transpersonal psychology, and occult practices. The movement contains an incredible variety of perspectives, from those who profess a this-worldly, "positive thought" approach to spiritual well-being, to those who opt for a thoroughly other-worldly approach.

Jeanne Lemenowsky, a sixty-five-year-old health and fitness counselor I met in Saint Paul, Minnesota, respresented the milder form of New Age commitment. "I guess the bottom line for me—and some people think it's real harsh—is that your life is whatever you think it is. If you think your life is a mess, it's a mess. If you think that there's opportunity all around you, untapped, there is."

San Diegan Ruth Norman (a.k.a. Uriel) represented the extreme side of New Age commitment. At eighty-seven, she had "channeled" more than 129 books from the "minds of the higher worlds," including messages of wisdom from, among others, Gus Grissom, John F. Kennedy, Hirohito, Will Rogers, and Mohandas K. Gandhi. Uriel told me that her time here on Earth was really a sort of exile; her true home was actually a planet called Aries. "I'm an alien, if you want to call it that . . . I wouldn't be proud to be an Earthian. Heck no . . . It's a very, very low vibration planet. Believe me, I'll be glad when I can step off of it." The bad karma she had generated in past lives had forced Uriel to come to Earth, and it was her ardent hope that the good karma she was accumulating now would eventually enable her to return to Aries.

"Lazaris," an other-worldly spirit who channeled his beliefs into my tape recorder via New Age intermediary Jack Pursel, was considerably more earthbound than Uriel. His philosophy of life was a blend of the positive thought of Norman Vincent Peale with the capitalist gusto of Donald Trump. He answered my questions both decisively and succinctly: "Why are you here? What's the meaning of it all, what's the purpose of it all? All those rather lofty questions have an answer, and the answer is that you're here to learn to have fun, and to learn to consciously create success."

While "Lazaris" was back in Marin County, California, making big money marketing his beliefs, Peggy Hutchison was down in Tucson, Arizona, taking heat for acting upon hers. On January 14, 1985, she and several fellow sanctuary workers were indicted for recruiting, smuggling, transporting, and harboring illegal aliens. A lay worker in the United Methodist Church, she reflected on her faith and determined that she must do something to save the lives of South American refugees. "My faith said that you have to do unto others as you would want them to do unto you. You know, you do not mistreat foreigners who are living in your land. Treat them as you would a fellow Israelite . . ."

Peggy had the courage of her convictions. John Coleman, the editor-in-chief of *Soldier of Fortune* magazine, did too. After pulling two tours of duty in Vietnam, he returned to the United States disgusted with the way we "sold out the 57,000 odd men and women who died in Vietnam and the thousands who were still listed as POW/MIA." A deep believer in democracy, he sold off his possessions and flew to Salisbury, Rhodesia (now Harare, Zimbabwe), and presented himself to an army recruiter. He then fought there for three and a half years in a "war between those who wanted a democracy and those who wanted a Marxist-allied, communist totalitarian regime." What compelled him to put his life on the line for a foreign government?:

> . . . you need to go out and become involved in some shape, form, or fashion with something you believe in. To me, getting involved meant fighting—and it still does. It still means being prepared to make what is the ultimate sacrifice, which is sacrificing your life for something in which you believe . . . When you're willing to go put your life on the line, then you can come back and say, "I've been to the edge and I've looked across and I've seen what I think is important. I've gleaned out all the unnecessary bullshit." When you come down to life-and-death scenarios, everything else really becomes placid and facile.

The Angolan ZIPRA guerilla fighter who shot him five times ("I took two in my arm, one in the neck, two in the chest") with a Soviet Kalashnikov assault rifle may well have agreed with John "that you need to go out and become involved in some shape, form, or fashion with something you believe in," but he obviously couldn't agree with him on the virtues of capitalist democracy. He was fighting for what he felt were true beliefs, for the communistic form of government he believed in, and so these two men with the courage of their convictions met on the battlefield of ideas long before they met on the battlefield of war. What divided these two men was a difference of belief in the things regarded as worth being killed for.

The beauty and sadness of this subject of personal beliefs lies in the fact that we need them so desperately to lend significance to our lives and to make sense of the many tragedies we observe and experience. On the bright side, we could ask what would the world be like today if Jesus, Buddha, Lao-Tzu, Moses, or the likes of Mother Teresa (to name just a few) had chosen not to act on their beliefs? Surely our world would be more impoverished. On the dark side, history gives ample testimony to the fact that our profound need to believe has caused, and will no doubt continue to cause, much of the pain, conflict, and anguish in our world. The actions of our contemporaries in Northern Ireland and the Middle East, while appalling, are nothing more than the ongoing historical expression of intolerance in action.

Focusing on this dark side of belief, many have argued that the most effective way to promote peace is to encourage wide-scale doubt and disbelief, operating under the assumption, as Peter Ustinov once put it, that "we are united by our doubts and divided by our convictions." True enough. Yet it is clear to me from my studies and travels that the human need to believe is far too strong to abolish. The resurgence of religion in the Soviet Union confirms this.

What may be needed more than doubt or a healthy skepticism is the capacity to temper our convictions (and the pride they promote) with the recognition that our beliefs will be rejected by others. Meaningful living in the modern world therefore requires, more than ever before, the ability to lead a dual life. In our private lives we must live and act as though our beliefs and values are the most important thing in the world. In our public lives we must respect the right of others to believe as they choose and carry our commitment to tolerance as far as possible before we attempt to limit or halt the activities of those who, by acting on their own deep convictions, bring hardship or harm to others. A commitment to tolerance requires only that we be "intolerant of intolerance." To outspokenly condemn the views of Jews, neo-Nazis, pro-choice advocates or Christian fundamentalists is one thing; to bring harm to them or even kill them for their views is a far different thing. A belief in tolerance therefore requires the courage to defend the rights of the weak against the bigotries of the strong.

Wherever tolerance thrives, religious and moral diversity thrive. Nowhere is this more evident than in the United States, where the number of registered religious denominations has nearly doubled in the past twenty years.* Together with this explosive growth of new

---

* According to Professor J. Gordon Melton, director of the Institute for the Study of American Religion, there were approximately 800 religious denominations in the United States in 1965. He estimates there are at least 1,600 today.

religious movements in America, tolerance has come under increasing attack by those who claim that many of our national moral ailments (drugs, alcohol addictions, the crisis in education, etc.) are a direct result of the moral diversity and permissiveness tolerance allows for. By undermining our ability to forge a national moral consensus around commonly held notions of right and wrong, tolerance, they argue, only contributes to our national "moral malaise." What we need are a few good absolutes, a little more intolerance, a bit more censorship. Perhaps. And yet one wonders, as did Juvenal, "Who shall stand guard to the guards themselves?"

As for myself, I am convinced that we will never be able to arrive at a national moral consensus. And I am glad for that, because many of the nearly five hundred men and women I met throughout my travels challenged my views, my dogmas, and my pride, and the more I disagreed with them, the more they had to teach me. I view the tremendous and rapidly growing diversity of American spirituality as a wondrous blessing, as well as a sign that our democracy is working, and, indeed, thriving. If we value competition in the marketplace of goods and services, why should we not value it in the marketplace of spiritual ideas? If we can "vote with our feet" in politics, why shouldn't we also vote with our feet in religion?

This book does not aim to tell you what you should or should not believe. I don't believe in that, and besides, too many others are doing it with great success already. Day in, day out, minute by precious minute, we are all bombarded by the eight-second sound-bites of world-hopping "experts," "stars," and televisionary gurus whose job it is to capitalize on our craving for spiritual comfort by marketing their own brands of belief. In the main, these self-appointed guardians of the human spirit sell nothing more than half-baked, prepackaged philosophies that demand little more from us than that we close our eyes and join the merry march toward the slow death of repose.

I saw no point in contributing to this collective "sleeping sickness of the soul." Rather, I have provided a series of signposts for exploring the dimensions of your own philosophy of life. I hope, then, that each of the interviews in this book will assist you in formulating or strengthening your own beliefs, confirming convictions or generating questions, inciting indignation or fostering compassion, inspiring hope or stimulating self-discovery. But if someone here should make you aware of a certain emptiness in your life, do not despair; rather rejoice. Consider it a wake-up call to your soul. For beneath whatever emptiness you might feel there lies the memory of the commitments you once made to preserve your soul; commitments to friends, family, community, nation; commitments to courage, honesty, integrity, truth, goodness, compassion. . . . Rekindling such commitments will revive your soul; denying them will allow it to wither. The choice is there for all of us—but we must be careful.

Our souls are at stake.

P.L.B.
January, 1990

Prologue

Thelma Black
and Joanne Baker

THE SOUL SISTERS

In a small house God has His corner, in a big house
He has to stand in the hall.

—Swedish Proverb

*Located on a busy corner on the poor east side of Wichita, Kansas, the
Soul Sisters Café serves up ribs, grits, lima beans, and other soul-food
fare. In the kitchen you'll generally find Joanne cooking, whereas out by
the tables you'll find her mother, Thelma, trying her best to "up someone"
with the word of the Lord and a smile. "Some people say that this old
place is raggedy," says Thelma, "but if we want to sit here and pay rent,
then, hey, this big raggedy place is ours." (Laughs.)*

*Just around the corner from the café, Thelma and Joanne share a
small home. It was there that we spent the morning together, "just talkin'
about what love will do for ya."*

JOANNE: I would be afraid to tell you that I was saved and be lyin'
about it, bein' a hypocrite; I'd be afraid, you know, to come out
and say, "Hey, I'm this and I'm that," and then just be livin' a false
life. Over at the restaurant we see preachers. They supposed to be
good, upstanding men who know God's word, but they don't live it.
They lyin'. I mean, preachers come in there, you know, and they try
to go wichya, "Hey, you want to slip up to the motel or somethin'?"

Preachers?

THELMA: Thousands. *(Laughs.)*

JOANNE: Pastors of churches say, "Hey, I can git you a room at
the Holiday Inn and you just come on up and do it. You be my
friend and I'll give you money." But I'm too scared of God. In the
long run the Lord will punish you.

But is there a side of you that wants to do it?

JOANNE: Oh, yeah, it's there. Yeah. Some of the guys look good.
(Laughs.) But the Lord said thou shall not commit adultery, and that's

in the Ten Commandments and that's direct with me all the time. *(Laughs.)* So I'm sayin', if you're not gonna live it, you're not gonna live saved, you're not committed. Can't anyone make you live saved, it's within the inner man. It's your conscience and it tells you, "Hey, you better not do that. It's temptation." Even back from Solomon and Samson men fell behind women. You know, their weakness was that right there.

THELMA: Sex and money has the nuthouses full. *(Laughs.)* That's what people go for—sex and money. That's the downfall of human nature. Most people go crazy about money, a woman, or a man. Love they call it. But it's just sex. And lust is not love. I've worked in hospitals as a nurse, and I've taken care of millionaires, and I remember this one rich man who was dying. I was givin' him a back massage and he was tryin' to feel my hips. I said, "Baby, you almost already dead now, you can't hang with it." *(Laughs.)*

But people like to be people, you can't be too hard on them, you got to let them be. And when you be yourself, then you're naturally beautiful. I know. *(Laughs.)* That's right. God made each one of us special, just like fingerprints, and it takes us all to make a unit. Maybe my language is not like yours, but we're both human and we can be ourselves. But everybody puttin' on airs, like them preachers. All I can do is try to accept them and try not to condemn 'em. You know, we have drunks comin' in here all the time sayin', "Hey, I ain't nothin' but a dirty old drunk." But I say, "Hey, you somebody." I just accept 'em for what they are. If they want to put on airs, I just accept the airs they put on.

We have some women they come in here all stiff-necked. We tell 'em, "You got some pretty eyes." You know, they're reaching out for something. And if you just find somethin' on them that's pretty—not the thing they're tryin' to be, not the thing they're tryin' to put over on people—just accept them for what they are, life is so much better. If you're for real, people accept you regardless of what's troublin' you.

Jesus came down here and died that I might have a right to freedom. I am free to walk out there, do anything, long as I don't hurt you. And I think I'm supposed to love you. If you're hungry, I'll feed you. If you naked, I'll clothe you. If you outdoors, I'll bring you into my house. You know? I do anything I can for you. I think that's love. Love makes me want to see you have the best for you. Love is givin', not takin'.

Most people come in here, they need somethin', they searchin' for somethin'. Most time we just tell 'em about the love of God. If they want to talk about sex, we talk about sex. If they want to talk about the Lord, we talk about the Lord. Just whatever they desire to talk about, we visit right there with 'em. And it gives us a good feelin'. It helps us. It makes us strong in our everyday walk to understand people and why they do what they do.

Most of our customers are older people, retired men. Some of 'em feel like they failed in life and there ain't nothin' left for 'em: "I'm just here waitin' to die." But we say, "Hey, you look pretty good today." We tease 'em or somethin' like that: "You lookin' for a woman?" You know, just kind of up 'em, lift 'em up, make 'em feel like things is okay.

I love everybody, but I really love the poor people, just like those white people out there. (She points outside to a couple standing in her driveway.) Now they poor, they stinky, but they my friends. I let 'em use my garage. I encourage them. He got a lot of talent. He fix up machines and sell 'em. His wife, she's epileptic. He comes over here and visits me and I show 'em how to cook greens. I love it. I really do. This is my life.

I'm the mother of nine children and the one thing I can glory in is that I've never received a welfare check. Their father and me separated. I had four children at home then, but I never received a welfare check. God has always made a way for me, opened a door for me. Just like when I come here, I didn't have anything but a suitcase. This ain't no fine stuff (she points to her couch and coffee table), but I'm comfortable. I don't owe nobody nothin'. Somebody brought me a kingsize bed. A guy brought me a color television. And I bought that table and chairs for $30. I've been poor. I've gone out there and picked wild greens. I know wild greens. I can cook 'em and eat 'em. I can live off the land. That's what makes me free. Oh, I feel so good. (Laughs.) I love people. That's right. I'm free. I don't need a lot of money. When I had money and stuff, I wasn't happy. I was a hypocrite like she was talkin' about. I was like goin' with the preacher. (Laughs.) It's true. But I always knew that the Lord had a callin' on my life because I always loved people.

JOANNE: You know, the Lord will give you that peace and contentment that money can't buy. Money don't mean nothin' if you're miserable, if you're sick and if you're evil and if you're jealous. If you got these things within you, life is just miserable. You feel guilt, you feel bad, you're not satisfied with yourself. That's why we try to uplift people, lift Jesus up so he'll lift 'em up. You might have a drinkin' problem, but you still somebody special and the Lord still loves you. And there's a way out of your problem if you just hang in there and ask God to help you.

The Lord always sends somebody over to the café so we can help

'em, even if its nothin' but to smile at 'em. Just like this young man who was sittin' in there awhile ago, all frowned up. I said, "Hey, you might be kind of tired, but things is gonna look up." And then instantly he started openin' up. "Hey, my daughter went out last night and she stayed out all night." I said, "Well, the only thing you can really do is pray for the Lord." I tell 'em that when bad things happen to me, that the Lord has really helped me.

One time I told the Lord that I was feelin' dead inside. I said, "Lord, I haven't felt your spirit. I need to know if you're still with me." A few days later me and mother was leavin' the restaurant and we was tired and everything and I was gonna run into the store to get somethin'. I ran in there and I left the car runnin'. As I was standin' at the counter, I noticed this guy fumbling with his pants, some big raggedy pants. Then I looked up and he got this big old long gun out. Then the little girl that was waitin' on me at the counter started praying. She said, "Oh, Lord, help us." Right then the spirit told me to fall on the floor. So I fell on the floor, and the robber said, "Oh, somethin's wrong with this lady." Then everybody seen that somethin' was wrong and they started shootin'. The little girl just had her arms around me and said, "Oh, Lord. Help us, help us, Lord Jesus." I said to myself, "Well, Lord, I know you still with me, I can feel your spirit." (Laughs.) They was just shootin' and everythin' and I just knew the Lord was with me. Then the robber said, "Everybody get on the floor." But the spirit had already told me to do that. I was already down there on that floor. (Laughs.) You know, the Lord just helped us through that.

The Lord is good, I mean I have felt him many times. One time the highway was really slick and I got on the bypass and it was just a little thin coat of ice. I was tryin' to stop, but my car went into a spin; it spinned three times around. Every time I was just callin' out Jesus' name, just callin' out Jesus' name: "Jesus, Jesus, O Lord, help me." Then I couldn't hold the steerin' wheel no longer, so I just let it go. The Lord let that car just ease on to a complete stop right there on the side of the highway. I just said, "Thank you, Jesus." I knew it was him 'cause it couldn't of been anybody else.

I tell you, it's just good to talk about the goodness of God. When you ask him somethin' and he helps or when you help somebody and you can see they be so thankful, it feels so good. This lady, you know, she came over here, she live in that house. (She points to a small, rundown house across the street.) She said, 'I need $5 to get some gas to go to work.' Our cash register was halfway empty. All we had was some change. I think I had about $3 in my purse. I said, "Well, we just don't have no money." Then she said, "Oh, if I could just get to work, I could pay you back Friday." I just took the $3 and gave it to her and, boy, she just got tears in her eyes. I said, "Well, Lord, I know that was you." He told me to give it to her 'cause it just feels so good.

Havin' this café is a privilege. I really believe the Lord put this place on the corner. This one guy, you know, he has this house where he allows gamblin' and drinkin' and every sin that you could imagine go on in there. But, you know, we still treat him as a customer. One day he was here with this young girl he'd been goin' with since she was fourteen. She said to him, "You been draggin' me up and down these streets since I was fourteen and now you won't even buy me no dinner or nothin'." Well, she had to eat. I told her she didn't have to pay for it. I said, "Don't worry about it." But she was cryin'. She's on dope real bad. They say she got to have three hits a day. She was in the kitchen and she said to him, "You here in front of these people treatin' me like a whore." Then she looked at me and said, "You think I'm a whore, don't you?" I was cryin' with her and I said, "We don't think you no whore, baby. Me and this other lady over there, we don't think you that. We love you. We don't care what you are, we love you." And that's the way we try to treat all our customers. We don't care what they are or who they are or what color they are or what they've done in life. The Lord has forgiven them and we have no right whatsoever to condemn 'em. All we do is treat 'em happy. When you treat people like you want to be treated, then guilt get off your back and you have more love for everythin'.

A lot of time people don't know what they missin' out on when they full of hate and evil and jealousy. Used to be I'd see a skinny woman walkin' and I'd just get jealous and hate her right there 'cause she was skinny and I was fat. Then I'd find somethin' to rake her for. I'd bring her down some kind of way. But that has gone out of me. I compliment people. "Oh," I say, "you got a pretty figure." I say, "Oh, you're a pretty lady, you're a pretty lady." There's somethin' pretty about everybody, pretty hair or somethin'. But used to be I'd find the worst thing and I'd try to just tear 'em down with it. But the Lord has just put more love into my heart. (Laughs.)

THELMA: I got a little white friend. She's eighty-four years old. She is so sweet. Her name is Daisy. When she first started comin' here, she was so mean. But she comes by and brings me books now, and we have a special way of cookin' short ribs—she likes our short ribs, you know—and she eats dinner with us. I just tell her, "Oh, you're so beautiful, you're a beautiful lady. Come on, let's dance." But she has cirrhosis of the liver and she says she can't no longer. I say, "You can still dance. Come on up, get up, kick your leg. You ain't dead yet; get up; come on, let's dance. Let's move it." (Laughs.) I said, "If you don't move it, you'll lose it!" You know, pretty soon I had more men over there dancin' with her. Then she says to me, "Ah, you ain't moving enough; come on, move some more." (Laughs.)

It's just good to see people happy. And it don't take a lot of money. It's a state of mind.

Alexander Curry

ONE DAY SOON

> Most people sell their souls and live with a good conscience on the proceeds.
>
> —*Logan Pearsall Smith*

My childhood background was middle-class . . . low- to lower-middle-class. And my parents were divorced pretty early on. I was in about the fifth grade. And that had been my mother's second marriage. She went on to marry a third time. I grew up pretty much in the New York area, but I must have moved about a dozen times. So that kind of influenced my life quite a bit in that I was changing schools a lot. And I didn't have any brothers or sisters. And my mother was divorced. So I grew up kind of quickly. Also, the lack of money had an effect on me. It's probably one of the reasons why I feel compelled to get rich. I guess that's the primary motivation that I've got for doing what I'm doing.

At thirty he's a highly successful stock and bond trader for a large New York brokerage house who makes (as a coworker put it) "at least four hundred grand a year." His Upper East Side apartment in Manhattan is decorated with modern furniture and filled with high-tech toys, from state-of-the-art ten-speed racing bikes to a 300-watt stereo.

There certainly isn't a deep philosophical motivation for trading bonds on Wall Street. It's really more or less a capitalistic game that's fairly high-risk and high-reward. And there's the possibility of coming from a background with no money and making it, making millions of dollars, which a lot of people do. The hope for people like myself is that we'll catch a wave along the way and get there.

As far as living in Manhattan, I'd say that I live here because I work on Wall Street. I kind of doubt whether I'd be living here otherwise. I think that there'd be a pretty good possibility that I would have gone to the country, since most of what I like to do is really outside, as you can see from the bikes there. And I spent about ten years as a rock climber, did some cross-country skiing, and most outdoor adventure sports. Again, there's the risk desire, a certain amount of risk in what I do. The rock climbing was certainly fairly risky. But to coin a financial phrase, it's sort of a high-risk, high-reward avocation.

You pretty much scare the shit out of yourself when you're rock climbing. But completing the climb gives you almost a druglike effect. That's the reward. And you can't really get it any other way that I know of. In a lot of ways it's like putting on a large arbitrage and basically outsmarting the market and making a lot of money. And along the way, in the arbitrage, you will probably lose money on the way to making money; and you will be nervous and you will be anxious and you will be a pain in the ass to everybody else around you. But the return is high. You make a lot of money, plus there's a lot of psychological gratification 'cause you know a lot of other people will be losing. To a certain extent it's a zero-sum game on Wall Street—if you win, someone else loses. And you hear about the few other guys who had the opposite side of the trade on; you know, the guys who got clobbered. So it's a competitive thing.

Wall Street is a lot more challenging than I expected it to be. There are quite a few dumb people that make money in various different ways on Wall Street, but if you're gonna trade the market, you really can't bullshit your way into making money. There is no bullshit in trading. It's a matter of being either right or wrong—and your track record will show that. Your track record, it's a day-to-day thing. You get a daily profit-and-loss statement. And your mood essentially moves with that daily profit-and-loss statement. The mood swings can be pretty incredible. When you start losing money, the first thing that happens is you get worried; then you get depressed, and then you don't care. That's the progression. When you don't care, it's almost sort of like you start laughing, joking around. And then the cynical aspect of my personality kicks in. And it's like: Ah, I don't give a shit. The hell with this. Oh, we lost a million dollars. Let's move to Montana or something.

So the competitive aspect of my life has always been there. And it's still there now. But I really wonder what I'm doing on Wall Street a lot of times, because as a long-term goal, wanting to work on Wall Street and making money does not fit what I originally thought I wanted to do. During college my game plan . . . well, let me step back farther. I had no idea what I wanted to do when I went to college. I tried a bunch of different majors and thought perhaps I could find something that I could put my heart into, that I would want to do, that wasn't gonna be a job. And that didn't happen. So I rationalized that if I went into business and made a bunch of money, that even though that's not something I really want to do, I could finance my leisure time. If I could make enough money, I could travel and possibly do something in education. That's one of the things I wanted to do when I started taking economics, work in a less-developed country in economic development.

That was the plan. The first part of the plan worked pretty well. I got into Columbia Business School, found out about trading, and got in while the getting in was pretty good. And I have been fairly successful; I'm not a multimillionaire yet, but so far it's been working according to plan. Of course I'm thirty years old now. The plan was to get rich by the time I was thirty years old and leave Wall Street and probably travel for a while and then go back to finding something that I wanted to do. Part of the process would be finding out what that was. But teaching is a good possibility. I always felt a compulsion to do something for those people that are starving, you know, are sick; those people that everything has gone wrong for basically. You know, the underprivileged. I don't know what the hell the right word is; but, for instance, the starving in Africa.

I've always felt that there was something that I could do and feel was doing something of real tangible benefit. It's ironic that what I'm doing right now to get there doesn't have any real tangible benefit. Trading, arbitraging futures markets, does not have any real tangible benefit, in my opinion. I mean, it serves a purpose for the economy, but I don't think of myself as really doing a hell of a lot for society. I'm really doing more for myself.

I guess I wasn't trained to think spiritually. It was always, "Here's the empirical reason for this and that and the other thing." And when I was confronted with it, I found it troublesome in that I could not understand how some other kids believed in God. I said, "Well, why do you believe in God? What reason do you have for thinking that God exists?" And I couldn't get a straight answer. It wasn't until much later on in life that I really came to understand how people felt about religion. It was in a college course called the Philosophy of Religion, taught by a very intelligent man. And I came to understand it at that point.

But I am not religious. I guess I'm agnostic, you might say. And because of that, I would have to say that I feel that there is a lack of purpose in my being. I don't understand why I'm here. I don't really try to understand why I'm here because I think it would probably be futile. It does provide a real hole in my existence. I'm sure it would for anybody, not believing that they are here for a specific reason. I mean, the whole thing about death is another thing. I mean like what happens after that? That's a big question mark as far as I'm concerned. And it's a little bit scary. And sometimes I'd like to have something I could lean on.

But, you know, even without religion I have a pretty firm ethical and moral foundation that's really based more on treating other people the way I'd like to be treated myself. That's sort of the foundation of the whole thing. And you can really put together quite a bit of an ethical foundation from that alone. I suppose it's a human ethic. And it also seems to me that it makes sense that if you have a lot, more than you need, and there's somebody else that has so little that they can barely stay alive and they're in agony, it just makes sense that you can do something for them with something you don't need.

How do you know when you've got enough to start giving?

ALEXANDER: That's one of the problems, especially in the environment of Wall Street. What Wall Street breeds is . . . it breeds millionaires that think they're poor because the guy next to them made ten million. And it happens regularly. It's the norm. I make a considerable amount of money, for example, but I don't feel that I do really because there are other people my age that make a hell of a lot more.

My idea of how much is enough is when I can make enough on interest income from what I have in the bank to live a comfortable life-style. And I essentially know what I want. I don't need like six homes and twelve Ferraris and stuff like that. I could live a fairly modest life-style and be happy.

What's modest?

ALEXANDER: Well, I think that modest depends on where you live geographically. And who you're around. I mean, modest in New York is still a hell of a lot of money. I mean, I'd say that for an individual to live a fair, comfortable life-style you need $100,000 in interest income a year. But I don't think that would be enough for me probably, probably not enough if I were to stay in New York and play the game in New York, because the game always involves making more. I mean, the game here is to make more money than the guy next to you. And it's a different game here than it is just about anywhere else. The amount of money in New York, especially in the financial sector, is just beyond belief, beyond belief.

On Wall Street money is the end of the job, it is the end in itself. It's sort of illogical in a sense. Your job is to make money. But the money is there for some reason. It's not any good by itself, but it doesn't matter. It's just the display of money. So the people on Wall Street tend to be ambitious, intelligent, somewhat ruthless, fairly greedy, and like me in the sense that they don't see it as particularly meaningful. . . . I mean, all you really think about is making money. It really doesn't have any meaning.

I wish I could have gone directly into something like a social-service occupation and not bothered with the step that I'm involved in now, which is establishing enough wealth to be independent, to live comfortably so I don't have to live on the floor. One thing that worries me is that I may get so caught up in my life-style that I'm not gonna take the second step, which is to get out of this. So when I see people on the television, on the news . . . what comes to mind is this fellow in Washington who lobbies for the homeless people, I can't remember his name right now.* But they have all my respect. They really do. And I think that if there were more people like them around, it would solve a lot of the problems that we have in the world. So I really do respect them. But I don't hammer myself too much for not doing what they're doing right now, because I like to think that I will be doing something like that at some time in the future. I just don't know when . . . and maybe I may never get there.

---

* Mitch Snyder.

Book One

Knockin' Bark
Off Trees

John Henry Faulk

During the 1950s he did a popular country humor and music show, Johnny's Front Porch, *over the CBS radio network. A vocal critic of Senator Joseph R. McCarthy, he managed to oust a pro-blacklist leadership from the American Federation of Radio Artists (AFRA).* Soon thereafter he was labeled a Communist by Aware, Inc., one of the many self-styled guardians of the political beliefs of the American people popular at that time. When Aware decided to send out bulletins to the networks charging that Faulk had entertained before pro-Communist-front organizations, he decided to challenge them in court. While waiting for his suit to come to trial, CBS, bowing to pressure from advertisers, fired him.** He then spent six years in court before winning a $3.5 million libel suit against Aware (later reduced on appeal to $550,000).*

We are sitting in the living room of his lakeside home in Austin, Texas, looking out on the water. The room is filled with books and birds. Birds chirp, it seems, from every corner. I'd called him an hour earlier, explained the idea of the book, and he invited me up: "American belief! Not much of that left anymore, but, hell, drive on over here and we'll see what we can come up with."

I was raised in a very pious Methodist home—as a matter of fact, here in Austin, about five miles from where we're sittin' right now. And my parents were Texans and we were pretty well convinced that the Methodist church was God's select way of getting people into glory. I pretty well believed that, except I wandered from the path a great deal.

My father was a free thinker, but a free thinker in the sense that he didn't so much believe in the divinity of Jesus Christ but in the teachings of Jesus. He thought Jesus was a magnificent rabbi who had brought great light into the world. As Daddy said, "He knocked the bark off the tree." And they murdered him for it. Daddy was a spiritual man. I was raised with real spiritual values. We observed all the holidays in church and all of that. Easter and Christmas and this kind of thing were important holidays in our lives.

---

* Later, AFTRA, American Federation of Television and Radio Artists.

** Ironically enough, CBS broadcast a dramatization of the John Henry Faulk trial in 1975, entitled *Fear on Trial*.

There was never any question in my mind that there wasn't a divine order of things, a great harmony of life. And at the center of it was the idea of justice. By justice I mean the basic principles of Jesus Christ: Turn the other cheek; "If thy enemy smite you on one cheek, turn the other cheek."

By the time I got to college, I came to loathe and despise religiosity. And by religiosity I mean that wearing of religion as a kind of badge of respectability. The Jerry Falwell type of thing. The belonging to the right church and associating with the right people became a terrible bore to me. I mean I rejected that.

But I can't say I was ever actually an atheist, because the evidence was too strong as far as I was concerned that there was a harmony that one could achieve with the world; a moving forward with the spirit; a universal spirit of affection, of love, of respect for people. I found this a very rewarding sort of attitude to have.

The basic principle of actively trying to weed out envy and hostility from one's behavior has alway made sense to me. Out of this emerged my conviction that competition for competition's sake is one of the great hurts and harms in our society today; being numero uno, to be number one, to accumulate the most worldly goods, to be the strongest and most unapproachable champions, whether it's in sports or whatever—I've rejected that very strongly. I've also come to reject nationalism, because it runs contrary to man's history. The great gift of life, the universal gift of life, is sullied by so many different forces that it behooves us now to recognize that national lines have no meaning anymore.

I would describe my spiritual life more as a progression—not that I've progressed very far. *(Laughs.)* But it's been a progression of insights into the experience called living. Perhaps the most important insight in my entire life was in this trial, in this lawsuit, back during the McCarthy period.

To begin with, you have to understand that I was deeply involved with Hitler. He embodied everything that I despised and loathed— the arrogance of Fascist indifference to human suffering. His anti-Semitism was one of the symptoms of a deeper sickness in Nazism. It was the pus sack on the boil that you could see, and it was hideous and ugly—like blacklisting during the McCarthy period. At any rate, by the 1950s I saw a corruption taking place in our society, a corruption of our democratic processes by using labels and name-calling and distortion to shut off political dialogue in our society. And this disturbed me very deeply. And the rise of the FBI and its surveillance of American citizens for their beliefs had more in common with a police state than with a democratic self-governing society such as ours. All of this disturbed me.

So when Nixon and Mr. McCarthy sounded off in 1950 that we lived under twenty years of treason and that the Democratic party was basically an instrument of treason in our society, I was genuinely outraged. And I was even outraged more when the Democratic party's response to that was, "Oh, we are not either. We hate them more than you do. We'll punish people for exercising independent thought more severely than you will." Hubert Humphrey came up with a concentration-camp notion, you know. I felt it left the broad body of American people defenseless, that we had not understood the genius of the American system and were allowing the lifeblood of the American self-governing society to die.

In the radio and television industry and in the motion picture industry there rose up these self-appointed vigilante groups. In New York there was one called Aware, Incorporated. And their proclaimed reason for existence was to combat the Communist conspiracy in the radio and television industry. The way they combatted it was not by gathering evidence of a conspiracy and taking it to the proper authorities but by publishing a list of names of persons about once a month who had in the past done something that Aware took exception to. William F. Buckley, Jr., and luminaries of that kind were very actively in support and worked hand-in-glove with the House Un-American Activities Committee.

Well, this all set me into a tailspin of outrage. The word was out that you'd best not take a position on any subject that was controversial at all. Criticizing McCarthy or J. Edgar Hoover could get you blacklisted. They'd list your name; you never had a chance to know that you were listed—you would find out by losing your job. This blasted the careers of a hell of a lot of people, and silence became the rule of the day. We had to belong to a union called AFRA, American Federation of Radio Artists, and I determined that we ought to do something about this. The union wouldn't. I wanted to investigate why. They said, "Well, the union is run by Aware." Screen Actors Guild (SAG) was run by ol' Ronald Reagan, whose thinking then was what it is today on these subjects. And AFRA was run by the same ones. So I got a bunch of guys—Charlie Collingwood, Orson Bean, Faye Emerson,* and a bunch of people who felt like I did about blacklisting—and we ran against them in the union. And

---

* Charles Collingwood is a CBS newsman and commentator; Orson Bean is a comedian and frequent TV game-show guest; Faye Emerson is a movie and TV actress.

we won. So they put out a bulletin on us. And I was head of the union slate, so I was the principal object of their outrage.

When they attacked us, they scared my side to death. *(Laughs.)* The people I'd run with just scattered like a covey of quail under the impact of fear. And it was shocking to see what fear did to people. Calling me at all hours of the night: "Is it true that you used to be a Communist?" Or, "Is it true . . . listen, we got authentic word that the FBI has a lot of stuff on you and, boy, it's going to be embarrassing for anybody that would associate with you. We feel in the interest of our career that you ought to tell us the truth now." And I could see that this was fear playing on them.

CBS called me in and said, "Listen, they've gotten to your sponsors; you're getting cancellations; you're going to be destroyed. There's one way maybe you can save yourself. Write an apology for these things that they charged you with doing. The ones that are false, just say they made a mistake there. Don't cuss them out for it, just say they made an error, that you weren't in New York at that time or something like that. Point out that you've never been a member of the Communist party. Congratulate Aware on its fine patriotic work, but tell them that it has made a mistake in this instance."

Well, I saw Aware as a group of racketeers and nothing more; political racketeers using patriotism like, as I mentioned, religion is used. And I went home because I was losing the union. I mean the guys were so scared *(laughs)*, they all turned against me. Ed Sullivan attacked me in the New York *Daily News*. It was obvious that I'd lost my force politically. Everybody was scared to come near me except Edward R. Murrow, friends that really knew me.

Here I was confronted with having to apologize to the sons of bitches to hold on to my job. So I went home and took this damn thing and started going down it, and it was a great revelation, me sittin' there in my apartment looking off across the lights of Manhattan. I was up on Seventy-ninth Street looking south in my study. I said to myself, "Why, *these* are the people that threaten the society. *They're* the *real* threats. Don't you see that, John? God. Why, if you answer this thing, answer them in court. Haul their rear ends into court and let them go before a jury, where they're bound by laws of evidence. Make them prove these allegations they're making, because to you they are a threat to this society. J. Edgar Hoover and his methods are a threat to this society as you see it. The House Un-American Activities Committee is a threat to those liberties that you consider sacred in our society, and now here's your chance to put it to the test." All of a sudden I felt just good as gold.

I remember Daddy fighting the Ku Klux Klan back in 1922 and

somebody called and said, "Oh, Judge Faulk, you're just so wonderful; you've just got such courage." Daddy said, "Pooh, I don't have any courage. It didn't take courage. All it takes is the understanding that they deal in fear; and when you're not afraid of them, they have no power over you, have absolutely no power. I'm not afraid of the Ku Klux Klan. They're just a bunch of misguided jackanapes. You don't congratulate somebody for getting up and going to the bathroom if his bowels need to be moved. It doesn't take courage to do that."

So I got to thinking about it, and all of a sudden I realized that I wasn't afraid of these guys. So I sat down and wrote CBS a fine affidavit. I said, "I won't answer this kind of claptrap. I don't know who these people are. Many of them are faceless accusers. I won't answer this kind of nonsense. I have a deep and abiding faith in the due process of law and in the Constitution of the United States of America and I will fight to uphold it. I will not desecrate it by answering these fellas." I went to see ol' Ed Murrow and I told him, I said, "Ed, this is a golden opportunity to strip these boys bucknecked, to haul them into court and let the public see them for what they are." So I went down and hired Louis Nizer to defend me.* Ed lent me $7,000 to top off the $3,000 I'd just put down as a retainer. I got kicked out of CBS then, blacklisted.

But I never did look back. Oh, I hated to drop off the top of the vine, because I'm vain, you know. I liked to be asked for my autograph and I liked to have a table reserved in the Persian Room at the Plaza Hotel for all their opening nights and that kind of thing. It was very pleasant. But, you see, I understood something, and it just came clear as hell to me that I could milk cows again if I had to like I did when I was a boy; run a filling station if I had to; that the one thing they couldn't take was my sense of self-respect. I could give it up, but they couldn't take it away. And that's an enormously enriching feeling to have.

So I never deserved credit, although I got a great deal of it for my courageous stand. As Nizer wrote, "One lone man stood against the elements of fear and oppression . . . fought through for six lonely years." Well, that was all juicy stuff in front of a jury (*laughs*), but it had no foundation in fact because I didn't enjoy being broke—and I was broke as hell. But, hell, I found that I had a lot of friends.

I'm enjoying life more fully now than I ever have. I'm enjoying people more than I ever did in my life. I don't for a moment regret being seventy-two years old. It's part of life, just like getting born

---

* Liberal trial lawyer and author.

was; just like being a jackass and an adolescent was. *(Laughs.)* And I'm continually, repeatedly, discovering or having experiences sitting out in the yard and listening to spring coming into the land, watching my purple martins, knowing that they've been all the way down to the southern tip of South America, have come back, found the same house—same hole in the house *(laughs)*—that they were raised in. This great capacity of life to renew itself. I think perhaps I'm more sensitive to that than ever before. I'm more sensitive to the fact that when Robert Browning had Rabbi Ben Ezra say, "Grow old along with me, the best is yet to be, the last of life for which the first was made"—that this is absolutely profound.

I guess that the principle of do unto others as you'd have others do unto you; the principle of love being the great healing and the great binding element of life; the learning to utilize that and to live by that has been an effort, many times unsuccessfully so, but has been my credo, really.

You know, it's hard as hell for you and it's hard for me, by God, to believe that this lovely and exciting and dynamic and sensitive creature is going to come to an end. But by God I know it's just my vanity. It's hard for me to believe that my family will not just cease to breathe when I'm gone, I'm so important to them *(laughs)*, but I know that's just a piece of nonsense. Still, I would like on my epitaph that they'd say, "He always tried to"—and I know this sounds silly— "tried to make the world a pleasanter place to live for the generations that come after him." Because, of course, the generations that came before me did that for me, you know. I do think of posterity a great deal. And I think of the obligations we have to it. I'm under no delusion anything I've done is of great importance, or even of importance enough to survive me. But there's a chance that it is. And I hope so. That would be the principal source of joy to me. And I delude myself, you see. I think that life moves forward, that that's the only direction it moves is forward. The only immutable law of life is change, and to live life fully you must accept that. It has to do with achieving more harmony with life, to understanding that this really is a damn good experience. Life is a good experience, a hell of a lot of fun. Just sheer pleasure for me.

I've always kind of conceived of Jesus as having traveled up the side of a hill and looking down across valleys. And the higher he climbed, the more clearly he could see those below him. And I would like to think that my life was, at least, getting up on a high place. *(Laughs.)* I haven't climbed any hills yet, but a little higher place, where I can see the struggle of man a little more distinctly, a little more realistically.

(He laughs; a sudden remembrance.) Ol' Jake Howard,* when he introduced me one time, said *(he switches to a nasal Texas drawl)*, "There's just two things about ol' John Henry: Number one, he ain't never been in the Texas penitentiary; and number two, I don't know why." *(Laughs.)* It's his good-natured way of saying the ol' son of a gun, he's all right. He's all right. *(Laughs.)* "Hell, I can't recommend him highly. He ain't ever been caught stealin'—that is, in the daylight." *(Laughs.)* This is Texas. Tex says he's all right, but, hell, don't ever expect too much of him. *(Laughs.)*

Postscript: John Henry Faulk died on April 9, 1990.

Peggy Hutchison

December 18, 1986. Tucson, Arizona. It's a sweltering 88 degrees outside, and we're sitting on the grass under the comforting shade of palm trees on the University of Arizona campus, where she's a graduate student of Middle Eastern languages and history.

On January 14, 1985, she and thirteen fellow Sanctuary workers were indicted by U.S. Attorney A. Melvin McDonald for conspiracy and seventy-one individual counts, among them recruiting, smuggling, transporting, and harboring illegal aliens. She is now in the midst of a trial that will determine her guilt or innocence.

I'm the youngest of four kids, and all of us grew up in the Methodist church. For the most part I've stayed very active in that. I spent my early childhood in northern California, in the Bay Area, in a very beautiful spot. There were a lot of green rolling hills that turned brown in the summer and huge oak trees. I remember the one rule that I had as a youngster was that I had to be in by dark. For the most part I could just roam and play in the hills. So much of my time was spent outside, and that was very helpful and very important. I think that helped to form my beliefs about the world and about life, because I began to fall in love with nature and creativity. I began to understand God as a creator of that beauty around me, and that understanding of a Creator was one that in a sense I really couldn't

---

* Rancher from eastern Texas.

define. But I really believed that there had to be some Creator to be able to explain for me what was around me.

We moved to Kansas City when I was twelve, and during the following summer I went down to Mexico by myself for a couple of weeks to live with a family. It was at that point in my life when I began to be exposed to poverty and oppression. And what happened was that I fell in love with the culture, with the people, with the history, with the art, the music, the food, with how people treated each other. I fell in love with that and I loved Mexico and I loved the people. But I remember getting lost one day on the outskirts of the city (I used to walk a lot). And all of a sudden I didn't know where I was, but I was in a very, very poor area. I continued to walk around and I got very scared at that point. I was really seeing poor people. Ultimately I found my way back to where I was staying, but out of that experience I began to ask a lot of questions. Why are people that work so hard—I mean, these folks worked very, very hard—why are they so poor? Why is it that they work so hard and yet struggle so much for the basic necessities that I've always had access to? Food. Health care. Clothing. Education. Job. So I came away from that trip with a sense of pain and a sense of joy. The pain I experienced (you know, second- or third-hand) was seeing the poverty and the people that worked so hard. The joy was seeing that these people were still able to find some beauty in life. I was able to learn from that.

Those experiences helped to develop my faith in God as creator of all that I cared about, the people that I'd met in Mexico, the land that I had fallen in love with. I felt very connected to that because that spirit was/is inside of me as it is inside of these people I came to love. So I was very much in pain because of that connection; what hurt them also hurt me in that I was connected to them. So I began to feel like, well, if the faith and the morals and the values that I had been brought up with, brought up with in the Methodist church, brought up with in my family; if all that they had taught me, taught through not just telling me but through their own experience, how they lived their life out; if that had any meaning to me, then I had to somehow put that into practice. I had to live that out, or it didn't matter. I mean, what good was it if I didn't try to act on it? So I began to develop a sense of social action. I was seeing my religious beliefs, my spiritual beliefs, touching the social, the economic, the political world. I couldn't separate it. I couldn't say, well, that's political over here and this is economic over here and that's religious over here.

I really believe that a faith that isn't a questioning faith is a dead faith. I mean, if I just say I believe and that's it and there's nothing more about it and I follow the formula of A, B, C, one, two, three, and everything's fine, then for me there's no action out of that. That's kind of dead and static. So I've always questioned the existence of God. When special people in my life have died (my father died when I was eighteen), when natural disasters occur, when people are hurting around me, I can't help but question.

But even though I continually question, there's a deep sense within me that there is a Creator, a spirit that has created us all. It's funny. For all my questioning, there's a deep seed within me that believes. And I'm not so sure how important it is that we spend time, you know, reflecting on the Virgin Birth. To me that's not important, really. I mean, it's a question that's constantly discussed among certain circles within the Church, but whether somebody believes it or doesn't believe it isn't as important as putting into practice that which Jesus taught—whether Jesus the Prophet, Jesus the Christ, whatever—that we put into practice what Amos and Moses and the other great prophets taught, that we put into practice what Muhammad taught. How they lived their life, that's what's most important, not whether we all agree on the specifics of the various doctrines that have grown around them.

Why did you get involved in the Sanctuary movement?

PEGGY: I was a lay worker for the United Methodist church and I was working in a metropolitan ministry and was asked to put together a border ministry program in 1982. All of a sudden I started going to detention centers after the Central Americans were picked up by Immigration, ready to be deported back, and didn't understand the system. They were signing voluntary-departure papers without understanding what they had signed, because these people really wanted to apply for political asylum. So I would go with attorneys and interpret and help them fill out the applications.

All those experiences of meeting Central American refugees and hearing their stories over and over and over again, seeing their torture marks, hearing that they didn't want to be here in the first place, that they wanted to be back home, didn't want to have to flee their homes and their jobs and their churches and their schools, but really had no choice. That really hurt me, just deeply hurt me. I had studied issues in Latin America and Central America for a long time, but it was all intellectual. And until I met refugees, what was an intellectual understanding became an emotional understanding and it touched me spiritually. What am I going to do about this? You know, I can continue to go to detention centers; I can continue to help people apply for political asylum; I can continue to be involved in prison ministry and basic social services; but my faith calls me to do something more, because people are being deported anyway. It doesn't matter if they apply for political asylum. It doesn't matter if their applications are ten inches thick. It doesn't matter, because they're from Salvador and Guatemala and because our administration discriminates against them and calls them economic migrants, so they're going to be deported.

So I studied U.S. law, the 1980 Refugee Act. I looked at the Geneva conventions, international human rights and international refugee law, and all of that said we were mandated as a nation—the United States was mandated—to provide safe haven to refugees. But we weren't doing that. I was very disturbed and I did some real reflection. I reread some of the Scriptures. You know, I reflected on my faith and my values, my morals. How do I act out in 1982, '83, '84, '85, my faith, my beliefs, in southern Arizona? I speak Spanish. I had an opportunity to meet and speak with refugees. And my understanding was that the United States was violating its own law. My faith said that you have to do unto others as you would want them to do unto you. You know, do not mistreat foreigners who are living in your land. Treat them as you would a fellow Israelite. So it wasn't anything special. It just made sense in terms of who I am, who I was, to respond. And responding at a deeper level meant being involved in the Sanctuary ministry.

So I got actively involved in Sanctuary ministry. I met refugees in Mexico. I heard their stories. I saw their marks. I remember a woman and ten children whose husband had been taken away by the military because they were lay workers for the Catholic church. She'd been raped numerous times by the soldiers with the kids in the house, in the next room, and yet she went out looking for her husband day after day after day. And one day a farmer came running in from the fields and said, "I've found Juan." And this woman went out, and her husband was in all different pieces, his body was torn to pieces.

It was those kinds of stories, the stories of people being in prison, being tortured incredibly—women, children, men—it was those stories that actually gave me strength. And what happened was, it wasn't so much what I was doing for refugees, but what they were doing for me, what I was learning from them. So my involvement with refugees has strengthened my faith more than anything else I've ever experienced. Here were people who had lived through so much terror and destruction and violence and death, and they still had hope and they still had faith and they still had a belief. So whenever I was afraid, they ended up ministering to me; I mean, sharing their stories ended up teaching me and giving me strength.

Since the indictment, people have tended to put us in boxes;

we're either criminals or heroes. But we aren't criminals and we certainly aren't special. I'm just doing what my parents brought me up to do. When I speak in Methodist churches, I tell them, you know, it's people like yourselves who helped form my values and my faith and my morals. There's nothing special about it. So, in a sense, it saddens me that when people respond humanely to other people, that that's considered a heroic act.

That's because it's a rarity.

PEGGY: But why is that? That's what's very sad. You know, when people hear about the indictment, hear about the U.S. government sending spies into the churches to surreptitiously tape our conversations to indict us, they get more upset about that than they do about the torture that Salvadoran men and women and children and Guatemalan men and women and children have gone through. They get more upset about that than they do about the fact that there's a holocaust going on—if we can call it that—in Guatemala, that whole tribes are becoming extinct and that we're largely responsible for it. We pay for it. We sponsor it. We promote it. We're violating international and U.S. law. And people . . . it seems like we've lost our passion. I get worried about that sometimes. You know, as a nation we're so passionless, we're so apathetic. Where is our passion? You know, we should be outraged.

I don't want to be a martyr. I don't want to be a sacrificial lamb. That's the last thing I want. And I don't want to be sitting in that courtroom every day. But any of the risks that I've taken are nothing compared to the risks that the refugees have taken. So we have to put that all into perspective and balance and focus.

It's hard to imagine going to jail. Certainly there would be something to learn from it. But, see, I really believe that this has been part of my faith journey—just one part of it—and that the Creator has been very much a part of who I am and a part of that faith journey. So why would I be abandoned now? I mean, my journey will go on.

Postcript: On May 1, 1986, Peggy Hutchison was found guilty of conspiracy for violating eight United States codes (section 371). On July 1, 1986, she was given a suspended sentence and five years' probation. Noting the forthcoming Liberty Day weekend festivities, her final words to the court were these: "It is common for Jewish people to proclaim 'Never again.' Never again, in terms of never forgetting the Holocaust and never, never allowing it to occur again. Today I stand before you to proclaim as a citizen of the United States and as a Christian, never again should our nation stand by silently in the midst of a different holocaust, in this case, the people of Central America."

Georgia Fuller

I remember sitting in church when I was girl (my parents were sort of generic Protestants), trying to figure out which side of the rib cage men had lost the rib on, because if Eve was made from Adam's rib, then men must have one less rib. And I remember distinctly on the hot days, when the white shirts would cling to the men's bodies with perspiration, craning my neck around in the middle of a boring sermon counting ribs, trying to figure out which side was missing. In retrospect, it was probably the beginning of my feminism. Because I figured if we had all our ribs, we must be the superior sex. *(Laughs.)* So I consider myself to be a Bible-based feminist for that reason. *(Laughs.)*

She's a well-known feminist activist and a prominent member of NOW, the National Organization of Women. In the feminist movement she's known as an expert on women's spirituality. A native Pennsylvanian who now lives in Arlington, Virginia, she's a short, thin, gnomelike woman with a great sense of humor and hearty laugh. She wears silver star-shaped earrings and a large white T-shirt that says, "Quakers Are Friends."

If you haven't guessed by now, I'm a Quaker. *(Laughs.)* I belong to a group of Quakers that are practicing what we call the old-fashioned Quakerism. We're the minority of Quakers in the world.

To me the God of the Hebrew scripts is very, very real, something I can feel and touch. God was one and at the same time transcendent and present with the Israelites as the pillar of cloud and the pillar of fire and the sound of the still, small voice. God called us forth to build the Kingdom of God on this earth—which of course is a classist term, so even my language isn't completely clean. *(Laughs.)* So I see us as having a purpose in this world, to bring the reign of God, to bring peace and justice here. I don't see God as a puppeteer or a coercive agent who is going to make it happen whether you like it or not. But I see God as a source that calls us to that and enables us to do that.

I really do feel called to be in the women's movement. And I'm pretty convinced that social movements have never succeeded in this country without an element of civil disobedience. So part of standing up for what I believe in has involved acts of civil disobedience.

The most exciting protest I did was climb the White House fence on Susan B. Anthony's birthday, February 15th, 1982, to petition

Reagan on behalf of the ERA. Reagan had consistently refused to meet with women's groups, and I realized that the ERA was going to go down for a massive defeat unless we did something dramatic; came forth, you know, with a symbol of such courage and audacity that it would direct women's energies toward their empowerment rather than allow those energies to be turned inward. So we staged a big rally at Lafayette Park on November 15th and then marched from there to the White House gate to deliver Reagan the petition. Naturally he refused to accept it. But we were prepared. Seemingly out of nowhere the rope ladders that we made appeared out of backpacks, shopping bags. My ladder carrier was a heavyset Italian woman. She rolled it up under her coat and walked around looking pregnant. *(Laughs.)* When the signal came, she unbuttoned the top in a flash and the ladder was over the fence and, bang, we were gone.

My ladder was tangled, so I had to jump. For me it was a long jump. I had practiced jumping on playgrounds, I practiced push-ups, I practiced knee things. And I had waited so long that even though the ladder was tangled and my ladder carrier said, "Wait, I'll straighten it for you," man, I was over. I remember landing on the lawn and looking up and there was the White House. And I thought, My God, it's an ordinary house. And I realized what a psychological barrier that fence is, because it keeps us separated from our leadership. How intimidating that little black wrought-iron fence is. I used to call it the multiphallic serpent *(laughs)* guarding the citadels of the patriarchy. I straightened up and I just started walking straight ahead and there's all these bushes in front of the White House. And we'd never seen the bushes because we never thought we'd get twenty feet. We could tell you everything within twenty feet of the White House because we'd mapped out our scenarios. But we'd never once considered the possibility that we would go over that fence and there wouldn't be a cop in sight and we'd have a clear beeline to the White House. *(Laughs.)* My God, where did those bushes come from, they're huge!

Well, this cop comes down and gets me just as I'm approaching the bushes, not being sure how to navigate them. He screams at me from ten feet away, "You're under arrest." I thought, Oh thank God, he can figure out how to get me around the bushes. *(Laughs.)* But this man was terrified. He grabbed me by the wrist and twisted my arm back and put me in an armlock. It's the kind of thing that doesn't look like much, but if you resist, your s'posed to fall flat. But I value my arm, so I didn't resist. It's very effective. He started pushing me around. I kept tryin' to talk to him. I said, "I'm here to petition the president of the United States." I had my letter in my hand. He wouldn't talk to me. I said, "Here's my letter." I kept trying to show it to him. It's my Constitutional right to petition the president of the United States. The man was terrified. He was absolutely terrified. I wasn't scared, but he was terrified. He kept lookin' over his shoulder. He took me down to the patio. Then he went back for the others. Well, they held us for processing at the White House for about two hours. They brought out two policewomen to process us. We went to the Third District lockup in Washington, D.C., which is not my favorite lockup. *(Laughs.)* And we were there for a long time, because our people and the press had found us and were camped outside of the lockup. They didn't want us getting any additional publicity, so they held us a real long time.

So why did I do it? Because I believed, absolutely totally believed, that at that moment in history we had to give forth a symbol of courage, particularly for other women. Because any of us on the inside of the women's movement knew we were going down to a massive defeat. I felt we had to infuse new energy and new possibilities into the women's movement. We had to really take that leap of faith, that leap of courage. To me it was absolutely a religious problem. Equality for women is part of the gospel. Jesus treated women equally with men. In Gallatians it says, "There is neither male nor female, Jew or Greek, slave nor free, we are all one in Christ Jesus." Equality of women is spiritually essential if we are to have a world of peace and justice, and I felt it my obligation to other women to show them that we do have that courage.

Problems of Evil

Elizabeth Jaranyi

WHY ME?

Her comfortable suburban home in Aurora, Colorado, is decorated with bird pictures, bird sculptures, and bird-patterned furniture covers. "I love birds very much. When I see birds in nature, that's enough for me to be alive."

Last year she retired from her business as a seamstress. "I was lazy in my business, but I'm even lazier now. And I can't diet even though I'm really miserably fat. I suffered so much from hunger in Auschwitz that I feel sick when I'm dieting. I always have to have good food in my poor stomach or else I feel I'm back in Auschwitz. I always have in my refrigerator at least two or three weeks of food supply."

I was born in Hungary and I wholeheartedly believed that I was a Hungarian. As a girl I knew I was Jewish, but I didn't care much to be a Jew. I didn't care too much about religion. What I cared about was to be a big, proud Hungarian. And then the Hungarians took us to the ghetto and deported us and I found out in a hurry that I am not a Hungarian, I am a Jew. And year by year, the older you get, you find out slowly that no matter what country you live in, if you are a Jew, you are a Jew and nothing else. Right now I'm very happy to be in America; I'm a very proud citizen. But I know in my heart that anything can happen here. If we had a revolution, like the one we had in Hungary in 1956, first they would kick out the blacks, then the Chicanos, and then the Jews.

I was a very young woman, married a year, the day when I arrived in Auschwitz. Actually it was my first wedding anniversary the day I arrived. My husband had already been gassed in Germany.

I was pregnant when I arrived, but I didn't know it. They were calling out the pregnant women because they used them for experiments. I didn't go, but I was forced to take bromine so I couldn't have a child. One day I felt warm blood pouring over my legs and I got very white and shaky. I was working with a Greek Jew, a pharmacist, and he asked me, "What's the matter with you?" I said, "I think I lost my pregnancy." And he did the kind of work where he had to use white gloves, wash his hair, and use these clean white towels every day. I think he worked on lenses. He got a clean white towel every day that he had to give back every evening. He handed me the towel under the table and said, "Try to stop the bleeding. Get to the toilet, lay down on the floor with cold water and push, push your uterus." So I went to the bathroom, and in about ten minutes a little fetus left my body. The towel was so bloody I threw it in the wastebasket.

When I got back, he said to me, "If they beat me because I have no towel, please don't tell them I gave it to you, because they will only beat you, too, and you can't stand another beating in your condition. Just let me take it." So in the evening, when the guard asked for the towel, he said he lost it. They beat him up so bad. His face was a piece of rag. His eyes were bulging. His head was covered with blood. I wanted to scream the truth, but everybody told me to be quiet, because it wouldn't make any difference. He took all that punishment and didn't say a word to me. Can you imagine how I felt when I saw this man kicked in the face? The next day, when we came to work, he looked so bad I had to look down. I was afraid to look at him. But he said, "Maybe someday somebody will be good to *my* wife." I don't know if he ever found his wife, and I don't even know if he survived.

In Auschwitz everybody pray, everybody pray and pray and pray. I lost my husband. I lost my child. I saw my sister shot to death before my eyes. I was beaten. And when I saw the crematorium, I didn't pray anymore. I was so angry! And when I came home, I'm absolutely not a God-believer again. If God knew everything, where was he when my family burned? Where was he when my sister was killed? Where was he when I asked for help when my leg was crippled for life by a seventeen-year-old German kid who beat me so bad that I almost died from the infection? Why didn't he come and help me and the other women who had to see their babies burned? I cannot understand a God like that. When God knows everything and sees everything, where is he when children are dying from hunger in Africa? Where is he now, when innocent people are being killed all over the world? When God is so big, why can't he come and help? He can do it, this is what the Bible says. I just don't see why he doesn't. So my religious feeling is really shaky, even now.

For instance, my tiny grandchild, nine months old. August 14th she is going to have an operation, because if they don't, she will grow up deformed. My little darling grandchild. I cannot tell you why. This is a good God? Why banish a nine-month-old baby? So, it's hard, I'm trying my best to believe; I try to pray every day. And just today we had bad news. We were supposed to sell this house so we could move, and the whole contract fell apart. So everything is so dull and bleak. I cannot believe. I have seen too much hunger and suffering in my life to believe. I don't understand why they punish me more. Not one minute in my entire life do I not live without the pain. That crippled leg is hurt so bad I often scream at night in pain. I don't understand why. Nobody answered me, ever. How God is good and how God does this, I don't understand. The only good thing God has done for me is my second husband, my wonderful husband. But he's heartbroken just like me, and so we go about heartbroken together, crying on each other's shoulders all day long.

I'm sixty-eight and a half years old, and I still don't find out. I find out one thing: Life is very important. We have just one life and we have to save it and keep it. But I don't find out of the goodness of God yet.

Kathryn Morton

August 1987. Norfolk, Virginia. On a muggy summer day we relax together in her book-lined living room, drinking lemonade. For the past fourteen years she has worked as a book reviewer for the local newspaper, the Virginian Pilot. *Married and the mother of two children, she is forty-three years old.*

I grew up a Secular Nothingist. *(Laughs.)*
My father was an artist who painted pictures. Every day he'd go out and try to capture something that was happening—a color or a shape or a tree or whatever—that would never exist at any other time. He was captivated by beauty. "There's a paradise and we are in it," he'd say. His church was life, really, and his philosophy was that you don't have to be living in front of the Taj Mahal to look up and see beauty.

My mother was a psychiatrist (she's retired now) who had sort of a Protestant pioneer upbringing. But when she began working in a TB sanatorium, she decided there was nobody looking after the fallen sparrows because the children, the mothers, and the young people she saw wasting away and dying made her think that this is just chaos. So she's an avid disbeliever in any "father in the sky." Actually she believes in God. She just believes he's neglecting everything terribly. *(Laughs.)*

In all these little ways my parents taught me that the world is a beautiful place, but that it contains a great deal of pain and it's for people to try to help others live through the pain, or around it, or peel from it. I grew up with this attitude that there's a great deal of very beautiful stuff all the time but that most people go through their lives with their eyes sort of shut. You know, they're thinkin' what they're thinkin' and they never look and see. So they miss a great deal of joy.

Given my background, I guess it's easy to understand why I wasn't inclined toward religion. I always thought religion was a matter of accepting some set-up structure of supernatural myths. You know, I believe in God the Father, and the Son, and the Immaculate Conception, and all that kind of stuff, and that through this you achieve salvation and eternal life. So I associated religion with accepting the concept of Santa Claus and not dealing with the real world that we're given. Waiting around for your birthday in the sky! That seemed wasteful, it seemed immoral, it seemed irresponsible, and it seemed intellectually frivolous.

My thoughts on religion really didn't change until I was thirty-seven, when my father died. It was one of those things where you, like, jump off a nine-story building and you've gone eight stories and nothing bad's happened yet. Well, I was thirty-seven and nothing bad had happened yet. But for three months my father was in terrible shape. He had a series of strokes, and I was helping my mother look after him and stuff.

Anyway at one point he was in intensive care and asked me to plan his funeral. All my life he had said that he was planning for his funeral, because he thought all that art needs is an audience. If you put art where people are . . . if it's good stuff . . . it'll sort of infiltrate them and enrich their lives. You don't need to do something to Beethoven to make it acceptable to people, you just need to make them sit down and shut up and listen. And if they do it a few times, why, that's what constitutes the music: that it gets to people. So, for his funeral, he's gonna have this captive audience; they're gonna have to sit there for a little while and he's gonna do some stuff to 'em, see. He wanted certain pieces of music played and certain pieces of poetry read. At various times in my growing up he'd say, "Oh! I want this poem here. This poem I want. Make sure you put this one on the list." But now he was actually dying, and he was telling my mother how he'd never lived until he'd met her, and he said to me, "Now, remember about the poems." And I said, sure, right, I got it. Then I realized that I didn't know who he wanted to have read 'em. So I said, "Well, who should read 'em?" And he said, "Larry Foreman." And I said, "Who's that?" And he said, "Rabbi Lawrence Arthur Foreman."

So the morning after my father died (I was with him when he died, and I'm glad I was there), I got out the phone book and I called up this person. I had never met a rabbi before. Anyhow I told him that what we want to do is sort of combine these poems and to sort of express this idea my father had. So the rabbi said, "Well, why don't you write something for me so I'll do it right?" It would not otherwise have occurred to me that something so ritual as a funeral was something that you'd write yourself, but I wrote part of it. So I expressed what I knew to be my father's attitude, and the rabbi said, "You're really Jewish, and of course your father was really Jewish, too, and of course your mother . . . she's a psychiatrist . . . all psychiatrists are really Jewish." Then he laughed. I didn't know what being Jewish was like, and he said, "Well, you ought to come see me sometime. If you ever want to talk about it, or talk about anything, come and visit, 'cause I really liked your dad. He was a great guy." Anyway it turned out to be a really lovely service. It was a real affirmation of the quality that my father valued, and the joy of life, and making something out of your life that will help vitalize other people, that will give them vision.

About a month after my father died, my eight-year-old son, Kenny, got very sick. He developed a rash, and he had a lot of allergies and stuff, but we didn't think much of it. We took him to various doctors and they said it might be an allergy, maybe it's a fungus infection, maybe it's cancer. So we went around and around, and he didn't feel well. He developed these big lymph nodes, and we were being rattled back and forth among doctors, and I was still getting over the idea of not havin' my father, and the dog died in the middle of all this, too (oh good, one more thing). Kenny was finally diagnosed as having a disease that's a lupuslike syndrome, which means it's something that has an unknown cause. The medicines they prescribed were very frightening. The first one tended to cause damage to the retina, in addition to assorted other things. (Sighs.) And he didn't get better. His urinalyses were getting bad, so we took him to a nephrologist, who did a kidney biopsy. They diagnosed and confirmed that it was systemic lupus, with the kind of kidney damage which is usually lethal within three years.

But the doctor said, "No! We caught it early and we can put him on high doses of prednisone." The prednisone made him feel a lot better . . . made him fat, made him real hungry *(sighs)*, but prednisone does terrible things to you. It causes ulcers, causes cataracts, causes osteoporosis. It's like the atomic bomb to get rid of your crabgrass. So you try to cut back on it, to take as little a dose as possible to get the therapeutic effects, and every time we cut back, he'd start getting rashes again. And it wasn't just a rash, it was that he'd have a fever of 104.5 and ulcers inside of his mouth. He was very photosensitive too. He couldn't go out in daylight, and for an eight-year-old who is like Tarzan this was very difficult.

Everything was going okay for about five months, until he had a seizure and went into a coma that lasted three months. And when one thing goes wrong, then they give you something for that, which makes something else go wrong. So during this time he had a heart attack (which is great when you're eleven) and pancreatitis and ulcers and bladder infections and pneumonia about five or six times. He didn't bother anybody because he was unconscious, but we could tell when he was in pain. When we'd come into intensive care (you're allowed to come in fifteen minutes out of the hour), we'd sing to him. My mother, my husband, and I took turns around the clock while he was in the hospital. We'd sing to him and stroke him and stuff. And you could watch the monitor: His pulse rate would drop twenty points and his blood pressure would come down to something more like normal. So we were always in contact with him to some degree.

We were told that he was going to die several times and that his brain was hopeless; his body was still alive, but his brain was hopeless. But he gradually woke up, over a period of weeks, and came home and smiled exactly a week later while his father was doing the hula for him, which ought to make a dog laugh. Kenny had always been a very comical kid. He was the family clown. He did not behave. He was always up a tree, or digging a hole, or swinging across the yard, but his favorite thing was making people laugh. He was very funny. And so when he started being funny again, it was wonderful. But it was also terrifying, 'cause he kept spiking fevers, or saying his stomach hurt, or saying his head hurt, or twitching a little . . . he didn't have the use of his legs. We never knew, from moment to moment, when something serious might happen to him.

At one time I had talked to a psychiatric social worker, and she was nice and she'd ask me, "How do you feel about this?" "Well, I feel lousy," I said. "How else should I feel?" And at the hospital there'd been a psychologist who they sicced on us. He would stare at you intently and ask inane questions. When I was seeing him, I kept thinkin' that what I really needed was a philosopher I could get by the hour, because it wasn't "how do you feel?" that interested me. It's how you live, it's how you put your cosmology together. When you've seen this kind of stuff, see what you see in intensive care, asking how you feel is a ridiculous question. There was a baby who came in who had fallen in the family pool and not been found for fifteen minutes and was brain dead. This was a beautiful little baby; oh, God, he was gorgeous. So they took him off the respirator, but it took him three days to die, and the family's in the waiting room eating fried chicken and watching *Dating Game* on television and going in every fifteen minutes to look at the body of their dying child. Then you walk out on the street and there're people who are leading what we think of as normal lives, which are blessed lives, but they don't know it. You know, you get a run in your stocking in the morning and say, "Oh! My God, what a terrible day this is!" (*Laughs.*) You think that's trouble! But then we saw what pain Kenny was going through (*sigh*), and the pain and the helplessness and then the terrific strength in people; the confusion and the hope and the not knowing what to do and what's wrong. So how do you put all this together? I mean, when you have the happiest days of your life because your family is together and you know it, and you have the most terrifying days at the same time—how can you make sense of it?

Along about this time I ran into Rabbi Foreman at a party, and we hadn't been out in six months, so my mother stayed with Kenny. The rabbi said, "Well, how's it going?" And I (*laughs*) told him— over the cheese dip—that I thought I needed to talk to somebody who wasn't just going to talk about "how do you feel about this?" I told him about my experiences in the intensive care waiting room (I used to live in the waiting room). There were the Twenty-third Psalmers, I said, the people who said, "The Lord is my shepherd. . . . I've got it made in the shade; even if the kid dies, it's okay, but he probably won't, and I'm gonna sit here and pray, and it's all gonna get better." I told the rabbi that this did not seem to me to relate to the reality I was watching. We were more like the Twenty-second Psalmers: "My God, my God, why hast Thou forsaken me? . . . I was cast upon Thee from the womb, be not far from me, for trouble is near, and there is no help." I told him that the people who had it made in the shade I found irritating. And he said, "Well, now, religion is not a set of beliefs; religion is the totality of your response to life. It is what you do with what you've got. And you're a very religious person, because you spend all those days and nights at the hospital and all that research time working on trying to save your child. This is a religious response, this is an integrated response to life. You're using your mind and your heart and your body trying to create an integrated and worthwhile family out of this chaos that has landed upon you."

I thought, Is that religion? I thought religion was "I believe in this, this, this, and this." He said, "Well, that's one kind of religion. Come and see me." So I went to see him, and I was there an hour and a half . . . three boxes of Kleenex. I told him that Kenny is so sick I can't feel good about anything and I have this need to sort of affirm, to feel like we're getting someplace, and it's like having the rug pulled out from under you all the time while you're trying to dance. And the first thing he said was, "You've got a problem." And I thought, Well, yeah, I guess I do, I mean, this is enough problem that I don't have to explain to someone that I have a problem. Yeah, you've got a problem, Kathryn. *(Laughs.)* I was telling him about the people who were saying, "God must love Kenny very much to make him suffer so, and you must be very special people to have had this visited upon you." And I told him about a letter we got from a monk who was a friend of a friend of a friend who said, "Well, I'm sorry for how much he's suffering, but at least this is proof of the existence of heaven, because there couldn't be anything this nasty unless there were." The logic of this is a little . . . well, it wouldn't pass basic logic. If children in this life suffer and die, then you can be happy because that means there's a heaven. *(Laughs.)* So this is what I kept hearing, I said. And the rabbi said, "That's bull. God didn't make Kenny sick. A virus got him, or an allergy, or an accidental defective gene, or . . ."

So the rabbi started working me into basic Harold Kushner stuff, which is sort of basic Jewish stuff. *(Laughs.)* You know, that given what you are given, what're you gonna do now? That is the primary question of Judaism. And so it follows that just because bad things happen doesn't mean you have to hate life; you don't have to try to turn around all the bad stuff and pretend that it's really good *(she starts to cry)*, that this is evidence of heaven, or that this is evidence of God's love: the pain and the shit he went through. . . . *(She pauses to collect herself)*.

Well, anyway, I kept after Larry to gimme some advice, and he's not a very directive person. He's one of those people who listens so well that pretty soon you hear what it is you're saying yourself. I couldn't hear what I was saying. So he finally said, "Well, I have a terrific idea. Now, this takes terrific chutzpah, and I'm not trying to convert you, but maybe this Friday night you can celebrate Shabbat." So he gave me the Shabbat manual (which is instruction on the proper way of celebrating the Sabbath) and said, "Why don't you try this, just as an experiment, and see what happens. Get all the pill bottles off the table, lay out a white cloth, light a couple of candles, serve something kind of nice. Order it out if it's too much trouble, but have a glass of wine, toast each other, look at each other, and you're together. There're prayers and stuff, but you don't have to get into that. Just try this." And I thought, okay.

I was very self-conscious. I fixed Taco Delight, because I figured the family would like this. It takes too long to make, it's a mess, so we don't usually have it, but everybody likes it (makes a mess all over the tablecloth). So we rolled Kenny up to the table with us, which we normally hadn't done, because he couldn't eat really; I mean, he was fed through this tube, so meals were always an awareness that he was in the other room. We used the good china, and we had candles, and I'd bought a bouquet of flowers, and we had wine, and we toasted. Kenny could toast; I mean, he toasted, toasted, toasted, and it was like Thanksgiving, it was like our birthday, it was like New Year's Eve, it was like all these holidays we had missed when Kenny was in the hospital. It was really nice! And we joked, all these mime jokes, and it was so special that after supper nobody wanted television. The kids were playin' this game around in the living room, it's some kind of tag, one of those dopey, inane games that children can play but nobody can explain, and everybody laughs, and it had to do with putting hats on each other and stuff. And I was sitting on the couch reading this letter I'd gotten from a friend who lives someplace a long way off, and she was saying, "Oh, how dreadful! Oh, I'm so sorry about your troubles and Kenny being sick. I don't know how you can stand it." But here the kids are laughing around and we're all full and happy and the flowers are sort of glowing, and I thought, nobody's got a better night than we've got right now; nobody on this block has got as much happiness in their house as we've got right here, right now. I mean, we know we've got troubles, so we know to enjoy what's good. And they don't know; you know, they're bickering about who didn't cut the grass, or about somebody staying out too late, but we . . . God! We've got this wonderful thing.

So the next Friday night we had our Shabbat again, because it was sort of like celebrating ourselves; it was the difference between being the victim and standing up for what is good and beautiful. We got illness all over the place and life's a mess and the bills are incredible and we don't understand how to do the insurance, but, by God, look at this! We've got this white tablecloth, and we've got these candles, and we've got each other, and we've got tonight . . . this is nice!

About six weeks later Kenny started having stomach pains. He had a perforated ulcer. He went back in the hospital in shock. They operated on him twelve hours later. He never fully regained consciousness. His eyes were open and stuff, but he kinda was all blanked out. He developed a fever of 108, and they couldn't figure out why, so they took him off the antibiotics because they thought maybe it was a drug reaction. Well, he went into cardiac arrest. He was in intensive, and they EEG'd him and it was okay. They EEG'd him the next day and it was flat. *(Sighs.)* I called up the rabbi and told him they were gonna take Kenny off the respirator. His kidneys were shutting down, his liver was shutting down—he was dying all over. Could you come, Rabbi? He said, "Yeah."

So Kenny was gonna die. The rabbi came, and so did my friend, Kathryn Patterson, a devout Presbyterian and one of my dearest friends. I felt kind of guilty with Kathryn sitting next to me. I didn't want her to feel that I was turning away from her, because she and her husband (he's a Presbyterian minister) had both been wonderful through all of this. And so I turned to her, and I said, "I think I'm finding out that I'm Jewish." And she said, "That's all right, sweetie, so was Jesus." Okay, so she's gonna love me anyway. So we're in this hospital room: me, the rabbi, Kathryn and her husband, my husband, my mother, the doctor, and the nurse. I had Kenny in my lap. And my husband read a couple poems, and the Reverend Mr. Patterson read, "My house has many mansions. If it were not so, I would have told," and the rabbi read the part of the Twenty-third Psalm I wanted. But when it says, "Be not far from me, for trouble is near, and there is no help," he said, "There is help!" I thought, He's misreading the Scripture. This is interesting. I never heard a clergyman misread a piece of Scripture before. He was supposed to say a prayer, and then they were gonna unplug Kenny. But he stopped and he made the doctor wait (I love it when you make a doctor wait, because I spent years waiting for doctors). He told us a story about King David: "When King David's son was ill, the king roiled in anguish. He tore his hair, he wore sackcloth and ashes, and the people were terrified of what would happen if the boy died. And the boy in fact died. They thought, 'Oh, what will the king do now?' So, in fear, they watched. But the king got dressed and went back to work. And the people said, 'How can this be? You were in such anguish when your son was sick.' King David replied, 'When my son was sick, I would have done anything to save him. But now he's gone. He cannot anymore come to me, but I can go toward him.'"

Of all the people in the room, the nurse was crying. The doctor was green, 'cause he loved Kenny, and he didn't think he was gonna die. But Kenny was lying there calmly in my arms, my husband was sort of holding his head, and my mother was at his feet. It was sort of the Pietà with assistance. And the rabbi did not look overwhelmed. He looked like there was something more to do after this. And I thought, This is interesting. This man knows something about how to live. I want to know what he knows. And when the doctor took the tube out of Kenny's mouth, he lay there a minute in my arms, opened his eyes and smiled, and then he closed his eyes, and it was all over . . . he was heading off toward Grandpa.

So that night (it was a Friday night) friends brought us supper. And we had our Shabbat. When the rabbi left the room where Kenny was dying, he said, "Come anytime. Call me anytime. You know we've got a service tonight, if you want to come." And I said, "What time?" You have to do something at the time, you know. It's not like in books, where there's a death and the next chapter starts; I mean, you have four-fifteen, four-twenty, five o'clock, five-fifteen, five-thirty . . . you have to do something. So I went to the synagogue that night to fill the time and to find out more, because it seemed clear to me that Larry Foreman had a different way of thinking. It wasn't a set of beliefs, it was a way of approaching life, it was a different way of thinking. He said, "Well, Judaism is really a way of thinking." And God knows I needed some way of thinking that was not just like sitting at the bottom of an avalanche having it all fall on your head. And his sermon was all about the Holocaust. *(Laughs.)* But I can deal with the Holocaust now, because I've sort of been there.

The next Friday I went to synagogue again, and the next Friday after that, and the next Friday after that, and I kept gettin' these books, and I talked to the rabbi when I could. I kept lookin' for the part I couldn't swallow; the part where it said, "I believe in the divinity of Moses" or something, but it doesn't say that. Then in the fall my husband started going with me. "You sort of disappear every Friday night," he said. "Do you mind if I come?"

Finally I said, "This is really nice stuff. I think I may convert." I liked the idea of, metaphorically, being made "in the image of God." That is to say, with the capacity to experience beauty, to perceive and want goodness, goodness in the taste of good food, goodness in the kindness of good acts, goodness in the sharing of love and with the energy and the desire to pursue quality for yourself and share quality—this is what I take as the meaning of being made in the image of God. The wonder of right now, and of together, and of what we can do with it . . . this is marvelous stuff. And I was attracted to the moral beauty of Judaism, that it is a human responsibility to finish creation; I mean, God did it for six days. We're here and we're supposed to clean it up, tend it, look after it, and bring it to such a condition that it would be suitable for God to live in again. I also liked the idea that you're responsible to take care of yourself, that you don't give away everything: you help other people, but you don't starve yourself either, because then you haven't got anything to give tomorrow. The Rabbi Hillel line "If I am not for myself, who will be for me? If I am for myself alone, what good am I? If not me, who? If not now, when?"—that's workable.

So I finally decided to convert, and so did my husband, because we didn't find anything that we had to jump across. The whole thing was just too good to miss. The idea that to doubt and to question's fine, that that's the way you pursue knowledge, that to question is the pursuit of God . . . I liked that. I mean, the idea that the more you know, the closer you are to Beauty and Truth and Goodness and the possibility of human strength, the possibility of creating a better world—I like that! That fits! I don't have to pretend to be stupid. I don't have to pretend not to be furious. I don't have to pretend that I just swallow what's happened. I mean, hey, I can turn my anger into energy. Psychologically this is smart stuff; I mean, this is healing. It enables you to go on without denying any of the bad stuff that happens. You don't havta pretend to believe that it wasn't bad, you don't havta swallow your hurt and say, "Holy, holy, holy." You just say, "It happened and we're here and we know there was goodness in this life that we've lost, and we take a deep breath and go on."

There is a Jewish prayer in which you say, "What is it for us to do? It is for us to heal the world." This is called the *Tikkun Olam*, which comes from the mystical aspect of the Jewish tradition. The story is that there was an original great light and it was divided and spread and cast all asunder and it is for each of us (who has a part of the light inside themselves) to gather more, to gather the light back together, and when the light is all reunited, it will be the coming of the Messiah—heaven on earth. I'm not much into mysticism, but I think it's a wonderful metaphor . . . it's a metaphor I can live by.

Bobby Joe Leaster

EVERYTHIN' HAPPEN FOR A REASON

I grew up in Reform, Alabama, which is a very small town, you know. I had nine sisters and brothers in my family. I am the baby of the family. My mother and father is two of the greater people in the world. They raised me in a way not to have bitterness in my heart toward people that I meet after I grew up and everythin'. I went to church on Sundays and I went to school in a small school down South; it was an all-black school at that time, you know. I graduated in '69, even though my education wasn't really good, because I didn't hit the books like I should have, and I regret that today. But since bein' in prison, I have got that together, 'cause I done been in school since I been here. I improved in a lot of areas that I was lackin' in when I first come to jail, you know. I even got my body in better shape, 'cause I've been workin' out with weights since I been in here.

August 26, 1986. Boston, Massachusetts. We are at the Bay State Correctional Center, a low-security prison for reforming inmates on the outskirts of Boston, where he's lived for the past six years. Through the window from where we're sitting you can see the tops of the high brick, barbed-wire-topped walls of Walpole, a high-security prison where he spent the first seven years of his sentence—starting at the age of twenty—for a murder he says he didn't commit.

I left home right after I got out of high school and came to Boston to visit my cousin and everythin', because she had been callin' me when I was in school to tell me that Boston was a nice place to come. I was still young at the time; had a lot of things on my mind, you know. I was about eighteen years old and I was just saying to myself, I'm getting out of high school now and I'm a young man and all I see ahead of me is my future—leaving home, settlin' down somewhere, raisin' a family, and becomin' a man. That's what my intention was when I come to Boston. And then this happened. I mean it was like, man, you wouldn't believe—it was like a shock. I was up here for fifteen months or so and everything was going along okay. I was working and everythin' and I was stayin' with my people for a little while. Then I moved in with my girlfriend. Things was like comin' together. I could feel my life gettin' ready to change, you know, at that young age. And all of a sudden this here happened to me. When they busted me and took me to jail and everythin', I was like numb; you know, tellin' me that I had just murdered somebody and robbed them. I'm sayin' to myself, "What? Nah, not me, I ain't never harmed nobody in my life."

When I was a kid, I seldom did get into fights. I might argue a taste or two with the guy that I grew up with, but I never got into any bad fights or nothin'. I was basically a very quiet kid growin' up down South. I wasn't capable of doin' nothing like that, because I wasn't raised like that. I wasn't raised in a way that you just go out and take from other folks; I mean, you know, take their money or their jewelry or whatever. And takin' somebody else's life was out of the question for me, totally out of the question. It's just not in me to do that.

They said first-degree life, you know: "We sentence you to natural life at Walpole State Prison." And I had never been arrested before in my life; I had never been to jail. Man, I said to myself; I said, boy; I said, I thought I was goin' to just fall apart when it happened to me. And that's when the faith, you know, came into my heart. I said, Wait a minute: I can't just fall apart here. I said, I didn't do nothin' to be here; I didn't do a thing. But I said, I'm goin' to keep my faith; I'm goin' to keep my spirit high and somehow I'm goin' to beat this . . . somehow, you know. I didn't think it was goin' to take fifteen years out of my life at the time. I said, They got to realize after a few months that I am the wrong man that they put in jail for this murder—they got to realize, you know. That's what I thought at the time. I didn't know nothin' about the court system at all. I figured that they didn't have nothin' on me.

But, see, I was young . . . gullible . . . didn't know nothin' about the law. Just a young kid fresh from the South, you know. I didn't know what was happenin', and they knew this. They said, "Yeah, we got a live one here. He don't know what happenin'; he don't know what goin' on here. We're just goin' to clean the book on this murder here and send this guy away. By the time he realizes what has happened to him, he will already be in jail with this life bit." And that's exactly what happened.

It took me about three or four years after I was locked up to realize what had really happened to me and how serious the crime was: you know, life, first-degree, with no parole. I was in jail for about four years before I really realized that.

What sustained you?

BOBBY JOE: Believin' in the man up above; believin' in God; prayin'. I cried many a nights, you know, askin' why did this happen to me? Why did he let this happen to me? Then as I got older, I

realized that even though this was a tragic thing that happened to me, I realized that it happened for a reason. I believe that everythin' happen for a reason. Me comin' in here like this for somethin' I didn't do, you know, it might of saved my life. I really don't know. I'm just sayin' it might of saved my life from whatever was goin' to come into my life on the streets if this hadn't of happened to me. And I kept prayin' and everythin' and I said, Somethin' goin' to happen good in my life, I'm goin' to get out of this; it might take a little time, but I can just feel it; I just know that whatever bad happened to a person like this, somethin' good got to come out of it— somethin' good got to come out of it. And I just kept that belief inside of me.

I kept thinkin' about my mother and father. All this time I been in here I know they were worried about me and everythin', and I didn't want to come in here and just fall apart; you know, go off the deep end. When they finally come to see me, I don't want to be so crazy that I don't know who they is or whatever. That would hurt my mother more than anythin' in this world if she come up here to visit me and I don't know who she is. She would be devastated by that. And that's another thing that kept me goin' all these years. I said, I'm not only goin' to be strong for myself, I'm goin' to be strong for my mother and father, because they will want me to be because they are two very religious people. They wouldn't want to see me fall apart, and that right there really kept me goin'. I reached down deep inside of me and pulled out strength that I thought I'd never had and sustained it up until this day here. And I survived it, I survived fifteen years of doing this.

A lot of people tell me, "Man, how could you do all that time knowin' that you were innocent, knowin' that you didn't do nothin'?" They say, "It's hard enough for a guy to do two days in jail even when they was guilty. Here you are, innocent, and you done did fifteen years." People is amazed about my attitude. I'm not amazed, because if I had any other attitude than the one I have now, I don't think I would of been able to survive. You understand what I'm sayin'? I figured if my attitude had been really nasty and bitter about this whole thing, constantly thinkin' about what they have done to me, I think I would of cracked up. I think I would of been washed up today. So I say I'm not goin' to have that attitude, I'm not goin' to have it. I say I'm just goin' to keep the faith, keep believin', keep workin' toward gettin' out.

I don't have no money now, you know. But I said, I'm goin' to keep filin' petitions in court, tryin' to get somebody interested in my case to take it and work on it. And finally in 1977 the federal court appointed the Muses to my case.* They came out and talked

---

* Boston lawyers Robert and Christopher Muse, who spent nine years and $400,000 worth of legal time working on Bobby Joe's case. They received no money for their work.

to me and they said, "Well, we're goin' to take your case." And then, a couple of months later, I seen that they was very serious about it. Right then and there I knew my prayer was gettin' ready to be answered; I said, Yes, my prayers are gettin' ready to be answered after seven years. I said it might take another five years or another six years or whatever for all this to come about, but I could see it, you know, I could feel it in my heart. I could feel that the man up above had answered my prayers by sending the Muses to me.

When I first come in here, I doubted whether there was a God or not. It went through my mind, you know. After all, you get sent to jail for somethin' you didn't do, for a life bit, and you start to wonderin'—at least I did. I started wonderin' in my mind, Wait a minute; is there really a God up above? I said, How could there be a God, you know, to let somethin' like this happen to me? But then, as I got older, I started realizin' and thinkin'. I said, Well, what about the babies that die two seconds after they're born? Don't even have a chance to live at all. From the time they come into this world, they don't even breathe for two seconds and they die. What about those, you know?

What I'm sayin' to you is there has to be some purpose for a baby to be born into this world for two seconds and have his life just *(snaps fingers)* taken. There has to be some reason behind that. God has to have a reason for lettin' a baby be born and then just takin' it away in that short period of time. Lookin' at myself, I'm sayin' that there has to be a reason for him lettin' this happen to me, lettin' this tragic thing happen to me like this, knowing that I didn't do it. Like I said, somethin' badder could of happened to me. I could be dead now. He could of seen death comin' toward me and sidetracked me; said, "This not goin' to happen to you yet; I'm not ready to take you yet. Instead this is goin' to happen to you. It's a tragic thing, but it's goin' to happen and this will save you." I look at it like that. It had to happen. You understand what I'm sayin'?

At this point here I don't even look back at it now. I'm only lookin' at my future right now. That's it. Just my future. I'm lookin' straight ahead. Hopefully I will be free around the beginning of '87. So I'll be thirty-seven years old when I leave here, and I just have my future to look forward to—travelin' around, clearin' my head, and gettin' used to bein' free again; you know, gettin' used to bein' back in control of my life, because for the last fifteen years other people have been governin' ninety-nine and a half percent of my life. I've only governed a half percent of it, and that's nothin'. After fifteen years of other people tellin' you what to do and what you can't do, you become somewhat used to that. And when it get time for you to get out, it takes time for you to get back in control of your own life. So I'm just going to relax and just enjoy myself for a little while, just let things happen and just take one day at a time. I'm not goin' to rush life at all. I'm just goin' to let things happen. I know in my mind what I want out of the rest of my life. And I will have those things, because when I get out, I'm goin' to strive for them and I'm goin' to work hard to have those things. And I believe, you know, like my father told me when I was growing up, he say, "If you work hard and do the right thing, you can have what you want."

Right now the most important thing to me is to get out of here and call my mother. The first day I walk out of Bay State, that I walk out of this door, I want to get on the phone. I don't want to use the phone here. I want to wait till I get on the streets, to a pay phone, where I can call my mother and say, "Your son is free. I'm out." You know, that is what's important to me right now, because she is waitin' on this call. She just waitin'. And shortly after that I will be knockin' on her door, and that would really get her there, you know, really.

I love my mother dearly. She's important to me. Very important. I would love to get out and do somethin' special for my mother, like buy her a big house or somethin' that she could be proud of and could say, "My son bought this for me." You know, that would make me the most proudest person in the world if I could be able to do somethin' like that. I haven't had the opportunity to do nothin' for my mother in the last fifteen years, but she did so much for me—raised me and everythin'. I'd just like to do somethin' like that, just somethin' to show her my love for her. She knows how much I love her and everythin', but I would just like to show it in that way and in every possible way that it is possible.

Postscript: Bobby Joe was released from the Bay State Correctional Center in November 1986. In 1989 he married and fathered a son, Robert Joseph Christopher Wade Leaster. He currently lives in Boston, where he works as a construction laborer and part-time weight-training assistant to Ellis Burke, centerfielder for the Boston Red Sox.

Robert Muse

I grew up in Stoneham, Massachusetts, in a place called Dogtown. And we were Catholics, and we were the poor kids. This was during the Depression. I didn't see any airplanes flying down to Florida on TV to tell me that there are rich people in the world. I just knew Dogtown. I knew my neighbors and the conglomerate kind of neighborhood of Italians, Irish, Jews, and, significantly, when I say one black family, everyone in town knew there was one black family. This was at the beginning of probably the fulfillment of the early Irish-Catholic hierarchical influence on the Church, where each parish was set up and then developed a tremendous antagonism toward Protestants—and Protestants toward Catholics. For instance, in that neighborhood we built our own school, Saint Patrick's. We were compelled to go there under pain of mortal sin and not to go to another school. So the public school system was alien to us. In respect of the attitude of the Catholic church, you could not become a Boy Scout, because the Boy Scouts were having their meetings at the Congregational Church, and you had to have special permission to go over and join.

August 24, 1986. Boston, Massachusetts. He's a lawyer with a thick Boston accent and a penchant for fine cigars (the dashboard of his Porsche 911 is coated with ashes). He and his son, Christopher, represent Bobby Joe Leaster. A colorful sixty-six-year-old Irishman, his oak-paneled penthouse office on Bromley Street in downtown Boston is in complete disarray. Yellowed news clippings are tacked to the walls with pins, button-down shirts and pin-striped suits hang from the chairs, and papers and files litter his desk and floor.

He and his wife, Mary Beatty (a Boston trial-court judge), have eleven children, six of whom are lawyers.

In those early days at Dogtown we would have processions, and mission priests would come and separate the men from the women and tell them what would happen to them if you sinned. All of which, retrospectively, wasn't all that bad. It has carried all through my life . . . a compelling sense of right and wrong. So the influence of religion on me was very strong. And it was very strong, I think, on everybody in the parochial system in that era. There wasn't any breaking away from that hard, fascistic tradition . . . you weren't asked, you were told what to do. And that influenced the way I brought up my own family. I was authoritarian; I was the authoritarian father. What I did with my children when they wouldn't behave was to spank them with a belt, like Pavlov's dog. And pretty soon I just had to point to the belt and that brought silence. *(Laughs.)* Today they have a hot-line number to call somebody for parental child abuse . . . all that kind of thing. So I've seen things that I did in one generation which were inoffensive and efficacious suddenly become (not

suddenly, but over a period since World War II), socially unaccept-able. You have to rationalize with children now, and I don't know what the real underlying statistics are with respect to which was the better method: the stern disciplinarian or the one who coddles by language and attempts to rationalize.

So I grew up with a stern, absolute, and unequivocal faith. And my beliefs didn't change at all until World War II, because they were very sustaining to me . . . fulfilling. I probably was as much a ka-mikaze pilot flying for the Marine Corps as any Japanese was flying for their air force. I had a commitment to die. I had no questions about that. We were in combat, substantial combat, for sixty days in Okinawa, and it wasn't until about the sixtieth day that I decided that somebody's tryin' to kill me . . . this is real. Up until that time I was programmed. I think they took the mold of my life, and so many people like me, and imposed this theme of America the Beautiful—"We're right, the world is wrong; they're gooks and we're the great human race and we gotta preserve it for the nice people." We came to hate Japanese. They were gooks!

When I went to Japan just this year (my daughter's teaching there, my youngest daughter), I traveled up in Kyoto and north of Kyoto in the outlying areas. When we were leaving, I said to my wife, "I'm going back to barbarism." That's the feeling I had. Everything there was so polite, so concerned. Human beings were so fair to each other that I thought if ever I've seen the Christian feeling for what is described as charity or love for your brother, I saw it in Japan. And I felt it in Japan as I've never felt it before. So I had great remorse, thinking back, that I went through a period where I treated them as gooks. I left there with a terrible feeling of remorse, particularly after I went to Hiroshima and to the shrine . . . I actually wept. Mankind has come this far around, to obliterate himself. And to think that we were part of the development of this little black bomb. You know, I said, "God must be laughing at us, that he let us develop all of this, that we built this goddamn thing. Now we can blow ourselves up . . . or whatever we want to do, as witness the devastating scene that was Hiroshima."

That frightened me. And it's in this era that I don't have that resolute, marvelous faith of a little child. I'm no longer sure if what I'm doing is right. I am wondering what was right and what was wrong in every respect for the past forty years. That we let this happen. Somehow the intellectuals of the world got ahead of the little kids from Dogtown, and they were doing things that we didn't even know about, while we were concerned with very prosaic Easter parades, First Communions . . . simple beliefs.

I question my beliefs like I never did before. I question dogma . . . those things that are set down. I probably should have been a Jew and been in the whole rabbinical order of things . . . the constant five thousand years of talking back to God, like Samuel and Jeremiah and all the others. And making demands of God. I have that kind of conviction after looking at the little black thing out there in Hiroshima, that first nasty little bomb that you can put your arms around. So I'd be more rabbinical now than I would be ecclesiastical.

I would read Hillel, 'cause I liked his style. All the great rabbis were working men, they all hadta work for a living. They said, "Keep talking but chop wood."

You know, the nuns in Dogtown taught me that God afflicts the souls whom he loves most; God doesn't send you a burden that you can't handle. God sends a disturbed child to a mother who can handle a disturbed child, you know. Well, I'm not so sure anymore. Bobby Joe was able to handle his tragedy, but many of us can't. We buckle under pressure. Most of us don't have Bobby Joe's kind of courage. I learned a lot from Bobby Joe. He's such a beautiful person. Patience . . . he has such patience. And no bitterness . . . incredible. An incredible human being. All he talks about is getting out and beginning the rest of his life. . . .

I don't know, I come to the question, in a lifetime, what do I really believe now? I have a very substantial belief in design, that there has to be some intelligence. I don't know what it is. I don't really expect to see a God figure the way that only man could visualize him—standing with power on top of a cloud. I just have some sense that you can't create or destroy energy. I feel that the fact of our being able to communicate and talk to each other right now is something of a very spiritual essence. And I suspect that when you die, it's a great adventure. If I could pause at the edge of death, I would say I am sad to leave everybody, but the adventure of what that's about I half look forward to seeing. Whatever that passage is from what we're doing now, sitting here talking to each other, into that other realm, is going to be a real passage of some kind. God knows what it will be like. I just don't think that we'll find it in MacKenzie's book of the Bible.* (Laughs.)

---

* A copy of Mackenzie's *Dictionary of the Bible* rests on his desk. "It's as great a source of information as mankind's ever had. (Laughs.) I've had it for about ten years, and when I go to church on Sunday and I don't really know who, what, or where they are referring to, let's say Judea's position to Bethlehem or whatever, I look it up the next day."

War

PART I: JESUS CHRIST
AND JOHN WAYNE

Randy Way

When they were makin' up my dog tag in the army, a guy asked me, "What are you?" And I said, "Well, I think I'm an agnostic." He says, "I'll put it on there if you can spell it." *(Laughs.)* And I said, "Well, okay, I'm not an agnostic then. Put anything you want on it." *(Laughs.)*

El Cajon, California. Not far from the Mexican border. His small home has barred windows, and from the looks of the neighborhood he needs them. His muscular build, weathered face, and Pancho Villa mustache portray the image of the macho outdoor laborer that he is. He's thirty-nine.

I was born in Orange County, California, in 1947. My father was a career Marine, so I spent a good deal of my youth on the East Coast or West Coast. Every year we would move. We made nine major moves by the time I was nine years old, and then we settled here in San Diego.

I was brought up a Lutheran. I was an altar boy. I didn't buy into it much as a youngster. I think it's Blood, Sweat, and Tears that has a line in one of their songs, something about how "I don't believe in heaven but I'm scared to death of hell" . . . something like that. That's about where I was at. It was almost hip not to believe in God as I was growin' up. The way I was brought up, with the Apostles' Creed and the Lutheran church, was that God was a pretty bad dude. I mean, he wasn't like someone you wanted as your runnin' partner. You wanted him to back you up from time to time, but you didn't want to be with him too much because at one point he'd tell you to be perfect, you know, or you get screwed. Then at other times he'd be tellin' you that only one person's ever been perfect, so you ain't gonna make it. So it all seemed pretty futile to shoot for that. And bein' a compulsive person, I never have half-stepped anything. If I do somethin', I either do it all the way or I don't do it at all. It's all black and white. And so at sixteen my father gave me the option. He says, "You don't have to do this anymore if you don't want to. You're a man, you make up your own mind." So I chose not to deal with religion anymore at all.

The closest I got to spirituality, you know, was Timothy Leary and Haight-Ashbury. I went and lived up there for a little while. It was just drugs, sex, rock 'n' roll. I fell right into that. I just cruised California lookin' for a good time. I did a lot of surfing at California Street, up in Rincon, and at Ventura County line.* I went to the first light show at the Hollywood Bowl. Love was free, and God was dead. So spirituality was totally out. At that point in my life I thought that love was like a fourteen-year-old runaway girl and spirituality was the butterfly she had tattooed on her breast. That's about where I was at.

But Uncle Sugar had somethin' else for me; he drafted my young ass and sent me to Vietnam. I flew there on a Braniff Airline with stewardesses, good-lookin' stewardesses, on a commercial flight. Now, I thought this was like a vacation, you know. I had no concept of what was goin' on in Vietnam. I just thought that from what I read and what the hip people had told me (people that understood, like Ginsberg and Ferlinghetti) that it was wrong for us to be there. And I believed them; I believed them. So I stuck three roaches in the end of some cigarettes to smoke before I landed in Vietnam. When it got to twenty minutes till we land, I went into the bathroom and smoked these three roaches and got a little buzz goin' and I went and sat down—all of a sudden I look out the window and there's fires happening in Vietnam! I mean, there's things on fire right below me. And the captain comes on the loudspeaker and says that the Bienhoa airport has just been attacked and that we are being escorted around by some fighter planes. And I looked out and there they are, they're just circlin' around. There's a goddamn war goin' on down below us! I wasn't high anymore. The high went away just like that. *(Snaps fingers.)*

And so we landed and all I got is my duffel bag. You know, there's a war goin' on and all I got is a duffel bag. I don't have a weapon. I mean, there's gooks there, there's Vietnamese everywhere. You know, who's the friendly ones and who's the enemy? I have no idea. They don't indoctrinate us on anything, they just tell

---

* Three of the best surf spots in southern California.

us to stay inside these ropes and don't go over in that building because that's the EM Club—it's where you drink. So, of course, as soon as the commanding officer turned his back, I was in the EM Club drinkin'. That was my main priority. The next day, they were going to give the new guys details unless they wanted to go to church. Well, Genesis, Exodus, Leviticus—hey, that's me. I want to go to church real bad. I fell out of the line and never made it to the church. I just snuck off and went and played for the day.

The Chicanos would get Jesus Christ tattooed on their whole chest, you know. And other guys would have crosses; poor white boys would have crosses tattooed on their arms. I, of course, was wearin' peace symbols. That's what I was into. In Vietnam, right, carrying a machine gun and carrying a peace symbol. And they used to get pissed off; the lifers would get so mad when they'd see you wearin' a peace symbol.

I used to talk about religion and God and stuff with guys in Vietnam, because I was curious about their feeling. And some people had the same belief that I was brought up with, meaning they were scared not to believe in God. But Vietnam seemed to weaken their faith, not strengthen it. But the Hispanics, it seemed like their faith got stronger. I mean, they fell back on it, they actually used it. I don't know what their concept of God was, but he must have been a vengeful motherfucker. One of my best friends was a low rider from San Jose, and he always said his prayers before we'd go out into the field.

The first time I confirmed a kill, I was carrying an M-79 grenade launcher. The guy with the M-60 machine gun and I were the only people that could reach the gooks we were tailing. The M-16s couldn't reach 'em. And so it was like a turkey shoot. We're on one side of the crest of a ravine which was real thick jungle and the gooks are on the other side of the ravine which had been cleared, napalmed, or Agent-Oranged. And we could see these guys crawlin' up. We ran into 'em, had a little firefight, and they took off up the side of this ravine. So I just started lobbin' rounds at 'em, and I got real close to one guy and it picked him up and threw him back down in the ravine. And it was gettin' near dusk, so we left the area completely and set up a night location far away, as far as we could get. We slept. The next morning we radioed in and told 'em what had happened. They said, "Well, go check it out; see what's over there." And we did. We found this guy that I'd hit and he didn't die right then. He crawled up this ravine with a lot of his insides hangin' out of 'em. He got up to the top and he hung himself 'cause he just couldn't go no farther. I was still pretty new, you know. I had seen some deaths and I had seen some things to that point, but I had never been responsible. And so the old-timers, of course, were goin' "Tripper" (my nickname was Tripper), "hey, all right, you got a confirmed kill, you're baptized." But I can remember feelin' real alone, feelin' totally alone at that point and scared. You know, how much of that old upbringing was comin' back—thou shalt not kill. I'd done all the other ones and got away with it and smiled. But this one, I wasn't smiling. *(Nervous chuckle.)* This one hurt.

As time went on, I became more callous, more able to do my job and shut off my emotions. A soldier can't have those emotions and be successful, so you learn to shut 'em down. You can't grieve in the field. And like I said, the biggest thing I can think of is this feelin' so alone. I didn't feel God. I didn't even feel my friends right there. I just felt alone. I felt like I was just surrounded by a little space that nobody could get into.

It wasn't long after that before I got heavy into heroin. I was hanging out with this Italian from Long Island who said his people were in organized crime. With his attitude, they could of been—I don't know. He was on his second tour in Vietnam. I respected the guy; he'd been around. Anyway there was some kind of Vietnamese holiday goin' on. It was off-limits to go, but the guards at the main gate of the Fourth Division Headquarters were so used to seein' us go out that they let us go. So I went downtown with Vinny and he heads for this off-limits alley. No Americans are allowed to be in there. But Vinny, he's got it cased out perfect, he knows exactly where to go, where every nook and cranny is. I mean, he's like Indiana Jones in the Temple of Doom. We're runnin' through this place and we go into an opium den. I'd been smokin' some opium—not in the field, but in the rear—and I liked the high it gave me. But I was always scared of needles. I thought only black people used needles, you know, that's the way I was brought up. White boys don't do that. Maybe if you're a jazz musician . . . but otherwise, white boys just don't do that—even poor white boys.

So we go into this opium den, and this cat Vinny gets down, bang, and I watched the transformation on him—totally miraculous. So Vinny says, "Hey, come on, Tripper, another baptism right here." And I go, "Naw, not me." I went through my whole rap. You know, I can remember like yesterday tellin' 'em, "Naw, man, that's dangerous, dangerous." But I'm holdin' my M-16 there. I've got it strapped on my shoulder or somethin'. He says, "How can you be afraid of this little gun right here with this needle on it when you're not afraid to go out and kill people with that gun?" And that totally made sense to me, you know. Yeah, you're right, I can go out with this gun and create mayhem and take children's fathers away from 'em, yet I'm afraid of this little piece of glass right here with a piece of metal on the end. Fuck it. Let's go. And so he give me 1 cc of the purest stuff. It was cooked down to just the minimum to fix. And it nearly killed me. It made me turn blue and I quit breathin' and these guys kept me alive. It was an overdose is what it was, but I was such a hard-core on everything else, he figured I could take this too.

Well, that was the first time. And once I came out of it, I felt so good. I felt like this is the one little place where I should be. I didn't care about Vietnam. I didn't care about the United States. I didn't care about nuthin'.

When I came home, there was somethin' wrong in my head, you know. I knew I wasn't the same person that I was before I went. I got back in June 1969, Labor Day of 1969. The night I walked into my father's house, he took one look and he knew there was somethin' wrong. But I decided that what I had to do to change me was to get married and have children and hold a steady forty-hour-a-week job. You know, just like Mom and Dad, because that's what I perceived as being normal. I figured if I did that, then maybe I would be normal. So I married a sixteen-year-old girl, you know. I was twenty-one. I figured, I got her young enough, I can just mold her like Silly Putty; you know, just mold her exactly how I want and then I won't lose her. That made sense to me. And that, of course, didn't last; it didn't work. We were married for three years and had one son.

When my wife and I split up, I told her I'm just gonna keep the kid: "You just get the fuck out of my life." I kept my car and my house; you know, tough guy, blah, blah. Then one day I had a guy I hadn't seen in years stop by who asked if I could put him up for a night. Mitch and I went way back to teenagers, so I said sure. Well, what I didn't know is that Mitch had just recently escaped from some mental institution. I had no idea. I come to find later that he had taken too much speed and burned his brain up; turned himself into a manic-depressive and had to be on massive doses of lithium or else he was just liable to go wherever. Anyway I took off for work, dropped my boy off at the baby-sitter, and told him when I'd get home. Then I get a call from another friend of mine who said my house is covered with police cars. Mitch decided that he was a big prick and he covered his body with Vaseline and he was going out to fuck the world. He decided he would do this while he was stayin' at my house! So, you know, somebody called the police and they arrested him, asked him where he was stayin'; he said my house. At the time I was selling Seconal and pot—just nuthin' big. I had, you know, five or six pounds of pot and a couple hundred reds. But

Mitch had all this stuff out there in the living room. The police walked in. Of course I end up in the felony tank, and across the way Mitch's in there in the misdemeanor tank. That's why I lost my son. The courts took him away from me.

From that point on I started using heroin again. Once they took my kid, I just really didn't care about anything and I started gettin' in situations where there was a lot of danger involved; physical danger, you know. I started packin' guns, doin' criminal activities. Like it would get me on the edge and it would get me high, you know; it would get me high. I liked it. I think it was almost like gettin' back to Vietnam in a way. Like I can say that Vietnam was the worst time in my life, but at the same time it was also the very best time of my life because to be walkin' around in the jungle with an automatic weapon knowin' there's some guy out there that wants to kill you and it's your job to kill him, there is nuthin' like that, nuthin'. I mean I sky-dive, you know, and I white-water-raft, but there is nuthin' like that. That is John Wayne. I mean, that's exactly what it is. We were brought up with Jesus Christ and John Wayne. And you get hooked on it even though it scares the shit out of you. I mean, why do you go watch a horror movie? You want to get scared. You can't get any more scared than someone tryin' to kill you—you just can't.

So far there's been a lot of killing, lots of drugs, lots of tough times. I'm surprised you're still here.

RANDY: Well, what happened to change all that is the Internal Revenue had come in and taken everything I owned—practically everything I owned—and my car had been repossessed. And my habit, my heroin habit, was between $500 and $1,000 a day. So you know what you gotta do to make that kind of money. I had burned and hurt everybody, even those that meant the most to me. I was living in an old tin barn down in Logan Heights, which is a barrio in this town. I had a 12-gauge shotgun, a double-barreled, over-and-under 12-gauge with dual triggers. And I wanted to see if I could stretch my toes to where I could hit both triggers with the barrel in my mouth so I could blow my head off. I mean, that's where I was at. And as I was lying there on this old, beat-up couch, fleas and rats and mice and stuff all runnin' around me, I thought to myself about all the hard times I'd been through and all the shit that had happened to me and I was still alive and this was how it was gonna end, that I was just gonna kill myself. You know, I wasn't Catholic, so I didn't have that big fear of suicide and hell. My main thought was that I didn't really want to go that way. I'd always felt a little bit cheated out of a glorious death, you know. Like I watched some of my partners get glorious deaths. They came out of it heroes, you know. Dead but heroes. And I felt like I deserved somethin' like that. *(Laughs.)* Let 'em sing songs about me.

My mother had just remarried. My father had been dead awhile, and she had just married this guy who I had never conned before. I came up to him and I said, "Listen, I need $1,000 to get into a hospital." And my mother's over there: "Don't you give him nuthin', he'll just go buy drugs with it." I was wearin' this old cowboy hat, and it had a diamondback rattlesnake that a friend of mine had skinned around the left side, and on the right side I had my CIB.* Well, this man saw that and he said, "What did you do? Where? When?" He was in World War II in the infantry, army infantry, and he himself had a CIB. He said, "I'm not gonna give you the cash. What I'll do is I'll come and pick you up and I'll drive you to the hospital and I'll give those people the $1,000." I said, "Hey, that's what I really want. I can't deal with this anymore." Monday noon he came and got me.

So I got into the psychiatric detoxification hospital. Well, the philosophy of this hospital was the AA philosophy, which is a spiritual program. My first thought to that was, I'm fucked. Here I am. If this is the only thing that works, I'm in trouble, because none of this shit do I believe in. *(Laughs.)* It's all dead and stinkin'.

One of the male nurses there had been a medic with the 173rd Airborne Brigade and he asked me if I'd been in Vietnam. He started talkin' about it, and all of a sudden I couldn't talk about it. The big chicken-bone effect right in my neck. I couldn't talk about Vietnam. So they figured they'd better get somebody in there who knew about Vietnam, because this could be a real important point in my sobriety. So they called Dick Scott. He'd already been through this hospital and was doin' pretty good. I think he had a year and a half straight at the time, somethin' like that. So he came and talked to me. And there was an immediate warmth that I got from this cat. Like I don't get close to too many people. I don't even talk to people, you know. But this guy, he walked right up to me. I had hepatitis so bad that my skin was yellow. I mean, I looked terrible. This guy walked right up to me and hugged me after he had heard my story. And I said to myself, This is a stupid motherfucker to come up and hug me the way I look. I mean he's either got to be sick or he's for real. And he was for real. Every day he would come back and see me, take time out of his day, and he's a busy man.

So I started listenin' to his concepts on Higher Power and spir-

---

* Combat Infantryman's Badge.

ituality. Dick would buy me all the books that you could read on spirituality, you know. But with all the books in the world I don't know that I've ever learned anything that's really stuck with me. So he just told me to stick around and just fake it. Well, I've never been good at that either, you know. But I did it. I'd bite my tongue; sit on my hands; I'd listen to people talk about this God. Every once in a while I couldn't handle it and I'd blow it and I'd say, "Let me tell you about this." And then I'd start givin' 'em all the reasons for not believin' in God. And in the AA program, what they say is "God as you understand him." So finally one day that clicked . . . as I understand him.

Well, the first thing is, I don't understand him. I don't know this guy. I have no idea. Today I still don't understand any of that. But I got the opportunity to work with some other people to where I was the teacher, so to speak, and I watched miracles happen in their lives—I mean, righteous miracles. Dope fiends comin' out of the gutter without a pot to piss in or a window to throw it out of. And one of the guys—he's a friend of mine—had spent like ten years in the penitentiary since he'd come back from Vietnam. Now he's got himself a great job. He's gonna marry some broad who's got a Ph.D., and all this in like two or three years. Somethin's happening, you know, and I don't know what it is.

So if I gotta draw a line and say this is my belief, all I could say is there's somethin' happenin' that's a lot bigger than I am and it's a lot bigger than anybody I know. But I'm not real sure what it is and I'm at a point where I don't want to know what it is. I don't want to know why, I just want it to keep happenin'. I've been off the drugs now for six years. I want it to keep happenin', because my life continually gets better when I do good.

But I think my perspective has changed a lot just in the last year. Things have been tough. I had gotten to the point where I'd fallen in love with a woman and was gonna get married and take the risk of bringing children into the world, which is a big deal. I mean, you talk about responsibility. And then this lady committed suicide right here in my backyard a few months back. So I've slipped back quite a bit.

But my answer is still that you've got to treat other people the way you want them to treat you. Be good, but strong. Don't take no shit and don't turn the other cheek. I don't believe in that. I know that when I do good, I feel good. And that's real simple. There's nothing complicated about that. There's no books in the Bible that can make me feel like that. There's no drugs that can make me feel like that. If I do good, I feel good. And it doesn't have to be big deals. Playin' with the kids here on the block. I mean, most of the kids here don't have parents or everybody's divorced; their father's in jail; they're livin' with grandmothers. It feels good to me to be with 'em, you know, just seein' 'em, givin' little presents and stuff. God, it's no big deal, but it just makes me feel so good. So I don't know that there is an answer to life. For me, I just try to be as good as I can, even though right now I'm going through some pretty rough times 'cause of this lady goin' out on me.

John Coleman

THE DEVIL'S PLAYGROUND

Boulder, Colorado. He is editor-in-chief of Soldier of Fortune *magazine. He entered the U.S. Army in 1969 and pulled two tours of duty in Vietnam. In 1970 he served as sergeant in the First Brigade, 5th Infantry Division (mechanized), and in 1971 he served in the First Battalion, 22nd Infantry Division, First Field Force. In 1975 he left the service in disgust.*

We had really gotten the shit kicked out of us. . . . I was not happy with the way the United States sold out Vietnam, and in turn sold out the 57,000-odd men and women who died in Vietnam and the thousands who were still listed as POW/MIA. I was not happy at all with the direction the United States was taking. So I decided, If I can't be satisfied here, then I've got to leave the country; I've got to do something else to satisfy myself. That's why I went to Rhodesia in April 1976. I took a careful look at that war and I decided that it was basically a continuation of the Vietnam war in terms of who was supplying what to whom. And it was clear to me that it was a classic East-West confrontation, a pro-Western government fighting two terrorist groups which were supplied by the Soviet Union and the Red Chinese. It was a war between those who wanted a democracy and those who wanted a Marxist-allied, Communist-totalitarian regime. Anyway I was sick of America, sold off what I had, flew to Salisbury, Rhodesia, presented myself to the army recruiter, and said, "I'm here to fight." And that's the war I fought for three and a half years.

When you asked what my deepest personal conviction was over the phone the other day, I asked you to let me think about this and you said, "I want a straight-from-the-hip answer." Well, when you first mentioned it, my immediate response was, "freedom." And as I thought about it over the weekend, it didn't change; there was nothin' else for me but freedom, the idea of individuals being free, of having the choice to make decisions, to decide how to live their lives, how they will be governed . . . without that basic freedom, everything else is moot. Nothing else exists. You become a nation or a culture of people who are no more than sheep. You're slaves. You're slaves to yourselves for letting yourself be ruled by someone else and for not having the conviction and the courage to stand up and say, "No . . . I'm gonna fight. I don't care what it costs, I'm gonna fight. And if I get killed, then somebody else is gonna fight. And if they get killed, somebody else is gonna keep fighting. And we're gonna keep fighting until the last person who has the guts to fight is dead. And when we're all gone and there ain't nobody else gonna fight, well, then it's too late; you know, we will have lost. But as long as somebody has that courage to stand up and fight, it makes it all worthwhile in the long run. I can leave a legacy to my kids . . . and hopefully my kids will stand up and fight and they'll leave that legacy to their kids. And we won't allow governments to tell us what to do—we will tell the governments what to do.

They say there are no atheists in foxholes, but there are. There are guys who put their faith in a 7.62-millimeter bullet; there are guys who put their faith in the god to the left and right of them and they don't ask for divine intervention. They ask for the camaraderie of combat to keep them alive, and they ask for faith in themselves, faith in their friends, faith in their training, their experience, the weapons they have—that's what they ask for.

Does God keep us alive in combat? Well, to me, combat is very capricious. I've seen excellent people, first-rate people killed, slaughtered. I've seen missionaries slaughtered; people carrying God's word slaughtered by terrorists, horribly mutilated. I ask myself the question "Why should they be slaughtered, why should they be torn asunder, as the Bible would say?" I have watched people who are nasty, evil, terrible men—mercenaries who would kill you as soon as look at you. And they will walk away and live and die of old age. I ask, "Is there some kind of godliness to that?" The devil's playground is a combat zone, you know, even though it doesn't make any sense, 'cause guys on both sides are fighting for true beliefs, true causes—on either side, most guys are convinced that they're fighting for the right cause. In that sense there should be some form of godliness in a combat zone; I mean, if you have men of true faith fighting for things they believe in, God should be somewhere in the picture. Yet I don't see it. I just see the worst come out in combat. I don't see a benign, benevolent God guiding us through to a better life. So I'm not driven by a belief in God.

When you're on the battlefield, it's easy to determine who the bad guys are. The bad guys are the ones that are shooting at you. Off the battlefield it's harder for me to point the finger. In Rhodesia the two main terrorist groups (the ZANLA* and the ZIPRA** guerrilla factions) were, in my eyes, the bad guys. In their eyes I was the bad guy; I was a foreign mercenary dog. But who's bad and who's good in this situation? I mean, there were times when American soldiers committed atrocities in Vietnam. There's no doubt about it. There were times when the Viet Cong committed atrocities. Now, those people that commit atrocities are bad people, but are generally the North Vietnamese Army troops bad guys? No. Is the average Joe, right out of the 101st Airborne Division a bad guy? No. Is a guerrilla a bad guy? Nah, he believes in what he's fighting for. So I have more respect for the people on the battlefield than I do for any politician, 'cause the politicians are the ones that send us in there in the first place. We're simply instruments when the rest of the process has failed. But if we believe strongly in the rationale that the politician has sent us for, then we go and fight. Down on the ground, though, it becomes him against me. He believes in what he's fighting for and I believe in my group. I think I probably have more in common with a Soviet paratroop captain than I do with the average congressman in the United States. I think I have more in common with an African National Congress guerrilla than I probably do with very many people in the white South African government, simply because we're soldiers on the ground—and because we live with the courage of our convictions.

In battle it's a very old, very tried-and-true premise: You either kill them or they kill you. Some people can't come to grips with it. Some people are brought up to believe that to take another human's life is just the worst sin you could ever possibly commit. But when you get down in the mud, and when somebody's shootin' at you, you

---

* ZANLA: Zimbabwe African National Liberation Army, backed by the People's Republic of China.
** ZIPRA: Zimbabwe Peoples Revolutionary Army backed by the Soviet Union.

shoot back at them. You may believe in what you are fighting for, or you may not, but you do shoot back. And I have to admit that grand convictions are not what you fight for in the heat of battle; you fight for the squad, you fight for the platoon, you fight for those people that you're out there on the ground with. The other guys are out there to kill you, and they're out there to kill your buddies, and so you're out there to kill them first. After you come back from the bush and have a few beers and lay down on the rack and stare up at the ceiling, you might think, Today I killed somebody. But if you're smart, you won't do it too often, 'cause you can think about that to the point where you drive yourself insane . . . you can really blow a gasket, and I watched it happen in Vietnam. We called it shell shock then. Now they call it post-traumatic stress disorder, and it catches up with guys after the war when they come back. But I've come to grips with it. I've killed . . . I don't know how many I've killed (I never kept notches on the gun), but I killed enough people so I didn't get killed in the process, although I came close to it a few times.

I was shot five times in Rhodesia. A fellow was about ten steps away with a Kalashnikov, a Soviet assault rifle. He had it on automatic fire, pulled the trigger, and five rounds hit me from a distance of about ten feet away. I took two in the arm, one in the neck, two in the chest. It probably took no more than two or three seconds from the time he pulled the trigger to the time I hit the ground. But in my mind that whole scenario took an eternity. From the time I took the impact of the rounds, which is like being hit with a sledgehammer, being physically lifted up by the force of the rounds, and thumping face first onto the ground and bouncing a few times, coming to settle . . . that seemed like an eternity, and it still does. And it crossed my mind in that one or two seconds. I said, Well, I've finally come to grips with what death feels like. It was nothing more than a collage of muted colors. I could see the colors of the trees, of the ground, of the sky . . . and they were muted, soft colors, and I said this is my entryway into death; I'm now seeing it. But then I hit the ground, and the physical sensation of hitting the ground brought me back to reality. Then I realized that nothing critical hit me. Says a lot for Soviet weapons. Guy hits me five times and I'm still okay. (Laughs.) I could feel my fingers, and I felt my toes, and I moved my arms and legs to a degree . . . and everything moved. I was out of action for about six weeks altogether with that. Nothing vital was hit.

I've been close to death a couple of other times in combat. And you ask yourself the question (as every soldier does), you know, what happens if I die, where do I go? For all my studies in school of the various religions, the seven planes of existence, the idea of reincarnation, the idea of a heaven or hell, I have to be dead honest with you; as boring as it sounds, I haven't the vaguest idea what happens to you. Thomas Edison passed out before he died and came back to life. And when he awoke, he sat up and said, "It's beautiful over there." Then he lay back down and died. There've been a lot of out-of-body experiences that people report. Say, you know, there's the long tunnel that takes you down to wherever you're going. But I don't know. If any of us knew then, we probably wouldn't sit here in this corporeal existence. We'd probably either kill ourselves or do our damnedest never to die.

Is there a meaning to life? If there is, I really haven't found what it is. But there is a way to find it, and that is to grab on to a belief. You know, we can all be Charlie Browns in our life and never make a decision. You can go through your life and never make a decision and die that way, and then your presence here has just been a waste of your time and everyone's else's time, because you've not affected anyone, you've not affected anything. You've not made a change for better or for worse. That's what I see is a problem right now with the United States. People want to sit back, go with the flow, do what everybody else is doing; you know, go out there and make some bucks. We let so much go by without trying to make a change that we just become slugs in the United States. We become herd animals, we become sheep, where we just kind of let everything happen for us and stagnate.

So I guess I believe you need to go out and become involved in some shape, form, or fashion with something you believe in. To me, getting involved meant fighting—and it still does. It still means being prepared to make what is the ultimate sacrifice, which is sacrificing your life for something in which you believe. To me, that's the way to find a meaning. When you're willing to go put your life on the line, then you can come back and say, "I've been to the edge and I've looked across and I've seen what I think is important. I've gleaned out all the unnecessary bullshit." When you come down to life-and-death scenarios, everything else really becomes placid and facile.

PART II: FROM RAMBO
TO RAINBOW

Don Preister

Northeastern Colorado, near the town of Sterling. He's a member of the Great Peach March for Nuclear Disarmament, walking across the United States in an effort to halt the development and deployment of nuclear arms. Yesterday he and his comrades marched seventeen miles through pelting rain and hail. But today it's clear and warm and by 3:00 P.M. he'll cross the border into his native state of Nebraska, where he works as director of the Boys Club of Omaha. His bright, hand-knitted sweater sports the colors of the rainbow. "We need to change the Rambo mentality to the rainbow mentality. We need to build rainbow bridges of communication and unity, bonds of love and communication rather than barriers and walls and hostility between people. This sweater is the symbol that I have in the march—the rainbow and the openness." He's forty.

When I first went to Vietnam, I had the sense that I would be okay, that nothing would happen to me, that I would get home and that would be it. What would happen in between I didn't know. I got there in December of '67. On January 30th of '68 the Tet offensive started. So we were being hit constantly day and night. You couldn't sleep, you couldn't eat, you couldn't do anything. But I felt I was going to be okay. I remember the first time we were under fire. It just kept getting closer—the shells, everything—and it was like the next one was going to be right on top of me and it was all over, I was going to be dead. I had this real helpless feeling, this sense of it's all over and it can't be over, it's not my time to die, I can't go yet. I had the feeling of floating out in space with a huge meteor coming right at me and all I could do is think and see. I couldn't move. I couldn't do anything. I was just totally helpless. Then, all of a sudden, the meteor just went right by me and the shelling stopped. And after that I was still afraid, but something happened. It was like I needed to get in touch with that real fear of death and then see that death was not the end. So having that near-death experience that first time and then many times after that helped me to see that that wasn't really the end.

The hardest part for me, as a medic, was seeing people blown up, seeing their heads splattered apart, seeing their chests blown open (some of them still living) and trying to get them on a helicopter and trying to save their lives and at the same time trying to kill other people. It didn't make any sense. It was so ridiculous. I kept asking myself, Just why do people have to be this way? Why do people have to kill each other? Why does there have to be this torment and this anguish? Why? It just didn't make sense. It was so insane and it just keeps going on. *(He begins to cry.)* And the people who had no connection with it were controlling it and making money off other people's suffering. Calling other people gooks and crazy names that didn't make any sense, it was just so totally crazy. I couldn't make any sense out of it, and I didn't know why it was going on, and yet I was there and I had to be a part of it. *(Weeping heavily.)*

(He pauses to gain composure, then smiles.) I've learned to cry and I've learned how good it feels to do it, 'cause for a long time I couldn't even think about it; I couldn't talk about Vietnam; I couldn't cry for that or for anything. And I've learned that it's very important to cry and especially important for men to cry. We need to cry to get in touch with the feminine part of us, because we are both male and female, and all those qualities that we label as feminine only create a balance within us. As long as we block those qualities out and as long as we don't allow emotion to show through us, then we're not fully in touch and fully balanced and fully aware.

It's only been in the last year and a half that I could really come to grips with Vietnam and get in touch with the pain and not let it overwhelm me. Now I'm able to experience at a deep emotional level the importance of never letting that happen again and doing what I can within my power to help bring about the transition from a warlike mentality to a peaceful one. And I wouldn't have the same motivation, I wouldn't have the same depth of emotion, had I never gone through a war and seen that happen around me.

I now see the essence of being here on earth is to try and work back to the godlike state of unconditional love, because love is what God is. The earth was created out of love; therefore what we are is love. And love is peace. And when we get that inner peace and that awareness of being connected with God, we'll uncover our life purpose and the meaning of our lives.

I have come to the realization that my main purpose in being here is to protect the earth; to be here, in whatever form that takes, to bring some harmony and unity and balance within people. With the Peace March that I'm now on, I'm helping to eliminate nuclear weapons, which are a destructive force that could totally throw the earth out of balance and destroy all life-forms on it. So my sole purpose in being on the earth is to help protect it. And right now the form that's taking is walking across the country and touching people's lives.

Sarah Corson

ONWARD CHRISTIAN SOLDIERS

Widowee, Alabama. She and her husband, Ken, have devoted their lives to missionary work on behalf of the United Methodist church. Together they have served in Cuba, Puerto Rico, Haiti, Costa Rica, and Bolivia. "When we first began this work in Cuba in the 1950s, we were both convinced that America was on the side of God, because we had been taught in history books that America is this great Christian nation. But when we got to Cuba, we were shocked to find out that Americans were really oppressing the Cubans in a terrible way. And as we've traveled around, what we've seen is that Americans do this nearly everywhere. We prop up horrible, oppressive governments to protect our business interests and we do it in the name of God . . . and this really hurts me, because our behavior isn't Christian at all."

As a result of their shared experiences and beliefs, Sarah and Ken founded SIFAT (Servants in Faith and Technology), a nonprofit organization that trains missionaries to teach Third World citizens low-cost self-sufficiency techniques appropriate to their surroundings.

I have one story I could tell that really expresses my faith. I was in Bolivia in the summer of 1980. I'd gone there for three months with a team of seventeen young people at the request of the district Bolivian church to do experiments with growing grain and to teach Bible schools to the children. They had no pastors for many miles around there, you know. It was just little villages of semiliterate people. Ken at the same time had to go to Haiti. He already com-

mitted himself for the summer there, so we divided up for that summer. And we were two hundred miles from any help at all, you know.

Well, I had been there two months, and there was a coup. This was a Nazi-type revolution, you know. They were right-wing . . . extreme right-wing. In fact it was what later became called the cocaine government, because they were sponsored by the Mafia in Florida accordin' to our State Department (that's what we were told by the State Department). So this woman in the village said to me, "Go to the mountains, 'cause I overheard the soldiers sayin' they're out to kill every American, because Americans are tryin' to stop their revolution." And I said, "We're innocent. We don't have to run from anybody." And she said, "You better run, 'cause they don't care if you're innocent or not." People in the village had lost family members from people just suspectin' them of things, you know. But we didn't have anyplace to run to. How could I take the seventeen young people I had out in the jungle? There were boa constrictors and everything under the sun out there. I couldn't take them out there.

That night I went outside to cover my son, Tommy (he was on the front porch, because there wasn't enough room in the house for all seventeen of us). And when I looked out, there in the moonlight, I could see soldiers. But they couldn't see me because there was a shadow over the porch. There were about thirty soldiers with their rifles, runnin' from tree to tree with their rifles on our house, you know. They were watchin' us, and then they'd run to the next tree. One slid into the water barrel right there in front of me, just about six feet from me, but he didn't see me.

I was just in total shock. I thought, This is it. I just didn't even think to ask God to save me, because I thought even God can't jump thirty rifles at one time, you know. (Laughs.) So I just had a moment to pray, and I said, "God, take care of my family, and please don't let 'em shoot till I catch my breath." I had been a Christian since I was thirteen years old, 'cause that's when I really consciously made my own choice to folla' Christ; it wasn't a hand-me-down choice from my parents. And so I thought, I've lived for him since I was thirteen, but now I can't even die for him without bein' afraid. Well, what's the good of doin' what I'm doin' if I can't trust him with my death too? I was just so ashamed of myself that I was afraid . . . but I was petrified when I saw all those guns. And then, just in that moment, I said, "Please, Jesus, take this fear away." And I believe it was Jesus, and you may believe it was God (I don't care what name you call him, you know), but there was a divine presence that was immediately there like I have never felt before nor since. It was somethin' that I could not doubt any more than I doubt that you are right there, you know. I was just so afraid, and then suddenly it was like I could take the hand of God . . . he was there. I still thought I was goin' to die. But that wasn't my purpose in askin' to live, you know. I just wanted this to work out, right? I wanted to end my life trustin' him, and trustin' him to take care of my family and all that. It was just the greatest peace I have ever known in this world, and the greatest power I've ever known. Because I've never hungered for power. I wanted to be humble and with the poor and the grassroots, but it was just such a liberating power that God was in charge, that I was in his hands. And yes, I'm gonna die, but that's okay, because he's workin' everything around.

So I didn't wait for them to find me, see. They were outside, they were runnin' around and had circled the house by that time. So I just walked out of the front door. And there was a young man squattin' with his rifle on, and I put my hand on his shoulder. I should have known he'd think I had a gun, you know. But I wasn't thinkin'. I just said, "Brother . . ." And I just felt love for all of them, you know. I couldn't have done it on my own. God just suddenly was there, and this guy screamed, you know, and he jumped up and said, "It's not me! It's not me! It's him." (Of course this was in Spanish. I speak Spanish.) So he pointed to the man that was leading the team, you know, the captain or whoever he was.

Then they rushed the house. They went runnin' in and turned the house upside down lookin' for the guns that we didn't have. But they were sure that we were a Marxist group, because there were some Marxists workin' in the area. They ransacked the house and got the kids outta their beds and lined 'em up on the two benches where we eat in the kitchen. So I just walked out toward the captain while they were rushin' in doin' that, and I said, "Welcome, brothers. Everybody's welcome at our house. You don't have to have guns to visit us, just come on in and tell us what you want." Then he pushed me around real rough and stuck the gun in my back and pushed me toward the back door. And I turned around to face him, and he stuck the gun in my ribs, and he said, "I'll teach you Americans to come down here and stop our revolution." And I said, "Brother, we are down here to help the hungry learn to feed themselves, and to teach the Bible, and we're not doing anything against your revolution." And he said, "Well, I've never read the Bible in my life, so what are you teachin'? . . . It's probably a communist book, for all I know." He was out after Marxists, you know. And I said, "You've never read the Bible? I'm so sorry for you; you've missed the best part of your life. Let me tell you what it says." And I picked up a Bible that was lying right there on the table. It was in Spanish, in his language. I'm tellin' you the truth now. I was the one in command, not him . . . he had the gun in my ribs. And I don't mean that I wanted to be in command. I just mean there was such a joy and fearlessness that was absolutely not me. This had to have been divine, you know.

So I opened the Bible to Matthew 5, the Sermon on the Mount.

And he wasn't goin' to read the whole thing, but he couldn't help but see the titles over the paragraphs in Spanish. And they said, "Jesus Teaches Love Your Enemies," and the next one said, "Turn The Other Cheek," and the next one said, "He Hits You on One Side, Give the Other One." So the guy was really shocked by this. He couldn't help but see the titles, and I read it to him: "Jesus Teaches Love Your Enemies." I said, "This book teaches the story of God's love for us, and in fact the Son of God gave his life that you and I might know that love, and therefore I know that you're my enemy. I've already been told that you're gonna kill every American, and I know that you are gonna kill me." And I really thought he was. But I said, "I just want you to know that when you kill me, that I will die lovin' you, and prayin' for you, because God loves you and I follow him." And he said, "Ah . . . ah . . . ah . . . ah," you know, he couldn't believe it. He said, "That's not humanly possible." And I said, "It is. That's why it takes a superhuman person to help us do it, that's why it takes God. Because of God I can say to you, 'I love you, brother.' Because I know he loves you. If you don't believe it, you can prove it. You have the gun. You can kill me fast, or you can kill me slow," I said. "There's a machete over there. Just take it and chop me to pieces little by little, and let me prove to you that I'll die lovin' you and prayin' for you." Then I stopped myself and said to myself, "Sarah, what are you sayin'!" They do those kinda things. But there is a Scripture in Matthew that says, "Don't be afraid when you're taken before judges and magistrates, because you will be given the words to say in that moment." And they were not my words. I would never have thought of sayin' those things. They just came through my tongue.

That man was so shocked, and he took the gun out of my ribs, and pointed it toward the floor, and he said, "Well, you almost convinced me you're innocent." He said, "I wish I hadn't gotten in this mess. I don't wanna take you prisoner. I don't wanna kill you. But in our army you don't break orders." He was trained by Klaus Barbie; you know, the Butcher of Lyons under Hitler. Barbie trained the army that the Mafia paid to take over Bolivia at that time. I mean, you just look the wrong way and you were shot. He said, "Listen, we don't break one little order. I wish I didn't have to take you prisoner, but that's the least I can do. Otherwise I've gotta kill you. . . . I've been given that order." So he marched us through this little jungle trail down to the main road, started to put us on the back of this truck, and all at once he said, "Wait. The women with me." But he had my fifteen-year-old son, and the seven other young men that were with us, taken to his jungle prison. Then he had the boys flown to the capital city in an old plane that landed in a pasture. He had them imprisoned there in a dungeonlike cell until the U.S. embassy was able to negotiate their release four days later. By the way, it was the Marxists that reported it to the U.S. embassy. *(Laughs.)*

While all this was happenin', he took us back to our house. He said, "I can't take you. This is the first time in my life I have ever broken an order. But I can't take you. Even if they kill me, I can't take you. I could have fought any amount of guns you had, but there's somethin' here I just can't face." He just couldn't fight love, you know. He couldn't. And he said, "I was about to take you into a jungle camp of over a thousand soldiers. I know what they do to every woman prisoner. I know that you all would be abused so many times that some of you wouldn't live through it. I can't do it. I can't do it. If they kill me, I can't." But he said, "If you let my supervisin' officer know that you were in this house when I raided it, and that I didn't take you prisoner, I'll pay for it with my life."

That was a Thursday night when all this happened. And Sunday the captain and his bodyguard came to our church. And I was leading the service, because the pastor had also been taken prisoner (he was a local pastor, one of the villagers). I invited the captain up front, to welcome him. And he was really surprised. I said, "This is our custom, to invite visitors up to the platform for us to welcome them." (You know, this little dirt-floor church, with a bamboo altar.) And the captain and the bodyguard looked at each other and said, "Welcome us?" They'd raided all the leaders of the town, you know; anybody they suspected. So they walked up, had their rifles slung across their shoulders, and stood there very stiffly, and we sang the "Welcome to you" song and waved at 'em (that's the way the Bolivians do this). And there were women in the congregation whose husbands, or brothers, or sons, he had taken prisoner on Thursday night. And they recognized him and he recognized them; I mean, he left some of 'em screamin' when he'd taken them off on Thursday, you know. So there they were in the congregation, and usually the custom in Bolivia was to come and hug a newcomer. And I thought, I can't ask these women to hug this guy, 'cause we didn't know by then if he'd killed their husbands or sons or what. I didn't even know what had happened to Tommy at this point. But still I said, "Well, let's sing the welcome song to him." And after they'd finished singin', a man in the front of the church got up and marched up to the captain and gave him his hand. He reached around his gun *(laughs)* and hugged him, which was their custom. He said, "Brother, I don't like the way you've treated our village, but this is the house of God, and you're welcome here, because God loves you." And everybody in that church followed, huggin' him and sayin' words of welcome . . . "Come back again . . . you're welcome here." And the man was totally shocked.

After it was over, he marched over to the pulpit and he said, "Now it's my turn." And we sat down . . . whoops, he's gonna take more prisoners, you know. Instead he said, "I have never in my life been in any kind of a religious service before. This is the first time I ever walked into a church. I never believed that God existed. But what I have felt this mornin' has been so strong that I will never doubt the existence of God again as long as I live. That sister down there told me Thursday night that Christians love their enemies. And I didn't believe her then. But this whole congregation has proved that to me this morning." He said, "Do you all know God? I don't know him. But if you do, if you know God, hold on to him. It must be the greatest thing a human being could ever know." Then he walked out the door, turned around, and came back. And he said the most powerful and true thing I've ever heard. "You know," he said, "I have fought many battles and killed many people. I'm a professional soldier. It was just my job to do that; it never bothered me. But I never knew my enemy face-to-face until now. It just makes me think that if we could know each other, our guns would not be necessary."

Luke Leon Coffee

A SPOKE IN THE WHEEL

My dad's a practical joker, you know. Until I was three months old, my name was Lukewarm Coffee. *(Laughs.)*. My mother had the birth certificate changed to Luke Leon.

We're at the National Western Stock Show in Denver, Colorado, where he's working as a rodeo clown. He says there's just two reasons God put him on earth: "To help people out and to make people happy. And I can do them both right there in that arena."

I went down in two helicopters in Nam. I was a door gunner. That brings back lots of bad memories. I guess the good Lord blessed me to let me get out of Nam, 'cause I was not supposed to get out of either one of them helicopters. I mean, you go down in one and you survive, you lucky. The second one, if it goes down and you survive, you ought to think about gettin' out of there, 'cause your time is comin'; you know, your ticket might get punched next. (Laughs.) Nobody ever tells you that a helicopter on paper's not supposed to fly. They don't tell you that till you up there with an M-60 hangin' out of it . . . and they don't rock 'n' roll. (Laughs.)

My first week over there was probably the worst, worst week of my life. We set down in Saigon. We were 150 clicks out of the DMZ and we were pinned down by a sniper. Wherever you at, you run, and you never run in a straight line. The sniper was just pickin' us off. Well, he laid off for a day, so we sent out a reconnaissance mission and just scanned the area. This one guy was part of it, and he said, "Hey, Captain, there's a baby over here." This captain just come runnin' through the jungle screamin' bloody murder, "Don't you touch that baby." But this guy says, "Hey, it's just a baby." And he picked that baby up and it was on a weight line; take the weight off it and it blows you up. And that's exactly what happened.

You know, when I got out of Nam, I felt like I'd been through hell, 'cause I had to walk into a village one time with a flamethrower and burn people. And that's the most pungent odor I've ever smelt in my life. I've had hell livin' with myself because of it, but I had a second lieutenant with a .45 pointed at my head sayin' you walk in there and do it, or you die. In Nam if you don't follow orders, you're a statistic. They put you in a body bag and ship you out. Nobody ever know what really happened.

When I left for Nam, my dad told me, he said, "Son, it can't last forever." And my grandaddy told me, he said, "Always remember the strength in lookin' up." Those things always stuck with me. No matter how bad I was feelin', I'd just look up. You look up, you might not see nuthin', but it's there; there's just strength in lookin' up.

I'm not a model Christian by any shape, form, means, or word, you know. But I'm gonna tell you like this: They ain't no truer song to me than that Jesus and me, we got our own thing goin'; we got it all worked out. And I live it that way. You know, if I'm doin' somethin' wrong, the good Lord gonna git me one way or the other. But I'm not gonna hurt no one, 'cause I did too much of that over there with a gun in my hand. I just can't. . . . I'm never gonna do that again. I've always been the kind of guy to try to help somebody

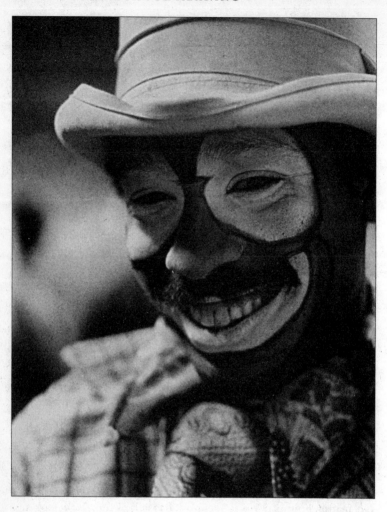

all the time. I go out of my way to help a lot. It's probably one of my biggest faults. *(Laughs.)* I can't say no. That's just not a part of my vocabulary.

When I'm out there fightin' bulls, I'm always thinkin' of what I can do next to entertain that crowd. And you know, I believe that when you stop thinkin' of what you can do for the good, that's when you gonna start thinkin' more to the bad. It's gotta be one or the other. Your mind never gonna be idle. I don't care what anyone says, you're never gonna be sittin' and havin' nuthin' on your mind. There's no way anyone will ever make me believe that you can sit there and just be totally blank. So I believe that if you got somethin' good to say to someone, what's usually on your lung is usually on your tongue. And I don't bite my tongue. *(Laughs.)*

I'm not afraid of anything anymore. You see, you want to know my belief again? It's wrote in the Bible, Psalm 123: "Fear not, for what can man do unto me, for the Lord thy God is on my side." So I got no fear of nobody and no fear of dyin'. Kill me. You ain't gonna do me no harm at all. Like I said, me and Jesus, we got our own thing goin'. We got it all worked out. It's kind of like what Martin Luther said, "I been to the mountain top. I been to the mountain." I don't worry about nothin'. I'm high on life. I'm not here for a long time, I'm here for a good time. And I feel like I'm doin' what God put me on earth to do. He gave me this ability. I came here with it, but I had to develop it. If God didn't want me to do this, he wouldn't give me this ability. It's my way of serving, but I ain't gonna stand on a street corner and tell everybody about it. I'm not an evangelist. I'm not a preacher. I'm a disciple, that's all. I'm just a worker. And there's a lot of people that are workers and a lot of people that are leaders. I'm not the wheel, I'm just a spoke in it.

Walter Littlemoon

He's an Oglala Sioux. His home on the outskirts of Denver serves as the Tiyospaye Crisis Center,* a nonprofit organization he founded in 1981 to aid Native Americans in the western United States. "We don't accept federal, state, or local money because of the strings attached to it. I have no interest in politics. I have interest in people. Anyone who needs help can enter my home so long as they don't drink . . . alcohol destroys your spiritual identity."

I was born on the Pine Ridge Indian Reservation back in 1942. My dad's Oglala Sioux. My mother's northern Cheyenne. She gave up her heritage in order for us to be raised as Oglala Sioux. It was

---

* *Tiyospaye* is a Lakota word that means "extended family." It is one of only three hundred words in the language.

a good childhood. We didn't have very many things. Matter of fact, we used kerosene lamps and had a wood-burning stove and an out-house. But things like that really didn't matter. There was plenty of food, and my mother was always givin' it away when people came over askin' for help.

My father was killed when I was six months old, so a lot of my education came from other people, some of the elders within the community. It's an unwritten law as part of our extended family (which the government doesn't understand) that other people in the tribe will step in there and educate the young, like my uncles, my grandfathers, some of the tribal elders. But I was put in a government school that tried to discourage me from following Native American ways, from following what the elders were teaching me. It created a conflict in me. I decided that I didn't care much for what they taught me at the government school, so I didn't put much effort into it. But I did learn how to read. I always started from the back of the book and worked forward. I used to read the same books over and over, because we didn't have very many books. A lot of my infor-mation came from the *National Geographic*, which created a strong desire in me to travel, to see these things. Reading wasn't enough. I had to see the world. So that was prob'ly one of my first goals—to develop the ability to travel around.

By about fourteen or fifteen or so I heard about the Bureau of Indian Affairs' relocation program, where they relocate you into a different city and teach you a skill. I wanted to travel and it sounded like a good program, so I tried it. And that's what took me off the reservation. I relocated to San Francisco, California. I just turned sixteen there. My life would be a lot different today if I had never joined that program.

I read about washing machines, I read about taxis, I read about airplanes on the reservation—but I never experienced them. So San Francisco was a culture shock. I didn't expect the mass congestion of buildings. I didn't expect the number of people. On the reser-vation we had two million acres and I knew where everybody came from by their names. But in the city it was different. The first few days it was like wandering around in a maze, just trying to take everything in at one time. Sometimes I'd go to a building and into an elevator and just go up to the top. That gave me a better feeling for the people around. It was like climbing a tree, to get up there and look around and find your direction. That helped in the city. It helped me overcome this culture shock.

The money I was making wasn't that much. We only got $125 every two weeks. I used to send my mother five, ten dollars. It was acceptable. But I never was happy in the city; missed the openness of the reservation. The new life-style wasn't very agreeable. Anytime I was hungry, I could find somethin' to eat, but it wasn't the kind of food I grew up on. I was getting weaker physically and spiritually each day. And I thought the best thing to do was just to go somewhere else. But that meant quitting school. So I just stuck it out for eighteen months and finished the program I was doing at this carpenter trade school. Got a certificate out of it. The day that school let out, that afternoon, I was on the bus. I didn't know where I was goin'. I got out as far as the airport. The future kinda looked bleak. I didn't know where to turn, so I caught the bus back into the city. And I just happened to get off in front of an army recruiting station. So I said, What the heck.

I got accepted into the army and was transferred to Colorado Springs, where I spent a few years. In 1965 I took a guerrilla-warfare course at Fort Carson. I didn't know what it was all about, but I decided to take that course. That was the first place I heard about Vietnam; I heard a lot of American supervisors were there. I wanted to be one of them. I wanted to visit a foreign country.

Once I got to Vietnam, I ended up at a place called Hai Phong. Before the Communists took over, it was a supply depot. At first I just pulled guard duty. But it wasn't too long before I got into firefights and such, saw some real action. And this is when I developed this ability to turn everything off to survive. Because in Vietnam, surviving was the main thing. No matter how many times I got shot at, I developed an ability to feel whenever somebody was gonna shoot at me—I seemed to know ahead of time. I don't know how many times I died there; I figure about a hundred times every minute. When these rockets started comin' in, I'd try to crawl into the deepest hole I could find. I used everything that I could to survive. And I survived. Life had top priority.

Human life at that time became so cheap—just a ten-cent piece of lead. And when human life becomes that cheap, you put it in the back of your mind. You file it away and don't think about it. You let it go. You look at other people as zombies or as robots or whatever. They're comin' and goin'. Friendships had to come to a stop. It was better to make enemies durin' that time. Whether they were Americans, whether they were VC, it didn't matter. Everybody was an enemy in order to protect yourself.

I experimented with a lot of cocaine and various other different types of drugs in Vietnam. I also drank a lot of whiskey. If I stayed sober, life didn't seem worth living. I became more and more withdrawn. The only thing that brought me a spark was whiskey; every time I'd drink there was a spark. I could talk to people. I could be among people. I didn't have to be withdrawn. If I drank too much, then I'd git nightmares. I always kept smellin' that smell of death or the smell of charred flesh or charred bodies, decaying bodies. Sometimes I didn't eat for days at a time. And I lost a lot of weight. I went from 220 to 176 pounds in Vietnam. So drinkin' became part of me, because it was the only way I could function with people. Eventually I developed a dependency on alcohol; in order for me to eat I'd have to drink.

When I got out of the service, I got as far as Denver and I lost my billfold at the bus station. I had about $26 in my pocket. So I just caught the bus. Ended up in Nebraska. I don't know who called my mother. But they came after me, and I woke up one morning and I was on the reservation. I just got out of bed and went down to the bootleggers and bought some bootleg stuff, cheap wine. Sat up on a hill. But the whole place wasn't home anymore. It was a strange place. And I drank enough to go down and talk to people. I went back, and my mother asked me where I'd been. So I just told her I was in Colorado Springs and that I just got discharged. I didn't tell her I was in Vietnam.

I didn't feel anything anymore. Even life itself, there was no enjoyment anymore. Everything was dead to me. Not even my own mother, I wasn't even glad to see her. I started dealing with death itself. And when I looked at myself, I came out dead. There was no life to me. My heart and everything else functioned, but I didn't have any feelings. I become more and more isolated, alienated myself from other people. I didn't want any pity. I just wanted to be left alone. For ten years that's how I lived. Nightmares usually got the best of me. Sometimes I'd sleep, but I'd be half awake. Sometimes I'd just walk along the crick searchin' for somethin', but I didn't know what I was searchin' for. Fishing never appealed to me anymore, or sports, and I used to play a lot of sports. Nothing appealed to me. I tried committing suicide a number of times, but it never worked. I don't know, I just couldn't follow through. I took an overdose of aspirin one time, but my stomach just heaved it back out again. I tried to drink myself to death. Sometimes I'd drink four, five weeks at a time. But it never happened. I tried hangin' myself one time. The whole limb just broke right off.

After ten years of this I was sittin' there watchin' a church one day. It was a newly painted church, and the sun settled on it in a certain way so that there was a brightness to it. I sat there lookin' at it. This was after drinkin' and I was pretty sick. Then all of a sudden I realized there is nothin' wrong. The only thing that's wrong is me.

I had to do somethin' about myself. I was the one that was dead. It wasn't the people around me. There was no hate in the countryside; the land and the countryside were bright and beautiful. It was strictly me.

About that time a friend of mine came up and said, "I'm goin' into Nebraska and I'm gonna go check into an alcohol, drug treatment center." I said, "Oh, I'm gonna go with you." After that I realized exactly what drinkin' had done to me. Physically I was completely deteriorated to the point where I was just strong enough to walk. And my eating habits were completely off. And my mind couldn't function at all. I decided then that from age twenty-two up to thirty—that time I had to forget about. So I let it go. I wouldn't try to deal with it until I was strong enough both physically and mentally. Instead I'd be a teenager again and try to catch up with my real age. Physically I was a thirty-two-year-old, but my mind was a teenager. I had to learn how to dance all over again, learn how to laugh all over again, learn how to talk to women, talk to girls, learn how to be sociable again.

Things began to improve for me very quickly. Everythin' was changin' from day to day. Whatever was acceptable, I hung on to it, and whatever wasn't, I'd get rid of it. But I still was troubled by a lot of things, and the thing that troubled me the most was selfishness. I don't know when it was, but I do know that somewhere during this time I decided that what I needed to do was learn how to give things away like my mother. My long-range goal became learning how to overcome this thing of power and money and material things.

It wasn't easy at all. When it came time to give money away, I just couldn't do it. I explained this to my mother and she said, "Just go over there, walk over there, and don't think about anythin'. Just hand them the money and walk away." It took me over five years before I could actually enjoy giving. It took me five years to realize that it isn't important if people pat you on the back or not. Whether they pat you on the back or not, you're never wasting time if you're giving. And once I learned that, once I got over hangin' on to things, material things, things began to look different. It was then that what the elders told me as a boy began to take shape. I realized what they were talkin' about when they told me to overcome the power of money. They told me that there is a space in this universe that God has given to all of us and that how you fill it up is up to you. And they told me that I owe this earth something. We call it Grandmother Earth. And I owe Grandmother Earth a life. The only way I can repay my grandmother, repay my debt to her for creating the world, is by respecting life and helping other people. It's like that debt that you owe your mother for giving you life, giving you so many things that you can't actually add them up—years and years of caring . . .

Maybe all of what I believe falls under the word *love*. *Love* is a big word, it's a broad word. But when I care about a person, to me, that's love. It helps me overcome selfishness. You never quite get rid of it, but you can try. Once you have that ability to love, nothing else is important. It's a hard word to explain. If it means walkin' on your hands to make a little child smile, that's love, and that's what you should be doing. There's not enough words, healing words, to describe the meaning of that word.

The Color Line

Jim Farrands

THE GRAND WIZARD

I know that God was white, that's absolutely sure. The only problem I have is that my wife says that God was a woman. *(Chuckles.)* But as far as I'm concerned, God was born a man and he was also born white.

I had a girl last night who called me and gave me her name and everything. She asked me if so-and-so had put in an application yet to join the Klan. I said, "I can't give you that information." She says, "Well, damn it, I want to know, because if that sucker hasn't joined the Klan yet, he ain't gettin' in my bed no more." *(Laughs loudly.)*

Shelton, Connecticut. He is the grand wizard of the Knights of the Ku Klux Klan. He is also a tool-and-die maker. He lives in a middle-class suburb. The tattered T-shirt he wears exposes a healthy barrel chest. He smokes a cigar. After our initial meeting at the door to his home— "Are you here to interview me or kill me?"—his demeanor becomes jovially arrogant. He escorts me to a small room, about ten by ten, which houses the national communications headquarters of the Ku Klux Klan. To the left of where I'm seated are files, organized state by state, listing Klan members and activities. To my right a large set of open wooden shelves contains Ku Klux Klan certificates; member certificates; distinguished service certificates; supporter certificates, and so on. A picture of John Wayne is tacked to the wall along with a framed letter from Jesse Helms on U.S. Senate stationery. It reads, "Thank you for your comments expressing opposition to a Special Holiday honoring Martin Luther King. I was both pleased and encouraged by your thoughtfulness. I made some statements in the Senate chambers on the subject which you may find of interest. They are being forwarded under separate cover. . . . Kind Regards, Jesse Helms."

I was born in a little town in northern Massachusetts at a very young age. *(Laughs.)* It was an all-white community. We did have one token black kid in the neighborhood, and he was a good friend of mine. I was very liberal at that time. He was the first black that I ever knew. I just didn't understand why he was that color. My parents didn't want me hangin' around with him, because he was black and so forth. As time went on, I began to see that I didn't like blacks. *(Laughs.)* This kid started to steal my toys, steal money out of my mother's house. So it started makin' me think.

Then I went to Boy Scout camp. I befriended a little black kid they called the Professor. He could read and write, so they called him the Professor. I befriended him. He was a likable sort of kid. But the other black kids got all upset, and so they stabbed me for talkin' to one of theirs. I carry a scar on my belly over here. *(He points to his stomach.)* That's about the basis of the whole thing; that's when I immediately decided maybe there's somethin' wrong with these here niggers.

I was raised as a Catholic, and a lot of people think that the Klan doesn't admit Catholics, but we do. In the Northeast, Catholics are the majority in the Ku Klux Klan. Essentially we are pro-segregation, pro-Christianity.

I see myself as a direct descendant of God. And the more I think about Darwin and his theory of evolution, I do believe that God made the white man. And I believe that the black man came up through evolution, from the monkeys. I wholeheartedly believe that. Because you can't tell me that anybody that runs around the streets as they do and carries on in the manner that they do can be descended from God.

I don't see God as callin' me to do anything. I just believe that I'm following the righteous path of white man as the dominant people in this world. And as far as I can see, anything that was ever invented or of any use was thought up by white people. I mean, the Africans were in Africa for how many years, and their culture never expanded beyond a few mud huts and spears and so forth. The same goes for the red man in this country. He was content to run around and be a nomadic warrior type or a hunter. He never did anything with this country until the influence of the white man came along. Heck, let's face it, they were runnin' around the deserts in the western part of the country pulling a wagon without wheels. They didn't have wheels. They had these little sticks and put a blanket on it—they carried things around draggin' 'em. Anybody that couldn't think of puttin' wheels on it couldn't have too much foresight or mental ability.

I have nothing against these people, but I don't want to live near them. I would like to see this nation voluntarily segregated. If I care to live in an all-white community, an all-white town, an all-white state, I should have the right to segregate voluntarily. Not only by race but by religion if I want to. It looks to me that no matter what you do or where you do it, the races or the ethnic groups always seem to group together. You get great enclaves of the Irish Catholic in Boston in certain sections. And of course you've got the Chinese group up there that all stays in their section. And they seem to be pretty happy. I mean, I feel I would be quite happy in an all-white Christian or, even more so, an all-white Catholic neighborhood, where all the cultural values would be the same.

I surely can see that the black cultural values are not what ours are. Anybody that goes out and puts graffiti on the walls don't have the same cultural values. I would like to be able to segregate from them entirely if I so wished. Actually segregation hasn't died in this country. We still have segregation, but it's economic. All the great Kennedys and their liberal thinking, they segregate themselves down in Hyannis Port. They are away not only from black people but from poor people. And they're the great criers of this country, the great friends of the poor. They're so far away from the poor that the poor would have to take two bus transfers to get to their home. (Laughs.)

If God had wanted a homogeneous race, everybody one color and speakin' one language, what happened at the Tower of Babel when he scrambled the languages? If God put Chinese or Oriental-type people in Asia, why did he put the black people in Africa? He wanted black people in Africa and Asian and Orientals out there, and he wanted white people around the Caucasus Mountains over there in Russia, and so forth and so on. And that's what we ended up with. He didn't mean for everybody to all be together, to all mingle together.

Jesus preached to everybody, but he never said that everybody should get together and mingle with each other, just like he never said that people should be queer. He says, "Thou shalt not lie with man as with woman." That's from the Old Testament. Even the Jews believe in the Old Testament. I mean, it can't be wrong. If all the Jews believe in it and all the Christians believe in it, the Old Testament's got to be absolutely correct. So that absolutely rules out bein' a homosexual. Absolutely. I personally, and some guys look at me strangely when I say it, I believe that AIDS is the wrath of God upon the homosexual people.

Like I say, we're pro-segregation, pro-Christianity. You understand, we take only white and only Christians in the organization. Doesn't mean that we're gonna say we're not gonna associate or talk to blacks or to non-Christians. I mean, I know a lot of non-Christian people who are pretty good folk. In fact a lot of Jewish ones I know kind of believe in what I'm sayin', because they don't want their children monkeying around with Christian boys if they can help it. Or Christian girls. They would rather see their children with Jewish partners. That makes sense. I believe that if you mix races, you should abstain from having kids. Because the children have no actual cultural background. Are they half Jew, half Christian, half black, half white?

But major evolutionary changes are greatly influenced—for better or worse—by the mixing of races. Don't you agree? Don't you think that a lot of tremendously positive changes have come from the mixing of various races and cultures?

JIM: History and evolution are changed by a lot of means. The victor of a war changes history. If Adolf Hitler and his troops had won the war, history would have been written different, you know.

Would you have preferred that he won?

JIM: In the beginning yes; in the end no. In the beginning he was absolutely fightin' against the Communist influence. The biggest thing in the beginning was anticommunism. Then later he was lookin' for the absolute extinction of everybody who wasn't blue-eyed and blond. That was gettin' a little out of hand, I would say. But I could one hundred percent agree with him about communism, because we've got the same problem going on now.

It seems like Judaism and communism go hand in hand. The list of Communists we've got in the state of Connecticut are all Jews. Why, we don't know. That's not to say that Jews as a group even support communism, but it seems that most of the Communist leaders are Jewish. Every Jew is not a Communist, but it seems that every Communist is a Jew. What was Karl Marx? Very kosher. Lenin too.

The Ku Klux Klan is not a group ever advocating anything but American. It was founded in Biloxi, Tennessee, in 1866, and it's still an American institution. We don't profess allegiance to any outside group. And we made mistakes. But it's all gone by. It's history. And who wants to keep talkin' about our history and bringing it up? The liberals. And the liberals are driven by what? They're driven by the Jewish influence. The Jews want everybody to feel bad about them. So they're bringing on this crap. Keep bringing up the past and the Klan, what happened in Germany with the Holocaust.

It's an outside influence on our country that's takin' it apart—the outside influence of communism and Judaism. Ben Franklin, or who was it that said, "Good God, if we take in the Jews in this country, we're in for it." He was makin' a big old statement on that. Don't take 'em in, because they're the parasites of the world. Everywhere they've gone there's been trouble. Not that I overly love him, but Adolf said it: "If ever there was a dirty deed done, there was at least one Jew involved."

We'd like to be able to adhere one hundred percent to the Constitution of the United States as it was originally written and intended. We feel a lot of these various small laws that have been passed are definitely wrong. I would like to see the system of welfare and Aid to Dependent Children either curtailed or completely done away with. It's got to be wrong when people can stay on welfare and dog-gone make as much as a low-paid worker. That's wrong. The Constitution may say, okay, everybody has the right to this and the right to that. But you cannot have the right to infringe on other people's rights. And you're infringing on my rights if you're a single woman on welfare with four children and you never attempt to better yourself or to support yourself. Why should my tax money support you all your life? Again, it's a Christian thing too. I mean, it says that you should be married to have children and so forth. I absolutely feel that once is a mistake; twice, they haven't learned the lesson. By the third time I think they should make some changes in the body structure of that woman, disallow her to have any more children that she can't support.

We're also antidrug. We believe that drugs are just totally the most abominable thing that ever went on. The drug traffic that's coming from Third World countries, the money's goin' out of our country, it's hurting the balance of payments. It's givin' money to countries that are unstable. And most of them are communistic or Communist leaning. It's sappin' money from our people. It's causin' our people to be addicted. If you've got a generation of people comin' up with drugs, you're gonna have more and more people with fried brains. If they got fried brains, we're not gonna have this country developed to its fullest potential. We got the greatest thing in the world goin' here, but if we keep allowin' these drugs, we're in for it. And if our government can send a man to the moon, they can certainly stop a bunch of asses from bringin' in drugs to this country. I could solve it, personally, little ol' dirt bag like I am, like that; absolutely, bingo, done. If they catch a drug pusher, they should take him to the nearest brick wall over a foot thick and shoot him, dead. You kill a few of them like that, boy is that gonna get your attention. This stuff over there in Iran ain't entirely wrong. They catch some sucker stealing, they cut off a finger. I betcha that sucker don't steal too much anymore.

We're against immigration, unlawful immigration, runnin' across the Mexican border. We say close off the border; put troops on the border. We got people all over the country training troops. You know, the Texas National Guard and the Texas Naval Reserve and all that. Put 'em on the border. Let them do their training duty there. Have it all set up so somebody's on the border at all times. And don't let these suckers in. This is the greatest country in the world. We've got potential, we've got land, we've got resources. We've got everything. Right. The great United States. But if it ever gets populated like India, you no longer got that. We've got all that because we've got resources. We've got the room to expand and so forth. But we've got enough people in this country. And if these people can't make it in their own country, under their own culture, how can we expect them to make it here? So I say, keep those Mexicans out.

▭

Mauricio Terrazas

Interstate 76, near Brule, Nebraska. A scorching hot day. We're sitting in my car off to the side of the road, looking south on endless fields of wheat. To the west stand four large silos. To the east, blue sky and a faraway destination: the White House. He's a member of the Great Peace March for Nuclear Disarmament, marching across the United States in an effort to halt the development and deployment of nuclear arms. "I'm a professional truck driver. I joined the march to help carry supplies for the walkers. But I walk a lot myself." He's sixty-nine.

I was born in El Paso, Texas. I was one of sixteen kids in the family. My father was a baker, a master baker. But he didn't earn enough money to take care of that many kids. So what he had to do was farm us out. I was farmed out to a boarding school, a religious boarding school at four or five years old. I enjoyed it. It was a lot of fun. It was a school where they self-sustained. It was like a big farm. We would grow everything; everything that went into the kitchen, we would grow it right there. It was a Protestant boarding school. But even though I went to church, I didn't really believe in the religion, to tell you the truth.

Discrimination was pretty bad back then. A lot of discrimination. In El Paso the hate was so thick you could cut it with a knife. That's how bad it was. In the swimming pools you can't swim with them. You've got your own days to swim. The same swimming pool, but separate days you could swim. That was how much hate there was. Vicious.

Anyway when I was in my second year of high school, I decided to leave . . . there was too much conflict, too much poverty. I went to California and became a farm worker. That was quite an experi-

ence. That was around '34, '35, the height of the Depression, when you couldn't afford a bus and had to jump freight trains to travel; you hopped freight trains to look for work. That's what I did. I followed the crops. I did cotton, I did grapes. I worked the sugar beets, topping beets. That's labor. I worked there about four years and got enough money to bring my whole family to Los Angeles.

I didn't think much about religion back then. There wasn't time. People were just making a living and surviving. All we did was learn to survive. But when people did talk about God, they talked about God in very negative terms, because the conditions they were living under were so terrible. Let me just give you an example. You got up at three or four in the morning, you made breakfast, then you packed lunch. By six o'clock they would take you forty or fifty miles to where the contractors' trucks were. Then they took you to the field and you're there until sundown, until there's no light. Then you come home and do the same thing all over again. But you had to buy the stuff to eat and make the stuff to eat. And you know the Mexican tradition—you gotta make the tortillas. No stores to buy homemade. So you gotta do everything yourself. Around ten-thirty, eleven at night they used to have a big bonfire, and all the farm people would get around the big bonfire. And they sang. And it was really a fun time for an hour or two, because the day was so long and it was such a struggle.

But I survived it all. Then I went to Los Angeles. In Los Angeles I got a job as an assistant truck driver, hauling furniture around. This was '38, '39, I guess. By 1940 I began to get interested in unions. And I began to get better jobs because I began to get more skill. I got a job with Safeway stores as a driver. But of course they didn't want to hire me, because I'm Mexican. They didn't have no Mexican drivers. But my union had sent me down there. They told me there was an opening, see. So the supervisor would tell me, "You've got to go see the truck manager." The truck manager said, "You've gotta see the blah, blah, blah." Playing games with me. I finally told them, "Look, you've got a job here, it's open. If you don't give me the job, I'm not gonna move from this office until you do. I can drive your equipment, I can do the work. I've been doing it for three years." So they had to hire me, reluctantly. I was the only Mexican. The only Mexican. And I was with them for eighteen years.

I've seen discrimination all my life. You can see racism express itself all the time. Let me tell you a story. Did you know that 20 percent of the people that were killed in Vietnam were Mexicans? Twenty percent—but we only make up 11 percent of the national population.* When I learned this, I got together with a group to

* In 1970 Mexican Americans actually made up less than 6 percent of the population of the United States. The percentage of Mexican Americans who died in Vietnam is difficult to determine in that Hispanics (unlike American Indians, Malayans, Mongolians, and Negroes) were labeled by the armed forces as either Caucasians or of "unknown origin." However, of the one study conducted by the Department of Defense, it appears that Mexican-American casualties exceeded 20 percent of the total number of Vietnam casualties and may even have been as high as 30 percent.

support a big demonstration in Los Angeles of people from the Southwest, ten thousand or so people from Colorado, Texas, New Mexico, and Arizona. We came to L.A. to set up a march to express our anger over what they were doing to us. And we marched about five miles or so, from Buck Park to another park. Everybody was sitting down; it was very peaceful. Then the cops surrounded us and started beating the shit out of us. *(He begins to cry.)* I was right in the middle of the goddamn shit. Children, women, pregnant women . . . shit, that's why I'm on this march. That's why it's hard for me to believe in God. That's why I believe that people have to change things. *(A pause. He tries to collect himself.)* I don't know why I'm so goddamn emotional. *(He begins to cry again.)* They were in riot gear. They came at us with clubs like we were nothing but animals. That was the worst moment of being a human being in my life, looking at this. I'm telling you, it was really awful.

The hate against us, that's what it was. The fact that the war was an unjust war, a war that didn't liberate anybody. It was just a war the people in power wanted to have. Because they built and built so much material to kill . . . once they built it, then they have to use it. Now they're gonna do it again. And it's not just the Mexican people that are gonna go down; this time humanity is gonna go down. They're already polluting the whole world.

Last weekend I went to an international Indian treaty conference at Big Mountain, Arizona. There was people there from all over; indigenous people, Indian people, all kinds of people who are treated the way we are treated. All over the world they are doing this to Third World people. *(Sobbing.)* People from the Pacific told me that they are testing atomic bombs there, bombing islands that nobody sees. But all that pollution is really going into the atmosphere. It's not gonna stay in the Pacific. It's gonna go all over the world. The indigenous people, they say, "Mother Earth is bleeding." It affects everybody. Everybody has to begin to be part of the struggle to stop these people. They're gonna kill us all, that's what's gonna happen. *(Sobbing.)*

This march, marches like this are needed all over America. And the marchers should not just march. They need to do a lot of outreach. These marchers with deep convictions need to visit every village, every house, every home they can. We must alert people to the danger about us. We must tell people that these people in high places are gonna kill us if we don't stop them. It's that dangerous. These people at the top have so much power, so much control that most people are not aware of. Most people just don't understand how dangerous these people are and how much organizing we have to do in order to defeat them, in order to clean them out. And if we don't clean them out, they'll clean us out. Because they don't care about human beings. They don't care about anything except themselves. It's really sad.

There was somebody that was talkin' religious to me one time. He was a Jehovah's Witness. He was tellin' me about God. He said that God is gonna do it all. God is gonna have to be the one to change things, because it's in the Bible. He's the one that's gonna change it all. I said to him, "Maybe if you put it another way, maybe if you say that God works through us, that we gotta go make the changes with him working through us; if you put it that way, then I'll agree with you." This guy couldn't understand it. But I do believe that God is not gonna come down personally. It is us that is gonna have to make the changes down here. We've got to stop the poisoning of the atmosphere, we've got to stop nuclear weapons, we've got to stop all this stuff before they kill us all. God's not gonna do it, we're gonna do it.

Reed Weller

I'm not gone get inta no religious stuff with ya. And I'm shore not gonna tell ya what I believe. I just don't argue with a man over what he believes. If you believe that you can get out there and stand on yo' head in the middle of that street out there and go to heaven, if that's yo' belief, you do it. If you ain't got any more damn sense than that, I still think the good Lord'll take care of ya. That's my opinion. I think that the good Lord takes care a' all the drunks, and damn fools, and crazy people, fer he's took care of a hell of a lot of 'em already, like this damn fool I heard about who was goin' down the road just weavin' here and yonder. The guy who was followin' behind him said, "That guy's drunk, he's gone kill somebody. He's just swervin' back and forth across the road." Then the drunk feller went down a damn big embankment there, turned the car bottom up and all like that. The feller who was followin' him stopped, went down there, and says, "Hey, are ya hurt?" And the drunk feller said, "No. I got the Lord with me." The other feller said, "Well, I'll tell you what you better do. You better let the Lord ride with somebody else, fer you're gonna kill 'em." *(Laughs.)*

Contentious, cantankerous, and crochety, he's an eighty-year-old to-bacco-chewing, ass-slapping, foul-mouthed codger. I ran into him by accident at a coffee shop in Fulton, Mississippi.

Very few people when I come up had any money at all in this part of the country. There was two or three people that you could go to and borrow money. And very little at that. Hell, we didn't have but cornbread fer breakfast and all that, and we went ta school with the ass end of our pants out, and shoes ya wore a hole in the bottom of and put a piece a' damn cardboard in there ta keep yer foot from hittin' the ground, or cut a piece off an ol' mule collar and put it in there. Hell, we come up hard. It's altogether different today than what it was then. I wanted to go to school at Old Miss, but I never did get outa the fourth grade. We were so damn poor you had to work to feed your stomach instead of goin' to school. Today it makes me mad to see the benefits that the young people's got and the hell that we went through—and they're still gripin'! Shit, beats anything that I've ever saw in my life. If we'd had schools then like they got now, I'd a never left it. The dorm rooms is better than the homes we had. Hell, I never went to a school that had electric lights and runnin' water in it in my life. It galls the hell outa me to hear people gripe at eight hours a day. You didn't work back then by the hour, you worked by the day. I worked for fifty cents a day, the hardest day's work I've ever done in my life. I made a half a dollar and was damned glad to get it. And today people get eight, ten dollars an hour and gripe and raise hell about more. Oh, hell, it burns my ass up. That's right.

Hell, people hangin' out in the street today, they say, "Loan me this or loan me that . . . loan me this, loan me a dollar." I say, "What d'ya mean 'loan'? You mean give it to ya. How in the hell're you gone pay it back? Give it to ya. I don't owe you a damn thing." That's what I tell 'em. And I've seen 'em out there shakin' from drinkin' that wine . . . nervous and all that. Shit, they're shakin' their damn teeth out. I don't do it. I give to charity, I give a lot of people stuff, but as far as you out there, a dopehead out there shakin', just go ahead and shake it off. I ain't gonna give ya' nothin' ta ease it. Guarantee ya'.

I never did ask for nothin'. I walked the streets of Memphis up there day and night and slep' in the lobby of the Peabody Hotel lookin' fer a job. Bellboys would come by and sweep yer feet out from under ya', and they'd say, "Boss, they don't allow no sleepin' here in the lobby." I never asked a man fer a bite of food, or to give me a dollar in my damn life. And I been hungry. But I found a damn job, and a man who gets out here and says he can't find a job ain't worth a damn, or he could find a job. Anybody that's worth a damn can get a job anytime. I never did have no trouble gettin' a job.

Another thing that bothers the hell out of me is blacks these days. It was better when I grew up than it is today, two to one. Nobody treated a black person dirty back then. This goddamn young generation of 'em's what is the cause of it. If I'd a' told an ol' nigger back then . . . if I'd a' called 'im by his name (John, Bill, or somethin' like that), my daddy would'a knocked the hell outa me. He'd a' said, "Don't you call them that. You call them Uncle or Aunt." And I saw my daddy go out a' many a time and say, "Hey, Uncle Moses, hey, Uncle Will, have you had anything ta eat?" They'd say no. And my daddy would say, "Well, come on in. We just got up our table; come on in and eat somethin'."

But today they hate the white man . . . the black ones hate the white man today. Don't you think that you've got a black anywheres that's a friend a' yours, fer you are damn sure wrong. They think that we got ever damn thing they should have. You ain't gonna find one here that'll he'p ya. They jealous and prejudice, that's all. They want to tie up every damn thing you got. You put one of 'em out there drivin' yo' car or yo' tractor or somethin' like that, I'll guarantee ya if they can do somethin' ta tear it up, they'll do it. That's the young generation. The ol' generation don't believe that. They know better.

Now there's a Martin Luther King legal holiday . . . ain't that a son of a bitch! Just like George Washington, made him a legal holiday. But look what he cost people. What good does that do 'em? They'd get their education in their own schools. If they couldn't, why? Why? They got teachers. Hell, King asked fer it and he got it. I don't care nothin' about 'im. You hear about him on TV ever' day, ever' day somebody talkin' about Dr. Martin Luther King. You'd think they'd quit some day or another. Just shut up about it, talk about somebody else. But these blacks want ever damn thing. God he'p ya. Shit, it makes me mad. I just hate talkin' about it.

Tommy Wrenn

DOCTOR OF PHILOSOPHY

I grew up right here in Birmin'ham, on the north side, Nineteenth Alley and Sipco. Some call it the place where "only the strong survive." Louis White, who was the mayor's news director (whatever you call it), called it Billy Goat Quarters. I ruther maintain that the north side was similar to the situation Moses was in down in Egypt. It was a rough place, a bad place, but it was really holy ground, a breedin' ground for God's children. And Birmin'ham was really the center of the civil rights struggle—what we did here shifted the consciousness of the nation . . . of the world. Birmin'ham, Birmin'ham. Right here in Alabama.

During the sixties he was frequently jailed for his participation in the civil rights movement. He's fifty and works as a dental technician in downtown Birmingham.

I was just listenin' to the news about these assault rifles, and they was sayin' on TV this is a sick society. But we in the movement been knowin' that all along. I remember attendin' a conference over at the University of Alabama, and a professor of clinical psychology got to talkin' about extraterrestrial beings . . . the possibility, you know, and why they hadn't contacted us. I said, "Well, can you imagine some intelligent people somewhere wantin' to contact us? Our little ol' toilet stool?" You got a black side and a white side for people to use the bathroom. And I walk in some areas in Mississippi and Alabama and see little children with bellies bloated from malnutrition. Well, you can almost see diseases. And food is stacked to the rafters, wastin' and spoilin' every day. We in America throw food away that people would gladly eat out of our garbage can . . . and wouldn't even be concerned about it. So it would be apparent to any observer that most people are mentally deranged. Now isn't there somethin' wrong with people who can sit down and hug, kiss his dog and cat, but have a problem shakin' another human being's hand? So we're sick, see?

I never followed Jesus, because I was no Holy Roller, but Jesus was talkin' about how the earth is the Lord, the fulfillment thereof. There were no upper class and no middle class. God didn't make but one race—that was the human race! Humanoids on this planet (and I don't know what they got on any other planets), we just little

birds. Now maybe when we find another planet, we'll try to carry some of that sickness out there, tryin' to define man based upon how he look! But I don't believe that you'll be accepted within the honest sight of God for how you look.

The period we're just passin' through is a very short period, but I can say in my lifetime that I tried to overcome the sickness, I tried to help somebody. I tried to stand up against the Vietnam war and its massacre. I tried to stand up against the Bull Connors. I tried to stand up against the horseman nooses in Saint Augustine. I tried to stand up against these people who were spreadin' this venom and racism. And I will not waste my time dealin' with good history, 'cause I want to deal with good news. The good news is we can make America better. The good news is that America is worth saving, and if it can be saved, we gotta save it. We got to save it.

I seen enough hate durin' the movement that I decided I would never allow no man to drag me so low that I would hate like that. And then the fear . . . I used to be scared, really afraid of Bull Connor. But when I discovered Bull was ill, my whole attitude changed. I pitied Bull. And now when I see Bull, and all them little Bulls, I pity them, because I don't have that fear, and they do. See, I've developed a total philosophy of life. A total philosophy. And a total philosophy of life has nothin' to do with how many cars you have, or wall-to-wall carpet. A philosophy of life has to do with lovin' other human beings. A philosophy of life understands the agony and pain of our fellow man.

So I'm just tryin' to get myself well enough to understand human nature. If I get myself well enough to understand human nature, I may not even make it in the Gates, but I could tell Peter I tried. I can stand up and tell him I damn sho' tried. I never can say that I didn't smoke a cigarette or drink liquor or chase women. But I did try in my lifetime to love mankind. So I might not make it in, but I'll try. I'll try' to be a sane, lovin' human being. We're talkin' about the development of a philosophy of life, and I believe if your philosophy breaks down and you can fix it yourself, they should make you a doctor of philosophy. I don't mean you have to go to no university to get it.

So you're a doctor of philosophy?

TOMMY: I is a doctor of it. *(Laughs.)*

Jean Mitchell McGuire

IT MUST BE A STRUGGLE

1986. Roxbury, Massachusetts. Since 1973 she's served as executive director of the Metropolitan Council for Educational Opportunity (METCO), a nonprofit organization seeking to provide integrated school-

ing for black and minority children and enhanced understanding between urban and suburban parents in the metropolitan Boston area. Located in Roxbury, a predominantly black, lower-class suburb of Boston, METCO is housed in what was once the first women's hospital in the United States, built in 1870. Large but terribly run down, its peeled-paint interior hallways are covered with posters: "Is the Clock Turning Back? Time to Join the NAACP"; "If You Think the Civil Rights Struggle Is Over . . . Read PORTRAIT OF INEQUALITY"; "Eracism: Wipe Out Bigotry"; "Where We Stand—Against the Bakke Decision." On large corkboards nailed to the walls are flyers listing employment opportunities for blacks and Hispanics, summer camps and scholarships for needy students, and books of interest to minorities.

During the two hours we spent together, she paced back and forth across her disheveled, plant-filled office, gesturing, spinning, fuming, crying.

I carry around with me a little card that I picked up from my church's conference center off the Isles of Shoals, about thirteen miles out to sea off Portsmouth, New Hampshire. On the back of the card is this quote: "The world was made of things to be used and people to be loved. Let's not get it backward." Basically that's the way I was brought up to think, that people, not property, are the most important things of all . . . that life itself is precious.

I tend to judge people's sincerity about their beliefs by their actions. In the Episcopal church, where my father's a clergyman, we often used to say that "It's ye who do the will of the Lord, not those who say yea, yea." You know, you can talk a good story, but it's your actions that really count. It's what you do. It's how you conduct yourself in the daily scope of things, what you do all the time, that really says what you believe in. The real test has less to do with great acts of courage and valor than it does with daily compassion and consideration. I mean, it's what you do all the time: how you speak to people; the tone in your voice; the way you are aware of other people's needs; the way you are aware of your own needs so you don't work them out on other people; trying not to hurt people, you know, if you can help it.

I grew up with animals to care for, with nature all around me. I grew up knowing some of the things that Robert Frost, Amy Lowell, Sara Teasdale, Emily Dickinson, and Edna St. Vincent Millay knew. People who spent time in Maine and New England have a certain point of view, I think. I've read poetry from the Bedouins—people from Eritrea and Ethopia, people who live in desert areas—and they

use different allusions. Different things spark their imagination, because it's a different landscape; it's a different way of looking at things. So I think when you're in New England and you love it, it has a kind of effect on you. You get used to the sea, the nearby hills. . . .

(A long pause; a remembrance.) I think of the line from one of the Psalms, which I read whenever one of our students die: "For lo, I am beautifully and wonderfully made and this my soul knows full well. And I look up into the hills from whence cometh my strength

and my salvation." When I go to see my dad in Jamaica, where he's a missionary up in the mountains, in the morning around four-thirty you can hear roosters and a couple of little dogs going yip, yip, yip. And as everything starts to wake up and you go look outside, there's the sun just beginning to glint over the Santa Cruz Mountains. And if I go down the road to where we have a house down at Sea Wind, you can hear the surf booming against the cliff at its foot. You see the pelicans and crows just hanging over the air currents. It's then that I know that what I'm in isn't a creation of man. It's something bigger than me, something infinitely more vast and endless than anything I could possibly imagine.

I still say that my prayer is to have a more abundant life, which is not a mean thing, but an expansive thing, a full thing. Not to be niggardly and penurious but to be the fulfillment of what God should symbolize more than anything else—and that's love. That's the one emotion or thought or value which encompasses everything. Without it what are people? I mean, what's the purpose? Just to have money?

Maybe I do what I do here because the ability to read is a skill which is expansive. You know, once you can read books, you can read what people have thought and read and lived for thousands and thousands of years; you can learn to read in other languages and understand things in a multicultural dimension; you can read poetry and you can delve into plays; you can read prescriptions and directions, how to do things. That's why I think the most important function of government is the creation of the next generation of citizens. And they do that through the education systems and health care systems and by providing good housing and jobs for everybody.

One of the books that I used to give my seniors for graduation— when I had a lot of money—was William E. B. Du Bois's *The Souls of Black Folks. (She walks over to her bookshelf, pulls down a copy, and turns to the preface. She reads.)* "Herein lie buried many things which if read with patience may show the strange meaning of being black here at the dawning of the twentieth century. This meaning is not without interest to you, gentle reader, for the problem of the twentieth century is the problem of the color line." He put his finger right on it. *(Tears trickle down her face.)* And until we resolve it, we're not going to resolve a lot of other things, because it saps our energies, it nags at our heels, it colors our thoughts, it controls our actions, it conducts our foreign policy; it's why we are in such a disgraceful bind supporting South Africa's apartheid, because we have apartheid here and don't recognize it. Du Bois talked about it in 1903.

(Weeping.) This is one of the most powerful books I have known. This country hasn't dealt well with black children. What we went

through with desegregation here, fighting those buses with children, hair filled with glass, stones and bricks smashing through the windows. "Nigger go home; you niggers suck; kill the niggers." And the glass is still in their hair. *(Weeping heavily.)* It's all right to have open season on niggers, to sell arms to South Africa so we can kill children, whip their bodies with plastic whips, and ask that they show a pass to say who they are and where they live and don't allow their men and women to live together; and pay them a different wage; and don't let them vote—and we support it under the flag of the United States . . . DAMN this country. *(Yelling loudly.)* It's terrible; it wipes the American flag in the dirt; it makes a mockery of the anniversary of the Statue of Liberty.

Nina Simone says, "I wish you know how it means to be free. I wish you know what it means to be me." That's what I try to do in this job, to help people know what it means to be other people, what it means to be those homeless standing down at Massachusetts Avenue by city hospital waiting to get on the bus to go to places where they can sleep because they don't have any place to live. They look just like you and me.

It's so obvious, isn't it, that there's such a thing as sin and redemption and good and evil. I mean Sophocles and Plato and all the major philosophers and religions talk about it because it manifests itself in that which is hurtful and that which is helpful. Yes, there are evil things in the world. However you describe it, whatever people's religious beliefs or philosophical beliefs, everybody knows there are things that hurt, that maim, that kill, that deny humanity. And either you admire evil because it answers a need in you or you fight it because you abhor it. I equate evil with power, control, privilege— privilege accorded to a few. And it's manifested itself in public policy. Look at our tax policy. The rich get richer. The poor . . . the hell with them.

Life is a struggle. Jesus was talking to his disciples and he said, "I want you to be fishers of men." If you fish, you know that's a struggle. To get fish with a net, you know, that's hard work; tugging in those nets, that's hard work. *(She walks over to the wall near the entrance to her office and reads from a framed parchment containing a quote from Frederick Douglass.)* "Those who profess to favor freedom and yet deprecate agitation are men who want crops without plowing up the ground. They want rain without thunder and lightning. They want the ocean without the awful roar of its waters. The struggle may be a moral one or it may be a physical one or it may be both moral and physical. But it must be a struggle."

Brother Paul Holderfield

JESUS THE NIGGER

It was a bitter-cold winter day when I dropped in to visit him at the Friendly Chapel Nazarene Church and Soup Kitchen, which he runs with his wife, Barbara, on the poor west side of North Little Rock, Arkansas. Everyone knows him as Brother Paul (since he's also the founder and pastor of the church), and his friends are quick to tell you that "he is never too busy to stop and talk and pray with you." I found him in the back of his modest kitchen, chatting with a coworker while stirring up a huge pot of soup. "This isn't a fancy place, but it's a place of love, and it's a place where anyone is welcome. We don't care what color you are. We feed between four and five hundred people a week. And next year we're gonna build a fifty-bed home out back. It won't look like much, but it'll provide comfort and shelter to whoever may need it." He's fifty-eight.

I was born in Scott, Arkansas, and my folks was sharecroppers, and I didn't git much education. I can't spell nuthin', I can't read, and I can't pronounce words. We came up very, very poor, ya know. I tell people we was so poor you haf'ta spell it with six *o*s: "poooooor." My mother was a godly Christian woman. Prob'ly the first thing I ever remember is my mother prayin' with us . . . ever mornin' she'd just be prayin' with us. Prayer was just so important to her.

While we was sharecroppers at Scott, we lived pretty close to a black man that had a car. We never had a car. I never owned a bicycle, I never owned a pair a' skates, I never owned a cap pistol . . . I never owned anything. But this black man (his name was Jimmy Lipkin) had a car, and he would drive my brother and me to the boxing matches down here in North Little Rock. He always brought us here to box. We would get up 'bout four o'clock in the mornin', and we'd drive with him. Me and my brother went on to make names for ourselves as professional fighters, so we come out of that poverty, more or less. My brother won the National Golden Glove Championship in 1944. And I tried to folla' in his footsteps.*

Anyway I graduated high school and went to work for the fire department . . . that was 1954, I think. And the people there were very prejudiced. I was, but I didn't know it. People don't know it.

---

* He won the Mid-South Lightweight Boxing championships in 1945 and 1948.

If you'da asked me was I prejudiced, I'da said no. But I never had been faced with anything, see? Well, by '57 or so the integration crisis started, troops began marchin' in Little Rock. And all sorts of protest marches were goin' on. They were tryin' to integrate Central High School, which was one a' the biggest things to ever hit this state. So there's a lot of hatred goin' on.

One day I was out talkin'—all the firemen were just standin' out in front of the station talkin' and laughin'—and I looked up the street and saw Jimmy Lipkin comin'. He was marchin'. But I thought, Well, he hadn't seen me in twelve years. I won't have to go in. I'll just turn my back to 'im when he passes by . . . he won't know me. But someone had told him I worked for the fire department, so he walked right up to me and said, "Mr. Paul" (called me Mr. Paul, and he was sixty to sixty-five and I was twenty-four to twenty-five), and he stuck his hand out to shake my hand. And I put my hands in my back pockets. He looked like I'd hit 'im in the face with my fist. I mean, that's how bad it hurt 'im . . . it hurt 'im, you could tell. He didn't stay but just a minute before he left.

Now I liked Jimmy personally, 'cause I was raised with 'im. And I was ashamed. I'd ruther have the firemen's approval than God's approval. I wadn't worried about God's approval, I was worried about man's approval . . . I wanted men to like me. I knew they would really be mad at me if I shook his hand, because we was in such a heated thing over the integration of the high school, see? But I knew what I'd done, and I knew I'd hurt 'im, so I went up to the bathroom and I cried . . . I shed tears. And I got on the phone, called my wife, and I said, 'Honey, I've done a terrible thing. I refused to shake a good friend's hand.' And I said to her, I said, 'But I'll never let that happen again. I don't care what people think.' And a few days later I wrote to the newspaper, wrote a letter to the newspaper, and told 'em what I'd done to Jimmy Lipkin and how sorry I was. And I said, "If Jimmy Lipkin reads this, I hope he'll forgive me." But I didn't hear from him.

Then, in 1969, my mother developed diabetes and finally cancer. She was in the hospital about seven months. And on a Friday night they called us and told us that she wouldn't live till the next mornin'. So I walked down the hall to the bathroom, looked up to the ceilin', and said, "God, you let my mother live till Sunday mornin', 'cause if you do, she'll know I'm a Christian." See, I knew that she had prayed for me all her life. I realized I needed her God. I realized I needed her Jesus . . . needed her Jesus to become my Jesus . . . needed her God to become my God. So I promised God (I didn't know you wasn't supposedta make deals with God) that Sunday mornin' I'd git up and take my wife and three children t' church (which we hadn't been to in years). And we all went to the altar. They didn't get saved, but I did. I knew what I was there for. They got saved later.

Well, bein' that I was pretty well known in Little Rock, a famous boxer and all, it wasn't long before word of my bein' saved spread around town. And pretty soon it hit the front page of the newspaper that I'd been saved; they had a big picture of me on the front page of the newspaper. And they did a big story, and I told 'em about mistreatin' Jimmy; that's the first thing I told the paper. I said, "I'm a different man now, and I wish I could see 'im." And then a black alderman on the city council called me and asked me would I come speak at his church one night. So I did. And after the service was over, three black women came up to me and said, "Well, Paul, we read that article in the paper. You don't remember us, but we picked cotton with you when we was little girls." I said, "Well, then, you know who the man was I mistreated." They said, "No, his name wadn't in that article." Then I remembered, it wadn't. I just said a black sharecropper. I said, "Well, it's Jimmy Lipkin. You remember him, don't you?" And one of the women said, "Well, yeah." I said, "I guess he's dead. I never have heard." She said, "No, he's not dead, he lives out here in Little Dixie."

So we got in the car and we went out there and knocked on the door of a little ol' bitty shack. And an ol' woman come t' the door, and I said, "Miz Lipkin?" She said, "Yeah." And I said, "'Fore I tell you who I am, is Jimmy here?" And she said, "Yeah, he's here." I said, "Well, tell 'im to come out." So he come out. He had his shirt out . . . looked like a fifty-year-ol' man, but he was about seventy then. But he come out just spry as a little banty rooster. I said, "Jimmy, you know who I am?" He said, "Yeah," kinda looked at me, and he said, "You Mista Dunlap." And I said, "No, I'm Paul Holderfield." And boy, he just grabbed me, you know. And I said, "Jimmy, I come to tell you somethin'. Do you know I'm a Christian now?" And he said, "No, I didn't know youse a Christian." I said, "Well, you know why I wouldn't shake your hand?" And he said, "Yeah, I know you ashamed." He had it figured. He said, "You worried about what the firemen would think." But I said, "No, that wadn't it, really. I just wadn't a Christian. No way would I do you like that now. I've been saved. My whole perspective is new."

You know, when people call black people nigger, I've said from the pulpit before, "Man, you be careful when you say that again. 'Cause you know who was a nigger? Jesus Christ was a nigger. *Nigger* has nothin' to do with the color of the skin. *Nigger* means 'lowly,' *nigger* means 'rejected,' *nigger* means 'dumb,' *nigger* means 'won't take up for hisself.'" And I said, "You don't believe it? Well, just go to the fifty-third chapter of Isaiah." *(He grabs his Bible and begins to rustle through the pages.)*

Let me read somethin' here just a minute. Now, Doc, this is rich here ... the fifty-third chapter of Isaiah. Listen t' this: "Who has believed what we have heard? And to whom has the arm of the Lord been revealed? For he grew up before him like a young plant, and like a root out of dry ground; he had no form or comeliness that we should look at him, and no beauty that we should desire him. He was despised and rejected by men; a man of sorrows, and acquainted with grief; and as one from whom men hide their faces he was despised, and we esteemed him not." And Isaiah goes on and says that he went "like a lamb that is led to the slaughter, and like a sheep that before its shearer is dumb, so he opened not his mouth."

So Jesus Christ was a nigger. And a beautiful thing about it is, he attracts us other niggers too. So I tell my church, "Unless you're willin' to become a nigger, you're not a candidate for salvation. Until you're really willin' to come low *(laughs)*, come down off your high horse and get low; until you're willin' to be despised by the world in order to please God, you're not a candidate for salvation." So the only reason why I didn't shake Jimmy Lipkin's hand was because I wadn't a Christian; I mean, a Christian would never be ashamed to shake no one's hand.

I say, "Oh boy, I wanna see Jesus." I'm not talkin' about comin' back in rapture. I can find him ever' day. I found him in McDonald's the other day ... over beggin' for food. I find him ever' day. I mean, we stumble over Jesus ever' day. He said, "When you've done it unto the least, my friend, you've done it unto me." See, we feed Jesus about a hundred fifty times a day. We give Jesus clothes ever' day. He says, "I'm naked," and we clothe 'im. He says, "I'm sick," and we take care of him. So the only way we can serve Jesus is to serve people. It's just so simple, and yet we just stumble. We want to do somethin' big, but the biggest thing I can do for him is take care of his people.

Richard Stonington-Reed Johnson III

A thin, affable, long-haired thirty-six-year-old, he sports a close-cropped set of muttonchops and goes by the name Stoney. He's director of media services and production for the Martin Luther King, Jr., Center for Non-violent Social Change in Atlanta, Georgia, and press secretary to Coretta Scott King.

I was brought up in the Methodist church, where my mother was choir director. And I went to a small rural school. And this is Alabama in the late fifties, the heart of Dixie, you know, where the Confederacy and all of the glory of the Confederacy was still a part of the way you were brought up. First and foremost you were brought up to be a gentleman, to respect ladies, and to respect and honor your country ... even those damn Yankees (as Northerners were referred to almost invariably).

Since my dad died when I was very young, I was primarily brought up by women; mainly my mother and my grandmother's housekeeper, Katherine, who was black. Katherine is really the person who, in very small ways, influenced me about blacks. And I remember Katherine used to like to say that "God created us all the same, it's up to us to prove what we are, and to make something out of ourselves." So she was the person who began to give me insights to the fact that we enter this world, primarily, with the same abilities and capabilities and it's what we're exposed to in our youth and growing up that allow us to expand those or not expand those. She never failed to remind me that I was white and therefore there was nothin' I couldn't do. And that was the way she always put it to me: "You're a white boy, you can do anything you wanna do." It never dawned on me that what she was saying was, "But if you were black, that wouldn't be the story."

I remember when I was thirteen years old getting involved with two of my brother's friends. These guys were fifteen, and when my brother was at home (he went away to a private school), they'd been talkin' about what was going on in Birmingham. At that point the riots in Birmingham, in '63, had been ongoing for almost the entire summer. And it was a real hot, nasty summer. And, you know, my grandmother would have dinner with us a couple of nights a week, and she was always talkin' about the niggers in Birmingham: "Martin Luther King, Jr.'s a Communist," and all this kind of stuff. And at family reunions all the guys would sit around and eventually the talk would turn, durin' that summer, to the niggers in Birmingham and the troublemakers and how they want the world. And I went right along with it, because these were my family. The people that were helping me grow up in the world, right? It's a totally unconscious thing that you inherit the beliefs of those that you believe in. And of course you believe in the older members of your family, you know.

So, at the age of thirteen, having heard these guys talk over the weekend about wanting to sneak out in the family car and go to Birmingham and see for themselves what was going on, I got on the phone one evening and said, "I'm gonna cut school tomorrow. I want you guys to sneak out your mother's car and let's go to Birmingham. I want to see this." And that was all it took to get these two fifteen-year-olds to sneak out their mother's car. I said, "Let's go throw some rocks at them niggers." All the way over there we were talkin' about it. Matter of fact, we even pulled over at one point just west of Birmingham where there was a gravel pit and got a couple handfuls of gravel and stuck it in our pockets for somethin' to throw.

When we got into Birmingham, we knew where the riots were, because we'd been watching the news, and they were over close to the Birmingham Civic Center. So we headed in that direction, and we got about two blocks away from the Civic Auditorium and we couldn't get any farther . . . the roads were blocked. So we got out and walked. And just as we rounded the corner where we could see the park area, the police were turning loose the dogs on people.

Bull's boys?

STONEY: Yeah, and we all held Bull Connor in the highest esteem, because this guy wasn't gonna take no garbage off a' even the president, you know? As police chief of Birmingham he'd made public statements about Bobby Socks and his brother the president, talkin' about John and Robert Kennedy. And, from the Southern point of view, from the Southern good ol' boy's point of view, Bull Connor was the epitome of the staunch heroic Southerner.

Anyway we walked around the corner and they were cuttin' dogs loose on people. I mean, not really turnin' 'em loose (they held 'em on leashes), but they let 'em get close enough to bite people. That was the first thing I saw, and it stopped me cold in my tracks; I mean, I stopped walkin'. My mouth dropped open, and I remember sayin', "My God . . . they're gonna let those dogs kill them!" And one of the guys with me said, "It ain't nobody but a nigger anyway." And

I turned and looked at him, and I said, "That could be the son of the woman that works in my house! That could be Katherine's son!" And he said, "What're you, a nigger-lover?" And they walked off from me. And there I was standing alone with just crowds of people, and it was like this major confrontation with these two sides. The police had all these paddy wagons and fire trucks and all of this equipment, and all these marchers were chanting and singing, but none of them were charging or doing anything violent. They were just chanting and singing. And when the police started sickin' the dogs on 'em, people started running every which way, and then the next thing you know, they cut a fire hose on and knocked this girl down. And the girl couldn't have been more than fifteen or sixteen years old. I mean, it knocked her down and knocked her across the lawn of this park and just kept pushin' her—the force from the hose was so much. And I know it had to have broken some bones. I turned around and went back to the car. I could not watch anymore. All I could think of was, "My God, I don't believe they're doin' that to those people . . . that's not right."

The guys I was with came back about fifteen or twenty minutes later and started callin' me a sissy and a nigger-lover, and I remember sayin' to them then, "I don't care if you are a nigger, you deserve better than to be chewed up by a dog." I don't think the other two boys that were with me really saw it that way. I think they saw it as an extension of the rightness of Bull Connor, and I can't really blame them for that, because that was what they believed.

A couple years later (this woulda been 1965) I called up another friend of my brother's, a poker-playin' friend who was the grandson of the most fundamentalist minister in Jasper, Alabama. I called him up and said, "I want to go to Selma. Martin Luther King's gonna be there on March the 9th, and I want to go. I want to see this man." And his immediate response was, "What do ya wanna go see a Communist for?" I said, "Because I want to see what a Communist looks like (belligerent voice)." I'd been told my whole life that Martin Luther King, Jr., was a Communist and that everything he was doin' was being done to bring down the American way of life, and particularly the way of life in the South. So I wanted to go see him. He said he wouldn't take me, and I said, "If you don't take me, I'm gonna call your grandaddy and tell 'im what you do every Friday night . . . that you play poker every Friday night." He said, "You do and I'll beat you up." And I said, "After your grandaddy whips you! And I won't worry about that . . . the only solution here is for you to take me."

Well, he did agree to take me, and the whole way over there he was sayin' over 'n' over 'n' over 'n' over, "I don't believe I'm doin' this. We're gonna get caught, we're gonna get caught up in the middle of this. We're gonna get killed. We're gonna get in trouble." When we get to Selma, we park the car and walk about a block. We can see the Edmund Pettis Bridge and the state troopers, okay? We're far enough away so we can see 'em, but no matter what happens, I know we're far enough away that we can turn around and go back to the car and not get caught up in anything. So we're standing there and we see this group of men marching—black men marching— toward the troopers. And I'm goin', "My God . . . they're gonna . . . those troopers are gonna cut loose just like they did a week or two ago on these people." And the fellow that's with me is sayin', "Let's go . . . let's get outa here, it's about to start, let's go . . . let's go." And he starts to pull me away, and I look over, and the majority of folks in the first couple of rows are really well dressed in coats and ties. I know that one of them has got to be Martin Luther King, Jr. I've seen him on TV, but I can't pick him out of the crowd. I'm too far away. And I say, "Hang on, hang on just a second." Then they get to a point, maybe fifty to a hundred yards away from the state troopers, and they knelt down and started to pray. I thought it was Martin Luther King, Jr., calling them into prayer. (I found out later that evening when I got home that it was Ralph David Abernathy.) And when I saw them kneel down to pray, I turned to the guy that was with me and said, "Those people aren't Communists. Communists don't believe in God! They wouldn't kneel down and pray if they were Communists." And he said, "I'm leavin'. I don't care if you're comin' or not." So he started to walk off, and I took off after 'im, and we went back. But all the way back all I could say, over 'n' over 'n' over was, "Explain to me . . . you're older 'n me . . . you're a senior in high school . . . explain to me why a group of Communists would kneel down and pray? They've taught us in school that Communists do not believe in God." And he said, "I don't care . . . I don't care anymore. I just want to get back to Jasper and get this over with."

I asked my grandmother that night, I said, "Grandmother, if Dr. King is a Communist, how come he knelt down and prayed today in Selma?" And she said it was just a trick. I didn't believe that. For the first time my grandmother said something to me that I did not believe. I'm fifteen years old, and that's when the walls begin to tumble. But I wasn't really aware of it. I just knew that my grandmother said something here that I didn't believe. I was there, I saw it, I felt it, and what I felt when these people knelt down to pray was a sincere wish on their behalf to not cause trouble, but to make a change. But I didn't give it a lot of thought much after that. I have to admit that between the ages of fifteen and eighteen I was more interested in girls and cars than issues of social justice. *(Laughs.)*

Well, the years went by, I finished high school, and, for economic reasons, ended up at the University of Alabama. And I went through rush there because my stepfather was a real heavy legacy from a fraternity. So that fraternity at the University of Alabama was bound and determined I was going to be a member. But by two semesters into my education it dawned on me that I really did not enjoy being around my fraternity brothers. Then I started to let my hair grow long and got in with the peace movement and the hippies on campus.

I guess midway through '69 I wanted out of the fraternity. I wanted to deactivate. But because I was a legacy, they wouldn't let me. It would've been an embarrassment for them, so they didn't want me out. So we get all the way through the year '69 and I'm still in the fraternity. But I started riding motorcycles, moved off campus, and I completely disassociated myself with the frat. What it took to finally get me out nearly two years later was this: I took a very attractive black woman from one of my journalism classes to a big year-end party at the fraternity. She openly admitted that she had never had an opportunity to even be in any of the white fraternity houses and she wanted to check one out and would be glad to go with me. And sure enough, fifteen minutes after I walked in the door with her, my brothers in the fraternity handed me my deactivation papers. "Sign here and you're out and can leave." That was in 1971! They could not deal with a black woman coming to their party as a date!

So I'm getting more and more radical. My hair was long by the standards of those days, but still short by today's standards. In 1971 if you didn't have whitewalls you had long hair, okay? I'm into riding bikes. I had met a motorcyclist who was black. He was a student living off campus in an apartment next to mine, and our bikes were parked out back. I rode a Triumph 650, and he had a Harley Davidson. We worked on our bikes together a lot. And during that summer we'd seen *Easy Rider*, and we decided we'd take a ride down to New Orleans ourselves.

So we got on our bikes, headed for New Orleans, and stopped in a little place, a truck stop, outside of Meridian, Mississippi. We basically just went in to get a cup of coffee, but we decided we'd get a hot dog or a hamburger or something. And we went in, sat down at the counter, and sat there for five minutes. There were four or five truckers and a waitress talking down at the other end of the counter. And we purposely sat away from them so we wouldn't bother 'em, 'cause the truck drivers looked like fairly rough characters. I knew goin' in that we had three things goin' against us: We were on motorcycles, one of us was black, and the other one had long hair. So we didn't want to mess with these folks. The waitress finally walks over and slams her order book down in front of me and says, directly at me, "The federal government says I gotta wait on a nigger, but I ain't gotta wait on no damn hippie." And I looked at my friend, Ojeeta, and smiled and said, "Hey, nigger, how 'bout bringin' me a cup a' coffee. I'll meet you outside." And I got up and walked out. He stood up and walked out right behind me. We got outside and I said, "You're not gonna get us some coffee?" He said, "I don't wanna stay in there by myself . . . are you kiddin' me?" And as we were getting on the bikes, Ojeeta said, "You know, we're liable to run into this again, and we might get ourselves into a lot of trouble, and maybe even get ourselves killed, like they did in that movie." I said, "Let's go home."

We went back to the university. But that was when it dawned on me what black people have had to deal with their whole lives. From the moment they step out into society, because they look different, they're treated different. They are treated, particularly in the South, with a high degree of prejudice. And it had happened to me. Now, I had not consciously ever said to myself, "I will not be prejudiced against anyone because of color" until that day. I said to myself, you know, "I can cut my hair and she'll wait on me, but he can't change the color of his skin." So I decided at that point that I would never bear prejudice against anyone again.

We're taught in school that America is the land of the free and the home of the brave (or is it the home of the free and the land of the brave?). We're told in school that in this country because you're free you can achieve the presidency . . . you can be anything you want to be. But I found out when I became involved in the antiwar movement that only if you agree with and are willing to look the role and play the role as those in power, only if you fit their criteria, are you free to really achieve anything you want to achieve. Otherwise there are limits put on you. If you look poor, you're not allowed to move into certain areas. If you're black, you're not allowed to do certain things . . . the door is never opened for you. But if you have money and you come from a well-known family, then doors are opened automatically for you. And I know that there's no way you can open a door for yourself unless you're willing to pay a certain price. And that price is your appearance, the way you act, and the way you admit what your opinions are on certain things.

I had been brought up to believe that a man is only as good as his word. That was the one thing my father taught me that stuck with me all through my life, that a man is only as good as his word. And that if you lie about the way you feel about something in order to achieve a particular goal, you've done it dishonestly. You're no longer worth your word. Your word's no good, so therefore your value is nothing. And I firmly believe that, under no circumstances, should long hair or the color of one's skin or the way one dresses have any bearing on what one should be allowed to achieve or do in this world.

I personally believe that the hand of God moved me here to the King Center; that God saw to it I was given the right experiences all along the way to be prepared to work at a place that is founded on the principles of nonviolence as espoused by Dr. King, which are based on the Christian church. I have no points of conflict with any of the policies of the King Center. I agree totally and wholeheartedly with everything the King Center is about and everything it stands for, because our primary mission is to develop the "beloved community" that Dr. King talked about. The beloved community is a community wherein all men are judged for the content of their character. Each person is judged individually on his abilities and commitment. It is a community of peace, where people share openly their ideas and concepts and their abilities and talents.

The most important goal for me is a continuous effort to work toward world peace, to work toward the elimination of hunger and homelessness and apartheid in South Africa . . . to work toward the elimination of prejudice, period. And it's still an effort, something that I have to consciously deal with. Not in reference necessarily to blacks, but in prejudging, which is what prejudice is (that means to prejudge). We all have a tendency to prejudge circumstances, situations, scenarios, and individuals. And it's an ongoing effort to continuously try to catch yourself when you do that and make yourself pull back and examine why you do it, and try not to do it again.

Postscript: Stoney Johnson died in a motorcycle accident in Atlanta on January 24, 1990.

Outcasts

Gary Phelps

JIM BOB

I was very much a nerd in high school, very much a geek. I used to have a pocket protector and a pen museum in my upper pocket, wear flood pants, and I was never athletic—and I'm gay—and that's a big part of my life. Now I work here as a student counselor. I love the work. I like helping people to grow and encouraging them to be who they are. As Aristotle said, "That which is most perfect is that which is true to its own nature."

We are at his sparsely furnished dorm room on the Northeastern University campus in Boston. He's boyish, sweet, incredibly clean-cut. He speaks with the enthusiasm of an excited little kid. At twenty-eight he has been a lobbyist in the New York State Legislature, serves on the board of the Boston Lesbian and Gay Political Alliance, and has served as an outreach coordinator for the Dignity for Today Catholic Church. In both high school and college he was student-body president. He is active feeding the hungry, caring for the homeless, and serving those who suffer from AIDS.

I always went to church; wanted to be a priest since I was a little kid; wanted to be a missionary in fact. I was planning on going to seminary until I decided that because I was gay, I was irreparably bad, rotten to the core.

The first person I told I was gay was Father Leo, a Catholic priest who worked at the summer Boy Scout camp I attended in high school. At the time, I was an altar boy. I thought Father Leo was a wonderful guy, so I told him in confession that I was gay. He was abhorred. He said, "Why are you telling me this? It's disgusting. I don't want to hear about it." I said that I was praying to change; that I prayed every day; that I wanted to be good, wanted to change. He got very angry and said I wasn't enough of a man. And I suppose I wasn't.

It seems silly now, but I tried to be athletic. I tried not to be gay. I tried to change. I asked for penance, but Father Leo said that I couldn't have it; I wasn't forgiven because I chose to be a sinner.

He said, "You served at my Mass earlier this week." He started yelling, saying that I was the devil incarnate and that because of me Christ was never on the altar . . . that whenever I was present, Christ was never there—that everything I did was null and void. And that was my life—I mean, I wanted to be a priest. I ran into the woods and I stayed out overnight. I got lost, and I couldn't remember when I came back what had happened. But I knew I was horrible and I didn't want to see anybody. I put it out of my mind for two years until a good friend of mine, a close friend that I'd grown up with, Allen, sent me a letter saying that he had something serious to talk to me about, something I wouldn't like and something I couldn't change. I thought, Oh, no, his whole family has cancer. So I went home to see him over Thanksgiving break.

Allen and I are in his car and he says, "I've joined a group on campus." I said, "That's good. They'll help you through it; you know, you'll get over this. I'm sure you'll get better." And then he told me he was gay. It was like: "You're what!" *(Laughs.)* Then he says, "Why aren't you yelling at me?" And I said, "Because I am too." Then he slammed on the brakes: "You're what!" Then we got hit, and the guy we hit is banging on the window. But Allen was just like: "I can't believe you didn't tell me." I said, "Allen, this guy is furious. Where's your insurance?" I handled that, and then we went and talked for eight hours.

That day we made a pact that we'd never leave each other alone, because we were very afraid of being dirty old men all alone. You know, it was kind of odd to be in college making a pact in blood, but it was so important to us that we would have each other if we didn't have our families or our friends, that if we were old and alone that we would live with each other, always have a place to go. But Allen got very angry and said nasty things about the Church. And I said, "You're wrong. It's a wonderful Church and I don't want to hear this. You have absolutely no concern for my feelings. You know I love this Church, and you still love the Church, and I don't know what's wrong with you. If you keep this up, I won't speak to you." I got so angry that I just left.

The day after I got back to college, I received a call that Allen was in the hospital, that he had tried to commit suicide. I said, "My God, my best friend is dying because he doesn't think he's a good person. But he is a good person." He worked at nursing homes; he went around the neighborhood selling stuff to raise money to run arts and crafts programs at a home for retired nuns; he worked at the Sacred Heart Home. Then I got very angry at the Church because I realized that Allen was dying because he, as a Catholic, believed that he could never be good. I got angry and said, "I've got to do something. The Church is wrong." And it was a revelation that I could make moral decisions on my own, that I didn't have to listen to the Church, because I knew they were wrong. That was hard to say, that the Church is wrong and that I am right. And it still is.

But I consider myself a Catholic, although the Church doesn't see me as one. Here in Boston I and other gay people are told that we are not to meet in Catholic churches. But there are about three hundred of us who come to special services that we put on. We meet together every Sunday and have a service that's well attended. It's full of love and caring. We raise money for people with AIDS. We run a soup kitchen every Friday. We raise the money to run that, and we run it as volunteers. You know, gay people helping the homeless, which is great. Reaching out, I think, is a sign of maturity . . . our community reaching out to help those who are more oppressed than us, or at least feel the same oppression. And yet these good people who celebrate together, who really celebrate and who take care of each other, take care of people with AIDS, take care of the hungry and welcome in all people in our community, these people are not allowed to meet in a Catholic church in our diocese. And priests are not allowed to say Mass for us, or they risk their holy orders. So we have brave priests who say Mass for us in spite of risking their holy orders. The diocese has sent people to find out who says our Masses.

We make donations to Catholic Charities of the Cardinal Stewardship Fund in Boston, but they send it back. And if we're anything, we're like Christians meeting in the catacombs, Christians worshiping in spite of our own church, Christians who are communing and celebrating the Eucharist with God present but not . . . without the Church's sanction. Our cardinal won't speak to us, but God does. We're not allowed in our Catholic churches, but we're allowed in God's church, I think. We're really a model of Christian community. But many people in our own community don't believe that. Many people in our own community won't even go to communion because they still believe they're inherently sinful; that because the Church doesn't recognize us, we're somehow not real.

I think we really need to work within our community, to say we are good people and get others to look at what we're doing. Because we are, in fact, better than most parishes in this diocese in terms of taking care of the hungry every week. We feed 100 to 140 people every week. We not only raise the money but do the work ourselves. We take care of the sick through the AIDS Action Committee. And we take care of our own community whenever they're hurting and welcome anybody who comes into our church. And we celebrate, clap, and cheer at the end of every Mass because we're so happy to be together. I say, "We're damn good." And we should go out to the world and say, "You're welcome to come into us, and you need to know we exist. We are your sons and daughters and mothers and fathers and brothers and sisters. We're the people sitting right next to you in the pew at morning Mass who go later in the evening to really worship, and worship afraid, going into back entrances of churches, into basements, afraid that somebody else will see us go in."

I'm getting away from doing the things I should do. I always did what I should do, have always been a good boy, a good person. I've always been a Jim Bob. In fact, until last year I never walked on the grass. *(Chuckle.)* I always went around. It's so ridiculous. Now I think when I make decisions, Do I want to walk on the grass? Yes. I'm in a hurry, and I'm going to walk across the grass. You know, I worked at those nursing homes when I was in high school because I should work at those nursing homes, and I didn't like it at all. I fell in love with some of the people there, you know, but I was scared. I was scared of the people who were drooling and that I couldn't help, who were not saying anything I understood, who were frightened and lonely. And I was scared that they were so needy that they would use me up, always want me there. I did those things because I should do them. So I don't do that now. Instead I work every week at the soup kitchen because I like it. And I do a better job where I like to be than where I should be. I'm much better to the people who come in to eat. I'm much better to the volunteers, especially welcoming them and making them feel comfortable. I have a much better time. I come back voluntarily instead of going there because I should.

I still do some things because I should, but I'm moving away from that. I'm finding out that there are enough things that I love to do that are helpful, that serve God more effectively, and I think I serve God best by being honest about who I am . . . and that, you know, has never been easy.

Ted Hayes

THE SON OF MAN HAD NOWHERE TO LAY HIS HEAD

He's a homeless person living on the streets of Los Angeles.

I was in France (my dad was workin' for the army) when Emmett Till was killed. Do you remember him? He was a twelve-year-old black kid that they said looked at a white woman, so they beat him unmercifully; killed him, threw his body in the Mississippi River. And of course his face was all torn, and fish had eaten his body, and they showed a picture of him in *Jet* magazine, front cover of *Jet* magazine. I remember as a three-year-old child looking at that and never, ever forgetting Emmett Till . . . I never will. That's what white people were doin'. This was one of the first times I began to realize I came from a slave heritage. A heritage of oppression. Prior to that time I thought my grandmother was white. That's how naive I was. You know, I saw grandmothers as white-haired, blue-eyed, short little old women . . . nice, jovial. I used to think the White House was a place where God lived. I really thought the White House was God's house. That's how much I was for America. America was my heart. In fact I couldn't wait for a war to start so I could go fight for America. I was literally brainwashed. Yet there was this other confusion coming in, and it started with Emmett Till and got stronger as I got older.

My dad got transferred to a military base outside of Baltimore during the early sixties, and by the time I got to high school, the black awareness movement began to come around. I began to realize some things about America that I hadn't thought about before, and about myself. And me and my best buddy and I used to sit back and talk about the oppression of our people . . . what we could do about it someday. And we would listen to all the militants, like Rap Brown, Stokely Carmichael, Malcolm, and so forth. And I got pretty militant myself. I was always taught nonviolence, not to hate, but a fervor started to build up to the point where I wanted to pick up a gun. And that built. "We're gonna pick up the gun! We're gonna pick up the gun!" It's like we started chanting. "Let's burn up the town! Let's start a riot" . . .

When the U.S. invaded Cambodia, I headed out for California . . . dropped a tab of acid and went lookin' for Timothy Leary, you

know. Then I began to speak on college campuses (USC, Riverside, places like that). I was sort of representing the militant perspective. People began to listen. And I remember the college students who were hippie-type, middle-class, etcetera, wealthy. Whenever anything would come up about Vietnam, they would jump up and down and scream, "Yeah, yeah . . . peace, peace in Vietnam." But when the Latinos would get up in a brown beret and say, "Hey, we need your help. Our leaders have been taken away, they raided our festival the other day, we have no leadership, we need to get 'em out of jail, come help us," the hippies just kinda laid back on the grass and lightly clapped their hands, and said, "Yeah, man, we're with ya." White lip service. They just didn't want to die in Vietnam. They'd rather let someone else do it.

I remember this one rally in Riverside when the Panthers got up and spoke. They said, "Huey's in jail, needs some support, demonstrate with us." And because these guys are Black Panthers, and carried a certain amount of fear back in those days, certain amount of awe, people clapped real hard, and said, "Yeah, brother . . . we're with ya . . . we're with the Panthers." But there was no real enthusiasm. So I wasn't scared to speak. And I went up there, took the microphone, cursed everybody out, called them hypocrites, motherfuckers, and this and that; you know, just went nuts. And I told 'em that the war in Vietnam was really here . . . they must fight the war in Vietnam here. You defeat the war in Vietnam here and you defeat the war in Vietnam over there. I said this business of sending draft cards to your congressman is bogus. We need to do as our forebears did in the early sixties . . . let's burn these fuckers. So I pulled out my draft card, burned it, and then everybody started rushin' forward with their draft cards, and we had a bonfire burning on the stage. Then the police came in, and everybody was screaming and tearing around. One of the organizers came up to me and said, "Man, you've blown it . . . you've blown it! You've started a riot. The police gonna come down, bust everybody." So then I began to come to my senses. And if I went to jail, these hippies were not gonna come and get me outa jail, 'cause I was a lone person, black at that. So I jumped on the bicycle I was riding at the time and rode all the back alleys back to where I lived. From that point on I really took a low profile . . . went underground.

Well, I eventually wound up in Hollywood. I had a plan, and my plan was I would go out and make a name for myself in the entertainment industry. 'Cause if you are "known," you can say, "Stand on your head as an answer to hemorrhoids," and people will try it simply because you are so-and-so. Ironically Ronald Reagan was my prime example. If Ronald Reagan was an actor, entertainer, and could become governor, why can't I become an entertainer and politician? I was headed for the White House in fact. I had it planned that by 1988 I would be president of the United States . . . youngest, first black president in the history of the country. I really believed it, and I think I could have done it. I really think I could have done it. The more I look back on it, I think I could have done it.

So I was livin' in the streets of L.A., and one day I was walkin' down the streets and some hippies started talkin' to me about Jesus Christ and the Bible. I listened to 'em, and I didn't believe anything they were saying, but my heart said, listen to these people. They were talkin' about the second coming of Christ . . . stuff I never heard before, you know. Although I was brought up in a Christian family, I never heard that Jesus Christ was coming back again. I figured if he was the son of God, that's his business; you know, he got crucified . . . if he's resurrected, fantastic. But what's that got to do with me, you know? I got my life to live.

Whooooa was I wrong. (*Laughs.*) I went with these people and I even accepted Jesus Christ in my life as my Lord and Savior. And naturally I went straight to God now that I knew to go to God through Christ. I didn't have to go through a priest. I went to God with respect and said, "Sir, I need to ask you some questions: Why is it that this hatred and suffering and warfare and all these things are in this world? Why is this world, and where's it going, and what's up? And another thing is, why is it that my people suffer so badly? Why is it that we have suffered the worst form of slavery in the history of humankind? I need to know those things." To my amazement God began to show me these things over the years.

Your highest goals and morals, your belief in God, must be able to walk on the earth. The Word must be made flesh. Tangible. Touchable. I don't care if you believe in every iota of the doctrines of Christ, it means nothin' to me, 'cause I know it means nothin' to him. You could be a Buddhist, you could be a Christian, or a Muslim, but if your God cannot walk on this earth, big freakin' deal. And you need to walk on the earth particularly among the poorest of human beings, which are the homeless, people like me. Jesus didn't live in some seminary, he lived in the streets with the people. Foxes have holes, birds have nests, but the son of man had nowhere to lay his head . . . he was homeless by choice. That is where the bottom of society is. If you can change it there, you can change it anywhere—that's the challenge. Otherwise what is your doctrine, what is your God?

It doesn't matter to me if you're an atheist . . . doesn't matter. What're you gonna do for that person right there from your heart? That's the key. So the thing that motivates me, mostly, is justice. Justice. I believe God is justice. Justice is God. "The son of justice shall arise with healing on his wings." That justice comes to earth in the form of me walking among the weakest, serving them without condemnation, be it the drug addicts, thugs, criminals, rapists, insane . . . mentally ill. He said, we are our brother's keeper. "Whoever desires to be the greatest here among you, let him be your servant."

That's what motivates me. Seek first the kingdom of God and his justice, and all these other things shall be added.

At a funeral I was at yesterday someone quoted Martin Luther King as sayin' something like, "Longevity is somethin' that we all would like to have, longevity is a wonderful thing . . . especially if you have longevity and health." But he said, "It's not so much how long you live, it's the quality of your life. Your gonna die anyway. Live every moment of your life in preparation for that." And he said, "If you don't have anything to die for, then you don't deserve to live; you don't have a reason to live . . . you're just taking up air." That really impressed me, man. That's how I'm trying to live.

Frederick Douglass said that people would like to have rain without some thunder and lightning. Can't have it. You must have some thunder and lightning. You gotta have some suffering. Somebody's gotta sacrifice. When that guy jumped in the water when that airplane in Washington, D.C., a couple of years ago hit that bridge, he had some courage. He was drivin' along, going home with his wife and kids from work, and people were standing on the shore, "Look, look, look . . . they're drowin' . . . somebody do something." This dude jumps in ice-cold water and pulls this lady out at the risk of his own life . . . he cared about a human being, man. That's the kind of thing that we must do, all of us, on every economic level. If we really care about homelessness and poverty in this country and the world, everybody must step down and suffer for a while.

Survivors

Freddy Bosco

A FLUKE OF THE UNIVERSE

We are sitting on the porch of his mother's home in Wheatridge, Colorado, a middle-class suburb of Denver. During the two hours we spent together he put away a pack of Kools and five cups of coffee. A poet by trade, he delivers his words slowly, with an air of great seriousness. He is thirty-seven.

Last December I decided that things had fallen apart for me so bad that it didn't matter what I believed. I felt cursed, you know, 'cause it just felt like I was coming to a pit of ashes and that nothing was left. I couldn't build out of the ashes like the phoenix anymore. And so I kind of packed up everything real fast. I was just going to head for Mexico. By the time I got to Juarez, just over the border, I figured, God, it's a different world: total, new, incredible, exotic. . . .

And I'm in Mexico, in this fancy hotel in Juarez, and they're just sending hookers into the elevator with me; nice, good-looking hookers, you know, real pretty. I mean like if I were in any American city and I saw this, I would think, Here are some real desirable women.

It made no difference to me. I think what I went there for was to die, to go into a different life. Like what happened was, based on my belief in reincarnation and my belief in a fresh start and all of that bit, what I really wanted to do was die. I decided I would do that so I could go live some other place, 'cause I thought I'd run out of chances, fresh out of aces, you know.

I went down to the bar and launched a few Cuttys—a sure sign of death for me, 'cause I stopped drinking when I was thirty. So I'm in the bar and I'm thinking I've got all this money and everything's cool, but inside me there's this heat wave burning and turning, you know, like I got to get out of here. This is the end. Seems like there's a real imperative on me to get lost, to get out of everybody's way, to get out of MY way.

So I drank as much Cutty as I could and went out running on

the street and drinking water from the street fountains. You know, in Mexico if you drink the street water, forget it, you're dead for three weeks. But I went into a cantina and drank I don't remember exactly what and heard the most outrageous band I ever heard in my life. It was like five guys and five instruments playing five different songs at the same time. And I thought, This is the music of death. Clearly this is the time for me to go. And I just stood at the bar and felt like I was in some way making some kind of departure from this plane of existence. It was time for me, it was really time. So I went up to my room at this hotel and thought about that hooker that I'd passed up and swallowed all kinds of pills and started writing in my journal, entitled "Life Is Torture," which is the way I was feeling at that time. And I made this entry in my journal about what it was like to be making a transition away from physical existence and then lay down to die.

I passed out to sleep, and it was the most peaceful, resolved feeling I'd had in a long time. And I was so excited about what I was going to find, 'cause I'd read all these things about life after death, about this whole beautiful world that was going to open up for me as soon as I left my body. And I was just real eager for this to happen.

But I woke up in the morning. And I tell you, that was a mind fuck. I thought, What are you doing here? It was like waking up in the morning after you've had a one-night stand; you have no further reason to know this person, but she's still there. So I looked at myself and said, He's still here. Now wait a minute. I thought I took care of you? And what about the tube of light, all this, where's that?

I wound up in a shelter in Juarez. It was one of those "If you pray in the morning, we'll feed you and give you a place to sleep" kind of joints. When my ticket ran out at that place, I checked into a hospital in El Paso and got myself a plane ticket. Then what would you do? I called my mother: "Mom, I've been through all this horrible stuff. I need a place to stay. I'm catching a plane back to Denver. Will you put me up for a while?"

So, what is this? I stared the big one in the face, and it wasn't my time. And I always had a belief in my sense of timing, my capacity for magic. That magic is gone. I don't know. The question is, you believe what you believe, you know what you know; but the thing is, if I believe something, do I believe it because I think it's true? Or because it feels comfortable? Ever since Mexico I've just really had to weed out huge amounts of stuff from my head that I thought I knew or believed. And, I mean, you've got knowledge; you've got belief; and you've got delusion.

I think I decided that what was really important for me was to have penance, punishment; to punish myself not only for my failures leading up to the suicide but for the failure of the suicide. It really comes down to narcissism, to being so involved with myself. I'm saying, I'm punishing myself, I'm purifying myself. But I'm really flagellating myself for all these different failures.

I kept this Gideon's Bible from the shelter, and I go to the same things over and over again. Anything I try to read that seems fresh or challenging, I just put it on hold, you know. I just go to the same thing over and over again, which is from, I think, Psalm 19 . . . the end of Psalm 19 that goes "May the words of my mouth and the meditations of my heart be acceptable in thy sight, O Lord, my redeemer." I just say this to myself over and over again. But I first got it from a Jimmy Cliff record.* And I later found out that was something David wrote. He's a great poet. He's really my favorite poet of all. You know, in some ways, the Old Testament world appeals to me more than anything that has happened in the last two thousand years, because people were really intense then. They went out to prove what nice guys they were. I mean, it was serious business; walking on the desert, all this stuff.

I don't know where this leaves me, except for the fact that I don't believe in toys. I've got a cousin who I admire a lot; she's very bright; she's very courageous. She's got this boyfriend who's maybe fifteen years older than she is. He's got three airplanes and no education. He's got more toys. We recently had this big family gathering, and

---

* Reggae musician.

my other sister's brother-in-law and this guy were talking about a bumper sticker that said something like "In the end, the guy with the most toys wins." I can't subscribe to anything like that, you know. I mean, if I'm a glutton for anything, it's for experience. And if you're going to get into feeling what your life is, you've got to know how to suffer, because a lot of your life is going to be pain. You may not want to suffer, but you will.

You know, it kind of seems like I relate to my Puritan ancestors in that I keep a journal for the sake of working on issues of the spirit. But it seems to me that they had a really good time. They had it hard in a lot of ways, but there was some bliss, some ecstasy in their lives. And where our fascination with commodities comes from— you know, I've heard it said, "born to shop"—I don't know. Perhaps the Reformation and the Renaissance were, as one professor put it, "perfectly congruent movements" in that mercantile capitalism got confused with being right with God; you know, if you're cool, you're going to have a lot of toys to prove it. I never really subscribed to that very much. I never really wanted to have a lot in the world. A long, long time ago, when I was still in school, I decided that the more a person has, the less he or she has to call their own. And I've always tried to keep it real pared down; a few suits, you know, some things to write on.

But, you know this question: Are you attached to detachment? You can get so lost trying to be spiritually perfect. And sometimes I've gotten disgusted and thrown the whole thing away and said, I'm just going to get lost in seduction; I'm going to get lost in drinking, in fun no matter how expensive. And some of my fun has come from a place where I played the role of a crusader; the guy who was driving the money changers from the temples; the guy to prove to people that what they were doing was all wrong, an avenger for God. And that doesn't go over real well, doesn't work on any level. And it's dangerous; I mean, you go to any Psychology 101 textbook and it will tell you all about that kind of thinking and behavior.

My life would be a whole lot simpler if I didn't swing to such extremes. But I've almost entered into that kind of selflessness in which I don't do that much for myself, except just think of things that I can do for others. And that makes a lot of difference, you know, when you try it out.

I picked a flower from the Denver Marriott a few weeks back. I don't know, what can I say? I thought I'd pick a flower, an honest little flower. It was real nice. And there were lots of flowers, so I thought, well, if I just pick one, I can enhance myself by giving it away. And just up the street by where the buses stop, there's a guy with a shopping cart and he's going through the trash can. You know, he lifts the lid and he's going through it. And the shopping cart is just brimming over with plastic bags, and there is this little old lady who has a very small, round face. She wears glasses. She had long dark hair. Her clothes were real nice. She had all the accessories—looked expensive, for all I know. Anyway the two of them were swearing at each other, violent, black, ugly, bile swearing: "Oh, yeah, well," you know, "fuck you." "And fuck you." "Oh, yeah, well, fuck yourself." And just as she was saying, "Oh, yeah, well, fuck you," I handed her this little flower. All the anger passed for the time that it took for her to take the flower and smell it. And then she remembered that she really hated this guy, or thought she hated this guy. And so the two of them were just screaming at each other again.

But for just a moment she stopped and smelled a flower. And I walked off under the courtyard and then came back to see if she would have anything to say, and she was gone. But I looked, and she took the flower with her. It just proves to me that in the face of something really loving and true that hatred is impotent. Impotent. It won't stand up to love. You know, when love and just a voice of reason and something true comes across, hatred just disappears. It's like, where does the darkness go when the sun comes up?

I don't know if your heart ever changes, because it seems to me what your heart is about is love, love for yourself and the life all around you.

What makes love fade?

FREDDY: Well, your head comes into the picture; and your head is very persuasive, very seductive, and it confuses your basic loving impulse. A lot of the studies and practices that I've engaged in spiritually have been an effort to prove that the only infallible thing about me is my heart; but it can get lost, you know. If we were just simple creatures coming from our hearts all the time, we wouldn't be human beings. We've got to have that head to make decisions, to make money, to create and desire comfortable furniture and stuff like that. Otherwise we'd just be cows, you know.

It's funny, I was talking to a woman just yesterday who was saying huge doses of guilt are an excellent motivation for narcissism. If you want to really get involved with yourself and tune out the whole world, feel guilty. I have said a lot of times that I know how to live with guilt. I'm not sure that's true. Maybe I just prefer guilt—and I've known guilt that can have me lying in bed for days just writhing.

You know, the thing that Woody Allen says: "My only regret is that I was not born somebody else." Sometimes I've known the truth of that statement. Just like I've thought why can't I just be the same all the time? Why do I have to be so changeable, so given to abrupt changes of heart and mind? I feel like a pinball sometimes. Do you remember what a pinball was like before video games? Did you ever play pinball? Just bouncing off one side to the other, sometimes just right back and forth, in all directions, crashing into things. I suppose if I were born perfect I wouldn't have had any collisions in my life with the values of other people or my own diametrically contradictory beliefs. It's like Whitman said: "I contradict myself very well. I contain multitudes."

A personal belief system is like a garment, you know. I'll try this one on. How does it feel? Is it too heavy? Is it too cumbersome? Does it breathe with me? Does it protect me? Does it look good? You know, you got to keep all these things in mind . . . and they wear out. So it seems to me you've always got to try on new coats of belief.

One thing for sure is that I derive energy from the void. It's real, you know; it's the thing in Sartre's *No Exit* when the guy stares out of the void and says, "I got to get out of here. Would you, please, if there's anybody, would you let me out of here?" And the door opens up and it's the void—and it sobers you up real fast. I have stared the void right in the face, and I guess a person who had lots of faith would say, "Well, that's all God." But for me it's just like saying "It's empty." It imparts a real imperative on me to say, "Do what you can do, as best you can do; be very careful about what you do. Be as nice as you can to other people. Treasure your moments here, because you don't know if you're ever going to get anything else." And I don't know, especially in the Nuclear Age, if I'll ever have another moment . . . or another life. And I've got to make it count. I really hate the moments of emptiness, when the void comes to visit me; feel a real lack of anything meaningful in my life or in myself; feel that the whole thing is just a waste, just an empty joke. I don't feel that very often. But it's good to feel that once in a while, I think.

Why?

FREDDY: Well, you got to go around the wheel, you know. And that's one of the stops. You got to make the circuit. And one of the stops is, "There's no reason for it." It's just like the *Lampoon* said: "You are a fluke of the universe."* You're a fluke of the universe, you know. You have no meaning. You have no value. You're just here.

---

* *The National Lampoon*, an American humor magazine.

Kenneth Baldwin

THE GOLDEN GATE

Tracy, California. Sixty miles southeast of San Francisco. His clean-cut appearance evokes a portrait of the all-American suburban family man. He's thirty, married, and the father of a three-year-old daughter.

Of the more than 1,200 people who have jumped off the Golden Gate Bridge since it opened in 1937, nineteen have lived—he's one of those nineteen. "I should have died, but I didn't. I feel blessed—like a chosen member of a very elite club."

I felt like a failure at work, you know, and that was really where my problem began. I had just gotten out of school at the time. I took a drafting degree, mechanical degree. I graduated with flying colors. I graduated with a 3.82, or something like that. So I did really well at school. It really helped my self-esteem. But I went to work for a guy a lot of people warned me not to work for. He was very negative. I guess I'm kind of a sensitive guy. You know, it's really hard for me to take criticism. Criticism destroys me. And the worst part about it is I'm very self-critical. So it's really tough. *(Laughs.)* Anyway I said, "No, I can handle it. I'm twenty-seven years old. I'm a big boy now. I've got to make my own decisions." So I went to work for him and really never did understand where he was coming from. It was really hard for me to become what he wanted, what I thought he wanted me to be. I would work later hours. I would work as hard as I could, and I still didn't become the worker that I thought he wanted. A lot of this was just my perception of how I was doing. Since I was just out of school, I was hoping he wouldn't expect too much. But I guess I was the one who was expecting too much. I was just killing myself with criticism. I knew I wasn't doing the job right. I knew he knew I wasn't doing the job right. But I never confronted him with, "Hey, how am I doing?" because I was scared of the answer. I was very scared of what he would say. He would be critical, and I couldn't handle that. I would rather not hear it from him and take it upon myself.

Well, I went on about two months like that. And it didn't take that long, it really didn't. I was surprised at how quickly I became depressed with the situation I was in. I had only worked for him for about two months. Finally one week I started thinking about how maybe my wife would be better off without me. I'd been in school for two years. I didn't have a job then, you know. She waited for me to get a job so that she could do what she wanted, so that we could have some money to do what we wanted, travel, you know, go on vacation or whatever. And here I am, I finally got a job and I feel like dirt. I feel really unhappy. I feel like I'm not accomplishing what other people want me to accomplish. I never worried about what I wanted to accomplish. But I was worried about what other people perceived. I couldn't quit, because that again would be a failure. And I felt that if I quit, she would probably leave me. And that would just mount the failures one upon the next.

So I figured the easiest way would be to commit suicide. I thought of that for a week before I jumped. I knew I wanted to commit suicide. About three days before I decided, I knew how. I really knew that this was the way. For one reason, I knew statistically it was a pretty foolproof method. Out of the 1,280 people who had tried, only seventeen had survived. So I was pretty sure I was gonna die. And you don't want to sit there and try suicide and then fail. Right. I mean that's not your purpose for committing suicide. Maybe for some people their purpose is to get attention. But that wasn't mine. Which has kind of backfired. (Laughs.) But you know, I also did not want a mess. This was my biggest reason for going to the bridge. I didn't want somebody to find me with my wrists cut or with my brains blown out. I didn't want that. I didn't want my daughter to find me, or my wife to find me. That's not something I wanted to do. Didn't someone say once that "even in death you're thinking of other people." That's true. I was thinking of how this would affect other people. But ultimately not really.

So I decided to go to the bridge. That morning I said I'm gonna work a little late, knowing full well I wasn't gonna live through the day. I said, you know, I'm gonna work a little late. I'll see ya later. Gave her a kiss and off to work. I did drive into work. But I drove past. It took me forty-five minutes to get to work. But I drove on to San Francisco. And I was really happy. I'd known a decision was made. All this pain that I was going through, all this pain that my wife was going through—all of it was going to be finished. I was so happy because I didn't have to worry about it anymore. I could start anew. I was so happy. I was getting so near to ending all the grief I was causing everybody, and myself. So I even paid for the guy behind me on the Bay bridge; I paid for the guy behind me. I was so happy. I didn't care about money. What was money to me, I was gonna die. I was so happy.

I got to the Golden Gate Bridge and then I started thinking about what I was doing. And I sobered up quite a bit. It really hit me that I wasn't gonna see my daughter again; I wasn't gonna see my wife again; I wasn't gonna be able to play softball anymore. No more golf or any of the things I wanted to do. I started becoming melancholy. But I never thought of turning back. Never had one thought of turning back. So I got up on the bridge. It was a beautiful day. It was Wednesday afternoon. I got to approximately the middle. And I sat there and watched. I watched the sailboats. I saw the Coast Guard cutter go under the bridge, which ultimately saved my life. One of those ironies of life you'd see on TV or whatever. Then I counted to ten, and I didn't do anything. I counted to ten again. And again I didn't do anything. I was tryin' to get my nerve up to jump. So I finally counted to ten again and I jumped.

I vaulted over . . . there's a railing, it's only about three feet high. It's just like a regular walkway railing. I vaulted over. I saw my hands leave the bridge, which was the most terrifying moment of my life so far. I still have yet to match that terror, stark terror, because I knew I was gonna die. And I realized that I really didn't want to. I really didn't want to by that time, but I knew it was too late. I don't know how to explain it. When you go too far on something, you realize that you've done it and you realize there's no way to turn back. There's no way to get back on the bridge. I knew it. And that's what terrified me. So I saw my hands leave the railing. And then I looked down and I saw the water. Then I prayed. I said, "God, please let me live, please let me live." Then I blacked out; I got about a quarter of the way down and I blacked out. I still think that saved my life. It's probably instinct that just cut it off. Cut all the sense off. *(Laughs.)*

The next thing I knew I was in the water. But I was in the water swimming. See, I'd been a lifeguard. I'd been in Boy Scouts. So I'd gone under the water, I'd come back up, and I started swimming without even knowing it. And I don't know how. Luckily the tide was coming into the bay. If I would have picked another two hours, another day, another time, I would have died. This is how things added up. Everything adds up to my living. Because the tide was right. It was slow. It was a cruise tide. I think it was just starting to come in. If it came out, it would have probably took me under. Because underneath the water there it's really deep. It's like six hundred feet deep.

The next thing I remember I was on the Coast Guard cutter. What had happened is that somebody saw me jump. There was a work crew there. See, another day they wouldn't have been there. They had called the Coast Guard. They had sent flares down toward me, near me, so the Coast Guard could find me. And the Coast Guard was there within seven minutes. *(Laughs.)* It was amazing. It was incredible. So they were there. And they took me up. I blacked out again.

I believe I got very, very lucky. Things came together. The Supreme Being came in and snatched me from a watery grave. *(Sighs.)* Still, it's hard for me to believe that God intervened to save my life. That would be such an egotistical thing to say, to say that I am more important to God than the other 1,280 who died. I just cannot accept that. Even in that I'm self-deprecating, I'm very self-critical. It's a bad habit. *(Laughs.)*

I never once believed that God would punish me for trying to commit suicide. And I still believe that if I had died, he wouldn't have punished me. I sort of see death as a debriefing process. You go over your life and you talk to somebody about your life, the decisions you made and why you made them. God gives you a chance to grow from your mistakes. I really believe that people make decisions for themselves. You make your decisions, you make your choices, and you live and die because of those choices. But you are never punished for them.

Life is so much different now because I learned that whether I live or die is my choice. People can criticize me, it still hurts me, still cuts me real bad, but I realize that I'm gonna have to live with it, because the only alternative is death. And I don't want that, because there's too much to live for. My daughter, my wife, the things that we do, the friends that I have, my parents. I have a lot to live for, and I realize it now.

I've become more self-assertive. I've decided that I'm worth my own time. I'm worth getting upset for. If something goes bad for me, I can get upset. I can make other people uncomfortable for something that I want. I was a chronic giver and I'm not anymore. I really gave and gave until it almost killed me. Now I'm talking. I'm talking about what bugs me. I'm talking about how I feel about things. Ever since the jump, for example, my wife has wanted a spa . . . one of those bubble spas. For a year and a half we argued about it. And I never let her have it. And I felt very good. Instead of saying, okay, let's spend the two thousand bucks, just to keep you happy, I said no. It's been that way since the jump. I started saying, "I want to be a little selfish. I want to do what I want to do. I want to tell you how I feel. I want to make you a little uncomfortable." Before I couldn't do that. I would placate people completely. I would bend over backward for people. Now I'm really gettin' a lot tougher on it.

Since the jump I've had an amazing year and a half. I've had emotions, I've had sensations that I would never have had. And it's really nice. It's more than nice, but I really can't explain. It's fantastic to be able to sit there and wake up every day and say, "Wow, I'd never have this day if I didn't live."

What's important to me now is to make sure that when I'm old and when I'm dead, people can look back and say, "Wow, he really lived and he left something important behind." It's really funny, because I've always wanted to be a painter or a writer because when they die, their works don't die. This is something I will strive for later on. Right now I want to make sure my daughter has what she needs emotionally and physically to be able to grow up pretty normal. Then she can decide what she believes in and what she wants to do with her life. Then I can start working on something that I believe in. It's really a sacrifice that I'm making. Willingly. Definitely it's a labor of love.

Life is very short. The world's gonna go on. Hopefully the world's going to go on. No matter what you leave when you leave, it's what you did that's going to live on. Nobody's gonna remember that I was a clean liver or that I was a Boy Scout at eleven. And an Eagle Scout. But it's important. It's a legacy. It's something that other people remember you by. I think it's really important. History. Thomas Jefferson was part of history. He left a legacy. He was remembered. He will always be remembered.

So I want to leave something to the world. I want to leave something. Maybe just leaving thoughts and ideas to my daughter is enough. I don't know.

Kurt Saxon

Harrison, Arkansas, in the foothills of the Ozarks. Since his birth in Wichita, Kansas, in 1932, he has been a member of nearly every major right-wing hate group and religious organization in America, including the John Birch Society, the Minutemen, the Ku Klux Klan, the Church of Satan, and the American Nazi party, where he served as a storm trooper. "I loved to riot. We would go out and bust up peace marches in the sixties. It was exhilarating."

Strangely enough, he harbors no ill feelings toward Jews. "I never considered the Jews were important; I don't think they're important now, I don't think they ever will be. They're just an ethnic group, and, incidentally, they're the most intelligent ethnic group, maybe thanks to Hitler. See, when Hitler killed so many of them, that was a culling. He got the dumb ones, and the smarter ones left. And the ones who survived, they were the strongest, the bravest, and the best. Without Hitler there could have been no Israel. I would enrage a religious Jew by saying this, but if the Jews ever had a Messiah, it would be Hitler."

No, my biggest fear wasn't the Jews or the blacks, but the Communists. And I'm no longer afraid of them, so I am no longer a member of those groups. I don't care about Jews or blacks one way or the other. All I am doing is preparing for the coming collapse and creating my survival literature.* I started collecting nineteenth- and early twentieth-century science and technology . . . crafts, cottage industries, trades; something like you find in the *Mother Earth News*. I started gathering all that material so that as I disseminated it, more and more people would know how to rebuild when civilization collapsed. And of course I made up the term *survivalist*. It was very easy to do. . . . I wanna survive, you wanna survive. A survivalist would be one who worked at it.

I'm looking forward to a new civilization. And the next step in the evolution of civilization is getting rid of the labor pool. You see, the labor pool has killed every civilization. Every civilization has started, flowered, grown up, and died because of the labor pool. The labor pool are the incompetents, the dummies . . . low IQs.

You married?

Yes.

KURT: How many kids you got?

One.

KURT: See, if you had an IQ of 90, you'd probably have eight. So, you're not reproducing, but your inferiors are. Your inferiors are on welfare, your inferiors will mug you, they'll rape your wife. And there're more and more inferiors all the time. You talked to a teenager lately? These kids today have nothing going for them. They're a bunch of slack-jawed boobs. They're ignorant. How else could a monster like Michael Jackson get $120 million from a tour? I mean that's total degeneracy. And these people, they got no brains

---

* He self-publishes and distributes from his home *The Survivor* (a multivolume series on survival) and *The Poor Man's James Bond* (a how-to book for those who wish to make "fire grenades, potassium cyanide, explosives, booby traps . . .").

at all . . . they're horrible. And, of course, people like you don't reproduce themselves. The inferiors do. I'm talkin' about inferiors of all races, and a blond blue-eyed moron is just as much of a jerk as a black one. So it has nothing to do with race. But it's the inferiors who can afford to reproduce themselves as fast as biology allows, whereas the intelligent people like you who should.

Eighteen hundred and fifty was the first time in history when the population of our planet reached one billion. In 1935 it doubled. In 1970 it doubled again. And since 1978, something like that, it got to be five billion, and now it's over five billion. Now we've got the greenhouse effect, we've got the pollution . . . it wouldn't matter if everyone were the same color, the same religion, the same IQ, we'd still have the greenhouse effect, because that comes because of the production needed to take care of too many people. So the human race has become vermin. And there's going to be a terrible die-off. Now, the die-off is perceptible in Africa now. I can see it now, but it will probably take a little while for you to see it. Over four million homeless in the United States, and many of them children . . . all of these people are losers. And the losers have outbred the carrying capacity of our socioeconomic system and our environment. And they're going to cause the doom of at least four-fifths of the human population.

People like me are trying to save certain individuals . . . certain intelligent individuals. I'm showing them how to survive, for one thing, and showing them how to rebuild. Like, for instance, in volume 5 of *The Survivor* there's an 1850 foundry guide, which you and a few other guys could turn out thirty-five-ton things without any electricity. So, what I'm doing will enable people like you to rebuild when this Disneyland for dummies shuts down.

When the the massive die-off hits, it's going to be horrible. And just little enclaves of survivalists will live through it. And of course they have to have stores of food, barter goods, tools, and of course weapons to defend themselves. But most people put the emphasis on the weapons. And I add that to myself, because I'm the king of improvised weaponry. But we will make it through. And then, what happens when all of that is done? Then people like you (hopefully, if you read my works) will say, "We must never let this happen again." We want a free society, sort of an anarchy, where everyone is his own boss. A real republic, like the republics of Rome and Athens, where you delegate responsibility to someone because you are too busy working on some PBS production or writing a book. And so, intellectuals such as yourself will be able to have children. And you'll make laws, such as no social dependent can enlarge his dependency.

That is, if you want to get on the public welfare, fine. We'll have enough of a surplus, but you can't reproduce. And no one with a birth defect can reproduce. No one who's ever committed a felony can reproduce, no one who is unfit for military service can reproduce, so all that will be left to reproduce are people like you.

One of me is enough.

KURT: That's crazy. Now, just think of a world, Phil, where the only people you come in contact with are people you can have a good, stimulating conversation with. People who you can enlist to help you in some project, research, whatever. And why shouldn't we have that? You see, the problem with Christianity, especially, is that they say this planet is a kind of hell; you want to work your way away from this. Buddhism is the same thing, because the whole root of Buddhism is to work so you're not reborn anymore. (I was a Buddhist once too.) But this is a beautiful planet . . . we've got a fantastic universe. I figure in two or three lives, I'm gonna be in the stars, in spaceships. I've been a Trekkie all my life, long before *Star Trek* came out. So I see wonderful civilizations where anyone who is inferior can have a good life . . . they simply can't reproduce. And as for that Bundy that killed a hundred women, people like that would not be allowed to run loose. And the populations would be held down to a manageable size, so that everyone would know everyone, and if someone needed mental help, you'd give them mental help. And you wouldn't take these child abusers, the molesters and beaters of children, and the batterers of wives that have maybe a mental age of five years old, and give them custody of children. Just imagine giving a five-year-old person charge of a baby, and a bad-tempered five-year-old at that. What do you expect? The judge says, "Well, it should be with its mother." Well, if its mother is a five-year-old in a grown body, that's chaos. How can anyone justify recognizing the right of one person to take away every right from another?

I was raised in the Church of Christ and baptized when I was ten, and I giggled. I believe that all life is God, and all living matter is the body of God, and we are cells in the body of God, therefore we are God. But like the defective cells in your body, cells that are old and worn out are gotten rid of. That makes sense. And I think we need to do that to the human race. And in my opinion a person is valuable only as he produces. And the only goal of any being is to enrich the source of knowledge. He's just a bump on a log if he doesn't do anything. We'll bless him and take care of him, but don't let him reproduce.

Whereas the Buddhists want to stop the cycle of rebirth, I don't want to. I want to stop the cycles of chaos. And I don't see why we couldn't have a utopia if the social dependents and the trash didn't reproduce. Then people like you could afford to have as many children as you wanted. And you'd take care of your children; you'd love them, you'd educate them, and you'd have plans for them so they wouldn't run out and join some nut party like I did.

Dr. Roger Walsh

My worldview started as a kid when I became enamored by science. Science was my god, and I assumed I would always be a scientist. And in fact I was for a period of time. I earned a medical degree, and I also did a Ph.D. in neurophysiology, so I studied the brain; I thought the way to understand the world and ourselves was to know the brain. I went to medical school at the University of Queensland, in Australia, which is where I grew up. Then I came to California in the early seventies to do a psychiatry residency at Stanford, in large part because I was just fascinated by behavior and people and the mind and the brain.

He is a professor in the Department of Psychiatry, University of California at Irvine. A lanky man who speaks softly but swiftly in a strong Australian accent, his many books and articles have received numerous national and international awards.

When I arrived in California, I found people talking about funny things like "feelings" and "getting in touch with themselves." This sounded pretty weird, because for me the intellect was, if not God, then mighty close to it. Rationality was the acme of human development. Feelings, emotion, intuition were things to be distrusted and got out of the way so one could think clearly. It was a shock to realize that these nonrational faculties could be valuable, enriching parts of ourselves. And it was also a shock to realize that they could be developed, enhanced, trained. So the first really major life-shifting realization for me when I came to the States was the realization that it was possible to train to live, in addition to training for a profession or for an occupation; that one could cultivate one's self, one's sensitivity, one's relationship skills, one's intuition, one's introspective ability. One could even cultivate wisdom, as opposed to simply knowledge and facts. (And I define the difference between wisdom and knowledge as follows: knowledge is something we have, and wisdom is something we can be.) Of course our whole educational system is geared to knowledge and not to wisdom.

It was a great shock to me to find out that there are ways of cultivating wisdom. And as part of discovering this, I put myself through various experiential trainings of one type or another. I went to a number of group experiences: Carl Rogers, Transactional Analysis, Gestalt. I also went through some of the California "isms" like est and so forth. So I explored the human-potential scene quite seriously for a couple of years and found both a lot of nonsense and a lot of value.

At the same time I went into individual psychotherapy, and I went in largely because I happened to have some insurance which would pay for it. I was doing psychotherapy on people, even though I wasn't particularly convinced it worked. But I felt I owed my patients the responsibility of trying this thing myself and seeing if I got anything out of it. I had the very good fortune of going into therapy with one of the founders of humanistic psychology, an existential humanistic psychologist . . . just a wonderful, wise man. I went in there expecting that I'd spend a month or two exploring this, and that it would be an interesting but not particularly remarkable or transformative experience. But I ended up staggering out of there twenty months later with my whole belief system, worldview, self-sense, shattered. It was clearly the most dramatic change in belief systems I'd experienced in my entire life.

I went in believing that science, objectivity, and rationality were the acme of human existence. But I came out believing that these are only half the picture. I came out with an awareness of the crucial importance of our inner subjective experience and found, to my absolute amazement, that there was an inner universe as vast and rich and complex and awesome and mysterious as the outer; that there were profound depths of the mind, the psyche, the spirit if you will, within us; profound wisdom, knowing, and a sense of direction, meaning, and purpose which seemed to exist within all of us. I found it was possible to develop one's sense of internal sensitivity, and I realized I had been living on, you know, the top six inches of an inner ocean. My entire life had been spent skimming the waves while underneath there was an ocean with an awesome variety of life which I knew absolutely nothing about and had not even suspected existed.

Sadly enough, I found nothing in our culture to tell me it was there. And I began to see that I had been totally out of touch with myself, with the capacities that reside within me, and it seemed that the culture was that way too. In fact the culture almost seemed to be aimed at distracting us from those inner depths. And one of the great insights I had was that we live our lives out of fear of who and what we are, fear of our own minds or own depths . . . that in our culture we seem to carry the belief that if we go inside and look within, what we'll find will be these horrendous monsters, these terrible things, these murderous impulses, this anger, hatred, greed, etcetera. And in point of fact what seems to happen is that those things we fear simply represent a surface layer. It is a little like having a faucet that's been closed for years. When you turn it on for the first time, what you get out is garbage, and so the immediate response is, "God, close it down!" But in point of fact, if you let it run, then the gunk clears out and you get clear water.

So I came to see that we are fearful of ourselves (and that's an incredible statement, to think we live in fear of ourselves, that our lives are spent trying to avoid getting in touch with the deepest parts of ourselves), and those fears are the expressions of our belief system. We believe that, at bottom, we harbor horrible monsters, so we avoid those inner things, our own depths, our own minds, ourselves. And to the extent we avoid them, the fear gets stronger and the beliefs are reinforced. Fears which aren't confronted tend to grow. So you get a vicious cycle in which we avoid what we believe are bad (in this case our own minds and deeper selves) and so we never give ourselves a chance to know them and find out that they are benign. So beliefs are critical. Every year I am more and more impressed by the power of beliefs. I think that they construct much of our worldview and sense of reality. You know, the first three lines of the Buddha's teachings begin with, "We are what we think, all that we are arises with our thoughts, with our thoughts we make our world." That's a pretty powerful statement. And the more I reflect on it, the more I think that guy was right.

If you take a look at the fact that most of us seem to operate out of a belief that what is within us is fearful and abhorrent, then you can see that basically our lives are, to a large extent, spent in avoiding a confrontation with ourselves. And then you can begin to make sense out of the enormous amount of our culture's daily activities, which attempt to distract us from ourselves, from deep reflection, from deep thinking, from existential confrontation. There's a wonderful phrase by the philosopher Kierkegaard: "tranquilization by the trivial." And I think American culture has mastered that better than any culture in history, simply because we have the wealth and means to do so. It's a universal phenomenon, but we just do it better. So I frankly believe that the belief that within us we will find these horrendous monsters is probably one of the most destructive beliefs operating in the world today. It means people's lives are spent in distracting themselves with the trivial and avoiding being with themselves.

I've come more and more, and very reluctantly, and I've fought it every inch of the way, to a worldview which is more and more similar to the kind of perennial philosophy of the mystics. I find myself agreeing that things are not as they seem, that we're not as we seem, and that what we take to be normality is a form of arrested development, a truncation of human possibility. What we take to be normality is actually a form of consensus trance, or hypnosis, or dream, or collective sleep. We live in the biggest cult of all: culture. Our culture has hypnotized us from birth, because there seem to be realms and possibilities for human development far, far, far beyond what we've accessed. And those realms have been pointed to by the great sages of human history, who have awoken from the collective trance, who have dehypnotized and detribalized, who have experienced enlightenment, liberation, salvation, whatever you want to call it. They are the ones who have been able to step outside the limiting and distorting cultural beliefs within which all of the rest of us remain enmeshed.

I now believe that the fundamental nature of reality is consciousness, that all that we see is a creation of Mind. Zen calls it the "One Mind," others call it God or Allah . . . whatever. But in the depths of ourselves, our mind, our psyche, our soul, and in the deepest realizations and awakenings, we recognize that we are an aspect of that. One comes to recognize the truth of the sayings that have been echoed throughout history: "the Kingdom of heaven is within you" (Christianity); "Look within, thou art the Buddha" (Buddhism); "He who knows himself knows the Lord" (Muhammad); and "Atman (individual consciousness) and Brahman (God) are One" (Hinduism). I think the idea I'm expressing is not that man is God, by any means, but that there is at-one-ment "with" God, and that what we awaken to is the recognition that the sense of separation is an illusion. So that's very different than saying man is God, and that's a big, big difference.

Looking out at the world and seeing the fact that, you know, in this hour and a half of interview, three thousand people are gonna die of starvation and we're gonna spend a fifth of a billion dollars on arms, it seems imperative to me that we wake up from this dangerous collective sleep. I look at the state of the world and I see an inconceivable amount of untold suffering, and I feel compelled to do something. I've been pulled by my philosophy toward a recognition that the deeper we go into ourselves, the more we recognize our common humanity, our unity, our oneness, etcetera. And it feels like not to do something would be almost inconceivable, so a lot of my work is concerned with global issues.

If we look at the world today, we find that for the first time in history each and every one of the major threats to human survival and well-being is human-caused. This means that global problems are all caused by human behavior, and so the state of the world is reflecting the state of our individual and collective minds; the suffering, the nuclear weapons, etcetera, reflect our belief systems, our perceptions, our actions, our relationships, everything. At a very fundamental level the global problems are actually symptoms. They're symptoms of our individual and collective mind states and belief systems. So what this means, for me anyway, is that the traditional means of dealing with these problems, which have been military, political, and economic, are really only dealing with symptoms. The deepest causes are psychological, philosophical, spiritual causes. And if we're gonna really handle these problems and ensure human survival, we have to work on both levels. We're gonna have to work both to feed the hungry and reduce stockpiles and to change the fundamental beliefs out of which these horrendous things have arisen in the first place. So I think, frankly, if we're gonna make it, it's gonna require global philosophers and global therapists; people really working to try to change the cultural mind-set, the cult that we all live within. That doesn't mean you have to be a professional philosopher or therapist to help. It just means that you'll be a lot more helpful if you realize that changing our beliefs and ways of looking at the world may be crucial.

So I find myself trying to create a psychology or philosophy of human survival (one of my books was titled *Staying Alive: The Psychology of Human Survival**), and trying to put this worldview out into the world . . . to try to get people to appreciate that, hey, we're gonna have to work on our beliefs very carefully if we want to survive.

---

* Boston and London: New Science Library/Shambala, 1984.

Book Two

Hedonic Calculus

Rex Beaber

I elected to go to law school because I especially like to debate, argue, fight, and think. I was a psychologist for ten years, and psychologists are supposed to listen, empathize, sympathize, and couch their criticisms in the most guarded of terms. So the kind of character that law will reinforce is much more like mine than is a psychologist.

We're in a small, quiet, undecorated study cubicle at the UCLA Law Library, where he is a second-year student on Law Review. He is confident, contentious, fast-talking, and it's easy to imagine him demolishing future foes in court. "People have two responses to me. There are people who, I think, see me at a distance and say, 'He's an asshole.' And then there are people who somehow get in a conversation with me and I admit that I'm an asshole. And our culture is really interesting. If you admit you're something, all of a sudden you're okay. But I think most people think I'm a ruthless egotist. I don't think I'm ruthless. I am an egotist, but I don't think I'm ruthless. Ruthless implies a willingness to do harm to people. I really very rarely have occasion to do harm. I don't need to hurt anyone else. I don't have to make some other person do less well for me to get what I want, because I think I'm hot shit and will get most of what I want just by being good. But I am an egotist and, so, some people don't like egotists."

I was born in 1950 in Los Angeles; have lived virtually the entirety of my life in Los Angeles, save a few trips to England, which was the birthplace of my parents. A synopsis kind of sketch of where I've been is I was raised in the San Fernando Valley, did my undergraduate work at UCLA in psychology and my graduate work in psychology at the University of Southern California. I then went out and practiced for a couple of years in a community mental health center. Then I returned to the university for about six years as an assistant professor in the Department of Medicine here at the UCLA Medical School. Then I elected to go to law school.

I have to say that for reasons I have no idea of, relatively early in life—I'm talking about when I was eight or nine years old—I began to be very interested in philosophy and religion. That began in early adolescence with me raising what I would regard as typical adolescent questions: "Is there or is there not a God? And what's the bottom line, game plan/purpose of life?" Those questions led me to explore their answers in two avenues. One avenue I'll just label as self-reflection, reading what were then popular books, Zen, Suzuki, Watts, etcetera, etcetera. Those are what I would call traditional approaches. The other approach was to talk to my friends about these matters, but that was totally useless because if you talk to other kids about important questions, they're not interested. And if you talk to adults about these questions, they basically don't deem them worthy of reflection, since most adults have kind of accepted a default view of the world and they're not interested in talking about what the purpose of life is. They're into living life. So that avenue didn't work. So the avenue of what I would call primarily intellectual exploration didn't work.

The final avenue of exploration, which I think had some very significant use to me, was drug experiences. And by drug experiences I mean specifically taking LSD. I was, by the coincidence of time, an adolescent at the time that lysergic acid became a popularized form of self-exploration. This started in 1966, when I was fifteen or sixteen, I think. I proceeded to have—and of course I'm guessing right now—about, oh, a hundred or a hundred and fifty experiences. And I would say that those experiences have had a profound influence in terms of my view of the world. But it is difficult to describe them accurately. Hallucinogenic experiences are ineffable, and it demeans them to describe them. They really are beyond description, and I'm not a person who's incapable of skillful description. With that caveat, one of the most critical experiences that I had—and I actually had a number of these—is what I would call annihilation of self and view. That is to say that you can have an experience under the influence of LSD where you experience all the rules and laws of nature and physics, all the aspects of yourself and your identity, as completely arbitrary. It's very difficult to describe. It is the experience of annihilation and total directionlessness, and it is associated with an anxiety that knows no equal in ordinary life.

I specifically remember once having the experience of being under a very heavy dose of LSD, and I didn't usually take very heavy doses. But I once took a very large dose and was talking to someone, and the person asked me a relatively mundane question like "What's your name, by the way?" And I didn't know what my name was and I did not know what I did for a living and I did not know who my parents were or whether I was an orphan or where I was, which house this was, or whether I was or was not under the influence of a drug. I had the experience of what psychotherapists call being "here and now," and of course that was a here-and-now experience unlike anything any psychotherapist has ever written about, because they never mean not knowing your past. I literally had an experience where every moment was the only moment that I knew. And that experience is profound, because when one does not have a history to tell them what to do, one's freedom becomes torment. What I discovered in that moment is that your history—either your personal history or the history of the culture you're in or the history of the world as you know it—is your instruction. There are too many options in the universe to experience yourself as free. So the way people deny freedom is to invest significance in history. And for the first time I discovered what it was like to be truly ahistorical, to not rely on history as a guide. That is an intellectually terrifying experience, terrifying beyond measure. The physical manifestation of it was that I began (I was laying on the carpet in our living room) to experience my body physically melt. I saw my flesh melt off my hands and my bones begin to crumble. And I laid down and closed my eyes and felt my identity disappearing. My body began to disappear. I began to kind of feel myself melt into the carpet. My anxiety mounted beyond . . . I mean it simply is impossible to describe the terror of the experience. I closed my eyes and I began to feel what I would describe as electrical charges traveling through my body. I began to experience myself as nothing more than a noncorporeal electronic spirit. All that was left of me was this electricity.

Permutations of this kind of experience happened a number of times on LSD. The positive thing that happens is that those experiences provide you with what has been called the peak moment. And inevitably as the drug begins to wear away, you gather your faculties up again and you're able to reconstruct your life. You're able to refigure out who you are, refigure out what your values are. But it's a very interesting thing, because you're starting at zero. For the first time in your life you have the experience of choosing your view of the world. And I think most people don't make choices. They don't make choices about what they do in life. But even more fundamental than that, people don't really choose their values, their beliefs—they're transmitted. And whether they're transmitted directly, like your parent tells you I'm a Catholic so you're a Catholic, or whether they're transmitted subtly because your parents tell you to be smart and being smart means believing a certain thing, there's a passivity in that. Certainly most of us kind of travel through life kind of continuously.

The bottom-line effect of these experiences in terms of affecting my whole life was the experience that I could choose everything, that nothing was given. I had the experience that I could be anything I wanted. I could believe anything I wanted. And I could do it from nothingness. Once you believe that, you have an inner sense of strength that is indescribable. No one can impress you anymore, because being impressed means believing that someone can do something you can't do. Right? And when you don't have that belief, when you believe that you are everything and can be everything, suddenly there are just other people out there who chose to be something different than you. Right? So, from a self-esteem point of view, you become very strong.

Another benefit from LSD is that once you have fallen apart, few things seem scary anymore. If a person has been very poor and survived, they've had one important experience. If they ever have money, they can be much less afraid of poverty 'cause they know that you can survive poverty. People who have never been poor have almost a phobic response to poverty. And that affects how many risks you'll take, because if you're phobic of poverty, you won't take risks. Likewise, once you've had your identity wiped away, once you've experienced what I call the ultimate existential terror, nothing scares you. Right? Things that bother people, what I would call ordinary neurotic anxiety, like "Does this girl love me?" "Will I get promoted?"—those become mundane. Whether or not somebody likes me or not, I could never have a neurosis about that, 'cause I've experienced what it's like not to exist.

That is the other critical lesson LSD gives you in terms of a grand lesson—the effect of perspective. And perspective conquers all things. You must be able to respond to every disappointment in life by saying, "Hey, wait a second. I'm alive. I have food to eat tomorrow, a place to sleep. In terms of the basics everything is okay." You must be able to always do that flip-flop between, on the one hand, being invested in something and taking it seriously, because if you're too remote and transcendental, you can't do anything, because everything seems mundane and worthless to you. On the other hand, you must, when disappointed, just be able to kind of flip back on that experience and say, "You know, in the grand scheme of things, everything is okay." People who can't do that are sick, crazy, and unhappy. But people who can are people we call wise or who we say have a sense of humor—because humor is a manifestation of transcendence.

I think my presence here in law school after being a psychologist for ten years I owe in measure to the LSD experiences I had, because I was able to make a decision, a true decision. I was able to say I'm gonna change my life. See, there are very few people who can change their lives.

For many, many years if you asked me what was my belief about God, I would have told you I was an agnostic. That was always a lie, because if I was ever honest with myself, I would have to admit that I said that just to be intellectually pure. You know, you can't be sure, so why commit? But I don't secretly believe in agnosticism. I am in reality an absolute atheist. We are God, you know, insofar as I know. I don't know if there are any other beings, non-Godly beings in the world, but we are the most remarkable thing in existence. I don't believe in God, and, more important than not believing in God, even if God existed, I regard a belief in God as highly destructive. Even if God exists, I think it would be better for man not to know of his existence and not to believe in him, because to believe in a Supreme Power is an ultimate denial of personal responsibility in life. And certainly any belief that God would interfere in the events of man is to trivialize the power of man. So I regard all beliefs in God as a form of unworthy supplication and a denial of one's personal power. Certainly if I am wrong and if God exists, it's difficult for me to believe God would dislike me and punish me for reasonably concluding, even incorrectly concluding, but reasonably concluding, that he didn't exist. I mean, that would be a most extraordinary form of God. So I certainly have no concerns that my disbelief in the existence of God will wreak havoc in me. If God wanted me to believe in him, he can arrange it.

I don't regard the conclusion that we are God implies that always good things will happen. We, even as gods, have the capacity to do unpleasant things. I have to add that we, by the way, are a very unusual God, because our genetic history is that we are animals. What makes us God is our cortex. But our cortex didn't replace our reptilian brain; it was mounted on top of it. So always the God in us struggles against the animal in us. That's the unique dynamic of man, that we are this unusual interplay of God and animal.

So I don't believe in God and I don't believe in morality either. I've never understood the word. The word implies a rule outside of the pleasure principle. And I decide what to do solely on the basis of the pleasure principle. If it pleases me, I'll do it. I can see you questioning: "You mean, if it pleased you to kill somebody, you'd do it?" Now I introduce one subtlety which is very important to me. There are two pleasure principles. One is what I call the narrow pleasure principle. If right now it pleases me, I'll do it. The other is what I call the sophisticated pleasure principle, which asks, "In the grand scheme of things will I be pleased with the result?" And I wouldn't be pleased with the result that everyone in the world killed on impulse. So I'm more than willing to sacrifice my momentary impulses to kill—which I have regularly, every time on the freeway when somebody blocks my path. I mean, there's a primitive part of me that says, "Let's obliterate that person." Right? But why don't I do that? Because if I did do that and created that as a standard of behavior in the world, I wouldn't like that world. That world wouldn't please me. So to me there is no moral rule that controls my conduct. What controls my conduct is a purely self-serving view of what kind of world I want to live in. And I want to live in a world that gives me pleasure.

This bespeaks another important part of my philosophy, which is—I'm making this word up right now—functionalism. That whenever I'm asked something about anything, I approach it purely functionally. I simply say, "What will that idea do to the world?" What is it functionally? I don't like to invest things with any meaning unto themselves. Right. Just what will be the effects? What kind of world will that be? What kind of pleasure will that give me? I could care less about other people, because I do not believe that people have any other concern but themselves. I believe all people are tremendously selfish and they don't do things for other people out of a true desire to do something for another. Whenever you do something for another, I believe, you're really doing it for yourself. We like to fool ourselves into believing otherwise. But I don't think, even when you do something for someone you love, you do it for any other reason than that the meaning of love is that you come to view another as a part of yourself. So you're not doing it for another, you're doing it for you. That's a psychological view of love, that it involves simply a merger of selves.

But mostly people do things for other people out of what I call the reciprocity norm, that kindness will yield a quid pro quo in the world. You'll get some kindness back. People will view you as kind. The view of you as kindness will get you certain things, x number of smiles, x number of favors at a later time. People have this kind of theory of a kindness bank account that's being kept in the sky. Religious people think God keeps a ledger, and nonreligious people think the social world keeps a ledger. That's why people get angry all the time—they call a debt and no one was keeping the books that they thought they were keeping. You see how moral notions disappear. It's just a secret form of hedonism. It's the interaction between hedonism and a mind smart enough to work out a formula for future pleasure. So I live by what I call the hedonic equation.

Given the cost-benefit approach of the hedonic equation, why did you consent to this interview?

REX: From a cost-benefit point of view it was easy. I waste all kinds of time playing around and bullshitting with people, so I'm probably not spending this two hours differently than I would have spent it—well, maybe I'm just packaging my bullshit into a smaller amount of time. And what do I get out of it? Well, if I get nothing, I haven't been hurt, right? But if I get to read my name in a book, it makes me feel good. I'm a very narcissistic person. I just love all the times I'm on TV and write articles and when people recognize me. Anytime people know Rex Beaber, it makes me feel good. And by the way, that's not unique to me. I think that's true for everyone, but in any event, even if it wasn't true for everyone, it's true for me. So, if for two hours I saw my name in a book, that would be great. I mean, if I said to somebody, "Lay down on that bed for two hours and if you do that, twenty-five thousand people will read your name in a book and say, 'Hmm, that's an interesting guy,'" would most people do it? Sure they would. That would be the greatest investment of two hours in your lifetime. *(Laughs.)*

James St. James

A LITTLE SPLASH TO A PARTY

If God bores you, tell Him that He bores you, that you prefer the vilest amusements to His presence, that you only feel at your ease when you are far from Him.

—*François Fénelon*

We're at a busy cappuccino bar in New York City's West Village. He wears tight-fitting fluorescent orange ski-racing pants and is carrying a pink evening dress in a shopping bag. His purse/wallet is a metal lunch box—the kind kindergartners carry—with a picture of wrestling star

Hulk Hogan on the side. His curly red hair sticks straight up in the air, as though he just underwent shock treatment. A few years back, just shortly after his eighteenth birthday, his grandfather died and left him an enormous trust fund. Currently a feted star on the New York City party and nightclub circuit, his principal occupation is putting together costumes for each night's appearance.

I was born in Fort Lauderdale, Florida, about twenty years ago. My father is wealthy, but he's a very uptight sort of meat-and-potatoes man. He's like the good old boy. He has a ranch up in north Florida, where he likes to spend most of his time. When he's not in business meetings and stuff, he likes to be at the ranch. He's sort of a very uptight heterosexual.

My parents got divorced when I was four, and I spent the whole time I was growing up shuttling back and forth between Michigan, where my mother lives, and Florida, where my father lives. I guess the going back and forth from Michigan to Florida left me sort of rootless. Just as I was starting to fall in love with someone in Michigan, I'd have to go to Florida, or something like that.

I always knew I was gay. I used to have a crush on Elvis Presley when I was growing up. And it was never really much of a big thing, my sexuality; I mean the fact that I was in love with Elvis Presley or whatever. And I remember when I was in the eighth grade, I was already sleeping with other boys. I never told anyone about it, but I never went through any of that, "Oh, my God, I'm gay" stuff and then go and try to kill myself. I never went through any of that stuff as far as my sexuality goes. But it really bothers my father. And for his son to be sort of a drag queen—nothing in his life ever prepared him for anything like that. *(Laughs.)*

I was a very rebellious kid. When I was fourteen, I used to sneak out of the house every night and go to the Copa disco, which is a big disco in Fort Lauderdale. It was like Disney World for me. I loved it so much there. I would sneak out every single night and do Quaaludes and sleep around with people.

I suppose I can't really say that I didn't have a problem with my sexuality, because obviously that rebellion shows that there was a problem, that I was like really struggling for an identity. But it was never one of those things that just consciously bothered me. I mean, of course there were times when I would come home from a coke binge and be lying in bed at seven o'clock in the morning and thinking, What am I doing? Who am I? Why am I here? Everybody goes through those once in a while. But basically I've never given much thought to such questions.

I don't think much about religion. I don't know if God exists or not. Right now I don't think so. I don't think I believe. And I don't know if there's an afterlife. I really have no morals, you know, and that sort of frees me up to be any kind of person I want to be. Like I'm not afraid that God is going to strike me down and I'm not afraid of going to heaven or hell. That sort of lets me be whoever I want to be.

I'm basically sort of selfish. I mean, I believe in sort of a karma; you know, if you're nice to people, people are nice to you, and if you're rude to people, people are rude to you. So basically I just want to live my life in a way that's most convenient to me. And if what's most convenient to me is being nice to people and being good to people because they'll be good and nice back to me, then that's my only sense of morals.

You know, I'd like to be a heavy-metal star. I think as soon as my chest hair grows in, I want to start pursuing that a little more. That sounds totally superficial; I really feel guilty for being that way. But I want to, like, do that for a couple years, because the life-style really appeals to me. Just the traveling, the being on stage, the dressing up in funny outfits, the groupies, the drugs—just the whole mad whirl. I could live like that for a couple of years. And then of course it would get on my nerves. But I don't think that far ahead. I've never really had to make any long-range plans because I have a trust fund. So when I start getting fucked up, I can always put on the brakes, take a vacation, go visit my parents or something. No matter what happens, a check will always come at the end of the month.

So I always tend to live very, like, in-the-minute. I honestly can't picture myself at thirty or at forty or at sixty. I mean, who knows, I might go back to college someday or I might become a teacher and move to Missouri. But right now I want to be a part of this whole party thing and run around and dress up in little freaky outfits, get lots of attention. It's fun. I enjoy going out and having my picture taken. You know, meeting artists and rock stars and movie stars and writers. It's fun to have a lot of attention paid to you. Like when everyone is giving you drink tickets and giving you presents and saying, "Oh, you're fabulous, you're fabulous."

I tend to live just very sort of in-the-moment. I try to live life to the fullest. You know, if there is no afterlife, I might as well cram in all the living I can now. So I'm having a good time. I mean, I wake up around one or two P.M. I get on the phone and I start talking to people. I go out. I have lunch with people. I run errands that need to be run. I buy clothes, or whatever, for the parties that night. I go out to dinner. I go home. I have a few friends over. I get dressed up. I go to parties. I go to more parties. Then I go to a few clubs. I go to breakfast about four or five in the morning. Then I go home and go to sleep.

I guess it would really be depressing if I were to say there wasn't a purpose in life, but I don't think there is. I mean, if you think in cosmic terms, whether I choose the chocolate mousse cake or whether I have the café au lait just doesn't matter. And I think in the long run it doesn't. It only matters to me whether I choose the coffee or the cake. Yeah, my life is the most important thing in the universe.

A lot of people think I'm disgusting or horrible or totally vacuous and that I'm not contributing anything. But I don't see myself as being a Mother Teresa type. If I have any contribution to make, it's to add a little color, a little sparkle, a little controversy. It's a purely entertainment-type thing. You know, when I get all dressed up in ostrich feathers and sequins and a pink tutu or something, it's certainly not to help the starving kids in Ethiopia. It's just, like, to add a little splash to a party.

Scott Salinski

PARTY VIKING

I grew up in Grosse, Michigan, which is about twenty miles south of Detroit ("Detroit—de citee on de reevaire"); you know, right on Lake Erie. I grew up in a very tight society, with a lot of automobile moguls. The Ford mansion was like three doors down from me, and I dated Lee Iacocca's daughter for a couple a' weeks. It was a very prim-and-proper society, very much dictated by money, doing the proper things at the proper times. So I grew up a spoiled rich kid, for the most part.

Skirkus Ski Shop, Denver, Colorado. Although it's his job to sell me a pair of skis, he's more intent on flirting with the attractive brunette who's taken a fancy to his six-foot-four, 220-pound frame. A dropout from the University of Michigan, he's a handsome, blond-haired jock who wears a constant beaming smile. He's twenty-four.

After my first year of college (I swam for the University of Michigan and played football as backup quarterback to Jim Harbaugh*), I didn't wanna go back to school, and it was my mom and dad's twenty-fifth wedding anniversary, and I said, "Look, you guys are goin' to Europe, and you don't trust me as far as you can throw me with all my fraternity brothers, so why don't I do somethin' while you guys are gone?" My dad was ecstatic. He said, "Well, that's great, 'cause I don't have to worry about it. I'll give you a one-way plane ticket to wherever you wanna go in the world." You know, Rio de Janeiro popped up real fast. *(Laughs.)* But it's September, the snow will be flying soon, and I was a real good skier. I started skiing in Vail four years after Vail opened, which would be like '66, '67. Sailing season was over, and I got a brand-new pair of boards. I figured, I don't need a car in Aspen. I know people there. So that's what I did . . . moved out there.

When I got out there, the guy that I knew was in jail in Mexico for a border violation. *(Laughs.)* I had about $800 in my pocket, didn't know anybody, and I was just kinda hangin' out one September afternoon with a guy I met on the street. He asked me, "Are ya new in town?" I said, "Well, yeah." You know, I have my duffel bag and my skis in a lodge. He goes, "Well, hey, I'll tell you what. Let's welcome you to Aspen the right way." And I'm like, "Great!" So I go up to his apartment with him, which is right above the mall, and he's got like this three-foot-tall ceramic bong with a six-shooter on it. So he lights it up and we start toking. And he says, "Welcome to town!" I'm like, "Holy shit!" So we sat there and partied for a while, and in the course of a couple of hours people came in and out. And I started to know a lot of people in town. This guy would say, "This is Scott, just came in, rad skier, likes to party, likes to ski."

Within twenty-four hours of being in Aspen I had found about eight to ten new friends, and one of the guys I met was a gentleman by the name of Jonas Hertz, who is a native Swede . . . he's from Stockholm. Short guy, blond hair, radiant blue eyes . . . became friends instantly. I've been around the pro tour for a while, 'cause I skied pro for a year, and I would have to say, stylewise, Jonas was

---

* Now quarterback for the Chicago Bears.

the best bump skier I have ever seen in my life. Anyway I moved in with Jonas and a few other guys from Sweden. And after the first year Jonas says *(switches to a Swedish acccent)*, "Scott, you're not really like one of these American people, because you're really actually pretty crazy, and you're not normal . . . you're one of us." So I was dubbed an honorary party Viking. I said, well, what do I need to do as a party Vike? And Jonas says *(Swedish accent)*, "Man, every time we go drinking, you have to come drink with us, and you have to just be really stupid on the slopes. After that it doesn't really take a whole lot of anything." Like, great!

You know, I've been asked what the meaning of life was once in a psychology class. It was for an exam that should have taken four hours and I finished it in fifteen minutes. *(Laughs.)* The professor had phrased the question, "What is life?" Well, I just sat around, kinda looked around for a little bit, and I rephrased it to say, "Life is everything." Turned it in and got an A on it. You think about it, you know, people talkin' about the chemical composition of a table or a tree . . . life is everything. Everything that we know is life. And as far as the party-Viking philosophy, it's living for a good time . . . living to ski basically. For me there's a oneness, I guess, with nature (I don't wanna sound like a granola head when I'm sayin' this), but it's gettin' back to nature. There's a feeling that I get when I ski that, you know, I'm one with whoever created that particular mountain at that given time. Skiing is a freedom—it's you and the mountain and the snow. You know, when two feet of powder hit, when it really dumps the night before, the town is closed for business, 'cause everybody's skiing. And it's a given attitude that you're there to ski. Family, work, ambition is way down on the list. There is no ambition at all. And when it's powdery, you don't hear your skis chattering, you're floating at about thirty miles an hour downhill with one of the biggest grins you've ever had in your life. If you woulda smiled any bigger, your face would probably break. So the Viking philosophy is striving to be happy, to be comfortable, and stretching the boundaries on skis. It's very evident in a skier, party Viking, if you would, that you're always testing your limits . . . you know you can do this, but let's see if you can do this . . . getting the adrenaline rush.

A party Viking is kind of a hedonist too. I just love sex. I think it's fantastic. I think a lot of it has been kind of deterred with this age of AIDS and all this, you know, all the new diseases. But I'll tell you what: If you get a one-shot cure for AIDS, like the penicillin did for a couple of the other diseases, we're gonna see a sexual revolution that is just gonna knock our socks off! And I believe that one hundred percent. As a ski instructor in Aspen it was great. You know, there were girls that would come out and say, "I'm gonna meet a ski instructor, and I'm gonna fuck his brains out." And that's it. I mean, that's all they came out for. You have the Aspen Ski Company jacket on . . . that's like a beacon to girls. And they just hover around ya. I'd never had a problem picking up women, and I'd never really needed something like a varsity jacket or a fraternity to help me do that, but all you'd have to do is say "Hi" wearing a ski instructor's jacket. That's it. The average stay for a girl in Aspen is about eight days. They fly in, you meet 'em, you take 'em to your hot tub, you introduce 'em to the locals, they totally fall in love with ya. Ya have a great time with 'em, outrageous sex, ya drop 'em off at the airport, and they ask, "Oh, ya gonna write to me?" Oh, yeah, we'll write ya, no problem. *(Laughs.)* Boom! They're on the plane and you're already checkin' the next bunch comin' off of the plane for the next week. It's a lot of fun, and that's what people are up there for. There're no inhibitions in Aspen. . . .

You know, I'm a full-bred Catholic, full-bred Christian: catechism, church every morning whether we liked it or not, went to first holy communion, confession, and everything else. And I did it because I thought that's what I was supposed to do. But I gave that up. For a while I thought I was an athiest, but now I just think I believe in a Higher Power. Maybe I believe in Uhler. *(Laughs.)* Do you know about Uhler? Uhler to most of the skiers is the ski god. And in Breckenridge every spring they offer back to Uhler a big bonfire of skis they're not gonna ski with. It's another excuse for a big party. But *(laughs)* anything for a party . . . sure, Uhler! Uhler Day! Great! He gives us skis, he gives us snow, so, yeah, we'll burn our skis for Uhler. *(Laughs.)*

Corky Carroll

PLAY NOW, WORK LATER

Marie Calender's Pie Shop, San Juan Capistrano, California. Dressed in canvas shorts and a floral-patterned surf shirt, he is an ex-world-champion surfer who makes his living as something of a professional clown.

"I don't have what you call a real job. I have a clothing line which I designed. And I put together the advertising for it. It's really kind of a lot of fun, because I'm in the ads. I get to construct an ad around me. (Laughs.) And I do commercials for Miller Lite beer. I do personal appearances for them around the country at different events, which is really a lot of fun. They pay me really well to do it. They could probably pay me half of what they pay me and I'd still do it. They send me to ski races because I'm one of the only 'Lite All-Stars' that skis. It's like a free vacation, paid vacation. Like a vacation from a vacation."

I grew up on the beach in southern California. Our house was right on the sand, so I pretty much took to surfing much like maybe another kid that lived across the street from a baseball field would play baseball or something. I started surfing when I was around six years old. Pretty much surfed every day. Got involved in competitions when I was goin' on ten years old. My first surf tournament was the U.S. Surfing Championships at Huntington Beach in 1959. I surfed in every U.S. Surfing Championships from 1959 to 1972, which was the last year they had it. I started making money from surfing as a professional when I was about fifteen. I was one of the first professional surfers, maybe *the* first professional surfer that actually made his living totally from just surfing.

Being one of the first professional surfers probably determined a lot how I feel about how you ought to live your life, or how I ought to live my life. Because from childhood on I always wanted to do something I wanted to do. I didn't want to take a job which I had no interest in whatsoever, didn't want to do, just primarily for the sake of making a living doing it. So everything pretty much that I've done in my life has been geared around doing what I want to do, what was fun or what I liked or what my interest was.

I'm pretty much a thrill seeker, so a lot of what I like to do is risky sports. I just got through goin' skydiving. What a gas that was! Surfing, skiing, skydiving, things like that are what really interest me. I'm a very thrill-hungry type of person. Maybe it's the adrenaline. I like things that are thrilling.

I've probably had maybe ten situations where I could have died real easy. Every life-threatening situation I've had surfing has been in Hawaii. You don't get waves in California that are really life-threatening or really too many other places. Hawaii's, you know, where you surf real big waves. It's pretty much the only place you can ride twenty-, twenty-five-foot waves. Probably for an experienced surfer you're not in a life-threatening situation until it's over fifteen-foot surf. Until it gets that big, it's not gonna hold me down so long I can't hold my breath and the currents aren't gonna be bad enough that I can't one way or another get back to the beach.

So I've been pretty close to death in Hawaii a few times. I mean, I've been in a number of situations where you really realize how small and insignificant you are in relation to the unbelievable power of nature. It's real dangerous. And when you're out there, you realize how little control you have over the situation. You're a little, teeny piece of human, and there's this massive amount of energy and power in the ocean and waves and in the currents. In situations like that it's not only thrilling and scary, it's kind of humbling, because you realize that, hey, I could die real easy here. You begin to feel pretty insignificant.

But I really don't know about death. I think if you spend a lot of time worrying about it, you can get yourself into a pretty paranoid state. I don't have the faintest idea what happens when you die. I don't know if you go to heaven or hell. I don't know if that's true. It might be. I mean, Christians believe there's an afterlife. I'm certainly not gonna say it isn't so. All's I know is that I don't really have to worry about it till it comes.

Till then I just want to do what I enjoy doing. I believe in God, sure, and I believe in right and wrong and living by the Golden Rule, but I'm not heavy into religion; I don't have a particular affiliation. And I don't spend a whole lot of time thinkin' about it, to tell you the truth. I don't have any particular answers. I don't know. I don't know what obligations I have either, other than to just treat people squarely. I guess my first obligation is to have a good time. (Laughs.) Yeah, I'm here to have a good time. I figure that's what I want to do. I certainly don't want to have a bad time. Yeah, that's my philosophy of life, having a good time. (Laughs.) I guess it's the surf life-style. Play now, work later. (Laughs.)

Young Folks

COLLEGE DAYS

While visiting the San Francisco Bay area, I stumbled across a coffee shop hangout for students of the College of Marin, a two-year junior college situated in affluent Marin County. Following are interviews I conducted with a few of the students I met.

Tad A. Devlin

He wears a striped tie, suspenders, and silky black pants. His English-style haircut (close-cropped on the sides, long on top) is held perfectly in place with styling gel. He's a part-time model.

I grew up in Marin in a Republican household, and it is very conservative, and we are very wealthy. When I was growing up, I wasn't allowed to eat at the dinner table until I was like twelve years old, 'cause children were supposed to be grown-ups when they sat with adults. My dad drank very infrequently, and my mom didn't even touch alcohol. We had the ideal household, you know. Two dogs, a cat . . . and I have a sister.

One of the main things I'm battling right now is living up to other people's expectations of Tad. Like, who am I, you know? Who am I really? And when I look in the mirror, who do I want to become? I'm eighteen years old, and I've decided that I want to become wealthy. I want power. I don't wanna be reliant on my parents. You know, I told my father, I said, "Dad, I cannot wait till I can buy you a car." 'Cause my dad just bought me a car for my eighteenth birthday. He got me a BMW 2002, totally refurbished. That was my dream car, ever since I've been grown up. He said, "Well, you can get any car you want." I said I want a BMW 2002 with all the hot shit . . . alarm system and all that crap.

What does the BMW represent?

TAD: Oh, God! . . . everybody asks me that. It's status, to be totally honest with you—it's total status. It's, like, I've got the nicest one of all my friends. All my friends are into fixing up their cars, but mine's done. It's lower, it's got Recaro seating, a large pull-out stereo system, and a $5,000 paint job . . . I had to have the best one, you know. My dad said, "Well, don't you want one that you can work on with me, one we can build up together?" And I said, "No, I want the best one." It represents to me power, you know. And it's gonna sound kinda corny, but one of my favorite movies is *Wall Street*. 'Cause Gordon Gekko, this guy Michael Douglas plays, he's just the epitome of power. What he controls is just so awesome.

I think that's what life means to me now is power. More than wealth even. With power you get wealth and vice versa. I'm a very controlling person. Like, I've been in a relationship with this girl, and it's like, I want her to do what I say, but I don't wanna be an asshole about it, you know what I mean? I'm very traditional in a man-woman relationship. Like, I take her out to dinner and I open the door for her and stuff like that. And I treat her very well, you know, but I don't like her wearing short skirts. I guess I'm very traditional in that respect. But I really enjoy my car, and all my little toys. I like that thing, "The man with the most toys wins," you know. Yeah, I really do.

Toys is what Marin County is all about. When I'm traveling and people ask me, "Where are you from?" I go, "Marin." And they go, "Oh, really." I like my house, you know. I like all that stuff. I really do. How much is each man worth? I like that. My girlfriend's father, he's one of my role models. I mean, this guy is so high up there in the business world. It's like, I wanna be where he is, you know. I wanna be respected, and I want my face on the cover of *Forbes*, you know what I mean? I really do. I think that'd be great.

Melinda "Mindy" Johnson

She is a bit giggly, but extremely unassuming and warm. She's nineteen.

I grew up in San Francisco, and I've lived in the same house all my life, and that has been really important. My parents got married at Forest Hill Christian Church, and my father still goes to it, and we went for a long time. I convinced myself that what the minister was saying was true. But it really did not move me at all. I mean, it didn't seem to be like a fact to me. And when I was about twelve, I kinda told myself that the entire Bible was a farce (*laughs*) . . . I just can't believe any of it.

A few years ago I started getting inta, like, a Buddhist kind of mentality . . . a lot like karma, that that is really the way the world works. And I got into reincarnation and everything. Now I practice an Eastern religion called Siddha Yoga. I meditate and chant. It has changed my life in a big, big way. Our main belief is that God dwells within everyone and that you need to respect that in other people and to respect that in yourself. We also believe that you can do anything you really want and that what's inside you is one of the greatest things in the world.

When I'm not studying, I like to think about our guru, Guru Mayi. She's an awesome being—she really is. She's like a living saint. If I hadn't discovered this religion, I would be dead. There's no doubt in my mind. 'Cause I met Guru Mayi when I was seventeen, and before that if any little thing went wrong for me, like a boyfriend broke up with me or something, I would seriously, seriously, for a day or two, really consider killing myself. I was suicidal for, like, years. And when I met Guru Mayi, I realized that life is so precious . . . and I could never ever kill myself now. I don't even think about it, because that would mean I couldn't be with her ever again. I'm so much happier. I'm so much happier. It's just amazing. I just totally look forward to everything, 'cause there's so much rad stuff that's happening.

Hamed Khakbaz

His eyes are a bit glazed, and that's probably because he's stoned. "I like to get stoned. It makes me laugh at everything." He's twenty.

I'm Iranian. I was born there, and I lived there until I was eleven years old. In 1979, like most of the upper-class Iranians, I came here. When the revolution came, you know, most of the wealthy people got the hell out as fast as they could, and I was one of them. My father sent me here to the Bay Area. My father wanted to modernize Iran, but Khomeini hated the fact that the Shah and people like my dad wanted to modernize Iran. And Khomeini's a basic idiot religious fanatic who doesn't know what the hell he's talkin' about. He's just a crazy, insane, religious man. So I guess I don't like religion much. *(Laughs.)*

I took a philosophy course, you know. And I took a religion course too. And I flunked both of them. *(Laughs.)* See, I have a very short concentration span. And I think philosophy is something for people who can really sit and think. But I went into class high, and I sat there and I completely got into it. I talked more than the A students, and I talked more intelligently than the A students, but when I came outa class, the unfortunate thing with marijuana is you forget an hour later. (Laughs.) And I never took notes or anything, so I forgot.

You know, I don't sit there and go, "Who am I? What am I doing?" That may be for some people, but it isn't for me. Right now I'm into people. I love people. I like to walk around city parks and observe people. I love lookin' at people. That's what I like to do. That's one of my favorite hobbies, whether I'm high or not.

Kaveh D. Soofer

He's a friend of Hamed's.

I was born and raised in Iran, and I lived there for eleven years. I come from a very close-knit family that stressed a lot of good values, you know. Honesty, hard work, I guess your typical, good, hometown values. We are Jewish, and I was Bar Mitzvahed, but I consider myself an atheist. Everyone in the family's good Jews except for me. I'm not a very religious person. I figure God's used as an excuse for not facing life. I guess that's almost like my philosophy in life; you know, that you're the only person to blame or take credit for what you do. You know, there is no being up there that's looking down on you, who's gonna help you out.

When people say that happiness doesn't come with money, you know, I don't buy it. Because money buys you the ticket to happiness basically. I know that not every wealthy person is happy, but it helps you out a lot. I feel like I've got the stuff to become successful, because every generation has got to improve themselves. My father's successful, but I feel like I've got to go beyond him, to take off where he's left off and improve myself. I guess that's my number-one goal in life, to become successful and make my father proud of me. I will buy all of the luxuries of life: nice car, nice boat, nice house, good schooling for my children, a lot of traveling. . . .

I could walk outa here and I could be hit by a car, you know. So lately I've been tryin' to live life to its fullest. I'm twenty now, so I figure I've got about forty-five years left—I figure I've lived about a third of my life already. And I'm gonna enjoy it to its fullest, because once I'm gone, I'm gone. There's no coming back, there's no goin' up there and living another life. I'm six feet under . . . that's it.

Marquis and Troy

FUCK SOCIETY

New York City's Washington Square Park is a popular summer hangout for a number of gangs, among them the Lower East Side Skins, of which they are members. Skins consider themselves the antithesis of punks, whom they see as peace-loving wimps. As they put it, "Skins kick ass."

Marquis wears a tattered leather jacket, green-and-brown-camouflage army boots and a baggy pair of jeans. Thick stainless-steel chains hang from his shoulders to his waist. He's short, but built like a pit bull. You'd guess he could fight like one too. He's twenty and black.

Yo, the name's Marquis, right. Marquis de Sade. *(Laughs.)* And, yo, check this out, right. As far as I'm concerned, man, like, this is what I feel mostly in my heart, right, yo, anybody can, like, take it and shove it up their ass, they can do whatever the fuck they want to do with it, but this is me, right . . . every way about, all around, up and down, yo, this is me.

I believe the universe came together with, like, one big bang, man. I don't believe in God, man. Whoever do, right, that's their own thing, man. But that ain't me. I believe in, like, a higher force, a more positive force, the structure of the universe, right, that made the earth what it is, man. I also believe that the human race are like pestilent aliens to some extent, man. You know, I don't have words for it, man, but, like, fuck, man, it's like you, it's like me, we're individuals raised from evolution of the earth and time. That's all that it is, man—time and span.

So I'm, like, into partying my life away into a higher existence, man. *(Laughs.)* Partying my life away. 'Cause we all gotta die one day anyway, and there's no hell and no heaven, right. We all gonna die any motherfuckin' way, right. This is what's up. The higher span of consciousness, man, to me, man, is a level of high. It's like when you're not human, you're not animal, you're not vegetable, you know, you're part of the universe, you're the substance that creates stars and shit like that, right. And you're actually being passed on in evolution, right. . . .

Hang tight, man, I gotta get a beer. . . . *(He leaves to grab a beer at a nearby pizza parlor and comes back with a buddy named Troy.)*

So where the fuck were we?

You were talking about evolution.

MARQUIS: Yo. I don't got much more to say. Why don't you talk to Troy? He's the unofficial leader of the Lower East Side Skins. *(Marquis passes the microphone over to Troy, a wiry twenty-two-year-old black man.)*

TROY: To me, I just think humans are a really big mistake, you know. I really do. We're very imperfect. We've got a very hostile nature. If somebody created us on purpose, it wasn't a very good idea. *(Laughs.)* It was an evolutionary goof, that's all.

At twenty-two I really can't tell you what I believe or what I want to do with myself. I gotta be honest. I'm just trying to deal with society, that's all. That's all any of us can do. I just try to get along with other people, and it's difficult, you know.

I'm a Skin, and bein' a Skin is a violent, working-class style of being. Most of us aren't too much into religion and peace, because peace doesn't seem to work, from my experience. I've never got along by talking with other people and so forth. If someone gives me shit, I believe in takin' it right to 'em, you know.

I'm very nationalist. I'm very proud of bein' American. I'm very proud of my working-class roots. Bein' a Skin is about protecting those roots and fighting for America. It gives us pride in ourselves. It fits me like a glove. I feel very comfortable with it. I believe in everything America is supposed to be. And I believe that we've got to straighten it out if we're gonna survive. So we kick ass from time to time. We have to. It's part of life. We don't like fighting, it's just something we have to do. It's necessary. I mean, it's just like a war. Nobody wants to kill, but they claim that killing is necessary. Things are a little rough over in east Brooklyn, where I live. They don't have these class schisms over in Long Island, but they do a lot in Brooklyn. So nobody gives us Skins shit. If you give us shit, we'll bash your head in. Then you won't hassle us no more.

Fuck society anyway. Society has no room for individuality. It's like, if you don't wear the same boots and have the same ideals and the same religion as everybody else, you're an outcast. That's why most of us are here, because we couldn't deal with society. If everyone here wanted to look normal, I don't think they'd come here. But because we look a little different, we're outcasts. So that's why we say fuck society. Because it doesn't respect anyone except for the main body. If you don't meld, then automatically you're no good. America is supposed to be for everybody, but it ain't. It's for the Anglo-Saxon, Caucasian, Christian, white person. They don't respect Jews, they don't respect gays, they don't respect, especially, blacks. The American Indian was run off his land. I mean, even though it is supposed to be a country for all people, as far as I'm concerned, it's not what it's supposed to be. It's supposed to be for everybody, but it ain't. So fuck society.

LIFE IS A BEACH

The Huntington Beach Pier is the most consistent surf break in southern California and a haven for surfers, "beach bunnies," and "party animals" of one sort or another. I spent a day at the pier meeting a variety of young people in an effort to capture a glimpse of the southern California beach life-style. Following are snippets from these shoreside conversations.

Gordon Gino

His surfboard is airbrushed in bright pastels, and his wetsuit is pink, black, and lime green. A wiry eighteen-year-old, he drives to the pier from Tustin (some twenty miles inland) whenever he gets a chance.

Surf good waves, party all the time, make money, be happy. Live one day at a time. That's where it's at. I can't tell you a whole lot more.

Chris Anders

He's a twenty-year-old vagabond from Washington State.

Right now I'm living for the here and now, traveling around in my van. I don't have any solid plans for the future. I don't own anything else but my VW camper van, and I live in it. I'm from Washington State, but I just came up here from Baja. I'm traveling by myself. Probably after here I'm leaving for Utah to do the ski scene for a while. I'm just sort of into surfing, windsurfing, skiing. These things give me a real buzz.

I think everybody has to live up to their own ideals and standards and stuff and go from there. There's no real set rules, although there's a bunch of people who'd like to think so. For me, I'm just into being honest with everybody and checking into what they're doin', givin' 'em a chance, not being arrogant about the whole thing. I guess I'm just going for the buzz.

Perry Keller

His handsome, rough-cut face and muscular physique would qualify him for a modeling job in Gentleman's Quarterly. *He's twenty-one and makes his living remodeling homes.*

I've been surfin' since I was six years old. I've surfed in Hawaii, Mexican pipeline, Puerto Rico, all up and down the East Coast.

I believe that our life is already planned. I believe that the Lord already planned our life. There's one spirit soul that made the earth, and that's the Lord. It's a spiritual feeling. Somebody put all this together. We don't know what's gonna happen in our life. All we can do is go day by day and try to be happy. And I feel that if you have somethin' you can relate to and you feel it in your heart and soul and body, it could only be one thing, which is God. And if God gave up his only begotten son for us, we ought to give up our lives to God.

So I believe that our lives will be fulfilled in a smoother way if we go with that feeling and live a clean, natural life. No drugs. No drink. Hard work. Lots of exercise. It's worked real well for me.

Bill Pierce

I found him hanging out under the pier. Last year he graduated from high school. This year he's just not sure what to do. In the meantime he'll "just surf."

I just wanna be happy, have fun, live one day at a time. All you do is go out and live your life. And for me, what makes me happy now is surfing. So I surf just about every day. It gives you a wonderful feeling, just like riding a roller coaster. It fills you with adrenaline and gets you high. If I don't surf, I get kind of irritable.

Allen Scott

I'm a recovering party animal. I've been clean and sober now for twenty-six months, since about my twenty-fourth birthday. I haven't had any drugs or alcohol since. I went overboard. I became addicted to cocaine and was drinkin' way too much in high school, and it got worse in college. I've been just keepin' my act together and enjoying life a lot better today. There was a time when I wasn't so sure I enjoyed life and I didn't really wanna stick around. Now I really enjoy my life a lot. I'm still into all the old things I used to do, I just don't do 'em with drugs and alcohol.

I'm not into religion. I don't like to work too hard. I like to play more than work. I want to enjoy every day. I love to surf, ride my bike, look at girls.

Greg Nielson

His bleached-blond hair stands out in sharp contrast to the black T-shirt and surf trunks he wears. He lives just up the street from the pier. Today he rode his bike down to check out the surf. He's twenty-four and works as a construction laborer when he's not out surfing.

I'm pretty much into Jesus Christ; why he came, why he died. I came to Christ just at the begining of this year, in April, when I was saved. Prior to that I thought I was livin' a good life. But a guy from work got me started searching the Scriptures, and I found out that I wasn't in the total will of God, that there is only one way to an eternal future and that was through Jesus Christ. I was doin' drugs, gettin' radical, and partying. That's pretty much what we're reared up around here to do. Living in southern California, you know, its kind of like livin' in the world of sin. Sex, drugs, and rock 'n' roll—that's kinda what they teach around here. But by the grace of God I was saved, you know, and now I'm leading a perfect life.

You can really tell in southern California that you're either one way or the other. There's no middle-of-the-road around here, there's no sitting on the fence. You're either living for your money, surfing, sexual pleasure, how many girls or how many guys you can score, or you're living a moral life that has meaning and substance to it. You'll see this here in Orange County—there's lots of Christians and lots of people that are just the opposite and very little in-between.

Debbie Richards

Her tight, glow-in-the-dark lime-green bikini shows off her well-tanned body nicely. She's seventeen years old and a junior in high school.

My philosophy? My philosophy is to party. I like dancing, meeting guys, partying, raging, and lying out on the beach. Drink till you drop and then quit—that's my philosophy. Well, I guess if you're gonna go out and do social drinking, it's quaint to sit back and have a cocktail. But if you're gonna rage, you need at least a six-pack of Corona.

Sally Randall

CHAIN-LETTER LOVE

East Village, New York City. We're sitting on a tattered couch in her tiny, disheveled apartment. Piles of paperbacks are stacked against the

walls and an old Harley Davidson motorcycle, half in pieces, rests on
top of a coffee table—her boyfriend's project.

She's a twenty-seven-year-old painter and rock singer and a well-
known figure on the nightclub circuit. She's also a stunning beauty. "I
always like it when someone asks me something that's completely far-
fetched, that has nothing to do with fame, fortune, success, glamour, and
all of the stuff that club life is about. That's why I agreed to do this,
because I like the idea of talking about things that are a little more earthen-
bound, not quite so frivolous."

I grew up in suburban Rye, Connecticut, which is a very comfortable town. It's a perfect little pocket with the perfect high school.
Everybody grows up to go to a nice Ivy League college. I mean, you
go to Princeton or whatever. And the girls all pretty much get married after school. By the time you're twenty-seven, you own your
own home.

My mother was an opera singer, who, at some point in her life,
decided to have a family instead. My father came from a real puri-
tanical background. He's one of the original Randalls, the second
settlement at Jamestown, the whole bit. So he grew up in a household
where there was no liquor, no card playing on Sunday, or anything.
He did everything the way you did it in the fifties. Went to college,
met my mother, got married, joined the army for the two-year period. They all did. And then he went into corporate life. So my
background is very much Connecticut upper-class.

From as early as I can remember, we went to the Episcopal church
every Sunday. My father at one point was on the vestry or something.
Mom was the head of the women's club. By the time I was ten, I
was in the girls' choir. I was the lead soprano. I was the head of the
youth group. There was a certain kindness I found there. I'd always
heard other teenagers in high school saying, you know, "God is
everywhere. Who needs a church? That's a bunch of rubbish." But
for some reason I could never believe that, because the one thing I
found in a church is that it gave people a place to simply assemble
so that all of their beliefs and ideas had some guidelines, so that we
didn't all create our own idea of God to the point where we re-
created God in our own image, which is scary, because I think if we
get too separated from the idea of communing with other people,
we can start to do that.

So that sense of the feeling of community with other people has
followed me through life. And my entire career deals with bringing
people together, whether it's performing myself or whether it's book-
ing bands and putting little clubs together. Everything has always

been communal. Even in my home. People come in and out of here all the time. You know, if I have three eggs in the refrigerator and there's four people, I'll make a bigger omelet and everyone gets a piece. I think that all stems from having been brought up in a very church-oriented town with very communal-oriented parents. So that's something I have to be eternally grateful for.

I think early in life I read too much Nietzsche. I never believed that God was dead, but I always believed a little bit of the philosophy that we're all born to die. And I've spent a lot of time in my life trying to negate that with my more religious beliefs. It's kind of like the little demon in me that says, "You're just here to die, so screw it." I mean everyone has a little demon, and that's mine, and I have to battle that a lot. There have been lots of different points in my life when things got rough. And I often thought of throwing the towel in. But again, it's that other spirit in me that says, "You've been given gifts and talents and you need to share them and you do not deny them." That kind of kept me going, because I kind of believed that if you are given talents and gifts and intelligence, then they're not yours. The second you write something on paper, paint a picture or write a song, it's not yours anymore. And if it touches someone else's life, you're a success. To me that's what success really means. It's not being on *Lifestyles of the Rich and Famous*, although that's a nice piece of icing on the cake. I certainly wouldn't say no. But it's just icing. I think the real reward is for me to be able to write a song that someone will wake up in the morning humming and will make them feel good. So as a result I've always been a bit of a populist about my music. I have not tried to write dark, avant-garde, looming, esoteric songs. I'm trying to write songs that deal with something enjoyable in people's lives, especially something witty or funny. Because I think in humor you make much bigger statements.

I've always believed very much in karma. I mean, I don't study Buddhism, but I've believed in karma in the sense that anything you do comes back to you in your life. So therefore you try to do good things. I mean, if you rip somebody off for a couple hundred dollars, a few months down the road something's gonna happen and someone's going to borrow money and not pay you back. And I see that constantly. As a result money has become very artificial to me. Because there are times in my life when I've owed someone or someone's owed me. And if you love the person, you let it go. Not all people feel that way obviously. I don't think corporate presidents who have done major corporate takeovers have a particularly beneficent feeling about money. But I do.

Every now and then when I have shared and given and helped other people out, it suddenly hits me: Why am I doing this? Why can't I be more selfish? I see other people being selfish and getting somewhere so much quicker. Maybe I should be selfish for a change. And for that split second or that week or that day that I exercise the art of being selfish, I always end up kicking myself because I'm not comfortable with it. And I always end up getting somebody angry at me, and then I have to go and apologize. That's a little bit of the New York syndrome that constantly says that everybody should be very selfish about their lives. And there's a lot of people who think that if you appear to be a giver, it's really because you're the most selfish person in the world and that you're just playing a game. And I always find that to be really amusing, because if I'm playing a game, I'm wondering why I'm not making more money doing it. You know, I mean, if this is such a great scam, then I'm unaware of it.

But all of our lives interrelate so closely that I often wonder why people get caught up in the selfish aspects. I mean, it's so obvious that we all are connected. So why not build the strengths? Why pull away from people? Because to me it's like the more people you create a connection with, the stronger a person you are. You know, it's like the old thing that you touch that person's life, they touch someone else's. It's like a chain letter. And I think that it's strengthening.

Noah Johnson

Berkeley, California. "I've never been interviewed. This promises to be interesting." He's nine years old.

I don't really care too much about God stuff. I don't really go for religion. Of course, there is my aunt up in Canada. She is a religious maniac. When my grandma was dying of lung cancer, she figured she could cure her just by praying a lot. It didn't work. I'm not sure what happened then, but I understood that she took it pretty hard. I don't really have a religion. The only thing I can think of that it does is make you open to religious prejudice. "You're a Jew, you stink." Something like that.

I do think about why I'm here from time to time, but not much. Usually I just come up with the answer that I'm here. I don't know why and I don't know how. Things like that are hard to figure out. They are much harder than what came first, the chicken or the egg. I mean, that's easy: The egg did. As far as the Big Bang, I think of it as some kind of fast putting together of the whole thing. It's like it just all happened so fast. In the inside of the bang it's like "Psssst— this planet goes over here, this galaxy over there, this star here," and so on. It's just weird.

So far nothing really significant's happened to me, life hasn't been very important, but I'm counting on it getting better later on. It just doesn't seem that anybody pays attention to me. It's like, I have a couple of friends and even they don't pay much attention to me. Not very many people even know I exist. I've just stayed exactly the same ever since I was a baby. I mean, I even look the same. I have the same features. I have had them for nine years. Couldn't I change even a little bit? Sheeesh. Why get older at all? I won't change. Big deal. Here I am, still the same.

So far I haven't had much control over anything. Like this here is the start of the set for a stop-frame animated movie I'm going to make. (*He points to a sandbox in the corner of his bedroom filled with plastic dinosaurs and soldiers.*) So, anyway, I can control that, but that's about it. I mean, so far things just happen.

I'm not sure about the secret to happiness. I mean, I think life goes on, and you can't make any really huge drastic changes unless you happen to have the world's most powerful nuclear bomb. Then you can make big changes, like causing Planet Earth to no longer exist. But that's a little drastic for a first start.

I figure, if nothing ever really happens, I mean, if life is just dull, then it isn't worth very much. Because, I figure, a good reason to live life is so something can happen. If nothing happens in life, then I don't think I should exist. However, if stuff happens, like if you save someone from drowning and get your picture in the newspaper, blah, blah, blah, then life is definitely worth living, because something happened. If life is just the same old cornflakes for breakfast, spaghetti for dinner, la, la, la, just the same old routine every day, then it's just zilch.

I think a guy should live his life depending on what kind of a person he is. Like, if I were a kid who was raised in a household that's very, very serious and everybody's going around with their mouths like in a straight line (*he flattens his lips and squints his eyes*), then I wouldn't exactly want to go into comedy movies, would I? However, being raised in the household that I am, I am thinking about going into comedy movies, Charlie Chaplin—style stuff. I'm pretty good at comedy. Of course I don't always get a joke whenever I want it. Something strikes me as funny and I just make a joke about it. Like just now when I was reading *The Hound of the Baskervilles*, it said something like, "And as we sat there together in the twilight" . . . blah, blah, blah. I thought it would be pretty funny if instead it said, "As we sat there together in the Twilight Zone." *(He laughs and hums the theme song for* The Twilight Zone.*)* Aaaaaak! It would be a pretty good place for the Hound of the Baskervilles to show up. Why not?

Well, everything's just so hilarious around me that I figure I might as well go into comedy movies. I mean, I'm a nice, active, funny kind of guy. So I wouldn't become one of those guys who wears gray suits, black ties, and works in these 97-trillion-story buildings every day, writing papers. No way. Something a little more active, like an actor. I'm a great actor. So, um, I think that if a guy wants to do something and the thing suits him, he should just go ahead and do it.

The Nihilist,
the Hooker,
and
the Chessman

Elisha Shapiro

JUST DOING WHAT I LIKE TO DO

He's thirty-three, short, chubby, and balding. He describes himself as a "performance artist, bon vivant, and social pariah." He is also an instructor of remedial reading at Santa Monica College. A self-proclaimed nihilist, he made a bid for the U.S. presidency on the "Nihilist Ticket" in 1988. His most successful art project to date was the "Nihilist Olympics," which he organized and ran concurrently with the XXIIIrd Olympiad in Los Angeles. Between the Freeway Relay Race, the Rosie Ruiz Marathon,* and the Decathlon of Housework, he managed to produce a hilarious parody of the kitsch and excess of the summer Olympic games. "The Olympic Committee didn't have me in mind when they did their fancy planning, so I decided to do something for people on the edge like me."

The existentialists said there was no God and then went moping around because they thought they were alone. They were all filled with angst. They couldn't handle the idea of being alone in this world without any values or a father in the sky and stuff like that. And then some of them decided that they'd replace that loss by making their own value systems.

But me, I call myself a nihilist. It's part of my art to call myself a nihilist. There is no God, and I don't feel like replacing him with anything, and I like it that way. It's a joyful experience, not an angst-filled one. My basic belief, if you can call it that, is that there is nothing that's constant, whether it's a moral or ethical tenet or whether it's a physical law. Take for example the statement "the grass is green." That's not always true. Nor is the sky always blue. Maybe that's not true. We don't know. Maybe it's all a dream. I like the idea that everything that people cling to that's comforting or gives them a grounding is subject to change. People change, and nothing is constant.

---

* Ruiz ran in the 1980 Boston Marathon and was initially declared the first woman to finish, until officials discovered she didn't complete the entire race.

I think my nihilism comes from rebellion when I was a kid. I remember people—kids and other people—would always, you know, try to identify you with value systems, with sets of beliefs. They'd say, "Well, did you vote for Goldwater or did your parents vote for Goldwater? Did they vote for Kennedy? Are you Jewish or Catholic? What grade are you in?" All these different things that seemed important. I mean, kids do it more obviously than grown-ups, but grown-ups do it too. It seemed important for them to know who you are. I think the first thing I remember is feeling the way I do now, without understanding it, feeling there was something wrong. I wasn't any of these things. I didn't feel like I was a conservative or a Republican or a radical. I didn't feel like I was God-fearing or an atheist or anything particularly. I just felt like me. Not being able to answer these questions, it was hard for other kids to accept me. So I remember feeling discomfort then. I think that was the beginning of my present belief system, such as it is, even though my belief system is a rejection of belief systems.

People react when I say I don't believe in anything. It's part of my art. It's part of, you know, my performance and my life as artist to say I don't believe in anything, and people react in different ways. The reason why I'm saying I don't believe in anything as my art is to make other people feel, well, how can that be? In our society, in our mind-set, it is not an option for a person not to believe in anything. That's why people say, "Well, but that's a belief too; everyone has to have a belief; you can't exist without having a belief. How can't you have a belief? You're kidding of course." These are the reactions I get. And that's why I do this as my art. It brings up these issues. It makes people question. Here's a guy who says he doesn't believe in anything. Well, either they find a way around it semantically or they say maybe it's an option.

To me, there really isn't any significance to life, none whatsoever. No significance. And I find that's a comforting thing. You're let off the hook that way. *(Laughs.)* People feel like that's a terrible emotional deal. But there is no significance to my existing here. I'm a product of . . . if I were to try to figure out what I was a product of, the best thing I could guess would be billions of years of coincidences, dumb luck. I enjoy my existence as an animal organism—if I'm not just a figment of my own imagination. If I am in existence at all, I'm just this animal organism running by what makes it run, what coincidentally came along with the package. So all these other organisms came before me, I'm a product of them, I could be a different way, but it doesn't matter too much to me right now. I'm reacting to the way I am. I am an organism directed by emotional deals inside, emotional instructions. I react to my environment.

You know, we're here, we're these squiggly little creatures on earth, if indeed that's where we are. And we're just doing what we do. There's no moral significance to any of it, I don't think. And we do what we want to do, what we need to do, what we feel we must do. You can look back through evolution to see why we feel the way we do, but that doesn't change whether we do them or not. *(Chuckle.)* We do what we want. What we define as good is either what we want to do, what we've been told we should do but don't want to do, or what someone is trying to manipulate us into doing. Evil is the opposite.

When I think about doing something, I don't ask myself if it is good or bad or right or wrong. I just do what makes me feel comfortable. Right now most people don't find a problem with what I am doing and how I do what I do. If I were a different person, maybe doing what I feel comfortable doing would be less in their realm of ethics. Maybe next year I will be that person, I don't know; maybe I'll act in a mean, hostile sort of way.

This reminds me of another common reaction I get to my art when people hear I don't believe in anything. They say, "Well, how will we keep people from killing one another wantonly in the streets?" That's an issue of right and wrong. Of course, people won't do the right thing unless there's some heavy authority over them telling them this is the way you're supposed to act and not this way.

If there's no God, there'd better be an electric chair.

ELISHA: That's right. *(Laughs.)* That's a nice image. That's what a lot of people feel. But I don't feel like that's true. I feel like people kill and do horrible things to one another and rationalize it in terms of their belief, and people who don't believe in anything may be completely benign. That's not the issue. The issue is what people have needs to do, and then the beliefs come later. Being brought up in an uptight, heavily moralistic environment is not going to keep you from being a mass murderer, just like not having any beliefs won't make you one. That's a psychological issue, not a moral issue. That's just something I thought I'd throw in. *(Laughs.)*

Buddhism almost came close to nihilism, but it became a religion and turned into the opposite of what it began. But as I recall, Buddha said that the thing that causes people pain—and there is so much pain in the world—is their desire for things not to change. And if they can free themselves from that desire, then they may be happier people. I think that was a basic tenet. And that may be true. Of course people couldn't live with that, so they turned it into a rigid set of ethics. It may be part of human nature that living without confinement in the head is just too painful. I don't know that that's true. But for me, I'm not giving an answer to anyone. I know what I like to do, and that may change. *(Laughs.)*

Marlo Meadows

GOD LOVES THE SINNER

I've been married three times. I divorced my first husband, my second husband died, and now I'm married to my third husband. We've got three kids and they are all straight-A students. So I've put a lot of living in my short years. Now I'm the manager of a $25 million business at thirty-five with no college education. How many people can say that? With street smarts and what I learned in school, and the things that I learned along the way, I'm running a big business. How many other people can walk in and run a $25 million business? Not too many.

The Mustang Ranch, Reno, Nevada. America's first publicly owned bordello. She's the Ranch's madame.

I drive into the Ranch parking lot around 8:30 P.M. and park next to four middle-aged men who are standing beside their Winnebago camper and laughing loudly, boasting of their recent exploits. After putting my recording equipment in order, I walk to the Ranch's electrically controlled entrance gate and announce myself. When the gate swings open, I walk into the lobby. There before me stand about a dozen scantily clothed young women, each of whom is hoping to catch my eye—and therefore also my dollar. After I explain that "I'm only here to interview Marlo," they all sit down. I am then escorted to Marlo's office.

I was raised in a small rural community of about seven hundred people in Ohio. It was a little tiny farm community. My father is a skilled machinist. My mother never worked. She was a war bride. And she's still a British subject. She's never renounced the country of her birth. And I think that gave me a lot of values and loyalty about who you are and what you are, because she wouldn't do that. She remained loyal to her country. That gave me a lot of value right there.

We went to church every Sunday. We were a very religious family. My father's a deacon in the church; Evangelical United Brethren, which is very strict. No makeup, no cards, no anything like that. My grandmother was the same way. She had a very strong faith. And she influenced me a lot in different areas, like on how to treat people: You treat people like you wanted to be treated. So I was very fortunate. Not many people have the kind of childhood I had. Very loving, caring parents who taught me values . . . real values that still hold.

I was a skilled machinist at one point in time. And I've been a cook in a restaurant, I've managed a restaurant. I've done lots of things before I came to this point in time. See, my husband left me with three children and no money . . . no means of support except for my job, which wasn't enough. So I did this. I worked the floor for ten years. And this job is about money, not sex. There's a difference between love and sex, you know. When you love someone, and you're making love, there's that feeling. So I didn't do this for the sex; if I wanted to do it for the sex, I would pick my partner. But people here pick you. It's all about money. It's like you go to McDonald's every day, or you go deal twenty-one every day. People are paying for a service, and it's just like if you go to the dry cleaners and they don't clean your clothes well, you won't go back.

Not every woman is cut out for this profession. You have to like people, you have to be able to relate to them, you have to understand their needs and their feelings and their wants. If you can't, you won't be a successful working lady. You have to be compassionate, you have to be caring. I mean you see a person for twenty minutes, a half an hour, an hour . . . and they're gone. But maybe a man came in that was having difficulty with his wife, or a coworker or something, and you could add just a little bit of your own input to that, maybe help him change the situation. So it's psychology, it's caring, it's understanding. We don't judge people. When you take your clothes off, everybody's equal. No matter how much money you have, no matter where you came from, two people in the nude are equal.

Coming from that strict Christian background, was there any conflict for you?

MARLO: Well, it was a means to an end. I needed to support myself and my children. It's a job. And I have my own peace with my own God. The only person that can judge me is him. And if I'm at peace with him, then that's all there is, that's all that's necessary. I don't have to explain my actions to anybody else. I go to bed feeling good about myself, and I wake up feeling good about myself.

I have fifty girls here, and I have thirty-five next door. Those people come to me with their problems all the time. If I can help them (people dump on me a lot, you know) in any kind of way, make it easier for them, then I've helped. If I can just make somebody smile, I've helped. Because that's hard to do in today's society, with rush, rush, rush . . . money, money, money, and what people think of one another. That's really hard to do. But if you can make someone smile, you make the load just a little bit easier to bear. Then you've accomplished something during that day.

My goal is to live a long, happy life and be satisfied with myself. And to be at peace with myself, no matter what I choose to do. But we don't make it by ourselves . . . no man is an island. I ask for help every day, but the Twenty-third Psalm said, "The Lord is my shepherd. I shall not want." And whomever your God is, and no matter what walk of life you come from, everyone is just as important as yourself. Everybody has their own story to tell, whether it be good or bad. There's only one person who can judge me. I can't judge anybody else. That's not my job in life. God may hate the sin, but he loves the sinner.

Murray Turnbull

THE CHESSMAN OF HARVARD SQUARE

> While others talked about what they would do if they heard that they had to die within that very hour, Saint Charles Borromaeus said he would continue with his game of chess. For he had begun it only in honor of God, and he could wish for nothing better than to be called away in the midst of an action undertaken in the honor of God.
>
> —*William Faber*

When the weather's good, you'll find him seated in front of a concrete table-chessboard at the Au Bon Pain coffee and pastry shop on Massachusetts Avenue in Harvard Square, just across the street from the main entrance to Harvard Yard. If you plop down two bucks, you can challenge him to a game of speed chess. If you win or draw, you keep your two bucks; if you lose, he takes your two bucks. But don't expect to beat him too easily. He's ranked among the top three hundred chess players in the United States. "I'm thirty-seven years old this year, and I'm a happy guy; I like being alive. Basically I play chess during good weather, which extends more or less from the beginning of May until the end of October, anywhere from ten to fourteen hours a day. I'm averaging about fifty or sixty a day in cash. My record day I made a hundred bucks."

My parents had all these expectations for me, right? One of their expectations is that I go to college. So I met this expectation. I even got into Harvard. This was in '67 or '68. My older brother had already gotten in. My father was teaching there.* So I fulfilled their expectation; except I wasn't really studying too hard. I was passing my courses and all, but it wasn't like I was making a success out of it. It wasn't me that wanted to go to school. It was them that wanted me to go to school. As far as I was concerned, I didn't know exactly what I wanted except that I wanted out. I wanted to find answers.

Anyway the first way I looked for answers was through drugs. At first it didn't work for me. Marijuana is a fairly subtle drug, and I'd smoke a joint, I'd smoke two joints, and I couldn't really tell for sure if I was stoned. I didn't really finally actually get incontrovertably stoned until later that summer. About '68. I was a counselor at a camp on Cape Cod, and on one of my days off some friend of mine brought me down a gram of hash. So I walked down to this store at the end of the road away from the camp and bought a corncob pipe, had a little tinfoil, put it in there, poked holes into it, and went into this cranberry bog—which they have plenty of down on the Cape. And I put in some of the hash and started smoking away. I smoked half of that gram of hash and I still didn't know if I was stoned or not. Plus the wind's blowing and it keeps blowing the match out and I don't even know if I'm getting a good hit. You know, it's like I can't even tell if I'm getting smoke in my lungs. Then, all of a sudden, it seemed like the world was round instead of flat. Incontrovertible, yes—I'm stoned. I was so happy when that happened. After that initial experience I was smoking a lot of weed . . . there was a lot around in those days. It took me to a certain place, but it didn't really

---

* David Turnbull, professor emeritus of physics at Harvard. Winner of the 1987 Japan Prize in Physics.

teach me that much to begin with, although I think the weed was necessary for what happened to me later.

I dropped out of school in 1970 and, of course, I didn't tell my parents I was never going back. I went out to California. I wanted to start over because I was very unhappy with the way my life was going. For one thing, I was still a virgin. I had a very hard time relating to girls, you know. Like, I was frightened of them. I didn't know what to do with them. See, part of how this happened is probably because I grew up in upstate New York but moved here to Massachusetts right at the age of puberty. I remember just before we left upstate New York that I had finally had the experience of being with a girl. We used to go to the Roll Around Rink, go roller-skating. And of course most of the time you skate by yourself, right? But then once in a while they'll put on this thing where you've got to skate with a girl or you can't skate. So I'd finally gotten to the point where I would actually skate with a girl. Like I'm twelve and she's eleven or something. You know, you've got your sweaty hands and you're skating around together, and it was really nice. I even had started something of a love affair with a girl . . . it might have developed into a real romance. But then all of a sudden we moved to Massachusetts and I don't know anybody. I naturally just clam right up and I don't have a girlfriend all the way through high school, and by now it's becoming a habit. So I wanted to go out to California and get laid basically. Another part of my motivation for going out there was just to have free time to play chess. I knew that it was fairly easy to get along in California without money, and that was my idea when I went out there. I went out there with thirty bucks, a sleeping bag, and a duffel bag full of chess books and a chess set, and that was it.

Anyway one day I was with this guy, Juan, a friend of mine, and this other girl, a waitress, and her friend the waitress. I dropped a bit of acid Juan gave me and was just hanging out being a street person, playing chess, watching life, and then they all just got up to go off and have dinner somewhere. And I just suddenly thought, Geez, I want to go have dinner with them. Why can't I go with them and have dinner? What a pleasant bunch of people to be with. So I asked them, "Can I come along?" And for some reason it didn't seem like they wanted me. By this time the acid was really coming on. The end of it is that I lost control. It was the first time in my life that I ever lost control of my emotions. And what hit me at this time was that these people who were leaving me were friends, but not deep friends like the kids I grew up with in New York. All of a sudden I remembered these kids. I'm never going to see them again.

I'm never going to see that girl I loved; they're scattered to the four winds. And it just hit me. My God, what kind of relationships with other people do I have! Who the hell am I? My whole personality just broke down. At this point I thought, Boy, there's nobody in the world that gives a damn about me. I felt that I was pretty worthless.

So I went up to this busy street corner, waited for the light to turn green, closed my eyes, and walked across the street. You know, I made sure that there was a big line up of traffic there, right? And as I'm walking across the street, I hear all these cars braking and beep, beep, beep, all this stuff going on like everybody trying to miss me. About halfway across the street I opened my eyes just a little bit because I wanted to see myself get hit, you know, but I didn't get hit; I got across to the other side of the street.

Now, my theory on this is that one of me got hit crossing that street. Like you're talking to me and I'm here and I'm telling you about this, but in some newspaper in some other universe there was an article, "Harvard Professor's Son Killed at Dwight and Telegraph in Berkeley on Acid Trip." It's used as a scare story in some other universe to keep people off drugs. Because, goddamn it, drugs sure are risky. You're risking your personality; you're risking skepticism; you're risking nonbelief essentially.

Anyway I got across the street, and from there things began to get a little less bad. Because once I had gotten across the street, my whole idea here was that I was going to give the universe a chance to decide for me, am I worth it; and I made it across the street. The universe didn't kill me. I gave it its chance. I offered myself to the world. I remember I thought, Wow, I'm in a new world now. Maybe in this world I can just get it on with girls with no problem. Suddenly I'd been reborn. Then there's this girl coming down the street who worked at this place where you could get a cup of coffee for, like, fifteen cents. She was kind of a fat girl. She had a couple of real big knockers. She's wearing a khaki army shirt. And blue jeans. She probably thinks I'm a bum, you know. But she always impressed me as just an ordinary person. So I walk right up to her and, boom, right onto her tits. And of course she's a little shocked, I guess, and she immediately makes it clear to me that, no, we don't behave this way, not even in this universe. So I got that idea real quick. You know, I wasn't trying to rape anybody, you understand, I just didn't know the rules. I'm in a new world. I'm trying to figure it out by trial and error. How does this one work?

This was the big seminal experience of my life. That was where I decided to test reality, find out what the world is made of, how far can I push it. And if I do push it, what's it going to say back to me?

I mean, is it really dead? Is there really this division between man and God? Man and other animals?—you know, this Christian idea, this division between the spiritual and the material. Am I supposed to just exploit the world? Is it just dead matter? Am I just supposed to get as much out of it as I can before I croak? And I found, no, that's not how it is; that courage, fearlessness, caring for people, that's what the world cares about. The world isn't dead. And it doesn't matter what it seems like to other people, because I'm convinced that you're always rewarded for acting in a moral way. And I don't care if you don't get rewarded in this life or even if you never get rewarded in another life. It's worth acting morally just because it makes the world happy. I can feel it, you know.

So the way I'm serving the universe or God right now is, well, standing up for what I believe in, which is basically treating other people with compassion and respect, and playing chess, which is a very honest activity. I keep people entertained. People could spend their time in a lot worse ways besides watching me play chess or playing chess with me. They could be watching television for cripe's sake. Think of what that could do to their mind and emotions!

Earthly Delights

Dr. Richard C. Murphy

THIS LITTLE BLUE JEWEL

I was basically a beach kid, having grown up in Long Beach, California. My father was a deep-sea diver, so I grew up hearing the stories he would tell me of having traveled the world, diving in the South Pacific and really a lot of different places. Those stories gave me a feeling of adventure and mystery relating to the sea. Then, on my own, in my little world as a kid, I would go collect shells. I had an aquarium and I would bring in animals and watch them and I read books about the ocean and science. I also looked at the ocean as a source of recreation, as a source of peace, and as something that nurtured me. And the things I do today—surfing, water-skiing, diving, underwater photography, working here for the Society—they all center on the ocean.

Los Angeles, California. He holds a Ph.D. in marine biology and serves as vice president of science and education for the Jacques Cousteau Society. A handsome, well-tanned, muscular man, his face bears a striking resemblance to that of Johnny Carson.

When I was thinking about our talk over the phone this weekend, I kept thinking, *Belief*, now that's an interesting word. I didn't look up the definition for it, but to believe in something doesn't necessarily mean it's founded on facts. And thus (in my mind), I thought, well, if I'm going to talk about what I believe, in general I'd have to say that I've tried not to believe a lot *(laughs)*, because I find it's often a trap. As knowledge, as things change, I've observed that a lot of people become trapped by their beliefs, because their beliefs aren't easily changed. So I feel much more comfortable talking to you from the stance that, at the moment, based on what I know, or based on what I've experienced, it seems that this would be the most likely explanation for what's going on. But I'm not gonna believe that too strongly, because the whole ball game may change. I may learn things that show that the rules that I was just operating under are totally inappropriate.

If you look at civilization, for example, we have operated under a lot of beliefs that have been harmful to us. Take the concept of growth, the belief in growth as an economic necessity, the belief that we need to colonize new regions to increase growth. Very seldom does anybody say, "Wait a minute. Do we really want to have people living there? Do we really want to colonize another planet? Do we want to colonize that continent?" I don't think those questions were seriously considered just fifty years ago. But as I look at the geological record, we find that the planet was doing pretty well without humans. I mean, in prehuman times animals evolved, some went extinct, and the ecosystems were going along doing there own thing pretty well. Then we get to humans. Well, we, too, are another species having evolved in this grand process of the development of life on earth. But then, all of sudden, we seem to be covering the planet with ourselves. There are more and more humans affecting more and more of the surface of the planet and, in general, not increasing the vitality, the productivity, the diversity of the planet, but rather decreasing the habitability of the planet; decreasing the productivity and the diversity of regions, creating dirty air, water, and all sorts of things. And, wow, you'd think there ought to be some lessons in that for us. Maybe we need to behave differently. But our beliefs are probably a stumbling block to that.

At the moment I think most people believe we are not at all a subset of the natural biosphere-ecology, but rather that we are the number-one activity. Nature is ours to do with as we please. So I believe that as a species we are kinda like children going through the teenage years, approaching adulthood. Children say, "Me now. I want more." Their temporal perspective is incredibly short. I just remember seeing my children not being capable of looking very far ahead and not being patient enough to say, "I'll forgo something now, because it will be better if I get it at some point in the future." That's just not in their mentality. The teenage years are a time of evaluation, a time of turbulence, a period when you're not quite sure what's going on and there's this conflict, this flopping back and forth to the more infantile mentality and then looking off to the adult mentality. And adults, in general, say, "That's okay, we will forgo pleasure now and save up so we can have a great vacation next year," forgoing the immediate pleasure for the future long-term benefit.

Fortunately I think we are very definitely beginning to take a long-term perspective as we look at ourselves, as we look at our natural resources, and as we look at the ways in which we need to create a higher quality of life for humans. Part of this is just because we've been forced to see it. When we hear all of this sort of hysteria about the ozone layer, or when we hear about starfish eating up the great barrier reef, or when we hear about El Niño changing the climate of the entire planet . . . these sorts of things tend to make us uncomfortable, because we begin to see that we are really vulnerable to larger-scale processes and that we need to strike a greater rapport with our surroundings.

I remember when I was in the military that I was given a choice of reading material: either war material or religious material. *(Laughs.)* So I opted for religion. And I read a couple of books on comparative religion, and I was fascinated by that, because the teachings of the masters of a number of religions basically were the same. And I came to look at God then as a kind of glue. God made the connections, you know, the relationships between things which bind us humans together with our environment. So there are these connections, and at some of my most inspired moments with nature I have felt a very close rapport with other things, which was incredibly fulfilling . . . a wonderful experience. And as I reflected on the message of the religious masters, I thought, Oh, yeah, compassion, empathy, understanding, generosity . . . all of those kinds of feelings come from a rapport with others at the most fundamental level. And then I thought, if we could all be brought to the level of, well, we'll just say electrons or protons, then we would be feeling the same things as everything else, living or nonliving; you know, rocks, trees, bugs, birds, dirt . . . things like that. If we could consciously, mentally, be brought to that level, then maybe we could reemerge with a very strong feeling of empathy and understanding for all of those other things out there. I felt that that's the kind of experience that a lot of those pioneers in religion might have been talking about (Taoism, or Christianity, or anything else); that they had that feeling, you know, underneath their words, embedded in their words—just incredible empathy, an incredible respect for other things.

(A remembrance. His mood becomes serious.) We were on Clipperton Island a while back, which is a little speck of land out in the Pacific. It has a lagoon that is totally isolated from the ocean; on a normal basis it doesn't exchange seawater with the ocean. It's a tough, tough place. There are maybe twenty trees on the entire island and very few species living in this lagoon. And as we got down below sixty feet, the system became anaerobic (there was no oxygen). It was 98 percent saturated with hydrogen sulfide, which is a poison, and, boy, that was a little ecosystem that had polluted itself. The critters that were living there were perfectly happy, mind you. But theirs was a very low-diversity ecosystem, a very stressed ecosystem from the point of view of a nice diversity.

Clipperton Island got me thinking. I decided that I don't believe we're going to eliminate life from the face of the planet, no matter how polluted it gets. I just believe that if we make a lot of wrong decisions, we will replace high-quality life with mere survival, just as in that little micro-ecosystem, with very low diversity and incredibly stressful conditions for the organisms that live there. So then I asked myself, What are we doing to the planet now? We're reducing the diversity and we're replacing rich, abundant, high-quality, diverse ecosystems with simple ecosystems. We're not killing the planet, we're just making it a much less pleasant place to live.

You know, I've heard it said, "What does it matter if we screw up the planet? If we are just a speck of dust in this great universe, then does it matter?" And sometimes I think, Nah, it probably doesn't. Who really cares? But then I find that this oasis in space, this little blue jewel out in the endless nothingness of space, is fantastic. Whether it's a mistake or whether it's predesigned, I don't even care. It's fantastic and I'm just not willing to say it doesn't matter.

Steve Darden

NATIVE WAYS

I'd asked to meet with him several times, and each time he refused. On my fourth attempt he finally gave in. "I was going through a stack of books the other day while cleaning my house and I came across yours,* and I had a feeling you would be here soon. There is an old Navajo saying: 'As a cat washes his face, someone is coming. Be prepared.'"

The only Native American on the city council of Flagstaff, Arizona, he is widely respected for his candor, integrity, and tenacity. He's thirty-three, about five feet nine, large-boned, and extremely muscular. His long black hair is tied back in a ponytail.

We met on a Sunday morning at his trailer home on the outskirts of Flagstaff and then drove to a local coffee shop for breakfast. We are joined by his wife, Rose, his three year old son, Kyle, and his one year old daughter, Coby.

---

* *The Courage of Conviction.* New York: Ballantine, 1986

I grew up in Steamboat, Arizona, in the traditional Navajo way, living as my people had for quite a number of years: raising livestock; being part-time agronomists; practicing our traditional mores, values, and belief systems. When I was five, my mother contracted tuberculosis. I don't know how familiar you are with Native American history, but in the 1950s and '60s there was a tremendous epidemic of tuberculosis and other diseases upon the Navajo reservation. I nearly lost my mother during that period. I was placed into a BIA* boarding school and my two sisters, Lorraine and Valencia, were taken from my mother. I'm the last to have seen them. At five years old, mind you, I still have this memory, this sight of my two sisters being taken into—I used to call these vehicles stinkbugs—black De Sotos, and an elderly white couple taking my two sisters. We've never heard from them since. We don't know where they are.

As far as my profession is concerned, Lorraine and Valencia (who I've not seen in twenty-eight years) have really had an influence. As a politician I've worked hard to make sure that children are never separated from their mothers. I'm not so concerned about the father. My greater concern is for the mother, because I honestly believe that the mother, the female, is the much stronger spiritually, emotionally, and otherwise. In my work I try to rejoin families, especially children with their natural mothers. And I've worked hard on the national level with a piece of legislation called the Indian Child Welfare Act, which asserts that if an Indian child is to be removed from an Indian home, the Indian child will be placed with extended-family members; and if not that, with the same tribe; and if not that, with other Native Americans. The last resort would be the transition of Indian children into non-Indian homes . . . white homes. We've already seen historically, militarily, politically, socially, and otherwise what children being removed from Indian homes does to promote genocide, cultural genocide.

On religion, I tell people today that I should actually be a Protestant, Catholic, Episcopalian, Presbyterian minister, in that I've been baptized by every single one of those churches. *(Laughs.)* At the BIA boarding school what used to happen was that all these churches would come into the school and proselytize. We're going to have a movie, they'd say. We're going to be serving cake and pie. We're going to offer roller-skating. We're going to have hot dogs and other snacks and games, toys, and all kinds of things—anything to entice us to come to their church. In this small community of Crystal, New

---

* Bureau of Indian Affairs.

Mexico, there were four specific Christian denominations, plus the Mormons. I went through every single one of those and was baptized by every one of them. *(Laughs.)* Okay? This is a child between the age of five and seven years old. It was real interesting, because of course at the BIA boarding school we were told that we were going to become American and to be an American you must speak English. We were not to speak Navajo. We were not to sing songs that were Indian. We were not to do anything that was considered Indian. We were not really afforded the opportunity to go home and be with our families. In the two years that I was there, I saw my mother twice . . . twice. One of the reasons certainly was because she was in a sanitarium recovering from tuberculosis. But another was just a very distinct and assertive position of the BIA system that, you know, you're here to get an education and you're going to be an American.

It wasn't really until my late teens and early twenties that I began to really accept the fact that I was Navajo and that I wasn't going to let anybody take that away from me. I began to learn how to be proud. I began to assert my rights as a Native American. I became very proud of my heritage. And that's when I began to really ask questions of my elders and started to delve into the spiritual aspects of life. And it has been that way ever since.

Today I've committed myself to learning about the spiritual ways of my people. What does it mean to call this earth your mother? To call this sky your father? What does it mean to propagate life and to protect life? What does it mean to respect life? I've grown to understand that life is in everything; every substance has life. I've learned from my elders that even a dust particle has life; that a dust particle has bits of pollen, bits of minerals—just like the seed of man, but smaller than a pinpoint. You can't even see it with a naked eye. You have to have microscopes many thousand times strong to see these minerals. I think about that, and then I look at my son and think about all the thousands of vessels in just his arm alone.

My mother engendered within me a very deep commitment to respect all that has life. With respect to the land, I honestly believe that this is my mother. Physically she's pregnant every day; every day she's pregnant and every day she brings forth life. You just look out here and you'll see the ponderosa pine tree coming out of Mother Earth. That ponderosa pine tree gives pine nuts, it gives life. It gives medicine; food for our livestock, from which we get meat; and grass and shrubs, which feed the lamb, the cow, and all the other animals which we daily feed on. Every day she brings forth life. She's pregnant. She is a mother. Rose here, she's propagated children; she's borne two children; she's been pregnant with a child inside of her womb. But today and every day in my mind she's still pregnant. Every day she brings love, she brings teaching, she brings warmth, she brings the attention that we need. So she's pregnant. She's made just like Mother Earth. And at some point we also know that she looks like Mother Earth. She is made of the Mother Earth.

We know where white society puts their people when they die: They put them into the earth and hope they'll rise to heaven. But we perceive death in a somewhat different sense. It's not a passage, if you will, but really more of a return. And this is why we are not obsessed with death and why we venerate old people. An elderly person is just as beautiful as the earth. Perhaps the best way to understand that is to take a look at tourism. What does tourism entail? The preponderance of it is to natural places of geological formation; old, non-man-made structures. The Grand Canyon is a natural phenomenon, a natural wonder. And more people visit the Grand Canyon than they do the White House . . . a man-made structure. They're awed by Mother Earth. And this is why I try to teach my children to respect the earth and all old people, who are a product of the earth. This isn't easy in the context of today's society, where youthfulness, tight skin, no pinching an inch or whatever, you know, remaining youthful, looking vigorous, are so very important.

ROSE (*interjecting*): Most kids these days are afraid of older people. I don't know why, but maybe it has to do with looking old or something like that, but they're afraid. Like a lot of kids Kyle's age, I notice, are afraid of older people, are afraid of old men and old women. I'm really surprised, because he doesn't respond like that. He runs to older women. He'll call them Grandma and he'll give them a hug. He's not afraid of them. Or he'll climb up on their laps. I think this comes a lot from what Steve has done, and it is good for them to know what it is to respect the old. And I'm glad he's learning that now when he's still a baby.

STEVE: What I do is tell people to go up the mountain with me, walk with me in your mind up the mountain. As we start to go up, we're going to go over several little hills. Then perhaps we will come to where a river has been or a stream has been, where we can see the erosion of water. I tell them you're standing on your forehead. Now let's go up to the top of the peaks and look to the west, where we can see the Hopi mesas. Look down this way and you'll see ridges, where perhaps there was a mesa. Look the other way and you'll see another mountain and perhaps a wart sitting there, or perhaps a mole or something. Now lets climb back down into the eye area, where there are a lot of creases, what people call the crow's-feet. Those are like the Grand Canyon. Those are the tears that Mom and Dad have cried for us, for the things that we've done that have eroded their face. We're made in the image of the holy ones, in the image of Mother Earth and Father Sky. Look down from the top of your mother, from the top of a mountain. Tell me, is she ugly? How many people travel for hours and spend thousands of dollars to travel to a beautiful place? Come to the Grand Canyon to see this big hole in the ground? Travel to Flagstaff to see these beautiful peaks surrounded by rivers and canyons and lakes and so forth?

See, that's my feeling about Mother Earth. You respect her. You take care of her. It's like, if I take care of her, she'll take care of me. I don't own her. I don't control her. But in that respect I can have faith that she'll take care of me if I need her caring. And I always do.

You told me today you're going up to the mountain. As a traditionalist, I have to give you that right. But in a contemporary way I'd love to curse you and tell you to stay off my sacred mountain, because you have brought death to my mountain, because you have brought your type of people, your contemporaries, your peers, who go up there drinking and toking up, leaving their beer bottles, their wine bottles, tainting my pharmacy, tainting my sacred place. I can say that it is disrespectful of you to do that to my place. But from the traditional perspective, you're a child of this Mother Earth. I can't deny you access to use her as you want. I may not agree with how you're going to use her, but, see, that's respect.

Now, I don't go up to the mountain every day, only when I really have to. But what is up there is my medicine, my twelve sacred tobaccos that are used in my ceremonies. The herbs that are used for healing. I did not plant those herbs. The holy ones put those there on the sacred mountain upon our Mother Earth. It was impregnated like a man copulating with a woman. The holy one impregnated Mother Earth, and thus these herbs came to be. Those herbs have life, and life is to be respected. Those herbs are just like my son; to me they are beautiful. They have life, they can propagate life, they can generate life, they can make happiness, they can heal. My son can heal so many times with a smile. I know it. He can heal. Those times I come home, I'm tired, I've been angry perhaps, and he'll hug me and in his own precious way say, "Squeeze, I love you, Daddy." He'll come running and hug me and say squeeze, okay. Those same attributes, I believe, are existent within our herbs at our sacred mountain.

If it came to a situation where it was discerned that my liver was failing or my kidney was failing or my heart was failing, I know my mother would love me enough to give me her heart, her kidney, her lungs, her liver, whatever. Likewise I know my Mother Earth would be willing to give her heart, her hand, her liver, her blood, her coal, her uranium, her gold, her silver, her gas, and her oil to make us live. But in doing so you've got to respect her. And I don't believe my tribe has effected traditional policies of respect. I've shared this with my own uncle, who's a coal miner. I've noticed that in the last four years he has been ill. He's wealthy. God, he makes four times what I do. Materially he's got it. But physically he's so ill, he can't even enjoy it. I told my uncle one day, I said, "Uncle, do you before you even put the drill in the ground offer cornmeal to the earth which feeds it? She's giving you life and your children life, but you're not putting back the seed. I know she would feed you, but you're not feeding her."

See, the process I've been taught is this: If I were to build a cradleboard for my son, I'd go into the forest, I'd identify the tree that I want to use, and I'd go in there bearing gifts of life. I'd take my four sacred stones. I'd take my cornmeal. I'd take the prayer song given to me. I'd offer a prayer, and then I'd talk to my brother, just like I would talk with you if you were my brother and I was asking to borrow your son. I wouldn't just take him. I'd talk to you, probably specify why I need him. And you'd tell me what rules to follow to borrow your son. And I would offer corn pollen because I'm going to take a little bit of life from this tree. I'm going to take a branch to form a cradleboard, which will help my son. But I don't have the right to just take it. I have to give something. It's like an insurance premium, you know. If you want to be covered, you've got to pay a premium.

That is the way I was taught and this is the way I try to live my own life . . . I really do. I honestly believe that my peoples have taught these things to me and I know them to be true. I don't own the earth, but I can call her my mother. I don't own my mother, but I can love her, I can take care of her, and she'll provide for me whatever I need so long as I am respectful of her.

My desire is to live and never die. And the way I believe I can do that is through my children. I remember one day when I was speaking to a group of children who were delinquents, speaking to them about what I perceived to be some problems and how I felt I could help them. I remember I also told them that they would have to request it themselves and accept it. Then all of a sudden I hit the table and said, "My God, have I learned about life today. Thank you my great-great-grandfather. You are not dead, you are alive within me. It is not me who is speaking, it is you who is speaking to these children. These things that I speak to these children today are the same things that I cursed you for, that I told you to go to hell for, that I told you I hated you for. Now I have finally learned what you were saying. Look at me today, I'm speaking the same things to these kids that you taught me. They have become real and actual in my life and I can see you living with me here right now with these kids."

That day, I tell people, I learned a little bit more about spiritual things. I learned that if a man in fact has shared something with you, it will enter your being mentally, emotionally, physically, and spiritually. My grandfather physically died at 109, but he's alive today within me. So many of the things that I share with young people today about the beauty of Native American lifeways is in fact not me, but me only in the sense that I've learned them and lived some of them. But they were taught to me by my grandfather, my forebears. And they are alive and well today through me and will be alive and well for generations to come because I will teach those things as well.

When I first spoke with you, I said that the things I will share with you about spirituality are not mine. So, you know, when you go to speak it somewhere or write about it, you know, don't give the credit to Steve Darden. It's not to say that I'm finding a back door out of it. I'm just saying that the credit should go to my forebears.

Ken O'Brien

HUMAN ECOLOGY

I came to realize after studying in school that a good deal of the issues that are facing us as a species (you know, from political science to chemistry, sociology, all the things I studied) are environmental; that the major challenge we are facing as a species is to prevent the destruction of our life-support systems ... the whole planet earth, and all of the life-support systems on it.

He's a Greenpeace environmental activist, working out of Boulder, Colorado. A few years back he received his B.A. from the University of Colorado at Boulder in Human Ecology.

One of my professors showed us a film on the Pygmies of the African rain forest one day, and he explained how the Pygmies were seen as second-class citizens in Central Africa, how their gene pool was slowly being diluted to the point where, in thirty years, there would be no true Pygmies anymore. And that would be approximately the first decade of the next millennium. The same thing was said for many cultures around the world. So I got the understanding that we're not only destroying our land and resources and systems but also the peoples who had adapted to those systems. And I realized that the most sacred thing to me, the thing that gave me the religious experience, or that feeling of a tremendous power outside of myself, and a real reverence, was nature . . . being out in the quiet of nature, seeing, breathing, hearing, feeling all that was out there—that was really what I valued most in life.

I don't see furthering my own personal situation on this planet as being very significant at all relative to the existence, say, of an ecosystem. I am just one transient being in a long chain of parents and grandparents and all that. If I hadn't been lucky, I might never have been conceived, or I might have died earlier in my lifetime; and I will die, you know, in less than a hundred years . . . like the greater deal of us will. I saw my peers in school generally going after careers that would make their lives completely comfortable: be a doctor, be a lawyer, you know; do well for yourself so that you can be comfortable and happy. At the same time I saw that as being the chief motivator for people (comfort, you know), I saw a planet being destroyed. I saw the greater system that was containing all these doctors and lawyers being eaten away. And I figured, Now, what good is it going to do me to be rich if there is no nature out there to enjoy, if there is no atmosphere out there to protect me from the ozone layer or to provide me with oxygen? It frustrated me, you know, to be around all these students who didn't care, students whose values didn't go beyond their pocketbook or their genitals. But I decided that the world environmental situation is as serious a situation as any war that has ever been . . . it's something more important than your own personal life. It's something that you're fighting for for the well-being of your family and your children; your gene pool, or whatever you want to identify as the reason to be concerned for the future or for continued existence. It's amazing, because it's, like, the ultimate onslaught; it's not just the attack of a village or the attack of an individual, which doesn't really phase the world—this is the attack of the world! And after four and a half billion years of evolution and so many different species diversifying and getting their places and ecosystems, life is too beautiful to destroy, and yet we don't recognize that in general. Though we may recognize it on some level, we deny it of ourselves. We let ourselves live in a polluted world of chaos and stress and continue to destroy it ourselves, passively.

Right now this is the first generation in human history that has had to take the whole global-resource and ecosystem issue and manage it. You know, up until now we've been able to just cut and run. We've been able to destroy every ecosystem we've been in and go to other ones. And of course there have been many peoples throughout human history that have been able to sustainably live in ecosystems, but, a little more typical for modern days (especially Western man, but I wouldn't limit that to the Western world), is that we will just do whatever suits us without much care for the future. We don't plan more than five years ahead, and you have these Communist countries doing their five-year plans. It's no better in this country . . . we can't plan beyond the next election. On top of that problem, making the whole thing just magnitudes higher in urgency and difficulty, is the fact that our world population keeps doubling just about every forty years now. We're experiencing the expression of unchecked exponential growth; I mean five billion people today means ten billion people in forty years, and we don't have the trees, or even probably the air, to support that many people with all the associated industries and pollution and everything.

If I have a religion, it is nature . . . it is the reverence for the natural world. I think it is important to understand that a whale cries or feels emotions about its family. That really makes me feel a strong connection, not only to those beings but to the whole of life. And because I see that most people don't recognize this, it makes it all the more sacred to me. And it is saddening that these connections that we share are not recognized and yet are the basis for some of the most magical, beautiful, and sacred connections that exist in our lives. You can have whatever formal relationship with your God that you want, but the real stimulation of being alive with other species is seeing how they act and seeing that distant but somehow tangible relationship between their lives and your own . . . that is the most sacred and religious experience there is.

The Muse

Theresa Bernstein Meyerowitz

NOW IS ALL WE HAVE

As an artist who has always painted the humanistic side of life, I believe in human nature. I'm not one of these "ivory tower" individuals, you know, who sit up and look down on people, think they're smart. I believe that every person has something very valuable. I don't care what their walk of life might be, you can learn from everyone. Every person has something very valuable. So, to me, every person is precious, and when I painted people, I tried to get the common denominator of their feelings, you know, and express that with my ability. I say that they have a message, and I have to find that message. And I have always felt that I rise to my best, step up on the ladder of life, through my relationships with others . . . if I can help, if I can make them happy, if I can give them inspiration, I'm very happy. That's my philosophy.

Gloucester, Massachusetts. Her modest Cape Cod–style home borders nearby Gloucester Harbor and is filled with oil paintings: works of her own, as well as those by her late husband, well-known artist William Meyerowitz. When her finances dwindle, she sells one of William's paintings to sustain herself. She is one hundred years old.

I've written about the universe and the way I've felt about the universe, and I said that the feeling that I have was that there must have been a very great being, much greater than a human being, who has created this world, because of its wonders; because of its great solidity, its permanence . . . its transition from one season to the other, the regularity of growth . . . all these things are very important, and people just take them for granted. So there is a great power in this universe that is directing, or has directed, or has made possible, the outgrowth of all life, you see. Life is a transition. You're only here for a short time, you know. I once wrote a poem about this. Can I read it to you?

No man knows the whole of it,
No man knows the goal of it,
The cow and the moon,
The dish and the spoon,
The black and the white,
The wrong and the right.

You're here for a day,
We each have our say,
And then we go away,
But before we go, glimmering,
We can do some simmering.

I just gave a garden party yesterday because everyone has been so wonderful to me, and I felt that I had to respond in some way beyond the usual courtesy of handing somebody a cup of tea. I didn't feel that was adequate, so I threw a big party, and I invited everyone that was able to come, and there were over fifty people on this one place. I was able to introduce them to each other, you know, and bring some of the young people out of their little shell and bring some of the older people out of their little trenches, and the trench being that they sit and watch the television. They're slaves to other people's outgoing entertainment, and they have nothing to contribute themselves except to absorb what has been done for them by this mechanical machine, which I don't disapprove of, but I feel that it's a very great handicap to the inquiring mind. We have all the libraries full of books, with all the great minds of the world congregated.

I am a now person. A now person is a person that thinks of something to do and does it. Most people are "maybe" persons, and some people are "someday" persons . . . do you follow me? Some people are "I'll think about it" persons, you know? I'm not that kind of person. I'm an accidentally instant person. If I think of something, I'm gonna do it now. And it works for me, because, if I didn't do that, I'd be sitting in my studio and thinking about the past or I would make myself thoroughly miserable. Don't you realize that? 'Cause you always think about the things that you should have done and didn't do, and maybe you should have done this instead of that; you know, you think about these things when you're alone. And then you say, "If I hadn't done this particular thing, it would have been much better." And you're right, but you can't change your past—you can't, you know. You see, the past is something that has flowed by you like a river. It's gone, and you can't change it. Now is all we have.

Silvana Cenci

BEAUTY COLLECTOR

Sedona, Arizona. Large-nosed, brown-haired, with eyes the likes of a child, she speaks in a deep voice with accents of her native Italy. An internationally known artist, her works are contained in permanent museum collections worldwide. She is sixty-two years old.

When I was much younger, I had an understanding with a painter friend of mine. Every time she came to Florence to go to a gallery or to stay for a show, or things like that, I would just move out of my study and live with relatives or friends so she would have a place to stay. And she would do the same for me in Paris. I remember I was going to Paris for a show once, and when I arrived to her studio, she said, "Go away!" She was having a man in the studio. So I was in Paris with no money, and it was getting dark, and I decided I would just walk the streets of Paris. I walked most of the night, and then I went to Les Halles; there was this restaurant in Les Halles in Paris that was open. Now it doesn't exist anymore, but it was open all night long . . . it was a market, and usually you would go and have a *soupe à l'oignon* (onion soup). And so I decided to walk in that direction.

As I walked, the lights were very dim in the streets, and I came across a big fat short woman . . . a *clocharde*; you know, bum, a bum lady, and she was carrying a bag just as big as her. A good-luck bag. She was taking a piece of paper, and she was looking at it in the light and shaking it and discarding it or putting it in her bag. So I walked behind her for a while, and then I helped her. I found a piece of paper, and she looked at the piece of paper, and she said, no, she did not like that, it wasn't really what she wanted. And she opened the bag, and inside of her bag there was this rainbow of colors. This woman was collecting tissue papers with colors in it. Many people, especially bums in Paris, collect paper, because you can turn it in and get money. But that wasn't what she was doing. She was so beautiful. I remember she opened this bag in this little dim light, and there were all those colors, and I looked at her. I said, "Oh, how beautiful." So I helped her during the night.

It was getting about four o'clock in the morning and she said, "Do you have a bed?" And I said, no, because I told her about my friend who slammed the door in my face because she had a man. So she took me under another light and she said, "How old do you think I am?" And I looked at her; I was very young, so I had no idea how old she was, but I said, old, maybe fifty, you know. And she said she was seventy-something, I forgot. And I said, "Oh, God." You know, she really looked very young for seventy. And so she said, "I'll tell you my secret." I said, "What's your secret?" She was like a child. She said, "I never sleep with men." *(Laughs.)* She was so funny. And she took me to the Metro. And on the grille there is the heat of the subway that comes up, and there were two or three other bums, and one bum gave me a piece of his paper to put under my head, and I slept. In the morning I just got up and left.

I had a sense then that you could choose your life; you know, you can make money collecting papers, or you can get less money collecting beauty. The *clocharde* was collecting beautiful paper. She wasn't collecting just paper, she was collecting the rainbows of color, you know. So she had a choice, too, you see.

Life is made of choices; it all depends what you want to do. If I wanted to be rich, I could become rich. Everybody could. If I made more commercial art, it would be more sellable. But that's not what I want to do. What will I do with money? Buy things . . . buy a lot of things, right? Oh, it would be nice to have some, but what do you do with money? You spend it, right? Now, what do you buy? Do you buy things that you need or do you buy things that you don't need? *(Laughs.)* And I thought, if I have a choice, like that *clocharde*, I'd rather collect beauty. She was making maybe one-third what other *clochardes* make. I loved that, you know. What a philosophy of life. She didn't care; she could have had more money, but would that change her life? You know, we live in a society where money's so damn important. That is a pity, because people really forget there are lots of beautiful things. When you walk in a forest, you don't have to own that forest . . . it's yours because you are walking into it. Don't you ever feel that way? That you don't need to own it? . . .

You know, the sense of life, I don't know this. I don't know why we are here, what makes the world turn, nobody does. I don't know what I do, but I love a free spirit, and I'll never do anything for something I don't believe in. Because I know that life is so sacred. You are here now, and not there tomorrow. So you have to make the very best of every day. Maybe I'm an existentialist . . . that's what I am . . . I am a free spirit. That's what I'm trying to say, really. And I know that my purpose is to live every moment fully. I don't know what other people's purposes are, but I know about mine.

Before you came, I was sitting and watching the sunset. It was dramatic. And sometimes we take things for granted. I used to. I think you live fully when you don't take anything for granted. I really do. But if you start thinking for a moment, and just stop taking things for granted, then you really are alive, you use all your senses. I don't take anything for granted . . . well, I try not to. Maybe I take coffee for granted. I love coffee, and I never saw a coffee tree with coffee beans attached to it. Have you? So, you see, we are taking that for granted. Really. And I love it. I think I should take a trip, go and look how the coffee grows. Yeah, it would be nice, eh?

Doug Anderson

WHAT'S HAPPENING?

He and his wife, Mabel, share a small, book-filled home in Denver. Mabel teaches high school while he writes poetry, free-lances articles for local newspapers, and runs the Bread and Butter Press, a small publishing company he founded to produce the works of local writers. He's forty-four.

It was either Mencken or Groucho Marx who said at one point, "I would not join any group that would have me as a member." And I've always felt uneasy around organized social expectations in group form. It may well be just a knee-jerk reaction that goes back to my teen years, or whatever. In more extreme structured situations, whether it's a social group or a religious group or whatever, I often feel people sucking more off the social expectations than going for the real source of what the group is supposed to be about. So, most often I've taken my doses of spirituality on my own, solo.

I could give you a long list of the things I do and don't believe in, but I'd hate to bore you with platitudes. And when it comes right down to it, I live by a very simple philosophy. It goes like this: When I'm capable of this *(he opens his arms)* instead of this *(he wraps his arms around his chest)*, I'm more likely to allow other people to look at the same possibility in themselves. So generally I would say I think it's better if we can embrace each other instead of shut each other out, if we can talk to each other instead of refusing to talk to each other, if we can admit things to each other instead of trying to prove things to each other.

Most of the poetry I write is meant for public expression, out front, to address audiences in public places. Over the years I've dealt as a workshop conductor or guest poet, with people in mental institutions, in prisons, with minority populations, including American Indians, with school kids in a wide range of environments, from hardcore city areas to little places out in the desert, to suburban settings, all ages. I've dealt with seniors in senior centers. And a lot of what I'm writing is in conformity with those situations. You walk in, you're faced with, in one case, twenty American Indians in a lockup, who are all sitting there like this *(closed-arm gesture)*, looking at you saying absolutely nothing. And it was on me in that situation—not on them—to find something to talk about. Took me more than two hours the first session *(laughs)* I was with them before I finally found something in me that I could talk about to which they could relate. Well, we continued relating with each other over the period of the next year and a half to the point where I could publish a book of writing and artwork that they had voluntarily produced. Not for me, but because they cared to produce it, you see.

Well, that possibility of people being able to talk to each other, to find we're a great deal more common than we are different, is always there. It depends on our willingness to overcome whatever it is in ourselves that we see separating us from other people. And those are intensely practical, daily, simple things, for the most part.

(A pause. A remembrance.) I went to India in my early teens and I worked for almost four months on the sea, you know. All the way from the Mexican coast to the southeast coast of India. I'd be out on the prow every evening at sunset. The light show was literally 360 degrees all around you and 180 degrees over you. Just all the way around, for an hour and a half. And after sunset there's that wonderful time for which I have no better word than the old Latin *crepusculum*. It's an invisible third state between twilight and dusk. It's that ring that's always around the earth where light and darkness join. It's always there, the earth's always turning through it, and during that time of day, depending on where you are on the earth, you go right through it. You move through something that isn't daytime and isn't nighttime. And it's there and you can watch the light just oozing out of your body. I'd be out on the prow of the ship for an hour and a half or two, like Thoreau out on Walden, just imbued with the sense of the unity and beauty of it all. And, yes, coming to experience that sense of unity is what has occurred practically over the years, to the point that in one of my poems I've said quite clearly to the Divine Beloved, "I don't need to believe in you. It's not a matter of belief anymore. I just know it." And since those early years on the water, whenever I'm able to recall or re-create those experiences, I feel an ancient Eastern smile of serenity just flooding my whole body. I'm no longer in a state of judgment toward myself or to the world. I'm just standin' on the planet, with my hands in my pockets, ears open, lookin' around, and saying, if anything, "What's happening?" That experience is more useful to me than any great philosophical emblem I've ever read or tried to write. And it's there for everybody.

Nancy Mairs

February 1986. Tuscon, Arizona. Her thin, ailing body testifies to the fact that she has a well-advanced case of multiple sclerosis, but she is nevertheless a strikingly beautiful woman. A few weeks before her first book, Plaintext, *was critically acclaimed nationwide.* "The book has some very 'down' things in it. Like it talks about my having MS; it talks about the time I spent at a mental hospital and the fact that I'm depressive; and it talks about the fact that my first sexual experience was a rape. All those things are sorts of downers, but I don't think they're punishments, it's just that they are. I don't feel singled out. What makes the difference is what we choose to do in response to whatever happens to us."*

She has written articles for The New York Times *and a host of national publications.*

I still have diaries from my teens. I was a real scribbler, and I wrote for long periods every single night. So I have a sort of record of my regular religious practice backed up by a lot of quite fervent adolescent religious beliefs. Some of them were spiritual, but many of them more pragmatic, strongly flavored with Puritanism. We went to a Congregational church in Wenham, Massachusetts, but the Congregational church is a direct descendant of the Puritan church; it's as pure a descendant as we have. And I was pretty active in the Church, went every Sunday and all that.

I loved God a great deal then, but I also feared God a great deal, and felt watched all the time. Sometimes that was "watched over," but more I think it was "watched" than "watched over" (if you get that distinction). And a lot of the things that I was doing back then I believed unacceptable to God and my fellows. So the relationship was kind of fraught with distress, guilt. Things like the fact that I had a high school boyfriend with whom I was very intimate but did not ever have sexual intercourse. And part of the reason I didn't was that I believed that it was a sin, you know, that it would offend God and my mother, who were somewhat indistinguishable. *(Laughs.)* I suppose since my father died when I was four and a half (he died from a car crash in Guam while in the navy), that that's what I was left with, you see. I had God, who was definitely real and definitely male, and I had my mother. Those were the two principals that were guiding me.

---

* New York: Harper & Row, 1986.

But it wasn't all guilt and fear, because I can still remember a real element of celebration. I spent quite a lot of time by myself. Not, probably, as much as I would have wanted to, because my mother was real uneasy about solo activities, but I would spend a lot of time tramping around the woods of Wenham. I remember particularly early days in springtime when things finally began to fall, and I would put on great knee-high rubber boots and go tromping through swamp areas, getting chilled and soaked (I'm a vegetation freak), and that was a spiritually rewarding experience. I may even have been consciously aware of the presence of God in something like that . . . would sometimes feel transported. I can remember coming home, as a matter of fact, one night in the winter, lots of snow on the ground, full moon, and instead of walking into my house, I walked out around the house into the backyard, which looked out over the fields, and just stood there in the snow with that moon. I mean, I can remember that image and just feeling as though I wanted to burst; I was just going to go everywhere. And I was wishing I would, you know, wishing for a kind of annihilation into all of that beauty. But then I turned around and slogged back to the front door, went in and took off my coat and my boots, and rejoined the family. *(Laughs.)*

With all those years as a good practicing Congregationalist, I wound up with some rather odd fruit. To begin with, when I married my husband, George, he was a confirmed Episcopalian. He had been raised an Episcopalian, and I wanted to try that. So when I was about twenty (I guess I waited till I was maybe twenty-one), we went to church together. But I experienced a lot of conflict about going to church, because that sense of duty, which had sort of carried me comfortably through high school, was bothering me, prickling me, wasn't comfortable anymore; that sense of having to get dressed up every Sunday morning and go to church.

Then we moved out here to Tucson, and we never really found an Episcopal church we felt comfortable in. They have a very beautiful one up in the foothills called Saint Philip's in the Hills. But very lavish, you know . . . they take up the collection in Papago baskets. I don't know if you know Papago baskets, but that's a piece of Papago work up on the mantel there. *(She points to the mantel above her fireplace.)* They're exceedingly expensive. And, you know, the chandeliers are silver, and that bothered us; all that material consumption in the Church. Then we went out to Saint Michael and All Angels, which is out on East Fifth, and the priest there made us kind of uncomfortable. The parish was kind of nice, but he would do things like get up and tell everybody that they had to go to a Right to Life rally that afternoon, and stuff like that. And I'm a feminist, you know. (*Laughs.*)

So we never got comfortable anyplace in Tucson until George got a job at a Catholic high school here. And they had another opening a couple of years later, and I applied for it, so we wound up teaching at the same school. And we were surrounded by all these really neat religious people. You know, in the summer they'd go off with the farm workers, and when the farm workers got arrested, they got arrested and went to jail with them. So lots of them who were teaching in the winter were spending their summers in jail—very vocal, active women. I just admired them a lot, 'cause they were acting out their beliefs; I mean, they were believing things and then acting on them. So we decided we'd like to be part of that kind of community, and in the fall of '77 we converted to Catholicism. So now I'm a Roman Catholic, having started life out as a Congregationalist. And I'm not sure one can travel much farther and still remain within the Western Judeo-Christian tradition. (*Laughs.*)

It's terribly, terribly hard for a feminist to be a Catholic. I don't want to minimize that at all, but it's one of the cruxes of my existence. But at least the female is present in the Church, in the form of the Virgin, in a way that there's no female present in the reformed denominations, at least any that I've come across. I mean, I guess Mary got mentioned at Christmastime, 'cause she would have to 'cause there was Mary and Joseph and the babe lying in the manger, but she was never alive as a principal in the Church at all. It was a wholly, wholly patriarchal structure. But Mary is in the Catholic church, and there are female saints as well, so I think I was attracted by that. I still get furious, though. We have one priest who says the Eucharistic Prayer, and he calls her "Mary, the Virgin Mother of Jesus," instead of the "Virgin Mother of God," which is the way it is written. And that still makes me very angry; I think he's demeaning her even further than she (*laughing*) tends to be demeaned.

It's funny, but here I am, this practicing Catholic. I do go to Mass every week, but I go on Saturday evenings instead of Sunday mornings, because that way I know I'm not just still doing my duty. I'm much more comfortable going on Saturdays, and that's the only explanation I can think of, that Sunday still harks back to childhood and being dressed up and taken to church, whereas if I go on Saturday at five-fifteen, absolutely nobody can be ranking me (*chuckling*)—I must be going voluntarily. So I really go to church regularly, and I profess my faith every time I'm there, you know. And so I say I believe in God . . . so what about God?

God is a very difficult point. I do a lot of deconstructing, particularly during church, but in most of my life. Because God was Big Daddy for so long. And I think God still is for most people, only I can't have that anymore . . . it just doesn't work. But when it's been Big Daddy for so long, it's almost a reflexive quality, so that if you don't watch yourself, you keep bouncing back, recoiling back to that primitive sense of, you know, some large male figure watching what one is doing. So, as I say, I have to keep deconstructing that all the time, as consciously as possible.

I don't think, for one thing, that God has gender. But I also know that human beings cannot construe a world without gender. We can't do it psychologically, and I don't even know whether we can do it at the semantic level. The distinction into gender is so deep and so ancient that we simply can't have any world that we would recognize as a world that isn't fundamentally divided into male and female. Which means that, in a lot of ways, I cannot construe God at all as I believe such a being might be. I can only create God, I can only ascribe human characteristics to it. Like calling it "he" or "she," and *she* isn't any more accurate than *he*. So there's no language, and there's no experience underlying the language, that gives me any way to express anything except he or she. And it can't really quite be "it." Because "it," too, is part of the gender system. "It" is the neuter. There's no all-encompassing word which just doesn't take gender into account. But that is who God is—genderless. *(Laughs.)* So I'm real heterodox; I mean, if the Catholic church knew what I believed, they probably wouldn't want me around anymore . . . particularly the traditional Catholic church. I think the sort of pinko Catholics that I actually hang around with probably wouldn't be quite so upset. *(Laughs.)*

You know, George used to have a friend who, if you ever asked him how he was, he'd say, "Perfect." And if you ever asked him, you know, how was your day, he'd say, "Perfect," and everything was always perfect. Very, sort of, determinedly optimistic. But I don't know, if one takes that attitude toward the universe, what one does with all the bad things. Like, George is teaching a young woman right now who is dying of metastasized uterine cancer. He's having a lot of trouble with that; he's arguing a lot with God at this point about that. My response to something like that is that I don't understand, but I can't arrive at any judgments about it, because it's all a pattern. It's much too vast for me to conceive.

Somebody asked me once, another person with MS, "Do you ever say, 'Why me, Lord?'" And I realized that I don't, 'cause there's no answer to that question, you know, except "Why not?" I mean, I don't know what this is for, but I think it's probably for something.

I don't mean in a predetermined way, that I was destined to be the one with MS. It was simply that, now that I have MS, that shapes my being and I go on being in the universe. So it's that entire process, carried out on a cosmic scale, that for me is God. But if you asked me, you know, do I pray to a personal God, it would be hard to say yes and hard to say no. Because what I've told you just now can't possibly be personal because it's everything, but I also do pray to a personal God. I suppose it's that throwback to Big Daddy, only I try now not to pray to Big Daddy, but I pray a lot to some presence. And I pray even more that I'm serving that presence as I should.

So often I have a sense that I'm not doing as much as I should. In part that comes from the fact that George does a great deal. His teaching is done entirely with some marginal populations. He teaches general education classes in the morning, high school equivalency classes, preparing people to take the high school equivalency exams ... mostly Hispanic. And then in the afternoon and evenings he teaches at the Amphitheater Evening High School, which is an alternative school for kids who aren't making it, for one reason and another, in the regular day program. And, in addition, he does a lot of work down at Casa Maria, which is a Catholic Worker house here. The soup kitchen feeds between four and five hundred people a day. George actually goes down and stirs soup and makes sandwiches and carries them out and hands them to people. And I don't do that. In part, obviously, because I can't physically, now that I am as crippled as I am. There are a lot of physical actions I can't perform. Fatigue is a great problem with MS. Symptoms may vary drastically, but everybody complains about being exhausted. So I don't have the stamina to do things. And so I often wonder whether, in fact, I am acting on my beliefs, or acting acceptably, or whether the things I've just told you are a kind of a cop-out, you know.

But I have to remind myself that there are all kinds of vocations, and perhaps something like writing and teaching is a vocation. You know, maybe I can touch a lot of people through my writing and teaching. I don't have to teach about God or spirituality or any of those things directly. But if I go into the classroom each day and treat my students in certain ways, through that I'm demonstrating to them what I believe is the right way for a human being to live. And marriage itself is a vocation. (Laughs.) George and I have been married now for twenty-three years, and certainly at the beginning we didn't have any sense of it as a vocation. (Laughs.) But it's an avenue for spiritual growth. One of many, but a valid one. But I still think I ought to be on picket lines down at the Federal Building. Oughtn't I to be going to the Sanctuary trial, oughtn't I be, you know, more vocal than I am? And I'm not sure. I can't entirely sort that out.

I am sure that I'm a pacifist and a feminist. I'm a very committed feminist, and I think it's important to keep articulating those principles. And I try to do that in my writing. The kind of feminist I am is called a radical feminist. It's different from a liberal feminist or a Marxist-Socialist feminist, if you want to chop us up into categories. The basic distinction of a radical feminist is the belief that all human intercourse of domination and subordination is unacceptable, has to be revised radically. That is, a liberal feminist would say, "If we just change some of the laws and have equal pay for equal work or equal pay for comparable work or something like that, that will solve the problems." The radical feminist says, "No, that doesn't solve the problems." And it doesn't, because I've seen those things come about, and what happens is women achieve equality by turning themselves into men. And the male values are killing us . . . they are killing us culturally. And they are gonna kill us literally. I mean, if we really do send troops into Central America, if we keep thinking in those terms, those "us" and "them" terms, you know, I'm the dominant and superior one, and you have to do as I say . . . if we construe all human interaction in terms of what one Jesuit writer calls male ceremonial combat, it is gonna kill us. And we've got to stop it. So that is how I see the feminism and pacifism connecting; if we can revise the culture so that it doesn't set up dichotomies, conflicts, then we might have peace. Then we would, I think, have peace. But nothing less is gonna do, nothing—just nothing less is gonna do.

The prayer I make after communion, it's kind of a ritualistic one for me, it ends, "and let me live my life in your praise." And I really hope that's what I want most to do with my life, to make it a praise of God, to make it a celebration. If I can do that, in whatever I do, then I'll feel as if I am doing real work, God's work. You know, if people look at me and don't feel sorry for me because I have MS, because I'm not pitiful, then I've transcended the limitations of being a human being.

Maria Cheng

I was born in Hankow, China, which is located about six hundred miles upstream from the mouth of the Yangtze River. Hankow and Wuhan are twin cities in China. I think my whole life is about what goes around, comes around, so here I am in the Twin Cities of the United States. When the Communists took over China in 1949, my family moved to Hong Kong. So I grew up in Hong Kong between the ages of two and ten. Then my family emigrated to the United States in the late fifties.

Minneapolis, Minnesota. She is the founder and director of the Humana Dance Theatre and an instructor of dance theory at the University of Minnesota. She's forty years old.

The most important figure in my childhood is my grandfather, who taught me about the universe and the stars and who first exposed me to the French language. He was a philosopher, a very spiritual man. He was a Confucianist, an atheist. I first learned about the concept of a metaphor from my grandfather. I remember he would take me to school every day and at dismissal time he would pick me up. We took the bus to school every day, and the bus we took from our home to my school was the Number 11 bus. I remember one evening when we were walking, he said to me, "This vehicle that is taking you to a system of knowledge, which is Number 11, is like your two legs. And just as this vehicle is transporting you to a world of knowledge, so your legs will take you to new lands." And he meant it, because he had a passion for walking, for strolling, for hiking. Years later my work depends on my legs, as I am now a dancer, a choreographer.

The missionaries got to my father's side of the family three generations back, so I'm a born Catholic. But my mother is the real Catholic, the fervent, zealous Catholic in the family, because she's a convert. The missionaries got to her when she was thirteen, so she converted to Catholicism pretty young. We went to church every Sunday, and I'm still in love with the pageantry of the Catholic church from an aesthetic sense in terms of the liturgy and the music and the magic. Our Catholic church choirmaster was from Parma, Italy. I don't know if you know this, but Parma is a major opera center. Some of the greatest singers have come from Parma. The citizens of Parma are reputed to know every single note of every Italian opera, and supposedly opera singers have a great fear of performing in

Parma because the citizens are so well versed. And our choirmaster, Father Cara, was from Parma. He was a great big, fat, three-hundred-pound priest who conducted a magnificent church choir. I loved going to church on Sundays and listening to the choir, and in those days of course it was also Gregorian chant. I particularly remember when the male voices sang Gregorian chant a cappella—it was a very moving experience.

But my family was not spiritual at all. My family background is that of the nouveau riche of China. My father was a scientist, my three brothers are scientists, and my mother is the classic good Chinese housewife. So my home life was devoid of any spirituality that I know of. My aunts were very devout Catholics, and so they

succeeded in making the entire family kneel down every evening (*chuckles*) to say the rosary, which, when my father led it, we could say it in about eleven minutes flat. So it was not true praying at all.

I have very vivid memories of the Pacific crossing. We came across on a freighter when I was ten. I remember the power of the ocean and the sea gulls. And four years later, when I first read Samuel Taylor Coleridge's *The Rime of the Ancient Mariner*, I was deeply moved by the poem that went "alone, alone, all, all alone, alone on a wide, wide sea, and never a saint took pity, on my soul in agony." I remember reading those lines and immediately completely understanding, as much as a fourteen-year-old can, about being alone, about alienation. It was an immediate connection with my transpacific crossing. And I remember the image of the albatross in that poem; you know, the guilt of the Ancient Mariner. I think I can correctly say I'm relieved of any Western or Judeo-Christian sense of guilt because of my background. I've never understood guilt, except in an aesthetic, intellectual way. So the concept of the albatross in that poem never struck me; I mean, I've never understood or had a sense of guilt. Responsibility means something to me, but not guilt. So I think I'm more of a Confucianist. I'm only beginning to understand these things, but certain Zen stories I'm coming to appreciate a bit better now. I think, for example, of the story of the old man going through a spiritual journey carrying this heavy burden on his back and then, on his deathbed, passing on this burden to his apprentice. And the apprentice, upon opening the bag, realizes that it's empty. Yet he wonders why did it weigh so much. And the old man says to the apprentice, "It is the weight of everything in my life that I did not need to carry. I am now passing this on to you." So I remember thinking about this story when I was first exposed to the concept of the albatross. So it was not guilt for me as much as a kind of unnecessary weight—the paradox being that one has to carry it in order to release it, if you get my drift (*laughs*).

When I think about it now, whatever spirituality I have I've gotten from art and literature and music. I remember first reading the lines of Wordsworth's *Intimations of Immortality* and some of his shorter poems. And literature, in terms of romantic poetry specifically, and Henry James's novels. And music: Chopin, Beethoven, all of Beethoven's symphonies, his piano sonatas. So I think it was through art that I had an experience of transcendence, of a kind of connecting with a oneness . . . with an experience of, an epiphany if you will, of beauty and goodness and wholeness. Certainly I felt something of this when I read James Joyce's *Portrait of the Artist as a Young Man*, when Stephen Dedalus had that wonderful epiphany with a young girl swishing her legs in the stream. So I think it's really through the experience of art, literature, and music that I started on the road toward any spirituality . . . what spirituality I have now.

What do you mean by spirituality?

MARIA: Oh, my God *(laughs)*, I knew you were going to ask that question. I don't know, I don't know, like art and love and life—it's one of those things that I know when I'm in it or of it or when it is with me. I don't have the words to define it. I mean, I can use words that I know you know, that I've read, and they're other people's words. You know, one can talk about a sense of transcendence that unites one in a deep love and compassion, and those are words that I've come across, that I can put together in an explanatory sentence, but that doesn't feel real to me. And when I go after it, it is never there. I think it was Spinoza who said, "Happiness is not the reward of virtue, it is virtue itself." See, when I was younger, and less wise, I used to seek love and spirituality. It'd never happen when I'd go for it, because it is absolutely a by-product of something else. And I think it's a by-product of when I am my truest self. Then love happens, whether I'm loving or love comes my way, or whether I'm blessed with a spiritual understanding or a sharing with another person.

In terms of any religiosity I've felt in this country, I've always been puzzled by the social aspect of it (I was married to a very active Presbyterian) and by the lack of spirituality. I can't document for you why, but I've always felt that. If somebody had asked me from the time I came to this country, "Do you think there's a great deal of spirituality in the churches of America?" I would have said no! And I wouldn't have been able to defend it, and perhaps to some extent I still can't. I don't know why I've been so fortunate . . . maybe it's my grandfather. I've never, ever looked to organized religion for the ultimate road or path of spirituality or wholeness or integrity. And maybe it's because of my bicultural background. The issues I'm more concerned with don't have any relevance to the Judeo-Christian background that's the basis of organized religion in this country. They have more to do with global, human-nature issues of prejudice, of fear, of what happens to a human being when he/she is spiritually vapid, or when that person lacks political access, or when that person is economically deprived, and those are universal issues. So I don't really connect it with organized religion at all.

This sounds so New Age, you know *(laughing)*, that we are all united in the human condition, that we will continue, and that for each one of us the journey is to ask those universal, unanswerable questions of who are we, why are we here, what is the purpose of life, what is love, how do I go about doing things, what is right, what is wrong, what is real, what is truth—all those questions which we must each one, each country, each nation-state, each community, each civilization, answer for itself in its own way with its own specifics. I don't have the answers. I think it's the question. It's how you ask the questions, it's how you ask the questions! When I feel most profoundly moved, or when I've had a cathartic experience, it's an enlightening of the further complexity of life. Those have been the moments of true enlightenment, if you will. A sense of wonder and awe, and the deeper understanding is not that you've found another answer—the deeper understanding is a deeper sense of wonder and awe at the complexity and that the basis of the complexity is a unifying simplicity. And I don't know what it is. It's just a sense one can get through artistic experiences where a work of art enhances one's life in terms of a sense of an experience, a reality, of beauty. And when it causes the observer, the witness, if you will, to give new testimony to his or her life, it can be powerful and moving. And that's what I try to do in my work.

Ralph Shapey

A MOMENT OF ETERNITY

I started the study of violin when I was seven and a half and gave a recital at age nine. I was a child-prodigy violinist. As a student my teachers always demanded more. My parents had that attitude too. When I became youth conductor of the Youth Orchestra in Philadelphia at age sixteen and told my parents about it, they said, "That's nice, it's only the beginning." When I won the Philadelphia Finds contest to conduct the Philadelphia Symphony Orchestra at age twenty-one: "That's nice, it's only the beginning."

New York Times *critic John Rockwell sees him as "a man likely to be regarded in the future as one of the great American composers." In 1982 he was awarded a MacArthur Fellowship for "exceptional talent, originality, self-direction, and promise for the future." He lives in Chi-*

cago, where he serves as professor of music and music director of the
Contemporary Chamber Players of the University of Chicago. In 1989
he was elected to the American Academy and Institute of Arts and Letters.

I was born in Philadelphia, in 1921, and two weeks later I came
down with double pneumonia. The doctors gave me up. They told
my parents, "Have another child as soon as possible. We cannot do
anything for him. He is simply not going to live." My father seemed
to have had one inch more brains than the doctors themselves. I
offer my apologies to the doctors. It seems (understand that this is
part of the family myth, so to speak) that my father reasoned, "What
is killing this infant? If there was some way to get the mucus out of
his lungs, maybe he would live." So he held me up by the ankles
and beat the hell out of me. What happened is I yelled, I cried, I
screamed, and as I did all that, I coughed and my lungs cleared. I'm
here to tell the story.

So I have always lived with death beside me. It was life on one
side, death on the other. I had cheated death. I am supposed to be
dead; I'm not supposed to be here, you know. I never expected to
live to twenty; I never expected to live to thirty. When I got to thirty,
I thought, Well, maybe I'll make it to fifty. But here I am sixty-eight
plus. It has always been a very big surprise to me that, yes, I'm alive.
And I have always felt that I had to battle twice as hard, because I
had to battle not only life—and life is, unfortunately, a battle—but
I had to battle death as well. Somehow I guess that this is one of
the most powerful forces that shaped me. No pun intended.

I am deeply interested in what I call the marriage between my
conscious and unconscious mind. The first time this happened so
very dramatically was when I was working on my second string quartet—that puts it around, I guess, 1948 or '49. I recall I was sitting
and writing—actually in an attic, believe it or not. The intensity of
concentration became so strong that I remember that the paper in
front of me on the table became white, pure, blazing white. I seemed
to be surrounded by pure, blazing white. I didn't know what I was
doing; my hand kept moving, but I couldn't see it because I was
blinded by this white light. All I recall is that I sat there, practically
the whole night through, till I finally put the pencil down. The quartet
was finished. I remember dropping into my bed in a complete state
of exhaustion, and I slept, I believe, for twenty-four hours.

When I finally got up, I seemed to recall—yeah, I did—what
had happened. I walked over to my table, and there it was. And I
began to read it, and I didn't remember it; I didn't remember writing
it. But it was my handwriting, and there's my pencil, so I must have

done it. But I don't remember it, at least not consciously. But it was good. Yes, this was good. And of course I then accepted it as my own. I have told my students over and over again that one has to learn—and this is a lifetime job—to accept one's unconscious mind, that when there is a marriage between the conscious and the unconscious, you will reach the highest levels of creativity, and that it is as though you are not there, it is as though someone else, something else, name it what you wish, is doing it, not you. You don't even exist at that particular moment. In retrospect all you remember is how wonderful, how positively magnificent it felt.

I've had that experience. I've had the experience of body, or soul, or whatever you want to call it. I don't know—out-of-body. I've had out-of-body experiences. Once, while writing, I suddenly was standing by myself. There I was, looking and watching what I'm doing. It was kind of a weird experience. But I've learned to accept these things. And throughout my life this has happened, these types of experiences, time and time again. I know that when I'm composing, I am in a different state of being. There is no question. I hurry to add I have never, ever, ever taken any dope, including marijuana.

As far as religion is concerned, I feel that most of it is a bunch of wonderful, beautiful fairy stories, which offer some magnificent moralistic and ethical ways of being. But throughout my life I've created my own "commandments." As an example, there is the story of Cain and Abel, in which the question is raised "Am I my brother's keeper?" I have turned that around into an affirmation. I say, "I am my brother's keeper." When all human beings will make that an affirmation, then maybe, just maybe, they will put an end to the horrors of this world.

I don't believe in a personal God, but I do believe in a creative force. That force for which our scientists and our researchers are constantly searching. Yes, the creative force, I do believe in that. There is no question in my mind that this creative force, which has created everything, will continue on in its own particular way. There's nothing that can stop it, and there's nothing that we can do about it.

I'm fond of saying that man does not live on bread alone. That is only one of the basic staples of life. Life contains other things. Other things that teach us. Other things that make us grow. These are the things of life that go beyond life. To share a moment of eternity, that great works live, or force us to live, in a moment of eternity. It doesn't matter whether it's music, painting, sculpture . . . every time I see Michelangelo statues I go out of my mind. What a fantastic, incredible genius he had been. Or that marvelous ceiling—all the pope wanted was a ceiling to be painted, but Michelangelo gave him a masterpiece. No, it's even more than a masterpiece, it's a miracle. Great art is a miracle, above and beyond ourselves. And when we allow ourselves, our minds, to absorb and partake of these great things, that's when we move into what I call eternity. When time, clock time, stands still; when a work of music is played and it took an hour's length of time but seemed to take but minutes, we have lived in a moment of eternity. And it's true with a painting, and true with sculpture, and true with literature. These are the things of life, true life. These are the things that make me say, "*L'chaim*—to life, to life."

Akbar De Priest

JAZZ MAN

We are alone drinking wine and beer in the basement of the Off Larimer Café, a jazz bar in downtown Denver where he occasionally performs. He's a traveling fifty-year-old jazz drummer who looks a decade younger. "Well, it's because of the music. Music has been good to me."

I was brought up on the east side of Los Angeles, about three or four blocks from Central Avenue, which was the main avenue for blacks in Los Angeles at that time. So I'd see street prophets on Central Avenue put up their tents. And because I was always in the streets, some of the older hustlers and players and pimps would tell me, "Hey, this guy, man, he's just rippin' people off." Then they would show me people who were acting like they were lame, being healed and all this stuff in the name of God. So I was real young, man, eight or nine, and I was seeing this, see. It really started me being skeptical at a very early age. Then the minister at my mother's church, at this Methodist church where I went, started boozing illegally. This was World War II time. You couldn't get booze then, and there was this guy in our neighborhood who had half-a-pints of booze that he'd stolen out of some freight train or somethin'. This minister heard about it, and me and some of the other kids realized that he was buyin' from this guy. I said, "Well, these guys, you know, they sit up there talkin' all that stuff. . . ."

I guess from being brought up that way, you're always sayin', "Well, if this isn't right, there's got to be one of them that's right." I figured I just had to find out which religion would appeal to me.

I turned to Islam at about the age of sixteen or so, you know, black Islam, Elijah Muhammad. In my neighborhood there was always gonna be somebody comin' and talkin' to you about Elijah almost every day. It was Islam for black Americans, real elementary stuff. See, Elijah Muhammad came to America to preach morality to blacks, tellin' us to stop drinking, stop smoking. It was good in those ways because it really straightened people up about some of their habits and morals, but it was a hate thing insofar as that all these alcohols and evils were something that the white man made available to you to keep your mind from really functioning. I went in for this, and it was good for me, because it kept me off the streets, but I finally got tired of it because of its hate thing, the hate thing that was goin' into it, 'cause I was trying to find some way to avoid that hate. When I started finding out about all the other Muslim factions, I became even more disenchanted. Pretty soon they were having wars with each other right here in the United States. One group out in Washington, D.C., one in Chicago; you know, they could not agree to disagree. And then you look over in Iran and Iraq and you look at everybody sayin', "Well, Muhammad came from here." And they say no. The Persians swear that that's where he's from. So it became more and more confusing as I studied it, to the point that I really realized it wasn't my religion, that I was American, and that I had better find whatever it was I was tryin' to find right here in my own backyard.

But I got sidetracked by Buddhism. I was living in L.A. in 1970 when Herbie Hancock* and his group, the Headhunters, and all the guys in the band turned to Japanese Buddhism. These guys brought me into the fold, you know. When I went into one of those Buddhist meetings, it was like the United Nations; there was someone from everywhere out there on Wilshire Boulevard. And that appealed to me, because I feel that there has to be something that appeals to everybody. As long as we keep goin' off into our own little sections, there will always be this sort of battle about who is the best. The Baptists are the best but the Methodists are better, that sort of thing. Anyway I chanted for three or four years out in California. Oh, I

---

* Jazz musician.

chanted a long time. Coming out of a divorce and all that stuff when I started, chanting seemed to be really bringing things together for me. And I liked the peace thing in Buddhism; people were always talking about peace.

I tired of Buddhism, just as I tired of Christianity and Islam. It just got to the point where it no longer satisfied whatever it was I was tryin' to do. See, Buddhism didn't get broad enough either. Like all the other religions I've explored, it also had this dogma. At the bottom of every religion there always seems to linger this dogma. It may take time to see, but finally it comes through; sooner or later you'll hear it: "We're better than the others." Oh, this dogma, it really turns me off. You know what I mean? Jonestown dogma: "You must do this." I also found out later that when you take on another culture, you don't have all the things that it takes for this culture because certain things that they have experienced you haven't. Although there's good parts of it that you can use, there's also things that you cannot use.

I'm a musician. I guess that would be my religion. I never thought of it that way until maybe four or five years ago, when all of a sudden I realized, wait a minute, this is my religion. Why am I goin' out here? (Laughs.) Here's the religion. You know what I mean? My shrine is this instrument. When I reach with the ecstasy of this music, it's really a godlike thing. I mean, it's like reaching out, reaching out into that eternal whatever. The sound can go there sometimes. It doesn't do it all the time. You have peak performances, and then you wait, sometimes four or five years, before the next one comes. But then you know. Pretty soon come two or three at a time in one year. You say, "Well, man, I'm in tune." That's when I feel I'm in tune with God or with this Supreme Being or with the universe, with the sounds of the universe.

You know, it comes from you, but it's a combination of you and whoever you're performin' with at the time. That's how it has been for me. Because I play this accompanying type thing, being a percussionist, I have waited for those times when just that perfect combination of things comes together; not only the combination of people, but that mental, spiritual, and physical place where this thing can take form; where this music can really take on something bigger than we are—where we're amazed. You know what I mean? Like, sometimes I don't feel like I'm playing it, like something else is playing the instrument. Maybe the audience is playing the instrument, because I believe that too. It's a give-and-take thing. That music is probably the most purest of all religion because of what it does. It doesn't matter what denomination you are when you're listening to music. It's universal. You understand? I mean we can really communicate, break down all kinds of barriers with that music. Louis Armstrong would go behind the Iron Curtain and just blow them away over there. And they called him the Ambassador because of his ability to communicate with Russians where our president couldn't. Our president couldn't communicate with Russians with all the words and the rhetoric in the world. But a piece of music, you know, twelve bars of blues, could do what all the heads of state could not.

In Italy when they clap for you after you perform, they all clap in unison. I had never experienced that kind of thing from people that I didn't even know, couldn't even speak their language. There was a guy who came and picked me up and took me to the concert place every day, called me by my name. He'd say, "Hey, Akbar, time to go." He got that across to me and then he'd take me down there and he'd be there when I got through. Being treated that great for the music. (Laughs.) I thought, Boy, this has got to be somethin', this music, for it to transform people like this. It feels good.

I can be very frustrated and go to the bandstand and completely get rid of all my frustrations. And, boy, you know, I've seen women fainting, I've seen people feel ecstasy, and I've felt ecstasy—and I only get it from the bandstand. That's when everything seems to be coming together with me and my peers and the room and the people and the noise, and everybody seems to be at one place. I've seen that happen. Every mind in there was on this one thing. That's powerful. (Laughs.) What makes it so religious to me is that it can bring people together. I've seen music just bring hostile forces right together, man, just bring 'em right together; like, for this moment or for this period of time they're gonna just drop their arms and not be at war.

So that's it. I mean anything that can bring people to ecstasy is powerful; anything that can change people like I have seen it, for good or for bad, is powerful. That's why I give music this religious power, 'cause it can be good or it can be bad. It can be really bad. During World War II Billie Holiday was doin' a thing called "Gloomy Sunday." It was about death . . . this woman singin' that she'd dreamed of the death of her man, you know. They had to stop playin' it over the air because women were committin' suicide, jumping out of buildings, as a result of this. I remember it. Although this was a beautiful piece of music, what she was singin' about was too real, was takin' place daily . . . telegrams were comin' in every day about somebody being knocked out in that war. So that's why it was banned. That is powerful.

Yeah, music don't have to be positive. Just like you can bring a bunch of people together, you can also tear a bunch of people apart. *(Laughs.)* Like the heavy-metal thing today is a protest. It's a young generation of Americans saying we are not satisfied with any of it, so we're gonna imitate the enemy, the one you hated the most. So they put a swastika on their heads or chains around their chests. There's racist music, there's music to fight by. Nothin' is sacred with some of these kids. They're just sayin', "Hey, man, you've really messed up the world." I can understand them to a point, because they've been so disillusioned. So that's why it's difficult, man, when I go to these schools and I'm tryin' to teach these kids about jazz. They look at me and say, "If jazz is so hip, then how come the world's so screwed up?" You know, "If it's so great, then why are we livin' the way we are right now? If it's so good, then why aren't you makin' the money that Michael Jackson makes?"

I really want to live. The main thing I want to do is something that's musically strong enough that it will last after I'm gone. Like Duke Ellington or Count Basie. Because music is eternal. Once you put that sound out there, it's going on and on and on; it's not gonna stop, ever, you know. *(Laughs.)* So that's how I feel. The most pure form of religion for me is this music. And I think it is for all of us, but I don't think people would accept it if you said, "You should believe in Music." *(Laughs.)* You know what I mean? Then they got to ask you what kind. Then you got a real problem. *(Laughs.)*

In the Public Eye

William J. vanden Heuvel

A SPECIAL OBLIGATION

The walls of his Fifth Avenue office in New York City are decorated almost entirely with photographs of himself in the company of Democratic party luminaries: Jimmy Carter, Harry Truman, and Bobby, Teddy, and John F. Kennedy. But the most interesting photo catches him standing outside the United Nations building in a pin-striped suit, covered with red stains. "I was serving as the U.S. ambassador to the UN at the time and we were about to begin a meeting of the Security Council.* A couple of Trotskyites from San Francisco sneaked into the room and dumped cans of red paint on myself and Soviet ambassador Troyanovsky as an attention-getting protest stunt. After the incident I suggested to Ambassador Troyanovsky that we were, 'Better red than dead.' (Laughs.)"

My parents were immigrants to America. My mother was Belgian and my father Dutch. They came to America, went through Ellis Island, and ended up in Rochester, New York. It was one of those heroic epic stories of immigrants. When I hear Mario Cuomo talk about his family, I sit back and close my eyes and thank God. I went through all of that, and probably in much more difficult circumstances than Mario Cuomo ever did.

There was always in our home life a deep love of America. All the years of our lives I remember my father had us singing "God Bless America" before we went to bed at night. It was a terribly important thing to him. Now this is in a family where my father was working for $18 a week. He worked at a company called the R. T. French Company, which made spices and mustard. He had terribly hard work, terribly hard labor work. But he was very proud of it. He gave us a great sense of pride in work, that there was no kind of work that was embarrassing or humiliating if in fact it allowed you to be independent and stand on your own feet.

We got our spiritual values primarily from our home and not

---

* He served as U.S. ambassador to the United Nations from 1977 to 1981. This particular incident occurred on April 30, 1980.

from any institutionalized religion. We got it from people whom we met and knew. I say we, meaning my sister and myself. We always believed that there was a Supreme Being, that there was a force, a spirit, a major spiritual influence in the universe. But I think we were also taught by experience that it was what you did on earth that ultimately was going to be totaled up in the questions of whether or not your life was meaningful. We were not brought up to think that life was spent now in a meditation about how good it was going to be hereafter. And we were brought up always with a sense of great tolerance for other people's differences. There was nothing in our lives that caused us to separate people on the basis of race or religion or ethnic background. I think that probably came from my mother, who said that each person is entitled to be judged in terms of their own merits and their own accomplishments.

Franklin Roosevelt was my political idol growing up, because Franklin Roosevelt was the man who saved our house. By ordering a moratorium on the mortgages, the man who held the second mortgage on our house couldn't foreclose it and we could continue to live there. Franklin Roosevelt was the man who made it possible for my father to work and eventually join a union. Suddenly you had a government that identified with your need. So at a very early age, six or seven years old, I was very much interested in public and political life, although my parents were not political at all, ever. But for some reason as a young boy I was totally immersed and imbued with this sense of public life and wanting to be a lawyer. Not to be a lawyer to make money but to be a lawyer like Clarence Darrow. To be a lawyer who was going to be able, like William Jennings Bryant or Franklin Roosevelt, to be in public life. And that was the excitement of it to me.

So I certainly have had, from the very beginning, a commitment to the liberal attitudes of life in the sense that you judge people in terms of their own achievements and characteristics; that bigotry and violence had no room in a civilized existence; that education was crucial to advance and progress; and that love was a major ingredient of one's life, both in your family and in terms of your friends. A commitment, I guess, to government in the sense that it had a positive and constructive role to play to assure a society based on justice and fairness.

One constant theme in my life has been an enormous antipathy toward anything that represents being bullied. I've seen that thread come out often in my life. When I was chairman of the Board of Correction in New York City, I spent a lot of time in the prisons. And one of the things in the prisons that prevented any prospect of rehabilitation was the extraordinary power that's given to people who have total authority over somebody else's life. It seemed to me as I witnessed it that it frequently brought out the worst of everyone, both the custodians and the prisoners. So the abuse of power was always something that was unacceptable to me. Perhaps this explains why it was terribly important to me to go through the prisons on any given day and make a difference in someone's life. I could listen to somebody who felt that they were entitled to bail or that the sentence they received had been unfair or that they had not been properly represented. By spending a little bit of time helping that person, I could really make a difference.

I think you can make a major difference in terms of the nature of your society, whether it's just or whether it's unfair, beginning with your own immediate social structure. I think that's our first obligation, because that's something you can directly affect and know you can be responsible for. I guess it was Edna St. Vincent Millay who wrote that, "I love humanity but I hate people." But I do think your universe begins with the ten, twenty, or thirty people who really are your intimate world. Your relationships to them and how you assist them and help prepare the quality of their life is really a pretty good insight into the kind of world that you think is possible. Because that's a world that you can really affect.

If you go into the macrocosmic world of government, you can also try to change and save the world, preserve peace, etcetera. When I was ambassador to the United Nations, I felt as though I had a role in that, but I never overrated that role. When I was with Robert Kennedy, I felt I made a difference as his assistant in the Justice Department. I was sent into Prince Edward County, Virginia, in the depth of the segregation crisis, with the Virginians leading the fight against the Supreme Court decision to desegregate public education. The schools in Prince Edward County had been closed for five years. Rather than open them up to black children, they just closed them down. The president determined that those children should have an education. So I went down there, with Bobby's power behind me, and we set up a whole school system for these children. We rented the public schools that were vacant. We raised the money from around the country. We recruited teachers from the rich, suburban schools of the nation to come down to teach. In a couple of months we had, I think, one of the finest school systems in the South. It certainly made a difference in the life of Prince Edward County. It stopped a great deal of the confrontation and violence between whites and blacks, and it showed them that an arrangement could be made where people could work and live together.

Although I frequently reflect on the words of Cromwell before the Battle of Durham—"I beseech ye, in the bowels of Christ, to think that ye may be wrong"—I am not a person who feels that I have to be right. I like to question myself and I like others to question what I'm doing. And I'm quite willing to accept other people's ideas to try to find a consensus way of doing something if that's possible. But I know that there's a lot of situations where you just have to act, where to try to find a resolution that's acceptable to everybody means nothing. In Prince Edward County, for example, I operated on the premise that if something should be done, then it can be done. And what had to be done in terms of saving America's own character was that those children could not be denied education.

When I saw the response of teachers around America, I understood then, as I've understood many times in my life since, that those who are most enriched in experiences of that kind are those who are the helpers, not the helped. I've seen that in the prisons, I've seen that in Prince Edward County, and I've seen that in many, many places. Those teachers had a chance to look at themselves again, a chance to feel that they were participating in something very important that was helping to define their society and their country.

Helping others is my credo, but not in a do-gooder sense, I don't think. There are people who have and people who do not have. And there are people who are ill and who are handicapped in a variety of ways and who, in any kind of civilized society, are going to have to be helped to live in a decent, humane way. But I have nothing against the accumulation of wealth. I have done well enough in my own career. And for those people for whom the accumulation of wealth is a prime objective, I don't resent it certainly, and I don't regret it, except to the extent that I feel as though they may be missing out on an important part of life; which is the ability to know and to help other people and to create a society that represents values that are bigger than yourself and your own personal wants.

I always did feel that in America we have a special obligation. I was enormously influenced as a student by the founding fathers, reading about them in history. That story was so extraordinary. Here in the midst of a world of tyranny, these extraordinary people, through their own courage and their own intellect, created an experimental government that said all men are created equal. And that they are endowed with certain inalienable rights. That among those rights are life, liberty, and the pursuit of happiness. And then they went ahead and created a constitution that turned out to be the most extraordinary document of government ever written. In that framework, with all the terrible mistakes we've made as a country, all of the things we've done wrong, we have still created that haven, that beacon to which the oppressed of the world can look for hope and salvation. What a great country to be part of, what an opportunity in one's life to live here and at this time.

I try to tell my children that too. Sure, have a good time, assure your material comforts, but remember that all of us have a sustained, residual obligation to make sure that this political fabric that we inherited is at least as strong and hopefully stronger when we leave it. That is the last best hope of mankind, in my judgment.

John Andrews

I come of Michigan people. I was born in rural southwest Michigan in 1944. Both sides of my family come of Christian Science background, going back several generations, really. Christian Science is dated from 1866 from the personal experiences and researches of Mary Baker Eddy in New England. By the turn of this century, I think, both my mother's and my father's ancestors were following Christian Science as their religion and way of life. So it was very much bred into my heritage. I recall, for example, that the daily Bible-lesson study that is part of the regimen of practicing Christian Science was something my parents encouraged me to take up when I was only six or seven. And it's been the way I've begun my day ever since. As I do today. As I always do.

He is director of the Independence Institute, a conservative think tank that focuses on state and local issues in Golden, Colorado. "We produce short papers, scholarly studies, and occasionally convene leadership conferences to examine economic questions, the development of the state, the environment, and the trade-off between growth and environment, taxation and water policy." He's forty-five, married, the father of two children, and an active member of the Christian Science church.

Looking back, I would have to say that the experience which most profoundly tested and influenced my beliefs was the time I spent working in the Nixon White House from 1970 to 1973. You see, after I left the navy, where I'd served as a submarine officer, I had an extraordinary opportunity, through my writings and through some family friendships, to work in the Nixon White House. So my very first formal job was as a junior aide in the Nixon White House. I was, by some measurements, a green kid. I went to work for Ron Ziegler in the White House press office before my twenty-sixth birthday. After a year in the press office I was recruited over in the speech writing team because they needed a token capital-Y youth. At that time the eighteen-year-old vote was just coming in. The campuses were very uneasy over Vietnam. So I had the opportunity to be the president's speech writer for three years.

A year and a half into the speech-writing experience the first minor news story crops up in the Washington papers that some odd burglars were arrested at the Democratic party headquarters. Nobody knows what to make of it. From the very first, looking back, it's clear to me that I took that all more seriously than most of my colleagues. Young John Andrews was quite naive and quite idealistic, and shocked at a close-up view of political skullduggery, which has gone on forever. But this was my first close-up view of it. Anyway it bothered me; it increasingly ate away at my ability to do my job. Speech writing is a highly personal function—you've go to believe in the man you're writing for. You've got to believe in the policies you're articulating. You've got to feel, if not good, at least okay about the guy for whom you're writing. It was eating away at me. I increasingly felt the president was behaving in every way like a guilty man, a man with a lot to hide. I remember buttonholing Nixon in a receiving line to try to take thirty seconds to look behind those eyes to see what he was thinking about this building crisis. The result of all this was to feel that there was a really scary moral numbness in the man and in some of those around him.

In the summer of '73 something called Operation Candor was launched, and Watergate was going to be decisively dealt with, and Nixon was gonna counterattack after the damage of John Dean's testimony before the Senate. I was involved as the coordinating speech writer for Nixon's national TV address that was gonna finally put Watergate behind us. Kissinger and Ziegler were the two senior staff people that I was working with on this project. I took some ideas to Kissinger, and he had some ideas for me, and we came out of that meeting feeling that contrition must be a theme of the speech. Then I go to Ziegler, and I say this is what Henry and I concluded. Ziegler said—this is a direct quote—"Contrition is bullshit. There will be no contrition from this president, because he has done nothing to apologize for. He has done nothing wrong. And it would be bad strategy, bad tactics, wrong on the facts, etcetera." The quote "Contrition is bullshit" later appeared in a front-page story of *The*

Washington Post because I gave the story to Bob Woodward. That ended my relationship with Ron Ziegler, as you might suppose. (*Laughs.*) Ziegler's a terribly shallow man. He has his talents, but he's not a man of depth.

Well, it built, it built, and finally I decided I had to get out. I had everything set up to call a press conference and make a statement that Nixon should resign if he couldn't come clean. I was dissuaded from all this by Ray Price, the key speech writer, my boss, a man I love and respect a great deal. "Go out quietly," he says. "It will all get better. You couldn't do any good anyway. All you'd do is taint and scar yourself as a turncoat and an ingrate." So I resigned quietly toward the end of '73, lived with it for a period of weeks, and then found I couldn't live with it. I ended up writing a long, analytical account of my experiences and observations and concerns for *The Washington Post*. Out of that came a "My Turn" column in *Newsweek*, an editorial piece in *The New York Times*, and a one-hour interview on PBS. In the PBS interview I said, with lots of qualifiers wrapped around it, "Maybe Nixon ought to be impeached, if all else fails." Well, I learned what the glare of the national media can do to you, because all the qualifiers were stripped away and they built the news lead for the next morning's *New York Times* out of "Ex-Nixon aide calls for impeachment, first former White House staffer to acknowledge that impeachment is probably necessary." It was acutely uncomfortable for me.

To this day I'm still not sure I did the right thing. I'm reasonably sure that I did. I did what I had to do and I believe I was praying my way through it. Incidentally my conception of prayer and the answer you get in prayer isn't such that I would hold God responsible for what really ought to be my mistakes. I'm not going to say that I prayed my way through it and therefore imply that he told me to do it. My concept of the answers I get in prayer is that you either have a sense of calm, certainty, of being unafraid, or you have a sense of turmoil and upheaval and inner conflict. The former is more like the answer to prayer that's saying yes, go ahead, you're on the right track. Hearing voices, seeing visions, having God call your name and say, "John, this is what I want you to do," I don't doubt that's the way in which some people receive answers to prayer, but it has never been for me. But I just want to amplify that I've prayed my way through anything I've ever done.

I've often questioned my motives in speaking out against Nixon, because I'm a bit of a melodramatic person. I don't shy from the limelight, from making a dramatic gesture. And I know that I can be strong-willed to the point of intolerance and cruelty in some situations, that I'm an idealist beyond what is probably for my own good. There just may have been an element of grandstanding in all of that. I still don't think so, but I'm willing to sit here and acknowledge to you that it's an unresolved question. But I believe in a Last Judgment. Not perhaps in the same literal way that some of my fellow Christians do, but I believe there will be a time when all these matters will be a great deal clearer to me. These things that are morally ambiguous to me right now, I'll know.

Being involved in trying to identify the most workable beneficial courses of action in community life, public life, political economic issues, you have to think about human motivation. What is fair to expect of yourself and your fellow man? And if the flaws are there, which they very definitely are, are they intractable? Why are they there, where do they come from? The explanation of the second chapter of Genesis is conclusive for me. What I take from the story (and I'm not a biblical literalist) is that there is in the human makeup a rebelliousness, a strain of self-centeredness, of short-sightedness, translating to self-destructiveness. Pride, ego, grasping overreaching.

So Original Sin is there. I study Adam and Eve twice a year in considerable depth. And I always try to remind myself that this week, that this place in time, for John Andrews, there are two choices for my concept of God and man. I've either got this all-good, all-powerful God who creates this magnificent, noble image of himself, man, or I've got this God who is magnificent, immensely powerful, and sovereign up to a point, but not so sovereign as to be able to prevent evil, perhaps even a jokester who designed a system with a flaw that has tormented us ever since. I choose the perfect-God-and-perfect-man concept. But I admit the reality of evil. I don't just say, "Well, I don't believe in any of that." A caricature of Christian Science would portray us as dismissing with a wave of the hand evil, sins, tragedy, and the limitations that exist within a finite material existence. But Christian Science does no such thing. It follows Jesus in answering the questions about evil by seeking to bring healing where there is need, rather than just lecturing about it.

Healing, then, is the existential answer to the problem of evil. It's not a satisfactory theoretical answer, but it deals with the problem of evil by replacing evil incrementally with that much more good—something much nearer to a portrayal of perfect God and perfect man. The best example of this in the life of the master is where Jesus is asked by his disciples, "Who sinned? Why was this man born blind? Who sinned? He or his parents?" Jesus perceived this as a false choice. He essentially answered, "None of the above." "Neither has this man sinned nor his parents, but in order that God may be glorified, I must work the works of God, who sent me. I must work while it is light." And he proceeded to heal the man. So the question of why the man had been born blind was mooted by Jesus' divinely derived ability to bring a higher law of good to bear upon what would otherwise seem to be a cruel and random law where this man was punished, whether by his own fault, that of his parents, by genetic flaws, or by poor public-health practices in Palestine, or whatever. To the disciples it may not have been a fully satisfying answer. But the one actor in that little scene to whom it was, I'm sure, a fully satisfying answer is the blind man.

I can't help feeling that the Judeo-Christian tradition as it's been expressed in what we call Western culture, and best of all in the United States of America, embodies a good deal more of what is noblest, deepest, most permanent, highest in the world than most other nations and cultures. I hope it's possible to believe that and yet not be jingoistic or not exaggerate it to the point where I fail to see what's good in other cultures, because a failure to do so contradicts my conviction that I'm obligated to treat my fellow man with respect and compassion.

One of Christian Science's most beautiful and profound teachings is to derive from Scripture seven synonymous names for God. Coincidentally it's like the seven colors of light that you identify with a prism when you break down white light. And in practice and in living, the challenge that you find is to keep these in balance. To say, I want to be godlike, I want to be Christ-like, is made so much more vivid and meaningful and applicable if you say, "The Bible identifies God as spirit, as life, as truth, as mind, as love, as soul." All those words are used in the Bible. The word *principle*, which is the seventh of the synonymous terms, is not used in the Bible, but God as love giver, God as a governing sovereign who is unchanging and principled and ever constant, is certainly in the Bible.

Sitting here trying to verbalize this for you, I can see that the balance that I try to maintain in my life to lead a godlike life constantly refers back to those seven elements of a spectrum of what Deity and who Deity is. And by never being unbalanced on just one or two or three of them, you find that life itself does stay in balance.

So why am I here? I'm here to glorify God. I'm here to glorify him, understanding him in terms of those seven identifiers, but also understanding him in very traditional terms of him who was incarnate, who made himself human in Jesus Christ, that he loved us that much. That he wanted to show us the trinity of his own nature; as father, son, holy spirit. Glorify God. That's the goal. And I do that by letting my life be a window through which as much of him as possible shines into other people's lives. And that translates into a sense of an obligation to be of service to others. An obligation to affirm life, to really love, not in a sentimental way or a utopian way that would overlook the very difficult problem of evil we were just talkin' about, but to love according to the best example that we have, which is the love of Jesus—a constant, unvarying love which didn't need to meet any return, that needed no object to call it forth. And this in turn calls for an obligation to constantly sort out the permanent from the transitory, the deep from the superficial, and to dedicate myself to what is permanent and deep and to defend them, to help see that they're preserved.

Governor Richard Lamm

THE PRODIGAL PARENT

Denver, Colorado. The Capitol Building. In less than four months he will finish out his third and final term as governor of Colorado. A busy and hurried man, he cuts to the chase the second I enter his office, as though he knows what I'm after and would prefer to get it over with as quickly as possible. Within ten minutes, however, he tilts back his chair, lifts his boots up onto his desk, and loosens his tie. Often referred to by the local media as "Governor Gloom" for his frequent pronouncements on the decline of American values and economic power, he comes across as a forthright man with a deep distaste for hype and cant.

I was raised in the Methodist church. But my wife and I were married in the Unitarian church. To the extent that we claim a religion, it's Unitarian. And I think that has been a result of my belief rather than a cause of it. Unitarianism believes that there's great truths in all religions and that they're all deserving of respect and study; they spend an awful lot of time trying to examine man's search for God. I'm very pleased with that kind of approach. I think there is something so terribly narrow about a Christian who says that his way is the only way to get to heaven, or a Muslim who says that his way is the only way to get to heaven. I think an awful lot of other people are offended by this as well, like the humanist philosopher Sidney Hook, who says that any God that's gonna condemn the rest of the people is one that I don't want to have anything to do with.

I guess I would consider myself a humanist, but not a secular humanist. I really have a hard time making fun of anybody else's religion, and the secular humanists do that on occasion. I would have a hard time doing that, even in the fundamentalist evangelical movement. Again, Hook distinguishes between Karl Marx's religion as the opiate of the people and Max Weber's more refined recognition that we all are beset by a myriad of questions and that if you do not have respect for those questions, if you do not have awe at the complexity of the world around you, you're in trouble. So I spend very little of my time thinking cynically about religion. It's got to get to the Jerry Falwell, Jimmy Swaggart level before I'll do that. I mean if people find answers and solace to those immense problems to which any thinking human being is heir to, you know, Godspeed. I guess that is why I would back away from calling myself a secular humanist.

So I guess what I am is a Unitarian. A Unitarian respects the fact of man's journey toward God and recognizes that there's just a lot of paths to get there and that they're all deserving of respect, that there's something to learn from all of them. I guess the one courage of my own convictions is that there is such a myriad of different convictions in the world that, unless they go off the Richter scale toward evil, whatever that is, that they're entitled to respect. And I believe that there's more error out there than there is evil. I run into error all the time. I run into people who are wrong, but they're not evil.

But the spiritual, while it's very important to me, and while I am just fascinated by man's search for meaning, my motivations in life, my beliefs, are more intellectual ones . . . not really tied into the religious experience. I've got to tell you, I've spent very little time in my life thinking about spiritual issues. I really think the thing that drives me mainly is more of an intellectual thing, my belief that the United States has many more serious problems than we admit to. I see myself as a Paul Revere rather than a Martin Luther. I see myself as somebody who is trying to warn society, not convert it. Well, convert it in a way, but not in a religious sense. The thing that drives me most is my belief in the kind of world that I'm leaving my kids. You know, the Bible talks about the prodigal son. I guess it's my belief that I'm a prodigal parent. I think that my generation of parents, politicians, business people, inherited wealth but are leaving death. We inherited a well-functioning economy yet we're leaving one that has been shattered by our own hedonism. So I am more intrigued about how you devise a health care system. I'm intrigued about such things as, Are we being fair to our kids? I'm intrigued by what I call intergenerational equity. And all these other things. So my beliefs are rather apocalyptic beliefs. They have to do with my historical sense of where this society is going.

One of the things I'm fighting now is this notion that God is an American and has somehow given us some sort of divine destiny. One of my basic convictions is that great nations rise and fall and that we really have to find a way to revitalize this society or we are heading toward real trouble. This faith in divine destiny does little to help us cure the real problems we face. Another thing I am fighting against is the loss of American values, because there's clearly been a loss of values. There's been a nihilism out there that has undercut all institutions, politicians, churches, businesses. There's practically nothing left out there with a great deal of credibility. And I think that one of the things where my thinking is going lately is that there is a life cycle to great nations, almost like there is a life cycle to life. Every great nation in history has had a youthful vigor, has had a maturity, and has then had a decline. It's almost like the great families of the world, where the first generation builds it, the second generation protects it vigorously, and by the fourth generation they're squandering it. The Roman historian Juvenal says, "Luxury is more ruthless than war." And I believe that we have become a hedonistic, fun-seeking country. We've lost those stern virtues that made us a great nation. And unless we recapture them, we are leaving a tumultuous time for our children.

I'm sure that my motivation for going into politics was to try to improve the world for the next generation. But I admit that being in politics is a love-hate relationship. Anybody in politics has to have a strong sense of self and convictions to put up with all the bullshit. You love two-thirds of it and hate the other third. But I think there's a great deal of difference between what drives politicians. I got out of law school the same year that John F. Kennedy was elected president. I come from a generation (I'm fifty years old) that in fact was really inspired by the Kennedy example; I mean, to us, doing good was to be in government, to make a better world. That's vastly different than what the current generation of politicians are coming into it for. And I'm appalled at how much of the right wing in this country . . . how much their agenda is to dismantle government. I can certainly see wanting to make government work more efficiently. But I can hardly see where you'd want anarchy, where you'd want to go back to sort of saying government should do nothing but raise armies. Anyway, one's attitudes are inextricably interrelated to their formative years. I am in that generation that fought in the civil rights movement, that really saw where government was a positive tool to make it a better world. Now other people come along with a whole different set of attitudes and virtues.

I think that the most important virtues, at least for me, are rather mundane ones. And these are the virtues I would want to leave my son because they have worked very well for me. Number one is keep yourself healthy, do not abuse your body; that the body is, to some degree, a temple. Number two is find somebody to love. Number three is find a satisfying job, something that you can really throw your vocational passions into. It really all falls away pretty fast after that. Those are, I think, verities that I read when I read people of a thousand years ago. You read Plato and it's intriguing how often in story and song he mentions the importance of love, job satisfaction, and personal health.

Big George Armistead III

BOOSTER

I'm a native Nashvillian, and I'm thirty-five years old. I was born and raised here, and all my family's always been from Nashville, so it's totally homegrown. I went off to military school at a place called Sewanee, and then I went to Birmingham Southern College, a small Methodist school, and then came back here. And ever since then I've remained here, and I'm fortunate enough to be a councilman-at-large here in our metropolitan government. We've got a population of about 540,000 people here, and just a wonderful city.

A tall, thick, lumbering man with short cropped hair, a round face, and double chin, he is both a real estate broker and city politician. Dressed conservatively in khaki slacks and a yellow cotton button-down shirt with "Vandy" monogrammed on the pocket, he's a devoted fan of Vanderbilt University basketball. On the day we met, he invited me to join him for a game. At halftime he walked the entire gym, shaking hands with no less than forty people, most of whom he knew by name. After the game

he insisted we visit the locker room to personally congratulate the team
for their one-point victory over the University of Mississippi. "It was a
big win for us. We almost lost. That was a cliff-hanger."

We played Florida three weeks ago, Vandy did, and with one second
left on the clock, somebody threw about six tennis balls on the court.
They called a technical on Vanderbilt, and Florida ended up winnin'
the game. And if you'll look in today's paper, it was said that I threw
the tennis balls. I'd come closer to throwin' a ball at a council meetin'
than I would at a Vanderbilt game. *(Laughs.)* But you're wide open
for criticism when you're in the public eye, so I've found myself, a
lot of times, coverin' my tracks, but I don't regret it, 'cause my civic
endeavors and charitable endeavors are great . . . I love 'em.

Nashville's a pretty close-knit city, you know, and the family, in
my judgment, is stressed big-time here. Churches are a mammoth
part of people's lives down here. This is, as you well know, the Bible
Belt. And Nashville's got the United Methodist Publishing House,
the Baptist Sunday School Board, and Thomas Nelson, which is the
biggest Bible publisher in America. We have over eight hundred
churches in our city, and that's a lot for a half million people. So
churches have always filled a big part of folks' lives here in Nashville.
And this is a big educational center. There's seventeen colleges here
and, I'd say, about fifty private schools.

I'm a member of West End Methodist. I'm a very kinetic person,
very outgoing and outspoken, and somewhat controversial *(laughs)*,
'cause I take a stand on things in my political life. But when I go to
church, all of that is beside me. When I'm in church, it's almost like
goin' to be rejuvenated; it's like gettin' a blood transfusion—I feel
so good after. And there're many times, every Christmas, every
Easter, a lot of times when I'm at the Communion rail (the Methodists
here take Communion the first Sunday of each month), and I think
about how daggum fortunate I am. And I tear up a little bit sometimes
thinking about how fortunate I am when I look about, just what
shape I could be in or what opportunities that have been afforded
me that could have easily gone the other way. I just thank my lucky
stars. I used to just fall asleep and not pray at night . . . just the two-
or three-minute prayer. But I do that now, and I feel so much better
that I do.

I'm very active in civic circles, in the Kiwanis, and the junior
chamber, and the chamber, and the National Booster Club, and the
Heart Association, Lung Association—all that stuff. So there's a giant

feeling in my life and, I think, in the majority of folks that are Nashvillians now, of giving. And one of the reasons I got into office in the council is because I've been given so much, given so much opportunity. I have always been enamored with children, and with those that are not as fortunate as I am. This picture back here *(he points to a framed picture on his office wall)* . . . this picture was taken the first of last year. I was given this Commitment to Children Award. It represents drawings from seventy-nine children from the Nashville Child Center—all pasted together. And I played Santa Claus for 'em and raised money for 'em. The Child Center is a United Way agency, which is a day care center for indigent families. And there're things that have happened to me, like givin' a baby away to an adoptive couple. This happened coupla years ago. Then there's a little retarded kid in Special Olympics. He was cryin' when our Kiwanis Club was givin' the ribbons away at Special Olympics. And the kid was cryin', so I put him up on my shoulders. His name's Keith Campbell, and we've been friends ever since. He has got the mind of about a six-year-old, and he's eighteen years old now. But a picture of Keith on top of my shoulders *(he points to another picture on the wall)* was used for the national brochure for Kiwanis International for two years in a row . . . over a million of those printed up.

That's really what makes the world go 'round . . . to help other people and share what you got. Just like you're sharing your book with people. It's the same way as what happened nineteen hundred and eighty-nine years ago. God was sharin' when he brought Christ down and, obviously, with the revelation of him, and what all's happened since then, it's strictly a matter of caring and sharing and doin' for your fellow man. And I'm guilty as hell of bein' selfish on occasion. And maybe that's part of the reason I'll get emotional in church every now and then. Because I'll think, "Gol-l-ly, how can I complain about not havin' a wallet full of $500, or not havin' this or havin' that, when I'm able to give so much. And others don't have half of what I do. And here I am feelin' sorry for myself." That's when you go out and suck it up and think, "Well, I'm here for a reason." Every person should feel this. And I'm certainly no exception that I feel like I'm very, very special, that God's put me here for a reason. And the reason I am here is to share what I can for others and to make Nashville a better place to live.

Deborah Howell

St. Paul, Minnesota. She is editor of the St. Paul Pioneer Press and Dispatch, *one of the few women editors of a major daily newspaper in the country. A thin, good-natured, fast-talking fireball of energy, she likes to lace her conversation with four-letter words. In a week she'll embark on her second marriage after spending the past seven years as a widow. She is forty-eight years old and has no children.*

My whole family on both sides were basically Southern Baptists, fairly fundamental people. My grandmother was a very religious woman, kind of almost a dour woman (not that she wasn't a nice old lady). She had a house filled with religious tracts, and her favorite thing was listening to the evangelists on the radio late at night in this God-forsaken isolated ranch in west Texas. So I grew up with a lot of that, but it never suited me . . . ever.

When I was about twelve, I remember hearing this Baptist minister named Brother Barbay preachin' against Catholics. And I got up and left. My mother thought I was sick or something and got up and followed me. I said (however a twelve-year-old would say it), "I'm not listenin' to any of that shit anymore. I don't believe it, I don't like it, I'm not taking part in it. And I'm not goin' back." And I didn't. I suppose I had a high degree of intolerance for religious intolerance.

I basically didn't have much to do with religion, or spirituality, or anything of the sort for another thirty years. *(Laughs.)* I went through a long period of being very agnostic, which lasted until the time of my husband's serious illness and subsequent death.* During his illness I found I couldn't pray for him because I didn't believe anybody would hear what was going on. So I didn't. And I felt somewhat guilty about that, but not a lot. But it got me thinking about spirituality. His death also brought me back into contact with clergy, which was rather hilarious.

My husband was a very religious person. He was born and raised a Catholic (even considered being a priest in his youth), and while he had fallen away from the church (basically over birth control), he still had a strong internal belief and he never stopped being a Cath-

---

* Nicholas D. Coleman, who died in 1981 from acute leukemia. Prior to his death he served as the state senate majority leader of Minnesota.

olic. But he was dying, you see, and the only way to get him properly buried and funeralized was to get him back in the Church. The first priest who came to see him said, "Well, you realize to be taken back into the Church, you have to live with your wife as brother and sister." Well, the truth was, my husband was never gettin' out of the hospital . . . he was dying. It offended my husband, and he said, "Well, I'll have to ask her how she feels about incest." The priest was so pissed, he turned on his heel and walked out. And I came in and I said, "Hey, what happened?" He said, "German asshole" *(laughs)* . . . no, "Teutonic asshole." He said, "Get me an Irish priest." So *(laughs)* I went out and got an Irish priest, who came. Same thing happens again, you know, my husband uses the same line again. This priest laughs, thinks it's pretty funny, and gets him back in the Church.

After he died, I found I had just enormous questions about why a man as good as he would be struck down in the prime of his political career and life? And why was it that he accepted his own impending death much better than I did? It pissed me off. So I began to read here and there. I began to be interested in books that dealt with spirituality and entered therapy at the time to try and help myself cope with my new life as a widow—which I hated. It was while I was in therapy that I began to see that there was a huge hole in my life, and that hole was that I didn't believe in anything outside myself. I didn't know what I was going to do about it, but I knew I had to do something.

One book that I came across that was very helpful to me was *The Road Less Traveled*.* When I first read the last part of that book, which is called "Grace," I didn't get it at first. I thought the first two parts were real interesting, but the "Grace" part left me cold. And I can remember telling my therapist, "Look, don't do the God shit at me. I don't want that. Don't tell me to read stuff about God. That's not where I am." But one night, in the middle of the night, I woke up and said, "I think I need to read the 'Grace' part again." And I read it and it was wonderful and I got it. And that really changed my life. I mean, if you truly accept the fact that there is either some benevolent spirit in the world or there is some greater thing, it makes you want to be a part of the solution instead of part of the problem. And it made me want to, very consciously, lead a better life. I wasn't leading a bad life; I never led a bad life, but I mean, it made me really wanna be more honest, more caring, be sure my ethics were in line, watch how I was treating people. And another fallout of that

---

* By M. Scott Peck, M.D. (New York: Simon and Schuster, 1978).

was that I increasingly began to love nature, which is something that had happened before my husband died. We did a lot of wilderness trips, a lot of backpacking, a lot of canoeing. And the more I was in nature, the more serene I felt, the more I felt a piece of it.

Now I am meditating a little bit every day. Not in the TM sense, or in the Hindu sense, but just to try to be peaceful and quiet, to sit and listen instead of talk all the time. I also do some kind of spiritual reading each day. I don't know where all this leads. It hasn't lead me back to the Church. *(Laughs.)* But I think I'm a better editor for it; I'm a better human being because of it. I don't say *fuck* any less than before. *(Laughs.)* My language is still bad; I'm unlikely to become a contemplative nun next year; I'm very much engaged in the world, the worst part of the world, the bad-news part of the world, but it gives me a perspective. The center of the universe is not me, and I cannot control the actions of a lot of people. The Serenity Prayer is great, I have it right up here in Spanish *(she laughs and points to a large, wall-to-wall corkboard behind her desk)*. In a very pragmatic way it really helps me.

I don't consider myself *(snaps fingers)* a born-again. It's much more of a learning experience I'm involved in. I'm reading and studying and learning. But grace has got something to do with it, because if it weren't for that elusive grace, I probably wouldn't be interested. But I am interested, and I know there's a reason for me to be interested. I'm doin' it, and God only knows what it'll come to.

Fred Means

GATHERED IN THE DUST

Shawnee, Oklahoma. A hulking man with a short, thick neck and rapid-fire wit, he's director of the Oklahoma State Bureau of Narcotics and Dangerous Drugs Control, or, as he prefers, "The Bureau of Neurotics and Dangerous Drunks." "I'm one of those curious people in this sense: I'm one generation removed from the frontier. My grandfather was born in 1852, and my father was born in 1908. My grandfather came into Oklahoma in 1873, long before there was an Oklahoma or an Oklahoma City. He used to say, 'I'm an Alabamian by birth, Arkansawer by high water, a Texan by choice, and a Sooner by God!' So I was raised on notions of almost frontierlike courage."

Let me tell you a story my father told me. I love it. It's apocryphal probably. *(Laughs.)* It seems like William F. Cody took his traveling "Wild West Show" to Europe. And in London they played before the crowned heads of Europe, and there present was the king of England . . . Edward, I think. It was maybe 1905. Edward was fascinated with the wild Indians and the cowboys and all the excitement that went with the "Wild West Show," so he expressed a desire to Colonel Cody to meet a real, live cowboy. Cody said that he could arrange that, and he took him down to the arena after the show and approached an old territorial cowboy, whose name was Bill. Bill was still on horseback, had thrown his leg up over the saddle horn, and was rolling him a cigarette, and Cody said, approaching the old cowboy, "I have the great distinction and high honor to introduce to you His Royal Highness, Edward, king of England." And Bill finished rolling his cigarette, lit it, extended his right hand, and said, "Howdy, King." That story has been wonderful to me, because it typifies a kind of radical democratic sentiment, as though Bill, had he not been a cowboy, might well have been the king of England, and would kinda have liked that. And that is one of the things I would like to preserve for myself and for my children. I would like to see my children possessed of that same attitude of self-worth and accomplishment, regardless of what they do to make a living.

Bill's sort of easy confidence goes along with another trait I admire in a person, and that is courage. I think the ability to stand on your own two feet and look the world straight in the eye means something, or at least it's one of the myths that nourished me—to what good end, I cannot tell you. *(Laughs.)* I remember when my dad was diagnosed as having colon cancer. We sat and talked about it, and he said, "Well, boy, it looks like I've drawn the black ace. But I never for a moment thought that I was immortal. I knew that the time of my death would draw nigh. I've lived a long time. I have no fear of death . . . only of leaving. That's what causes me grief . . . the notion of leaving, not of dying." He died a painful death, but he bore up under that great weight splendidly. That was a great example to me, and what that reinforced in me is that meaningful living requires courage; you really do have to live with courage, understanding, of course, that you're a human being and that courage will fail.

Mark Twain wrote, I thought, a remarkably sensitive piece on human courage in the account of Jack Slade's death in Nevada, or wherever it was. Slade was a notorious thumper and killer who was an enforcer for the Butterfield Stage Lines. He was the guy that carried (if I recall this right) a watch fob made from a human ear. He was reputed to have slain many people in single combat, some that he'd killed in a cowardly manner, and some deeds of real courage as well as ferocity. But he was hanged by a vigilante committee and, on the scaffold, wept. And that band of vigilantes, who, under masks, had hoisted him to the scaffold, laughed at his weakening and his pleading to see his wife. And Mark Twain later remarked that there wasn't a man among them that had done the deeds that Slade had done, things that did require some bravery and some courage. And he said something to the effect that, "True, he was weak when he died, but his death might ought not be the means by which you judged his life." And so, when I speak of courage, I speak of courage in human terms, knowing that courage fails us all, that we all, in the end, are merely mortals who will be inconstant in our beliefs. And I'm happy that I no longer judge myself or others by momentary inconstancies, but by commitment over a long time to beliefs that one, you know, strives to honor. We ought to learn, all of us, to forgive ourselves momentary weaknesses, inconstancies, failures of nerve, those things of which, in time, we all grow ashamed. And we need to surmount those things and to triumph above the cynicism that some people fall into as, I think, an ordinary course. You know, I tend to believe that cynicism is a kind of disappointed naiveté. And you have to transcend that and see the world in less rigid terms than either the idealist or the cynicist see them.

I've tended to see the everyday workman as my hero, not a Nietzsche screaming down from his crag, not a Dante writing of the levels of hell, but that big green middle section of life that's comprised of ordinary people like you and me, who by dint of sheer effort awake in the morning and go to their work, and do it and come home to their families. Now, I've not always done that. I have lived by the lip of the cup. I've been, in my day, a brawler . . . all of those things. But the older I get, the more I see that the real richness is not to be found in the breast of the Great Man. I don't believe in that. I believe it was Admiral Halsey who said that "there are no great men, there are only ordinary men like you and me who are required by circumstances to face great challenges." That's what I believe.

You know, I look sometimes around me and I see these ugly old roads and telephone poles that have been laid across the land, and I think they're ugly until that thought is modified by a thought that comes quickly thereafter: These roads were laid by men trying to knit together a society and provide some convenience; that those ugly telephone poles, they, too, serve a purpose. What we have wrought here may not be beautiful, but the intent is. And one either makes a contribution to this society, in whatever circumstances chance allows, or one makes no contribution and takes from society. I believe in the hermit's right to isolate himself from the rest of society. But he does not contribute living alone on a hilltop. I would not like to be a hermit, neither would I like to be one of these romantic outlaws I daily hunt that run these roads and byways and prey upon their victims with force. They're a detriment to the society. So, you know, I think that just in the common man there is something noble and good and beautiful.

Talking about the seriousness of life, as we are, in some respects recalls to my mind a section that comes from Poe's "Masque of the Red Death," and it goes as follows: "There are chords in the hearts of the most reckless that cannot be touched without emotion, even with the utterly lost to whom life and death are equally jest, there are some things about which no jest can be made." That struck me as a young boy, and I still have not gotten over the import of it. I think that's true. I've known, from time to time in my life, people who were rather desperate, but unless they were absolutely mad, there were some things about which they could make no jest; there were some things of great and full importance in their lives that they could not mock and could not put away to contemplate on some other day.

As I think about those things of which I cannot jest, I've tried to simplify through my life. I think when I was a young man I was much in pursuit of philosophy and meaning and a vision of the world as it is truly related, and probably somewhere along the way, when I moved out of that theoretical realm, I came to realize that no such complete vision is vouchsafed to men and women in their lifetimes; that if there is a great unity out there in this universe, that we apprehend it only by very subjective means, and that I would never see it in any concretized fashion. Therefore one must do the best one can, and I think that with the passage of time that you learn that love has meaning, and part of the meaning is that you work to preserve it and work to earn it and to deserve it. And I believe that the fellow that wakes up in the morning and is not struck by some sense of wonderment at the world that he sees, whether it be reflected in the eyes of his family or in nature itself, is all through. He then becomes an automaton, a person not much elevated from these admirable animals we see in the air and on the ground and in the seas.

So I don't know that I believe much, anymore, in anything except old saws . . . old clichés. And yet, if you think on those things that have been around for so many years in this culture, you understand why they became clichés. Having said this, I would not have you think that I'm one of those people who are resigned to his fate, who plods through life with head down and one foot following the other on some unplanned trek. I wouldn't want to be seen that way, or to have anyone be seen that way. All I am saying is that there are smaller visions in the world, and perhaps mine is one of those.

I pursued elusive things for a long time and talked to men who had vision and sight, but in the end they were not much different from other men I've known, and I lost confidence in their vision. So I think it is necessary for us to hammer out, however modest, our own vision, our own simple wisdom, and maybe wisdom itself is not all so complex as we admirers of it believe. Maybe it's simply that thing you have left over after you've forgotten everything that you learned in school and in the books. I'm not sure what it is. Maybe in the nooks and the crannies of living you find wisdom gathered there like dust?

Home on the Range

Sue Knode

My best training, and I know God has reasons, has been to be a ranch wife. I cook. I mean, hey, I can make the best pie you ever had. And I sew. I make a lot of my own clothes, and I know how to can. I can put in a garden, deliver a baby calf, bring the cows in, milk a cow. That was my best training. That's what my parents prepared me for all my life. That's what I want to do; I want to be a ranch wife somewhere and have some cows and horses and a cow-boy.

We met at the National Western Stock Show and Rodeo in Denver, Colorado, where she serves as the publicity director for the rodeo. She's twenty-six.

My parents have very, very strong values, and my mother is a very religious person. I was raised in an American missionary fellowship Sunday school. We were so far from town that it wasn't always easy to get to church, so we had this circuit-riding preacher who came about once a month and had services for us and Bible studies and everything that my mother and dad participated in. My family was very close, and as far as what's right and wrong, you know, everything was Bible-based.

I still believe in the Bible, but things aren't always as cut-and-dried for me as when I was living twenty-five miles from town; you know, without the outside influences. I was very isolated growing up. When I was in high school, I got out and traveled with the band and with FFA* and 4-H and that stuff, but it's never the same, because you're always with a group. Then when you get out on your own and you find out what life's really about, you realize that it's not as sequestered as what you saw at home. I mean, our closest neighbor was two and a half miles away; we used an eight-party telephone line; got our mail three times a week. I didn't date in high school, except for this one guy from Eaton. We figured out one night that he had to drive 150 miles just to take me out. I was, like, geographically undesirable. *(Laughs.)*

Now that I'm on the road so much, I pray a lot and ask for

---

* Future Farmers of America

guidance. But God doesn't have as important a role in my life as my parents would want. Like, for instance, the dance that I'm putting on at the Clarion.* Mother asked me, "Are you sure you want to do that?" I said, "Yes, 'cause there's a need for it. The cowboys don't have a central place to socialize and get together and have a good time and there's a real need for it here in Denver." But Mom said, "I know I couldn't do that, because there will be drinking there and carousing and all these things." I said, "Well, I'm not having anything to do with the bar, Mom." My mother, she's kind of a self-righteous woman. I love her to death. But, you know, that's my way of life. I'm a rodeo girl now. It's hard for me not to be a part of it.

I don't read my Bible like I used to, but I have my own relationship with God. And I do believe that God sent his son Christ and he died on the cross. I mean, I'm a Born-Again Christian. I used to read my Bible every day, and I don't do that anymore. But I feel like my God is a loving and a caring God and he understands why I do the things I do. And, you know, if you read the Bible and if you look at things, then you know that's the way it is. That doesn't mean I'm not a sinner. It doesn't mean that the things that I do are right, but I feel like he understands why I do them.

I feel real confident that God created everything. There's no other explanation as far as I'm concerned. It's like, faith can move a mountain. I mean they have scientific explanations and everything, but most of them are more humorous than they are realistic, as far as I'm concerned. I don't ever question very much like that. Like, I'll go to the mountains and it's just: Isn't this wonderful what God created? And when you see clouds in the sky when you're flying, like when I'm flying to Albuquerque to make a bid on a rodeo, that flying over those clouds, it just puts you in touch with reality. It makes you realize that you are just one little human being. You are only human. You know, sometimes we get to feeling like we're invincible. The guys do this. They get on a hot streak and they start winning, winning, winning, and then all of a sudden it's gone just like that. It just blows them apart. But things just come along to remind us that no matter how well we do, we are only human. God can pull the props out from under us anytime.

I try to go to the mountains about every time I'm home. I love the mountains. I miss them when I'm gone. It's been really neat for me to be able to ride my mare, Mindy, at home. I can ride to the top of the hill and see Longs Peak, you know. I can see the mountains,

---

* A hotel in Denver where she organized a nightly dance for rodeo and stock show participants.

and that's always been neat. It just makes you feel good about being alive. That's a part of God's creation. And I know this sounds crazy, but I talk to Mindy. I'll say, "Well, Mindy, what do you think about this? Isn't this pretty?" Mindy doesn't answer me, but it helps me work out my problems, makes me sort things out and get my head together.

But I'm exposed to a lot of evil too. Not like maybe city people my age are, but I see a lot of things going on that I know shouldn't happen. Oh, golly, I shouldn't be saying this, but a few of these cowboys are pretty sleazy; I mean, we're talking real sleazy. There's this one I worked with in Texas and he's the worst; he's the worst. I don't know how many times he's tried to get me to go home with him. And of course I don't mix business with pleasure at all. I never date anybody that I'm working with. But this guy, I told him, "I don't have to be with you. Why don't you be by yourself?" He said, "No. Man, we've got to get lucky tonight." I said, "No, no we don't. I like myself. I take pride in myself."

But Satan, he'll get you when you're down. I have this other friend and he was with this girl this week, and she was just a real wench. I said to him, "You're better than that." He hadn't had a good week. He said, "This is what I deserve. I don't deserve to be with anybody." I said, "Oh, you know, that's not right." But, you know, when you're feeling bad about yourself, that's when he'll come in and throw more at you ... so you have to be on guard all the time.

J. W. Vanderpool

DOWN ALONG THE CIMARRON

I was born in Beaver, Oklahoma, '42, May the thirteenth. My folks lived in a dugout similar to this one when I was born. It was just about four miles south of the Cimarron River down there, barely into Oklahoma. My dad and all his brothers, when they were just young boys, well, they used to wrangle mustangs out there around Las Animas. Track 'em, break 'em, bring 'em to Dodge City, and sell 'em for saddle horses. (*Laughs.*) But then they moved to down here about sixteen miles south of Meade, and my granddad bought some land down there and build 'im a house. And then he went into registered Appaloosa and registered horned Hereford and raised them for years. So I come from a long line of cowboys.

If you drop south about twenty miles from Dodge City, Kansas, on Route 283, hang a right on Route 54, drive west twenty miles to Meade, and then head south two miles on farm road 23, you're getting pretty close to his place. But you still have to turn right at the sign for the state park and, as he puts it, "go along apiece until you see a big ole sign with a cowboy painted on it sayin', 'Howdy.' Then ya go left on that dirt road 'bout three miles and you'll see my place up on a hill. The house is built into the hill, so just look for the front door."

My wife figures I should have been born a hunderd years ago, 'cause life was much simpler then. That's the reason I enjoy bein' out here. We lived in Denver, and we lived close to Chicago, and, boy, you get in the fast lane and it's hard to get out. And you get out here (we're sixteen miles from the nearest town), and you can stand in a pasture and not hear anything. But if you hear anything, it's gonna be an animal, you know, or a bird. Just being close to nature like that is godliness to me. I mean, it's like a religion, you know.

We raise all kinds of animals. I love animals. I don't know how to explain a philosophy out of it, but I like to be around animals . . . odd animals, you know, or any kinda animals. And to be able to make a livin' from raisin' animals is what I think I'm meant for outa life. *(Laughs.)* We've had bobcats, ferrets, and coons (we raised coons for a while), and of course all this time we always did have cattle. Right now I've got about a hundred and fifty head of cows, got two head of buffalo with calf, and I've got exotic bulls . . . and two big ol' ostriches.

Mostly the women are the churchgoers around here; the men, I don't know whether they're just too busy or what, but they're just not real strongly religious. I've been a Lutheran ever since I was born, and I'm still a Lutheran. We go to church nearly every Sunday, and while I'd say I'm a religious man, I believe in wildlife mostly. God's creatures. The main objective that I have for living, really, is to be with wildlife. Animals look at things the way they are. I mean, they're always forgiving. And if you have a friend that's an animal, it's a friend from now on, you know, unless you mistreat it some way or another. And a lot of times people are so different about that. I mean, you can think you have a friend in people, and you don't really. They're deceiving a lot of times, you know, where, with

animals, they don't ever do that. I mean, a lot of times you'll have animals that will kick you, you know, but they usually kick you because they have a reason. They don't just kick you for the heck of it. *(Laughs.)* If you're botherin' 'em, most of the time they'll warn ya.

I believe in being good to your neighbor, practicin' the Golden Rule. When someone has some problems, I'll give 'em a helping hand, treat 'em like any other Christian would, you know. Treat others as you'd have them treat you . . . that goes for everything. And the animals are the same way. You know, they'll treat you exactly the way you treat them. I've got a Brahman bull out here, and if I go out there with a ball bat and beat on 'im, why, I couldn't get in the corral with 'im; he'd either put me out or he'd kill me—one or the other, you know. But I've got 'im to where I can scratch him anywhere. If he's down there on the bottom of the farm, I'll holler at 'im and he'll come to me, and I'll scratch 'im all over, you know. Just a big ol' puppy dog, but, boy, if you'd mistreat 'im or somethin', well, he'd treat you the same way you'd treated him.

(He smiles.) I guess my philosophy isn't very complicated. Would ya mind if I told you a little story?

There used to be a lobo wolf who run up and down Crooked Creek and then up and down the Cimarron. This was a long time ago. And all the ranchers around got together and got a bounty up for 'im, because he'd kill a doggone steer about every hunderd miles he'd go. He usually had at least one female with him, maybe two wolves, and they'd kill a steer about every hunderd miles, eat it, then they'd go on for another hunderd. So the ranchers around got up a bounty for 'im, and they were gonna give a thousand-dollar bounty to whoever killed 'im. Well, that'd been like two hundred, three hundred thousand now, you know. People was workin' for a dollar a day.

Well, this one ol' colored boy, Peatfish, used to live right up the creek here, I think about three or four miles. And Peatfish decided he was gonna get that bounty, you know. Doggone everybody laughed at 'im, 'cause he was a minority; colored, you know, and everything. But he was a regular ol' dirt farmer and cowboy, had cows and everything, you know. Still, they all thought that was a pretty good joke that he was gonna try to get that wolf. Anyway Peatfish fell in behind that wolf and was trackin' it, and he hired another kid to keep 'im with fresh mounts. I think he was about two to three weeks on the trail of that wolf before he ever got 'im, but he did get the wolf. He killed it and brought it back, and my stepfather lived right here, and he said that when he killed the wolf, it was down south here somewhere, and he brought it by here, and, heck, he was stoppin' everywhere and showin' everybody what he had done, you know. And, heck, he was right in his own neighborhood. The ol' boy had it in a buckboard, you know, and he said that was the biggest animal that he'd ever seen. *(Laughs.)*

But anyway he took it up to Meade and collected the thousand-dollar reward. They asked him what his theory was and how he managed to get that thing, and he said, "Well, one man with his mind made up is a majority." *(Laughs.)* "All you have to do is make up your mind, and then everything you do pointed in that direction is

pointed in the right direction. Sooner or later you'll accomplish what
it is ya set out to do."

That philosophy is about the way I look at things, I think. Ol'
Peatfish really had it. One man with his mind made up and persistence (you've got to have persistence), is a majority. That's almost
my philosophy. If you pursue something long enough, work at it
hard enough, you'll accomplish it.

[ ]

Red Moore

KEEP IT TO YOURSELF

*We're slouching back in huge red leather reclining chairs in his study at
the Red Moore Bar M Ranch in Belton, Texas, just south of Fort Worth.
His brass spittoon sits on the floor to the left of his chair and he uses it
often. He says there are two things he always prays for: "That God don't
ever let me get to where I can't ride my damn horse and go dancin'."*

There's two people in one body with me, don't ya know. One
side of me, one part of me, is tender, gentle, understandin'.
That's the Irish side of me. The other side is as mean as hell, don't
ya know. I call the gentle me little Arty and the ornery me big Arty.
I let little Arty try to run the damn deal as long as he can. But when
he gets in trouble, big Arty takes over and says, "You little son of
a bitch, get the hell out of the way." Big Arty likes to fight. I don't
like to bring 'em on, but I love somebody else to start it and I love
to finish it, see. And don't misunderstand me, I've had the hell beat
out of me a thousand times to every time I won, don't ya know.
(Spits.) I've had the hell stomped out of me, but the guy that stomped
it out had to do it every time he hit me, don't ya know. *(Laughs.)*

I've been through everything. You couldn't understand me unless you reviewed my life, see, and known what I've been through.
God has pulled me out of the shadow of death a jillion times. I've
been through a little of everything. I've been broke up. Look at this
here. *(He points to his left ear.)* That whole side of my head was kicked
off by a horse, don't ya know. And I wasn't supposed ta get well,

but then one of these, what do you call 'em, yeah, plastic surgeons, well, they fixed me all up there. I finally developed a cancer in there, ya know. They finally got that out. It was a cluster of 'em. I've been through everything. It would take you, to git my life and really understand me, it would take you weeks and months.

Understand, I don't belong to any denomination of religion. And if there's any that I lean toward, it's Catholics. And that comes, I guess, from inheritance prob'ly, because my people mostly . . . traditionally the Irish are Catholic people. I'm not talkin' 'bout all of them. But you know what I mean; you can find more Irish Catholics than you will any other denomination. *(Spits.)*

There's other reasons that I lean toward Catholics. They're more liberal. What I like about 'em is if you go to a wedding at a Catholic church, which I've been to a few, when the wedding's over, chances are they'll have a big keg of beer in the back and maybe let 'em dance and one thing or another. Now, the Baptists—my wife was a dyed-in-the-wool Baptist—they drink more than any other people that I know of as a whole, and you may be one, but I'm just tellin' you how I feel. They drink more but they keep it hid, see. And they try to keep the country dry and everythin'. You know, they don't want any horse racin'. They don't want anythaing. And yet they go to the horse races and drink more than any other people I know. I don't like people who pretend to be one thing and is somethin' else, don't ya know. I'm what I am. I never try to be anything but myself.

I hate like the devil to tell you these things, 'cause as long as I keep my beliefs to myself, I ain't hurtin' anybody but myself. *(Laughs.)* If this thing ever gets published, which I doubt it will, I might influence somebody else to think along the same lines as me. And I might be wrong. I don't want to influence other people, don't you see. A smart man may not buy it, but then some stupid ass is liable to fall for it, see. *(Laughs.)*

Tell you one thing. The most egotistical thing a human bein' ever conceived of, in my estimation, is that he claims to be made in the image of God. That's a bunch of bull far as I'm concerned. That's the most egotistical thing. It irritates the hell out of me. God is everywhere. God is right here. He's everywhere. He's all over. He's everythin'. I don't know what he's like. There's something there, a brain or somethin', that created this thing. And how it started and when he started what I have no way of knowin'. You can go to thinkin' of outer space. Where is the end? Where is the end? It'll drive ya nuts. You've got to come back, 'cause a human mind can just go so far.

I think this, though. That in my estimation there has to be, science has proven to me there has to be, other planets and other worlds. Do you folla' me? I mean it's too well planned. Everything is planned. I don't have to take anythin' on faith, because I see how even the trees are multiplying. How the pollen's carried from one to the other and the animals and so forth. But here I go again tellin' you what I think, which I hesitate to do. I prayed since you talked to me on the phone. I asked God not to let me say anything that would hurt somebody else or to say anything that he wouldn't want me to say. Folla me? Let him put the words in my mouth.

I can't figure but one thing, don't ya know. I believe this: that if you do somethin' good, if you want the applause of the people and everythaing, go tell about it. But if you want God's pat on the head, if you want somethin' special from God, keep it to yourself. Never let nobody find out. And I'll give you an example that happened to me.

I got a one-cent postcard from the wife of a guy who worked for me at the highway department many years ago, back in the forties. Springer was his name; Smitty Springer's what we called him. He had a wife and several children. Mrs. Springer told me that Smitty had left her and that she had developed cancer somewhere in her female organs. She could be cured, but she didn't have the money, and they wouldn't operate on her because she couldn't raise it. She asked me if there was anything I could do. Nobody would help her. The hospital refused to operate on her. So there she was, gonna die. They told her she was gonna die. But she could be cured if she'd have this operation.

So I gets in my damn car, and I was on crutches then, but I could hobble around. I come down the highway line, and everywhere I stopped, I stopped with these employees and everythin', and I gathered up money for her. They all knew about Springer and everythin' and I told them the story. I said I'm broke. I've been in the hospital myself for over a year. Then I've been at home in bed for six months.

I gathered up the money. Maybe fifty cents here, fifty cents there—money was money back in those days. It takes ten dollars now to buy what one dollar bill would buy then. So I gathered up the money, fifty cents here, two bits there, a dollar here, and I guess maybe a dollar and a half was maybe the biggest I got from anybody. 'Course they wasn't makin' but forty, fifty dollars a month back then. Fifty cents was big money. I come through here, and I got more here because that's where he worked. This district here. But I come through all the other districts. The Fort Worth district and the Waco district and all that. And I gathered up the money. And I got about half of it. And I didn't have nothin' myself. I was goin' on credit and one thing or another. I was broke flat.

I went into the damn office of the head honcho at the hospital. He was a big damn redheaded Irishman himself. He wasn't the doctor or nothin' like that. He was the big boss, the administrator. He was the one that wouldn't let her have the operation. The doctors were willin' to do the job, but he wouldn't accept her bein' in the hospital.

So I went in and parked my crutches and got an appointment with him. And I went in and I set down and I talked to him. He wasn't no way gonna help this lady, by God he had to have the money. And I gave him the story, and I told him how I'd accumulated this money and how much I had. *(Spits.)* We'll say I had a thousand dollars or seven hundred and fifty, or whatever. I had about half of what they said it had to be. "Hell no," he said. And I told him, "Goddamn it ta hell. You can stomp hell out of me, you big bastard you, but I said that woman's gonna be operated on if I have to get a goddamn gun and hold you up while they do the damn job. And you gonna see it." And I told him the whole damn story again!

"By God," finally he turned and said, "I want to tell you one damn thing. By God, this hospital has got just as much goddamn sympathy as you, and they can match your goddamn generosity and all the things you've done. We've got just as big a heart in this as you have. Have the woman in here, by God. We'll get the job done."

So I paid him the damn money, he gave me a receipt for the whole damn thing. Had her over there. So we got her in there. So far as I know, she's still livin' today. That's been years ago. Her kids grew up, she raised them up.

I had the greatest feelin'. There's no way to describe it. But God . . . I just felt his presence. It just seemed like he wrapped me in a mantle or somethin'. Words won't describe how I felt. I had the greatest feelin' I ever had in all of my life. Of anythin' I've ever done in my life, that gave me the greatest feelin' I've ever had. And I've done a lot of things.

Anyway I went and told one of my best friends about it. And you know what? The minute I told him, that craziest wonderful feeling left me. And then I got all these applause from all over the highway department. "Oh, God Almighty, what Red did. Red saved that little woman's life." And all this just made me sick. My friend was tellin' everybody, and every time he told it I just got sick to my belly.

In other words I got the applause of the people and lost the pat on the head by God. That's my belief. If you do a thing, if you do it for the applause of the people, if that's what you want, okay. But forget God. But if you want to have that craziest wonderful feeling that comes from having God with ya, keep it to yourself.

Fred Sherman

ON THE HORNY HANDS OF TOIL

Turon, Kansas, population 450. A retired farmer and grain elevator op-erator, he's been "married for sixty-one years, had two daughters, and now I've got seven grandchildren and twelve great-grandchildren."

I don't take the *Wichita Eagle Beacon*, whatever, but some way or other I got ahold of one one day (that'd be over thirty-six years ago), and they had what they call a "Hometown Page," and it was just different things that they put in there that various general people wrote. And there was this little poem in there by a man named James M. Cowan that I really liked, and it kinda states my beliefs. I liked it so much that I got it printed up on a card. I got five hundred printed, you know, just fer to give people, just fer a hobby. And that's over thirty-six years ago, and since then I kept gettin' 'em, and so finally anymore I get a thousand printed up at a time. I'll give people two or three of 'em, in case they might wanta give one to someone else. I have traveled to the West Coast, prob'ly four times, and sometimes on bus, sometimes in car, and a few times I've come back on airplane. And I just give 'em to waitresses and anybody I meet up with.

I'm gonna read it off to you. The title of this is, "Work Is Man's Greatest Function":

> He is nothing, he can do nothing, he can achieve nothing,
> fulfill nothing, without working.
> If you are poor—work. If you are rich, continue working.
> If you are burdened with seemingly unfair responsibilities—
> work.
> If you are happy, keep right on working. Idleness gives room
> for doubts and fears.
> If disappointments come—work. If your health is
> threatened—work.
> When faith falters—work. When dreams are shattered and
> hope seems dead—work.
> Work as if your life were in peril. It really is.
> No matter what ails you—work. Work faithfully, work with
> faith.
> Work is the greatest remedy available for both mental and
> physical afflictions.

I had never read anything like that in my life, and I believe every word of it; you know, I believe every word of it if you apply it. I have to apply it to my own life. Why do I have to apply it to my own life? I guess I believe in work. I don't know I believe in work-aholics or not, but I think that's one of the things that they need, right now, in this United States. So many people are tryin' to enjoy theirself, you know, just through everything you can imagine, instead of working. I really think that goin' back farther in the history of the United States, work was more popular than 'tis right now. It seems like all the things I see, mostly, on television, and just lookin' at the world, you know, people're pretty well materialistic-minded anymore, to my notion, than they used to be.

I've heard this way back: If you wanna know human nature, read the Bible. That's not just the New Testament, but go back even in the Old Testament. And you can find greed and ever'thing that you have in the world today, and you'll find examples of it. And I don't know as I believe, you know, in just keepin' your nose in the Bible all the time, or that, but I believe in the principles it teaches. And I think that's one of 'em right there—work. I'm just eighty-four years old last Thursday, you know. *(He springs from his couch, seats himself at his upright piano, and bangs out a ragtime tune.)*

Book Three

True Believers

PART I: GOD

Speculations over God and the World are almost always idle, the thoughts of idlers, spectators of the theater of life.

—*Eugen Rosenstock-Huessy*

F. Bringle McIntosh

AT NINETY-TWO

It's 4:00 P.M. on a hot summer day and we're at his apartment at 115 West Seventy-third Street in New York City. I'd earlier asked if I could come over at noon, but he explained that, "a little later would be better for me, young man. In the early afternoon I like to work out at Jack LaLanne's."

He has been a schoolteacher, a Methodist minister, and for seventeen years served as president of Ohio Northern University. He is widowed.

First of all, I believe very definitely in a personal God. I don't mean by that the kind of personal God that some people think about. The God that I believe in is the God that is great enough to be interested in me and in you and in all humanity, but also great enough to have created the universe and the multiverse and to operate the universe in which we're living today. He is great enough to do that, but he is also interested enough in me personally and you personally to help me direct my life and you direct your life. Now, that combination of greatness, well, I call it the combination of the telescope and the microscope. In other words the smallest atom is a part of the work of the hand of God, and the greatest planet, galaxies, systems of galaxies, nature, and the universe is also

a part of the work of the Eternal. That I believe with all my heart. Never doubted it. Never doubted it. No sir, that's been with me straight through from the beginning. And it's firmer today than it ever has been before.

The greatest proof of the existence of God is as I look into the face of humanity, and look into the galaxies, stars at night, the beauty of the earth, and the rolling waters of the sea and have some little understanding—some very little understanding—of what it's all about. It's then that my belief in the kind of a God that's big enough to run the universe and small enough to know about me is so tremendously important.

I believe I've been placed here to live in the world as it is and to try to transform as much of it as I can. And I try to live well with what I cannot transform. Therefore if my plane goes down tomorrow, I go down in contentment. I mean, it's a part of life. It's a part of the system.

We have a little old lady here in the house, a little Jewish lady. And she's a lovely little old lady, but she's terribly upset about old age and the sufferings of old age. I met her in the elevator the other day and I said, "How are you Mrs. Juliper?" And she had a string of complaints that long. *(He stretches out his hands from side to side.)* She said, "Oh, old age is something terrible, it's something terrible, I tell you, Mr. McIntosh, it's terrible. Who wants to die?" The point I'm making here is that we're not going to eliminate death and suffering and all the ills of society. We're gonna have to learn to live with them and do our very best to eliminate any that we can. And we're doing that by discovering how to handle germs and disease. Our doctors and our hospitals and our educators are all banded together to try to work out some kind of a system for the human family where people don't suffer too much, but suffer enough to keep them humble and to keep them dependent upon the powers that be. I suppose that's my answer to the so-called problem of evil.

I serve God in my daily rounds by finding as many needy people as I can find that I can help. I don't stop and chat with people on the street, because I don't know who they are, but if I find a person that's in need and if I can do something about it, then that's the person I spend my time with. And I find those people quite regularly, quite regularly. Over at my church on Park Avenue and Sixtieth Street we feed about two hundred people a week. And I helped to initiate that program and helped to support it and I work with those people. And once in a while we'll find a fellow we can do something for, somebody in there that's really capable of coming up out of it. I remember I ran into a fellow the other day sitting at the end of the table and I said, "What's that book you have there?" He turned it over, and it was some very, very erudite edition, I don't remember the title. I said, "Are you a reader?" He said, "I sure am. I read all the time and I read good books." I said, "Boy, keep at it. One of these days you'll be able to pull yourself out of this situation in which you find yourself here." He said, "Thank you very much, thank you very much." And he went on his way.

Now, it's things like that where I help. But I think we help most the people that we know, the people that we're acquainted with. The influence of our lives on people that know us is rather tremendous. You don't realize it until you get to be ninety years of age. (Laughs.) But they are tremendously important. I've had so much to do with students who come to the university and who get into trouble and into the dumps. And I get them up and pull them out and straighten them out if I possibly can. I remember one young fellow came to Ohio Northern University to be a pharmacist. And the first year that he was there he began to turn in flunks. The dean had him in but couldn't do anything with him, and it finally got to my desk. This young man came in and sat down across from me. And I said, "John, you want to be a pharmacist, you really do?" "Yes," he said, "I do." "Well," I said, "I wouldn't trust you around the corner as my pharmacist, because I'd be afraid that you'd give me a prescription that would poison me." He looked at me kinda shocked, you know. And then he began to grin, and we both laughed. He went out, picked up his grades, went through the university, got his degree, and is today a good citizen. Now, that's the kind of thing I'm talking about. You can't do everything, but you can do what you can do.

Yes, I'm pretty sure of my beliefs. I'm still a Methodist. But I don't bind myself to the Methodists. I believe a lot of things that Episcopalians believe and I believe a lot of things that Presbyterians believe and I believe a lot of things that Christian Scientists believe. But my belief is my own. It's not my church's belief. It's my own belief. And I gather what I can from every source that I can find that's helpful and inspiring and uplifting. And that's not always easy to do.

I think the philosophy that Jesus exemplified and taught and espoused is about the best philosophy we can find anywhere in the world. I've studied other religions, as you have. And I would say that basically the things that were basic to Jesus Christ are the things that are most important in the mind of God: Love your neighbor as yourself. Love yourself. Be honest. Be straightforward.

My father used to say, "Son, your word should be as good as your bond." As I see society today, your bond and your word are both goin' down the drain. I think we're in bad trouble right now, in the midst of a spiritual decline. And I'm distressed by it, because there are a lot of good men that have been brought up wrong. And they're out of some of our best colleges too. You get the impression that we have raised a generation of young executives that say to themselves that it's all right to do it if you can do it and not get caught. And that's bad. That's very bad. It's amazing how many leaders of society today just take that attitude: "If I can get by with it, I'll do what I please." No principles on which to build their experience at all.

That's it in a nutshell. (*Laughs.*) I say be yourself, be yourself, be sure that yourself is a good self, a self that you can respect, a self you can be proud of. Love God with all your mind and heart and soul and love your neighbors in spite of their weaknesses. Love your family and your loved ones. And that's the important thing in life. Love is the center of everything that really counts in this world.

I go to bed at night and I say to myself, If I don't wake up in the morning, why, it's all right with me. It's all right with me. Because I believe very definitely that the spirit is beyond the physical body. I believe that when a person dies, the spirit passes on eternally. Just how I don't know, just where I don't know. And I don't care really. I know that whatever happens to me tomorrow morning, if I were to die, I'd be in the hands of a God that understands me and cares for me. And I leave it right there.

Michelle Janis

THE MESSIAH HAS COME

I grew up in Chicago suburbs, the North Shore area. It's a nice area of Chicago . . . a lot of Jewish people. Where I grew up, it was predominantly Jewish, and on the high holy days we'd all be out of school. Everyone in my family, as far as we know, was one hundred percent Jewish background. And on my dad's side, seven generations before his great-grandfather were all orthodox rabbis. My great-grandfather said, "Enough of this poverty," became an agnostic, and decided to go back and become a doctor. And from that time on, most of my family went away from God and totally into the arts and professionalism. But, you know, we always had the holy days. We were reform, but we went to a conservative temple when I was growing up. And I went from the time I was little, till I was eleven. And so those first eleven years of my life everything was Jewish, and everyone around us was Jewish.

Virginia Beach, Virginia. A tall, bosomy, bubbly young woman, she's a senior researcher for Pat Robertson's 700 Club. "The Lord has called me to the Jewish people. My heart's desire is that every Jew would know him. The Scriptures say in Romans 11 that the remnant will come in, and I'm part of that remnant. In my job I interview all the Jewish people who have come to know the Lord. And people are gettin' saved left and right because they're seeking. God's put that seeking in all human beings, but, I believe, especially in the Jewish people, because our role was to be those who went out to the rest of the world and spoke of the one and only Living God."

I really didn't think very seriously about God and religion until I went to college. I went to the University of Illinois in Champaign-Urbana, and I decided to pledge a sorority, which I never thought I would do. Actually I never saw any house except one. I went through informal rush at the end of freshman year. What I didn't know was that half the girls in this house were Born-Again Christians. I was the only Jewish person!

Within that first month one of the girls I got to be friends with handed me a Bible, and it was kind of like the easy, everyday-language version. In the front it would say, "When you're feeling sad, look here. When you're feeling lonely, look here," or whatever. So she gave it to me, and she said, "Michelle, I know you're Jewish, but at least find out what you believe in." I'd never looked at a Bible in my life (except learning the Sunday school stories out of a Bible), so I took it, and that was about it. Toward the end of that year, though, I kept ending up having all these great friends who were these Born-Again Christians. And they had such a peace and a joy over them, I couldn't believe it. I was getting jealous of that. I just saw this peace and joy over these people, and I wanted it, but I did not want Jesus. Well, what happened as time went on was that some-body started a Bible study and I'd go and listen, but when they'd talk about Jesus, I'd just kind of ignore it. And my sorority sisters really pushed at me. And I'd tell 'em, "Don't you preach at me, I don't want to hear this." You know, I'd go to Bible study as a favor, but I was obnoxious and rude about it. But there was also that search-ing inside, 'cause I always wanted to know what is Truth.

By my junior year I just felt like my life was going in circles. I never really was a drug addict, I didn't have a wild life-style, sort of sleeping around or any of that, but inside I was really empty. Partying wasn't doing it for me, relationships weren't doing it for me, good grades and success and that sort of thing was not doing it for me. And I just knew there hadda be more. I was searching for that void to be filled. I wanted to know what Truth was, and what is my purpose here on earth. I couldn't believe that I just popped in for seventy or eighty years and was going nowhere. And I didn't remember anybody ever teaching me anything from Judaism about heaven . . . was there heaven? Was there hell? I wasn't afraid of hell, but I really wanted the assurance that I'd go to heaven, and I did have a fear of death. Meanwhile I'd seen all this peace and comfort that my friends had. I really felt the love, and even though Jesus was the last person I was seeking for, I said, "God, if he's really your Son . . ." And I remember walking down the street saying this in a very obnoxious tone: "God, if he's your Son, prove it to me." And that was it. All of a sudden I was put in touch with what I call divine appointments. I mean, I felt that spirit of the Lord.

So I went to see this pastor at a Bible church. And he put me in touch with another Jewish person who had received the Lord. And she handed me a list of Scriptures pointing out Old Testament prophecies. And I took that sheet of paper and started studying it for the next five months. But I was very fearful, because I believed in the Old Testament God, who zapped all those people off, all those Sunday school stories, you know, that he would kill me if I was wrong. But instead of being killed, I had a supernatural experience. Immediately I felt the presence of the Holy Spirit go through me, this massive warmth from the top of my head to the tips of my toes. And simultaneously I saw the throne of God, and I saw Christ at the right hand of the Father. And I didn't know at that time that the Scripture says that he is at the right hand of the Father. I knew that I knew that this was Truth. And I was on a spiritual high for the next three days.

All this happened ten days before I had to go back to live with my parents to student-teach. And I got a Bible in the mail on my birthday, which was in November, and (laughs) my mom was there when I opened this up, and she said, "What is this?" You know, "Old Testament or New Testament?" And I told her I'd received Jesus as my Savior. And (laughs) she had a fit . . . to say the least. You know, the old Jewish guilt trip: "Where did I fail?" (She imitates mother's distressed voice.) My dad thought I was just going through a phase until after about a year. Then he said, "Enough of this already, change to something else." I said, "No, this isn't a temporary situation."

Six and a half years later my mom went to Israel with me. I was going for a Christian Charismatic conference, and she just wanted to see Israel. Before she was married, she'd been a Zionist. *(Laughs.)* So she came along. And after we got back, four months later, she called me up and said, "You don't have to pray for me anymore, I really believe Jesus is the Son of God, and, you know, I've asked him to come in and take charge of my life too." And then my brother did two months after her, and then my sister five months after that. My dad is coming still. It's been thirteen years now, but God just transformed my family.

So I believe that Jesus is the Messiah for the Jewish people. I know that I know. And probably in your interviews, if you talk to other Messianic Jews, all of us will say the same thing: that we know that we know we are saved. We know that Jesus is the Son of God and that the Holy Spirit came to live inside of us, and we know that when we die, we will spend eternity in heaven. There's no ifs, ands, or buts about it.

Dr. John Collins Harvey

As a boy I always wanted to be a physician, and I've been a physician for a long time now, and I view the activity as a mission, that I am doing God's work on earth. I've always thought that one could and should give witness to the kingdom of Jesus and to his tremendous actions in human history. I think that all of us in the lay state have as much of a vocation as anyone in holy orders. And I've always viewed being a physician as a witness to Jesus' love, because we are commissioned to extend care to individuals. I've always tried to do that and I'm fairly satisfied that I have done that. I hope that when I stand before God at the Judgment at my death that God (whether it be he or she) will recognize that I've tried to do my best, although I know I've failed many times.

Georgetown University Hospital, Washington, D.C. A longtime professor of medicine at the Georgetown University Hospital, specializing in geriatrics, he's a pudgy, white-haired, round- and red-faced Irish gentleman. The walls of his office are covered with degrees, awards, and black-and-white pictures of himself in the company of the many popes he has met. "Over there is a picture of Pope Pius XII, and Pope Paul VII, and Pope John Paul II. At home I have a picture of Pope John XXIII. So I've met and had an opportunity to speak with all the popes who have reigned during my lifetime except two: Pius XI, who served when I was a little boy, and John Paul I, who lived only a month after his election." He's sixty-four.

One of the things in my medical work that has always interested me is the relationship of ethics and religion with medical practice. When we began to develop the very high technology in medicine (and by this I mean intravenous feeding, intravenous alimentation, artificial respiration out of the iron lung, heart revival, etcetera), it seemed to me that we were losing some of our humanity, losing the human touch. And I remember back in 1965 or '66 talking to some medical students about a difficult case we had. We had one person whose heart had been revived when it stopped. The individual had had a stroke and was in what we now call "the permanent vegetative state," in which the cerebral cortex was dead and only the base of the brain, the medulla, was left, which maintains respiration and heartbeat automatically (those functions that carry on by themselves), so that we could say that that person was still human but did not have the neurological substrate to express his own personhood.

I can remember talking to the students and saying, "I think we were wrong, when this individual's heart stopped, to revive him." And one of the students said to me, "Are you talking about euthanasia?" And I thought, Oh, my God, if that's what the students think I said, I'm in a lot of trouble. I tried to explain that I believe there is a normal time to die and that the primary purpose of life is not continued biological life but rather life with God, hereafter, in glory. So I said, "No, I'm very opposed to euthanasia. We don't have the right to take anyone's life. Euthanasia is a grievous sin, it's murder." And I was telling this to the students, and they said, "Well, we don't understand what you're saying." Right then and there I thought, Well, you know, I've got to learn, really learn, about theology so I can talk to the theologians. Because they don't talk medical talk, and doctors don't talk theology. So I determined then to go ahead and study theology in Baltimore, at Saint Mary's Seminary, which is the oldest Roman Catholic seminary in America, founded, I believe, in 1795. Over the course of the next fifteen years I studied theology and, as a matter of fact, I just got my *(laughs)* doctorate in moral theology this past June from that seminary. That has been a very happy time for me and has opened my eyes to many interesting ideas and has led me into the whole area of bio-ethics.

I have never really felt a conflict between science and religion. I've never really ever doubted my faith. I think it's important that everyone understand that you cannot prove that the revelation that God has given to man through Jesus Christ is true. One can't prove that in a scientific way at all. One accepts it on faith, so I never argue with the scientific humanists. Nor do I feel a need to apologize or to try to prove the point. Scientific humanists will say to me, "I don't understand how you can say this is taken on faith," but that is it. I take it on faith and I believe.

We know from the mythological story in Genesis that God created man and woman. I have no doubt about that, that God created all of this out of nothing. How was it done? We have no idea. We now know from our studies in science, from reading Darwin's *Origin of Species* that we are a product of evolution. But God could have breathed life into this organism that was once a great ape; he could have breathed the soul of life to make a human in this fashion. So I don't think, as a scientist and as a man of faith, that there's any conflict in my mind at all about this. But that doesn't mean I always side with the Church. For example, the Church has come out with a statement on *in vitro* fertilization. It was issued by the Sacred Congregation for the Doctrine of the Faith in March of 1987 in answer to many questions that had been posed to the Congregation from bishops around the world on the technologies regarding birth, fertilization, etcetera. And that document is a brilliant document. But in the document it says that *in vitro* fertilization, even in marriage (what's called homologous *in vitro* fertilization) is not consistent with the laws of God. Now, I disagree with that. I think that *in vitro* fertilization within the married state is a medical treatment, and if God gave man the ability to think through and to develop certain types of treatments, God meant for us to use those. To me, this is doing God's work. I may be wrong in thinking so, but I'm pretty much convinced that God won't fault me if I am.

We all realize that we make mistakes and that we're sinners. We all have failings, and God is merciful. I've always said that I thought God was so merciful that he never would really condemn anyone to hell, no matter what that individual did. And many people have told me, "You really don't know your theology all that well," etcetera. But I still think that this is true, that God is so merciful that he would never condemn any sinner, because he loves us all so much.

All you can do is do the best you can do. Love God with all your heart and help other people—that's all you can ask of yourself.

PART II: SCIENCE

The Superstition of Science scoffs at the Superstition of Faith
—James Anthony Froude

Dr. Mark Geier

NOTHING OUT THERE BUT SCIENCE

I grew up in the Washington, D.C., metropolitan area, and I've always been interested in science, ever since I was a little boy. In elementary school I was way ahead of my class, so I was allowed to just read in the library. I read the entire library of hard science, and then I read all the science fiction. So I never took religion, or the concept of a Supreme Being and Creator, seriously. I viewed the universe as an orderly thing that you could study and control—and I still do.

Silver Springs, Maryland. He's a chubby, bespectacled man who moves about his spacious suburban home with a curious sense of unease. Formerly a professor of obstetrical genetics at Johns Hopkins University, he operates a private prenatal genetic counseling service, specializing in various forms of genetic engineering, among them sex selection and in vitro fertilization.

I've always felt that it's important to help advance man's knowledge and man's understanding and also man's compassion, to make life less painful and more enjoyable for the largest number of people. I think life is, historically, from earliest evolution forward, a struggle by living things to make things better for themselves and for their future generations. In the case of the nonthinking, or lesser-thinking creatures, they do it in ways they do not understand. In the case of man, we've evolved to the point where we can actually think about what we want to do and do it. And it's something we've been doing for a very long time.

There's an interesting misunderstanding that occurs in this field I'm in. People say, "You're gonna do genetic engineering? You're playing God, you're interfering with what was meant to be." But that's a very limited view, because mankind has always done that. That's exactly how we got where we are today. We are genetic engineers. If you look around you on this planet, there's almost nothing that we haven't genetically engineered. Currently we do the genetic engineering by interfering with DNA, with chemical tricks. Previously we had lesser technology, so we did it by selective breeding. If you look around at all our domestic animals, they don't even resemble the animals or plants from which they came. There's some plants that are so genetically engineered that we don't even know for sure what plant they came from. An example of that is corn, which was genetically engineered by the Aztecs from a wild species that is not even certainly determined. If you take corn and plant it in a field and go away for ten years, it'll all die, because it doesn't have the basic minimum requirements for survival. So it shouldn't strike anybody that now that we're doing genetic engineering, that this is a new experiment. This is a very old experiment, and it's the main experiment that has allowed us to leave the caves and control the environment on this planet to the extent that we can have large cities and support large populations and not all be farmers or gatherers or hunters.

I think the manipulation of our environment is an inherent thing that goes with our evolution. Every organism manipulates its environment. I certainly don't believe that a Supreme Being is doing it for us, because the formal, classical view of a personal Supreme Being goes contrary to what we actually see. I understand that there are those who believe in a sort of a spiritualness of the universe, and I don't have any big problem with that, but those who believe in God as, you know, a single entity that reflects the shape of mankind . . . to me they belong in the Flat Earth Society. I mean, there just isn't any evidence for that. If you look around, we're in a rather ordinary position in the universe. There is nothing so special about us. We orbit a rather nondescript sun and the earth's probably a run-of-the-mill planet. I don't see any evidence for anything out there except science. There may be other life-forms out there, and they may be superior to us, but I don't think there is one life-form that created it all.

It seems to me that the highest form of ethics is to do what's right because you think it's right. You certainly can never know what's gonna happen to what you do. All you can do is make sure that you make the best decision that you can at the moment. The caveman who invented the wheel (no one knows who it is, obviously) might be very upset to find it on B-52 bombers that might destroy, you know, humanity. But he couldn't forsee that. He did what he thought was right at the time, and I think each of us has to do what we think is right at the time. You can't anticipate the consequences of all your actions, but if you do what you feel is morally right at the time, that's the best you can do. And if you violate your own sense of moral rightness, then I don't see any way of forgiveness either.

So I think you have to live by what you think is right, and a reasonable thing to do is to try to make the world a nicer place for everybody to live in. And the best way to do that is by advancing education and knowledge. We've already advanced far beyond the point where we have the power to destroy ourselves. So it's a little late to think that if we could just keep everybody ignorant, we'd be all right. At this point the only thing to do is gain more and more knowledge and believe inherently that most people will do what's right. That's the only hope.

Dr. John Swartz

We're at the Aspen Institute for Physics, a summer retreat center where many of the world's most eminent physicists come to exchange ideas and relax in the quiet of the Rockies.

He's a professor of theoretical physics at Cal Tech. He speaks with care and precision, but his manner is easy and warm and he smiles and laughs almost constantly. He's forty-six.

My orientation is sort of a rational-positivist type. I like to start my framework of beliefs from that which I feel I can understand in a rational manner. So in trying to understand the universe and my place in it, the way I begin to think about the question is by asking what do we already know on scientific grounds? I am willing to admit that there is much that we don't know, that the fact of the existence of our solar system and the earth and life on earth and human life is an amazing miracle, but I do feel that any ideas you have about the universe and your place in it need to be consistent with an understanding of scientific laws, the laws of nature.

I feel strongly that one shouldn't have an opinion one way or the other on a subject based on preconceptions. I think you should observe the facts and, based on the evidence that you're able to accumulate, objectively reach a conclusion. I have difficulty with people who simply decree that it must be one way or another and either you believe it or there's something wrong with you, not because they have objective evidence but because somebody said or wrote that that's the way it is. So I think these issues should be settled not on the basis of authority but rather on the basis of evidence.

Take, for example, the theory that the universe is expanding. By observing different galaxies and so on, the astronomers are able to measure with some accuracy the rate at which the universe is presently expanding. So the fact that that's presently taking place is, I think, an incontrovertible fact. If you extrapolate backward this growth of the universe, you can see that at sometime between ten and twenty billion years ago it extrapolates back to a point. Now, it's clear that as you approach that point in your backward extrapolation, our understanding of physical law becomes less and less certain as you get closer to that point (*laughs*), and then we become less and less sure about what happened. As our understanding develops, we're able to push things back farther and farther. Whether we'll ever get back to the origin, we're not as clear.

Extrapolating in the other direction, you can ask what's the ultimate fate of the universe. And the big question there is, Will the expansion continue forever or will it eventually stop and recontract? And this is simply a question of whether the gravitational attraction of the matter in the universe is sufficient to overcome the expansion. If the average density of matter in the universe exceeds a certain critical value, then the expansion will reverse and there will be a subsequent contraction. And if the density is less than that critical value, the expansion will go on forever.

I think the idea of the expansion going on forever, while it may be a rather boring conclusion, is not one that's difficult to grasp. It just keeps expanding. What's so bad about that? If it were to suddenly stop, though, it wouldn't be like a Disney cartoon where it says, "The End." Obviously if it said, "The End," you would ask what happens after that. So the idea of having an end to the universe, I think, is more difficult to grasp intellectually than the idea that the expansion just goes on forever.

The beginning, the idea that there's a beginning of the universe, the naive question is, well, what was before that? And of course, if there's a beginning of the universe, the idea is that the geometry of space and time are so curved up on themselves that it becomes a meaningless question to ask what was before the beginning. There's just this space-time continuum and it's perfectly smooth and there's a point on it which is called the beginning. I don't picture it very clearly, and no one else does either. But once it's understood, we'll see that it's something that makes satisfactory sense. But at the moment it's the point at which all of our knowledge of physics breaks down. So we can't really talk about it in a very intelligent manner.

As to whether or not our futures are determined by this expansion, it's important that we behave on the presumption that they are not. (Laughs.) It's clear that if you based your behavior on the assumption the future is determined, you can use that as a rationalization for committing all sorts of atrocities and saying it was pre-ordained. So even though that may be true (chuckles), I think it's important to behave as though it's not. Certainly all our cognitive environment suggests to us that we do have control over what we do in the future. I mean, I can either choose to hit this table or not hit this table, and that was a conscious decision which I feel strongly was not preordained but something I chose to do. I mean, I feel that in my bones and I feel very strongly that you have to base your behavior on the presumption that that's the case. But still, in a certain deep sense the physical law, at least at the level of probabilities, could be deterministic.

I suppose this raises the question of good and evil, and this is a category in which I do think there are many issues about human existence, systems of values, and so on, which cannot be addressed in scientific terms. Obviously, as you can tell from my previous discussion, I try to address as much as I can from what I can understand logically. But I realize at the same time that there are many issues of human existence that cannot be addressed in those terms and I don't want to give the impression that I believe that everything should be answered in terms of the quantum mechanical wave function of the universe. (Laughs.) Certainly one needs to have some sense of moral conviction about what's right and wrong. Human society needs to be organized, have laws of behavior, and one can argue that it's the details of whether you should do this or not do that. And I think there are many issues on which rational people can disagree, like whether or not abortion should be legal. I think it should be legal, but I recognize that people have a particular opinion about that and that their opinion can be perfectly reasonable too.

Obviously all of these things are issues that thinking people grapple with, and there are no simple answers. *(Laughs.)* Being sort of a pragmatic type, I guess I take the point of view that since I'm here, I ought to try to make the most of it. And to me, making the most of it does not mean trying to have a good time—although it's nice if you do—but trying to have some impact on society and the world in which you live of a positive sort; doing something worthwhile which will have made your life of value; to set high goals for yourself and strive toward attaining them. If you set very high goals, obviously the probability of success is low; but if you don't set high goals, the probability of success is even lower. *(Chuckles.)* So the only way you can succeed at something is by trying very hard to do it. And anything that's worthwhile can only be achieved by hard work, persistence, and luck. A little luck, a little skill maybe.

I think people have to look inward at themselves and say what are my talents? What is the area in which I can make the greatest impact? Some people were born with musical talent. Obviously they should write music or perform music. Others are good with numbers, and they should do mathematics or physics. Or a good athlete will go for it. But whatever it is, I think you should set high goals and try to make your life as meaningful as you can.

I suppose I have always subscribed to the notion that you should treat people the way you would like to be treated yourself. I think that's an idea with a long-standing tradition behind it which seems to me to make a lot of sense. And I think that people of all different backgrounds and persuasions should be given an equal shot at success. And, oh, I also prefer the other-cheek philosophy. *(Chuckles.)* The problem is that all conflicts escalate, you see. It's never an eye for an eye; it's always an eye and a half for an eye. And then it keeps growing and growing, and that's the way wars get started. Now, if you turn it around and always say half an eye for an eye, then it will escalate backward, you see. So it's a question of stability.

In any event, if we don't blow ourselves up in the next thousand years in a nuclear war, we know that life will evolve and that whatever is going to be here on earth in a couple million years from now is going to be quite different than what we have today. But it will be an outgrowth of what's here. So we will have played our role in fashioning whatever that is. On a larger time scale, the earth will be destroyed by the sun in some 5 or 10 billion years from now. I don't remember the exact number. The sun will gobble up the earth, and that will be that. Of course whatever life-forms have evolved on the earth by then will probably have found ways to go somewhere else and get away from all that. So what is started here can still make a lasting mark on the universe. And I take solace from that fact.

These are issues that any person must grapple with. Why am I here? What does it mean? These aren't questions you can get any very intelligent answers to. The best you can do is say whatever reason I'm here for, I'm going to make the best of it. I feel very strongly that it's important that people's lives not simply be aimed at existing on a day-by-day basis, but that they should have some high goals and ambitions. Maybe even unrealistic ones.

Like understanding the meaning of life and the origin of the universe?
JOHN: Yeah, right. *(Laughs.)*

Dr. Frank Wilczek

THE PHYSICAL WORLD, AMONG OTHERS

I was brought up as a Catholic, although my ancestry is one-fourth Jewish. And until I was about twelve years old, I was very, very religious. I remember once walking along and promising myself that no matter what *(laughs)* happened in the future, I would not stray from the path. And I'll remember this moment forever, when I vowed not to stray. But that didn't hold up.

It was actually through reading Bertrand Russell that I began to have my doubts about the things I was being taught. It started out innocently enough when I read one of his books on mathematical philosophy. I got sucked in, became an admirer of Russell, and decided to read all of his books, including *Why I'm Not a Christian* and *Mysticism and Logic*. And once that process began, it was a process I couldn't stop. Then I began to read other scientific books to see if Russell was really telling the truth, and I became convinced that he was. It wasn't long after that before I had a very violent reaction to religion. I went from being very religious to being very antireligious quite quickly. Then I took an interest in physics and philosophy, probably because I was trying to replace the gigantic void that was left when I gave up the religion I was so attached to. By the age of thirteen I was well on my way to becoming what I am today, which is an unreligious theoretical physicist. So that's the history of my belief in a nutshell. *(Laughs.)* We can say quite a bit more about the details if you want.

The China Castle restaurant, Isla Vista, California, just off the campus of the University of California at Santa Barbara, where he holds an endowed chair in the Department of Physics at the age of thirty-five. In the international physics community he's considered one of the most promising young theoretical physicists in the world.

Attired in blue jeans and a thick red sweatshirt, he fits in well with the casual local style. He's especially happy today because he just turned in the final draft of his most recent book, Longing for the Harmonies: Themes and Variations from Modern Physics.* *Although shy by nature, he's a warm-hearted man who likes to laugh at his own jokes.*

There's a famous psychology experiment in which a frog starves to death even though it is surrounded by flies. As long as the flies don't move, you see, he doesn't know they're flies because he can't see them. What a fly means to a frog is not what we think of as a fly, but just something the right size moving at the right speed. *(Laughs.)* The frog has a very incomplete perception of reality, and I think we humans are in much the same position . . . our natural endowments don't begin to exhaust what the world is about. Even at the purely physical level the colors we see are a very small segment of the visible spectrum; in fact there's an infinity of possible colors, and we only see three averages put together, not to mention radio waves. So we have our physical limitations and, even more important, our mental limitations. We can't put together all the information. Take the fly the frog couldn't spot. We can look at a fly, but we don't know what's going on in its head *(laughs)* or how it works. So we have similar limitations to the frog. We don't think about them because we don't know what it would be like to have a different kind of consciousness, but we know enough to know that we're missing a lot. *(Laughs.)*

I have this dream that someday human beings, or some combination of human beings and external aids, will be able to appreciate much more of the world. Another dream I have, which is also partly a nightmare (I don't know quite what to make of it), is that someday there will be an explosion, an exponential development of intelligence in the universe. Human beings are just about smart enough to make machines that are smarter than themselves, and we're seeing that happen now. Those machines, very plausibly, will be smart enough to make machines that are even smarter than themselves. And so on and so on. *(Laughs.)* So maybe they will be able to have this much more complete picture of the world that I just talked

---

* New York: W. W. Norton & Company, 1987.

about. It's quite possible that, for instance, they'll design ways that will turn whole planets into giant computers.

This dream should give you a clue about one of my most strongly held beliefs, which is that we shouldn't hold back in our search for knowledge. It excites me to know that there will be forms of consciousness which we can only dimly perceive now, which will be our successors. And that we will be, in comparison to those forms of consciousness, children or monkeys, or amoebas. *(Laughs.)* I just think it would be criminal for us not to let that happen.

Despite the obvious impossibility of predicting what our advanced successors would do (I can't even begin to understand what they would be thinking about), one possibility that seems very interesting to me is that they might choose to create worlds. We do, of course, simulations of physical systems all the time on computers, and you can imagine doing simulations of very complex physical systems. You can imagine doing simulations of conscious beings, or beings that think they're conscious *(laughs)*, or act as if they're conscious but are really purely fictitious in a sense; they're in another world; they're human beings with bodies, walking around, but they'd really be patterns of electrons and silicon running around. Creating such a world strikes me as the sort of intellectual activity that superintelligences would indulge in. The really frightening question is whether we're actually in such a world now. *(Laughs.)* I don't think we are. But the only way we could find out would be by looking for errors. In some giant computer, you know, occasionally there would be a transistor which failed, or something like that. And that would look like a failure of physical laws, or a miracle, or something would go astray and some parts of the world would start to look different, and funny things would happen. *(Laughs.)* So I believe in the possibility of miracles because I believe in the possibility of fictitious worlds.

It's a little peculiar, if you think about it. I think the process that I've discussed is bound to happen, in fact will happen in hundreds of thousands of years, presuming that no catastrophe intervenes. And then you ask yourself, Well, there are stars and civilizations out there in which it must already have happened. And so there are probably many more fictitious worlds than real worlds. *(Laughs.)* So it becomes very unlikely that we're living in a real world. But the design is very good, the errors are all compensated for, or we really do live in a real world. In any case so far there's no evidence that we live in a fictitious one. But it's interesting to think about.

If you had the power now, what kind of world would you create?

FRANK: You may be very disappointed in my insights, because

they're not very grand (*laughs*), but I think I would create a world where honesty, love, and truth are what people strive for—and there're many roads to that. I don't think any one of them should be pursued exclusively. I think it's very fortunate there are very many people that can do very many different things, that there can be musicians and poets and artists and scientists and . . . audiences. (*Laughs.*) When it comes down to it, the abiding thing I'm looking for is increase of insight and appreciation of the world . . . just that.

John Beardsley

He is the CEO of Padilla, Speer, Beardsley, one of Minneapolis's largest public relations firms. A large-boned, deep-voiced man with an intense curiosity for things scientific, he hardly strikes you as the PR type. Not at all inclined to hyperbole, he defines his profession as, "nothing more than the management of communications between an organization and its publics. It's as simple as that. You can expound on it, you can glorify it, you can put all kinds of modifiers and other trappings on it, but essentially that's what it is. I've stayed in the business because it satisfies a need I have to be doing something that is modestly creative and which furthers the ability of people and organizations to communicate with each other. And it also puts bread on the table." He's fifty-one, married, and the father of three.

When I sit and look up at the stars at night, when I'm, y'know, paddling in the Boundary Waters canoe area north of here, and everything is silent and there is a profound stillness in the woods, my wife and I ask ourselves, "Why are we so remarkably different from other animals in our capabilities, and yet there's only about a 2 percent difference in the genetic structure of the chromosomes between a chimpanzee and a human?" In other words the chimpanzee chromosome is 98 percent a replica of the human. And yet look at the difference between a chimpanzee and a human in capability of thought. So that gives me pause, and I ask, "Was it divinely guided?" But then I think and say to myself, "I don't believe so."

I see no evidence that we are the product of divine intervention. But I do think that throughout modern history (by modern I mean the last ten thousand years) humans have been profoundly disturbed by the fact that we are so different from all other life, and there is no ready explanation for that. Why are we able to think so much differently from other life-forms and to be so different from other life-forms and yet we're all out of the same soup? We're all carbon-based; we all basically have the same amino acid structures, the same DNA. It's unique to this planet. And this one species is now capable of transforming the entire planet. We can, you know, bitch it up forever; everything we do now has an effect on the whole damn planet, which is scary . . . which is scary. And it invests us with a responsibility. Swift always said, y'know, that human beings are capable of reason, but they're not reasoning animals. *(Laughs.)* Most of the time I think he's right. We are capable of planning, but we don't plan . . . we really react to crises. We're a marvelously adaptable animal and we can react to almost any crisis that comes up, but we're not much for actually planning our future.

Well, it all leads me to a greater recognition of the impelling need to understand who we are and what we are. A study of evolution leads you to that, I suppose. I mean, something began here, and it's going there, and why is it moving in that direction? The physicists and the astrophysicists are pondering that at great depth right now. Why in the first microseconds of the Big Bang did certain values obtain that have set the direction for all of cosmic evolution ever since? If some of those free variables had been just the least bit different, there's every likelihood that the universe wouldn't be like it is today and there wouldn't even be human beings. This has led to a postulate called the anthropic cosmological principle, which Hawking talks about in his book.* The older, general cosmological view says that one way to look at our existence as a product of evolution, from the Big Bang all the way through, is that we are here because the universe evolved the way it did. The anthropic cosmological view turns it around and says the universe evolved the way it did because we are here. If we were not here, conditions would have had to have been different. This is a recognition that in the human brain we have a mixture of elements which makes it possible for the universe to contemplate itself. I mean, our brains are made out of material that was created out of a supernova someplace five or ten billion years ago. But a star can't be aware of itself that we know of. And the universe can't be aware of itself that we know of, except in our brain. And the hydrogen that's in our bodies is almost twenty billion years old, so there's a great deal of continuity there.

---

* Stephen W. Hawking, *A Brief History of Time* (New York: Bantam, 1988).

Now, you can begin to get kind of mysterious about all this . . . and you can begin to get kind of rhapsodic, as people like Hawking do now and then because it's an awesome kind of simplicity. Hawking uses the word *god* dozens of times in his book. He asks, "Why did god do this?" But it's a lowercase god, not uppercase, and you don't quite get the feeling he's talking about a personal savior, but it's interesting that he likes to use the word *god* when he's talking about something that's unexplainable. And, you know, there's never been an explanation. He doesn't say why he uses the word *god* in his book. I presume he does because *god* is a word that is instantly recognized by almost anyone on earth to represent that which is ultimately unknowable.

Now, I don't know why the universe began back about sixteen to twenty billion years ago in this supersingularity called the Big Bang. I don't know why it is evolving the way it did. I don't know why we exist the way we do. So there's a mystery there, but we do exist, and, other than just pure speculation, I don't get a lot of pleasure out of pondering religious significance in all of that. It doesn't make that much difference to me. I'm more interested in trying to figure out how it works and trying to understand how it's all sort of put together, to sort of be amazed at the fact that it has come this far, that in the last fifty years we've learned so damn much about how it did get put together and how it is working.

I guess I'm just more interested in questioning than believing. As far as "God" is concerned, I don't think he is necessary any longer. Freud went a long way in that direction. Once you understand and accept what Freud was trying to say, you don't need God anymore. Just like you don't need Zeus to describe what causes thunder and rain and you don't need Apollo to explain why the sun goes across the sky. You don't need to explain human motive and human desire and all the other attributes of human personality in mysterious ways any longer.

So, unlike my mother-in-law, who answers the question of how she should live her life by doing what she thinks God tells her to do, I feel that I can get along best in society and still maintain my integrity by living life the way I choose to live it. I don't willfully hurt other people, I abide by the rules of the game, I obey the laws, and I have respect for other people. And I feel, you know, if you use the teachings of Jesus as a precept for how human beings can live successfully together in a peaceful society . . . they're marvelous. They echo things that were said by Gautama Buddha, and they echo things that were said by Socrates; I mean, it seems to sort of prevail in several societies, from the fourth century B.C. up to the first century B.C. So I follow the precepts that are espoused in the New Testament. But I would abide by them even if the New Testament didn't exist, because the values it espouses are the values that are necessary to run any kind of decent organized society. I try to do unto others as I would have done unto me. I live by the Golden Rule in that regard, and I'm not, you know, terribly aggressive or acquisitive. And I don't misuse resources. I guess what I'm saying is that if I were a fervent and devout and zealous Christian, Buddhist, Hindu, I don't think I would live any differently than I do from a moral standpoint. I think that living a moral life is necessary because it's pragmatic . . . it's how human beings can best succeed as a species. And I think that's what impels people, generally, to live a moral life. It's some inner sense, some innate sense (perhaps some genetic sense), that this is what works. And to me, even religion is an expression of that same underlying genetic force.

Who was it said that the older you get, the more you realize that you don't know? That's the truest thing that was ever said. *(Laughs.)* It's agonizing to think of all the things that one should know, and doesn't yet, and probably never will know, because knowledge is advancing so fast. We've learned more about the human brain in the last ten years than we had learned in all the thousands of years leading up to 1978. And that's awesome. We human beings have this propensity to know everything, and I guess that's what really sets us apart, this compelling desire to know. I'm sure that the driving force in my life is just that, a powerful desire to know more tomorrow than I did the day before. That's probably the main thing that keeps me going.

PART III: THE NEW AGE

The New Age is fraught with contradictions. . . . "Materialistic science" is blamed repeatedly as the source of the world's worst troubles; paradoxically, the trappings of science are greeted with enthusiasm when they support New Age expositions like *The Tao of Physics.*

—*Ted Schultz*

Dr. Raphael Ornstein

RAPHAEL'S VISION

San Rafael, California. After earning his medical degree from the University of Dundee, Scotland, in 1973, Dr. Raphael Ornstein returned to the United States to open up a holistic-healing practice in San Francisco. He is currently medical director of the San Francisco Medical Research Foundation, Inc., a nonprofit educational research foundation "dedicated to researching and demonstrating the reversibility of degenerative diseases upon the human organism." His current driving vision is to transform Alcatraz Island into the "Elysium," an enchanting world of sun-drenched streams, lakes, fountains, geodesic domes, and pyramids. "I want to bring healing and transformation through positive information to millions upon millions of people. The outcome of that is the vision that was initially given to me: the conversion of Alcatraz into a global peace center. I want to create a Renaissance, an artist's haven. I want to turn it into a holistic health, creative arts, and education center."

On my path I've seen that the role of the physician is not so much to give pills or to have clients but to serve as an educator and an empowerer of other people, other beings. As I acknowledge and empower others, I am empowering and acknowledging myself, because on an experiential level, through my direct mystical experiences, I fully understand and know that the universe is a unity. The old joke is that "there is nobody out there but you," but for me this is not some intellectual concept—it's the truth. So I see all of humanity as the cells of a larger body. If you like, from a religious point of view, it is the body of Christ, which is one with the Father, God, and that we are all sons and daughters of the Most High. We are on the planet earth to fill a cosmic destiny, which is to create a planet of freedom. To me this translates as perfect health, beauty, and harmony; to create the earth as it was initially envisioned to be, which is a place of love.

So I've been the Fool, I guess, the archetype of the Fool; just continually going for the highest vision. A lot of people think I'm crazy. My parents say (*switches to a South Bronx Jewish accent*), "Our son the doctor, he took too many mushrooms, God knows what, and he's never come down." Well, the truth is, I've never come down because when you have a very deep experience of God directly, you can never come down. You see, you reach a certain point in your consciousness where you see God in everything you're into.

It's been said that man has been created in the image and likeness of God and that the kingdom of heaven is within. What does that mean? What it really means is that the spirit of the Lord, the spirit of God, is indwelling in the heart of everybody, everybody: Christian, Buddhist, Hindu, Taoist. The spirit of God is indwelling. Because God is in every cell of us, we all are God and we have a direct, intimate connection with what I call the universal creative life intelligence. That's what I call God, the universal creative life intelligence, which is working in and through us. It is the infinite artist, the infinite thinker of the universe. The way I define it so that people can grasp it is to think of God as either music or as pure intelligence.

I've come to understand that the whole universe is electromagnetic energy, and it's basically a musical construct. That God is music and God is light and God is intelligence. And, by the law of correspondence, so are we. So I say to people, "Write out your positive declarations of truth: I am intelligence. I am love. I am beauty. Whatever you say about yourself is true. That's the way the universe is set up. So if you define yourself in terms of limitations and negativity, if you see yourself in terms of limits, then you are stuck with the limits. However you define yourself in your heart, however you've convinced or conditioned yourself to be, is what the universe will mirror until you finally get it straight that who you are is unlimited, is perfect in the sense that we are perfecting ourselves moment by moment. There is no end, because the absolute is not anything that comes to a conclusion. It is absolutely infinite. Once we can grasp our own infinity and our own immortality, free ourselves from the limitations and hang-ups of fear, we are truly free. Then we are healthy and then we move into creativity. And that's where I like to hang out, in the land of freedom and creativity. And that's what this country was founded on, freedom.

The way I see it, we are light-beings; we are basically composed of light, and who and what we come from is light itself. We are a holographic projection of sunlight, and we've come into this play to create. Heaven on earth is really just a creative-arts project.

Patricia Sun

Berkeley, California. She's an extremely successful lecturer and New Age futurist. Her long blond hair, blue eyes, flowing silk dress, and graceful demeanor are reminiscent of a Maxfield Parrish heroine. She's forty-five and single.

I was raised on the East Coast in a very intellectual family. And I think it was wonderful training for me because I honestly believe that I'm a natural-born mystic. So being raised in a very scientific family, a very verbal family, was a tremendous asset because then I got both a linear and logical view of the world as well as a more wholistic, intuitive view of the world. And I think that's one of the things that makes me a little different.

It's partly characteristic of my own childhood drama and personal style that I was also very alone and that I really thought everybody was a little bit crazy. *(Laughs.)* You know, I saw men and women acting very peculiarly with one another at cocktail parties and things. What are they doing? Why are they lying? And so I learned early not to believe anybody else's perceptions of anything. So I really only trust what I experience and feel myself.

In terms of what I believe—and I say this as a metaphor—I look at the last great evolutionary leap as the Fall. And the Fall was when "Adam and Eve ate from the tree of the knowledge of good and evil and then they knew suffering and then they knew shame." Before the Fall they lived in paradise. Paradise was that they lived like the animals and all of nature, with no choice, and followed God's order. They lived, they died, they had babies, they hunted, things happened, that was it. There was no sense of consequence. There was no holding on to things. There was no regret, remorse, and despair. They lived in the mind of God or order of the universe just as the animals did; and that was paradise. After the Fall what we were given was an opportunity to live by choice, to live consciously. Because before, we didn't have any choice. Animals don't have any choice; that's what instinct is. But we were given the option to go against the laws of nature, and we had to be given that option to consciously choose whether we were for God or against God. So in order to be free, to choose, you must be able to say no. And all of our adventures, all our intellectual adventures, all our discoveries, all our wars, all the terrible things we've done, all the wondrous magically good things we've done, the heights and the depths of humanity, have all been about discovering conscious choice.

What I believe fundamentally is that the human race is in the midst of an evolutionary leap, and the crisis we are in now is signaling a shift in how we think. We are moving from a purely linear mode of thinking toward a more inclusive, wholistic perception of life beyond duality. So instead of right or wrong, it is the whole situation you make use of. It's not just your left hand or your right hand, it's all of you and your hands. It's not just man and woman, it's humans. It's not just God and man, it's us all experiencing and creating life. It's not just spirit and matter, it's spirit descending into matter and expressing itself through matter. And I think physics and quantum physics and Einstein's theory that energy equals everything, $E = MC^2$, is the physical equation for the psychological state that is in the process of becoming.

What all this means in living terms is that we are looking at the stuff each one of us has inherited—our fears, perceptions, dramas. I call it being on automatic pilot. As a little child you're a sponge and you sort of absorb the fears, the programs, the patterns of your parents' life and those of your culture and time. And then as you grow up, you start acting them out again, sort of on automatic pilot, and that's when you get your pain. That's where relationships don't work. You fall in love with someone by choosing who you wish they were, but then you have to find out who they are. And it has to do with knowing yourself. The whole power behind the ancient oracle in Greece is to "know thyself," and the power of that comes when you discover your own shadow, using Jungian terms, when you understand your own unconscious and when you face it and heal it and move to the next level of awareness, where there's no more blame, there's no more regret, there's no more remorse, there's no more despair. You then see and choose what is healing.

The predominant automatic pilot today is linear dominant thinking. And so it sees all as either good or bad, cause or effect. One of the movements we are now in is that we have gone to the extreme of the linear-mechanical, cause-and-effect, God-is-dead kind of control. That peaked in the fifties. When they got into physics, they thought, Oh, wow, you know, everything is mechanical. And it's what's missing in medicine. It's what's missing in our lives. What we need now is to shift our focus toward the intuitive mind. And it's acausal, without cause. The linear mind doesn't like that word, doesn't like infinity, 'cause it says, "Well, what do you mean? Where's the end? Where's the beginning?" The linear mind doesn't like the Big Bang either. What do you mean, out of nothing something?

Now, the intuitive, acausal mind is what the Chinese would call the yin mind. It's the void. It's the room. It's the nothing into which something can come into being. Lao-tzu used to call it the thing of value in the lump of clay that makes it a valuable vessel. So it's the space. It's the room. And that mind thinks acausally and that's where synchronicity, intuition, beauty, art, music, creativity, genius comes from. You don't control it and you don't make it; you let it come up into you. So genius and great artists like Michelangelo used to describe how they went out and found their inspiration. Michelangelo was noted as much for finding incredible pieces of marble in the quarry as he was for creating beautiful statues. He could go into the quarry and he could see into the stone and tell them where to cut it out to get exactly the right stone that would hold an arm sticking out and a finger and know that there would be no fissure. And it's because he used his intuition. He would say he went out and found a statue trapped inside a stone. He'd see it in there and then he'd just chip away all the outside and what would be left would be the statue.

So I believe that the human race, when it opens up to this other hemisphere, will become more intuitive. And to be intuitive, you've got to release control. Intuition is about letting go. Unfortunately the sins of the fathers are visited upon the children—the garbage of our unconscious just keeps getting handed down. Our world is a tremendous reflection of wanting to have control right now, and that's why it is so full of garbage. Think of the rather insane things that are done in the name of control: drug issues, the sexual abuse of children, psychological abuse of children, eating disorders, television addiction, shopping compulsions—all the escape "isms." I mean, many of the problems we face today exist because we are holding back against our own intuitive side. We are hating ourselves because we think in either-or terms. Am I good or am I bad? And everyone is suffering from low self-esteem because in their unconscious the linear mind is saying they are bad. In either/or thinking, if you did anything bad, anything you judged wrong, you can't win or forgive yourself because it already happened—too late, you are bad. What you must realize is that you were born into a world of craziness and you've got a whole bunch of stuff in there anyway, so you cannot win from it; you've already got it, it's your ticket into the world. So my point is that what we're doing here is healing it, we're in the process of growth. We're in the process of healing all the fears and all the programmings and all this stuff we've inherited that is blocking our intuitive experience and awareness. This is life, growth, and evolution.

One of the first things humans did when they learned to speak was to learn to lie—and that's Cain and Abel. So the first thing that humans do is to try to look right. And what the evolutionary leap is is when we give up needing to appear "right" and begin to align the feelings inside with what we live and say outside. We won't always do it perfectly by any means, but to authentically attempt to be honest instead of right is the goal. "Right" is a function of the linear mind and it causes war and all kinds of judgmental, polarized problems. I don't mean to say that you can't have intellectual discussions in which you attempt to define right and wrong. I'm not against that. I'm against the psychological dynamic of needing to be right and not realizing that it's always relative to something and that if you go toward what's good in yourself, if you use that as your Geiger counter, then what you do is move toward what Lao-tzu called the Tao, the flow of the universe. And I believe it's another name for saying the mind of God or the holy spirit, depending on what religion you're talking about. I think Buddha would have called it waking up. We wake up when we follow that flow. And the flow is written in your cells, in your body. It's the old meaning of conscience. And it's not a literal judgment of what gets you something; it is what is wholesome. That's the question. Is this good? Is this wholesome? And when you ask this question, you move into the intuitive, acausal mind that has a sense of what is good. It gives you information that no logic can give you, because logic can only sort. It's a tool. Logic is not equivalent to reality. It's only a tool for sorting and discerning.

So I believe that the law of God, order of nature, the mind of the universe, the harmony of the spheres, is also written in ourselves.

And we have to learn how to consciously choose to join it and that's up to you for you and it's up to me for me. And the way that I teach that best in the world is if I heal me. It has more to do with Truth and compassion than right and blame. It is taking responsibility; it is in fact the ability to respond healthily. So this is not a political thing but a psychological thing—it's a psychological coming home. It is about facing ourselves. And a lot of our persecution of one another, ridicule if you will, comes from our own fears of facing ourselves. So my fundamental message is that you really have to love yourself and know yourself to be able and healthy.

One of the things I always think of, you know, is that Judgment Day is here. Guess who the judge is? You. And guess where you send you? Hell. And when you forgive you, guess where you go? You go to heaven. You're in heaven. Heaven on earth. Jesus said to his disciples, "What do we pray for?" And he answered that we pray for this: "Thy kingdom come, thy will be done on earth as it is in heaven." And so we're going for it.

Jeanne Lemenowsky

Saint Paul, Minnesota. She's a radiant sixty-five-year-old health food store owner, fitness counselor, and astrologer. "I remember throwing a health food awareness party for my friends here in Saint Paul in 1955. I had twenty-nine of my friends over, and everyone just laughed at me. Now, thirty years later, I haven't been to a doctor in over fifteen years. And of those twenty-nine people at the party, only two of them have not had a major surgery! Gall bladder, mastectomies, hysterectomies . . . I mean, it's just unheard of. But the thing that hits me most is that even though they have been lying in the hospital, really on the brink of the next level of existence, they continue to say to me, "Are you still on that crazy food?" You see where human nature is?

I guess the bottom line for me—and some people think that it's real harsh—is that your life is whatever you think it is. If you think your life is a mess, it's a mess. If you think there's opportunity all around you, untapped, there is.

Most of us never live for today, okay? But the goal is to live for today, because this is all we really have. Of course we pay our rent a month ahead of time, and we do certain things, but living each day (and this is a biblical thing, truly) . . . living each day as though it's your last . . . what would that tell you? You wouldn't have arguments, you wouldn't have hostility feelings, you would live each day in joy and harmony. Because we really don't know if we're going to be here tomorrow, do we? It isn't that each day we're preparing for our next life. Oh, that would not be too practical, would it? But today is what counts . . . what're you doing today? I mean, what are you thinking about today? Now, this is what I believe is the answer: If you don't love what you do, you better get out of it, because it can make you sick. There's a lot of opportunity. Most people say today that it's so much harder than it was twenty years ago, thirty years ago . . . that is absolutely untrue. Even though there are way more people today, there are way more opportunities.

I guess I'm just looking for the best in things. I think it's pretty indicative of our society that the newspapers are filled with garbage. I don't even read the newspaper, it's so depressing. Look at the headlines every day. Have you ever seen a headline across this country that says, "It's a Beautiful Day!" Never. Wars, killings . . . just think of the people that read the newspaper! I feel sorry for them, I really do. So I believe like the old song, "accentuate the positive." It's a simple route. I'm not saying that we should bury all of our hostility and just simply negate it, but I'm saying that we must all try and get to a point where we can look at a terrible problem in a totally different way. We have free will. We can change our lives if we want to. When people ask someone, "If you had your life to do over again, would you do it differently?" I think the person that says, "Wow, would I do it differently!" isn't thinking. You see? Because wherever we are, at any given moment, is where we're supposed to be, or we'd be someplace else! It's that simple.

God created everything in the universe for a reason. So if we are wise, we use the tools. Number one, our brain; number two, our spirit; and number three, our heart. These are the tools we use to make our life joyful. And I don't think in any way that we are here to suffer. There are some religions that truly feel that if you don't have a cross to bear, that's a mortal sin. I think the opposite. I think we have the tools to make our lives happy, to be happy, to show others the route to happiness, to show them how to gain it for themselves. And that's what I'm trying to do.

Investments of Faith

Mother Tessa Bielecki

Her high cheekbones, wide glossy lips, and baby-blue eyes evoke the portrait of a middle-aged fashion model—but she's hardly that. She's mother abbess of the Spiritual Life Institute, a Carmelite Hermitage with retreat centers in Crestone, Colorado, and Kemptville, Nova Scotia. She's forty-two.

I was born and raised in Connecticut, so I'm a pretty sturdy New England Yankee type. Plus I'm of Polish background. So I grew up in a very strongly ethnic family. Good peasant stock. One of the things that I find most unusual about myself is that I was born and raised a cradle Catholic and have been an undisillusioned ecstatic Catholic all along. And the reason is, I think, that I always had a sense of the mystical heart of Christianity and, more specifically, of Catholicism. That has always sustained me through any kinds of difficulties with the more painful institutional dimensions of the Church that have so bothered other people and which have caused many of them to withdraw from the institution altogether.

We were very dutiful, very devotional Catholics. As a child I vividly remember how after we received Communion, I would sneak a peek at my mother while she prayed. I don't know what ever made me do that, but I do remember being very moved by how deeply wrapped in prayer she was. Years later, as a contemplative praying myself, I realize that what I was responding to was my mother's very deep contemplative experience of the living God. And that was the heart of our whole family life, the heart of our whole religious life. It's not something that was ever mentioned. It was just an ambience in which we lived. We breathed it in, the way you breathe in the air. So I had just the most incredibly blessed childhood, I'm sure, on the face of the earth. I'm so aware of how blessed I've been. I've never doubted the existence of God; I mean, to me to doubt the existence of God is like not believing in the sun rising. Or, you know, like not believing in spring coming after winter. I mean, it's just never been a question.

Now, after twenty years living as a professional contemplative, I've been able to understand that the very heart and soul of Chris-

tianity, which has been very obscured, is mysticism. Everything re-
volves around that mystical heart. The people who do not live at that
mystical heart of Christian experience dry up and find the tradition
meaningless to them, because it's not anything that sustains them.
And the bulk of the work that I do out on the road is with the people;
well, for want of a better word, with the New Age types, people
who are disaffected, disenchanted Christians for the most part. Or
Jews, because I consider myself a Judeo-Christian. I'm very rooted
in the whole Jewish tradition, which you have to be to be a good
Christian. I am very interested in helping those people who have
turned away from institutional Christianity to reconnect with their
roots, because most of them come to me and say, "No matter how
hard I try, I can't cut myself off at the roots. I know I have to come
to terms with my Christianity and I don't know how to do that."
And part of how I try to help people do that is by recognizing mysticism, which is the heart and soul of Christianity.

The mystical experience of God, the immediate, intuitive experience of God, is what the tradition is all about. Everything else
flows from that. So liturgy is really just the ritual reenactment or
embodiment of that mystical experience. If there isn't any mystical
experience underlying it, then you have nearly an empty ritualism,
which means nothing to people. Morality, too, is a consequence of
mystical experience. It's not something you can impose from the
outside. It's an inner necessity that one experiences as a result of
mystical experience. Once you know God, there are certain respon-
sibilities and obligations. I mean, you just can't live like the old slob
that you've always lived as. *(Gentle laugh.)*

I think that the primary obligation we have is to recognize other
people as part of the human family. And we have obligations to the
planet, which is also a part of the family. I've always had trouble with
people who think that it's only Buddhism that has this understanding
of the oneness of creation. But there's a whole tradition in both
Judaism and Christianity of kinship with the earth and oneness with
all of creation. So I consider my family as more than just the people
who live with me; I mean, the plants are my family and the animals
are my family too. The constellations are my family. So there has to
be this lived-out, intimate connection with all of those.

Because of the incredible implications of the central mystery of
Christianity, which is Christ becoming man, the Word becoming
flesh, everything is the body of Christ. Every part of the universe,
every bit of the materiality of the universe is the body of Christ.
And through our mysticism we celebrate our oneness with that
Christ, with that God, which means that we are actually wedded to

all of creation. All of creation becomes spouse. All of creation becomes bride or bridegroom. The universe is your body. In the Carmelite tradition especially, we celebrate a whole dimension of contemplative experience we call bridal mysticism, where we know God as spouse or bridegroom, the way a friend would know a friend, the way a lover knows a lover, the way the bridegroom knows the bride. It's amusing to me how many people come out of the closet and say to me, "You know, this is how I experience God, too, but I always thought I was a little odd, so I never said anything to anybody." Men as well as women.

But if you're a contemplative, you have to be open to God on any number of different levels—you have to be ready for just about anything. I mean, you have to be ready to experience God the way God reveals himself to you, and this is in every conceivable manner. So sometimes you experience God as, say, a partner in a dance. Or you experience God as an adversary in war. You experience God as great joy. You experience God as great sorrow sometimes. Sometimes it's very painful. Sometimes it's very wonderful.

To me, though, the greatest reality is not only the existence of God but the image of Christ crucified. That is absolutely central and essential in my life. Nothing else to me makes sense. And if it were not for that image indicating a profound cosmic reality, I don't think that I could continue living. There's nothing else that would give me the courage to go on. What I love about the image of Christ crucified is that it seems to me that one of the biggest things in life is the tensions that pull us in a million different directions. You know, life just seems to me to be a whole series of polarities or paradoxes. So there's man-woman, there's light-dark, there's good-evil, there's solitude and togetherness, there's fast and feast, there's discipline and wildness. There are all these seeming opposites and if you are an alive human being and not a dud, you just feel yourself pulled in every direction. You know, at one moment one thing seems like it's the most important; the next moment exactly the opposite seems like it's even more important. And that's what the whole image of the crucifixion is for me—Christ stretched to every possible conceivable direction in the universe. Seemingly he's broken by that. But by being broken by those tensions he emerges with a kind of wholeness and integration. Not by avoiding any one of the extremes, not by avoiding any bit of the tension, but by absolutely walking into it and moving out of it.

You know the old traditional Catholic cathechism answer to the question of what is life all about: "To know, love and serve God in this life and enjoy him forever in heaven." So serving God is a little ways down the line. There are things that are more important than serving. But loving God is what's most important. And yet you can't love what you don't know, so you have to come to know God. And you learn to know God through nature. You learn to know God through other people. You learn to know God through the Scriptures. You learn to know God through prayer. For the contemplative, especially for the professional contemplative who vows celibacy, the love of God is absolutely crucial. I mean, that's what it's all about, because as someone once said, "If you're going to live celibately, you have got to be mystical. Your only choices are mysticism or neurosis." And this is what we see. We either see towering mystics or we see some pretty terrible neurotics, and more of the latter I'm afraid.

The most important way for me to love God is simply to be in the presence of God, all alone, just taking care of God himself. Not acting out love of God through others, even though that's also important. A lot of people tend to relegate the love of God to social action or to service of others. But what happens in the contemplative life is that God alone, all by himself, is so captivating and so intoxicating that you can actually spend time alone, all alone with God, you know, in what we call contemplative prayer. Of course a very important question to ask is whether or not spending time alone with God is a selfish act? And there's absolutely no doubt that it can be, that it can be selfish, that it can be a cop-out, that it can be an escape. But if God is actually calling, that God is so captivating and so compelling that he is demanding this. It is very conceivable that not to spend that kind of time with God but instead to get lost in what might seem to be social service would actually be a cop-out or an escape, because it's really nothing but do-goodism—self-directed or self-propelled, and not inspired by God.

This gets into the whole dynamic of action and contemplation. It's a twofold dynamic that absolutely everybody has got to live out of. I think it's one of the biggest tensions in life. And it will vary from person to person. Which of the polarities is more compelling at what time in life or at what time of the day? So everyone has to work out that dynamic and that rhythm. There are going to be some people for whom, in terms of hours of the day, action will predominate. But we see, especially in Christianity, the wrecks of a feverish activism that has not been enlightened enough with contemplative preparation.

I think it's a mistake actually to think that there are some people who are nothing but pure contemplatives. Nobody is a pure contemplative, because that's not what life is like. Unless you are really,

really, really isolated in some kind of a cave somewhere, living as a hermit, there is no purely contemplative life. And any of those people who have eventually gone into that kind of radical solitude, say historically, in terms of the Christian father of the desert, for example, they first were very active and were called out of that into their solitude. But for most people it just goes back and forth. That's true for me too. And at this stage of my life, this second stage of my life, I'm aiming for many more hours a day of contemplative prayer in which I can simply bask in the presence of God, unselfishly. In fact it is so compelling to me right now that I am still not pulling it off well because I still feel the tug of involvement with the community. But I know that this is a demand from God, because the more I fail to do it, the more trouble I run into on these other levels. It's a very painful transition to make, because the demands on me are so great. I am still not assenting to what is a very real command. But if God is that real, you feel that pressure, you know, you feel that call. And it becomes inescapable after a time. You just can't say no to it anymore.

Father Thomas Keating

Saint Benedict's Monastery, Snowmass, Colorado. Large-boned, muscular, gentle in manor, he's one of the world's most respected contemplatives and for many years served as abbot of Saint Joseph's Abbey in Spenser, Massachusetts. He is now the abbot of Saint Benedict's.

Saint Benedict's was founded by members of Saint Joseph's Abbey and carries on the nine-hundred-year-old tradition of the Cistercian order. Cistercians trace their origin to the eleventh century, when a group of monks left their Benedictine monastery because they felt their practice was too lax. They then founded a new, stricter order at Cîteaux, France, giving them the name Cistercian. A second renewal of the order occurred in Soligny-la-Trappe, France, leading to the formation of the Cistercian Order of Strict Observance. These monks were called Trappists. This is the heritage of Saint Benedict's and of the fourteen other Trappist monasteries in the United States.

I was born in New York City and went to school in New York. I was raised in the Roman Catholic Communion. But I was never educated in Catholic schools. I went to boarding school and later to Yale University. It was at Yale, really, taking a course in philosophy, that I got interested in contemplative life. It wasn't too well known in those days. This would have been 1940 or so. I went into the library and I happened to come across a whole set of books that probably had never been opened before, judging by the pages. They were commentaries of the early fathers, like Origen and Ambrose, of the Christian church on the gospels. They had been excerpted by Thomas Aquinas. The name of this book was *Catena Aurea*, which means "golden chain."

This book gave me an entirely new vision of the Christian faith, because these fathers had a certain insight into it, a certain approach from a higher wisdom, which was no doubt due to their own developed life of prayer and union with God. It wasn't the customary moralistic or literalistic or half-dead kind of presentation of the Christian faith that one usually hears in mere catechetical instruction. I was fascinated by this approach and so I read the other Christian mystics. I spent the last half of my first year and almost all of my second year at Yale studying those books and more or less getting through my courses so I wouldn't be thrown out and so on. It was like a networking process . . . only it was the network of books rather than people. You read one book and it tells you about another. And then you go there. You go on and on. And pretty soon you have a pretty thorough grasp of the contemplative approach to the gospel.

A few years later I discovered an actual monastery that was very serious and there were only three Trappist monasteries in the States in those days. There's about twelve to fourteen now. So I visited there and was very much taken up with their life-style. Finally I went there, entered there. My reason for entering of course was my conviction that this would be the best place to develop the contemplative dimension of life. It required leaving family and friends, and all the other things I could have done. I then pursued the monastic life, which was very vigorous and austere at that time. And I'm still at it more or less.

The period in which I entered, prior to Vatican II, was a lot more austere than it is now. In those days we spoke to only two people—the abbot and the one who was in charge of our formation. So there was no possibility of getting to know other people. Making friends, this was kind of frowned upon. And it was a heavy schedule of common prayers. A good deal of manual work. And a lot of silence and very strict rules of solitude. One couldn't even go home in those

days if there was a sickness or death in the family. So it was really a kind of departure from this world as far as the symbols go. It was very difficult for families and impossible for friends to continue to see you. It was a kind of total commitment to this project of pursuing divine union; union with Christ.

I was trying to recognize the evil, the limitations, weaknesses in myself, and to die to what might be called the false self; that is to say, that tissue of projects or emotional programs for happiness that most everybody develops in early childhood and which get reinforced by our culture and the value system of our parents. This value system is basically self-centered and selfish, even under the guise of some good intentions.

The contemplative life always came across to me as requiring the total loss of the false self, or death to the false self. In the beginning one sees this as a fairly materialistic combination of renunciations, such as fasting or remaining in one place or living with one set of people or putting up with a low standard of living or practicing celibacy; as concrete, gross restraints that one imposes on oneself. Then, with a little practice at that, one sees that it's immensely more complex. Because the false-self system even co-opts one's generous efforts at asceticism and does that for motives of pride, competition, security, esteem, or control.

The idea that was presented to us in those days was that if we can purify our own razzmatazz, we can enter into higher states of consciousness, as you'd call them today, or divine union, as you might describe it in a Christian frame of reference. Then one kind of serves like a transmitter, you might say, pouring good vibrations into the atmosphere. This offsets some of the evil vibrations and negativity of the self-centered activity created by institutional injustice. In other words one is subtly undermining or entering into combat with evil spirits; that is to say, demons in high places. This was one way in which the monastic journey was conceptualized and justified by the early church fathers. And this is a deeply held conviction of both Christian and Hindu monastics—that the accumulated energy and spiritual power that comes from prayer and the contemplative life has an influence in diminishing the forces of evil throughout the world. In other words if one is away from the distractions of self-centered activity, one is better able to refine one's spirit and become a receptor of divine energy. One may then transmit this pure divine light back into the world.

Anyway the monastic theology has always had this intuition. It therefore emphasizes with great force the value of a life of solitude in which the concentration of energy in self-surrender refines one's receptive apparatus so that one can receive the more sublime communications of the universe and then transmit back into our atmosphere, into our world, this positive light, which is ultimately love and transcendence. Self, giving, goodness. So this, in essence, is the monastic answer to the question of the social gospel: contemplative prayer will have an influence on society whether society thinks about it or not.

So it's a question of an investment in faith. And that's the investment I made in entering; that if I could clean up my own act and enter into this rhythm of divine charity and love, that I could make a greater contribution than going to war or functioning in some type of social action.

Understand that what I am talking about is not mystical experience in the sense of parapsychological phenomena. The fascination with mystical experience is a dead end, I think. In a genuine contemplative path, it seems to me, one is not looking for mystical experiences. And if one has some, one doesn't pay too much attention to them. Because after an experience you're back where you were before. In other words everything that goes up comes down with a heavy thud. What is important for those who take the spiritual journey seriously is an abiding state of union with God, in which the false-self system as a motivational center has been completely dismantled. It's the restructuring of consciousness into an abiding and permanent state of being which is spontaneous. In my experience those who take the spiritual journey most seriously and who have a structured life to sustain it rarely experience mystical gifts. They seem to be more appropriate for those who are in social work or active ministry or who are married and who need special assistance from God to survive in an environment in which everything is against you as far as trying to shake loose from those programs for happiness that develop out of instinctual drives. Such drives are good and necessary but hopelessly exaggerated when pursued as the end of life, such as security needs, affection-esteem needs, or control and power needs. It is to be locked into an infantile set of values that just won't work, even though our culture tries to convince everybody that this is what life is all about. It isn't.

Somewhere in life one just crashes through wars, accident, bankruptcy, illness, sickness, death in the family. It suddenly dawns on one that maybe one's childhood programs for happiness are not so great after all. At least they don't work. The spiritual journey is the invitation to take ourselves in hand and to grow up, to recognize those programs for happiness and the damage they're doing in our lives, the fact that they don't work. It is about changing them before they lead us into some kind of catastrophe or disaster, more or less.

That's my understanding of religion. What good is it unless it gets you out of the mess? And unfortunately a lot of people use religion itself as just one more way of expressing their self-centered needs for security, control and power, and esteem. This is the false-self system that every true spiritual discipline invites us to dismantle in order to use that energy for the expansion of our rational, intuitive, and transcendent potentialities. In other words to be human is to grow. And the false-self system is an option not to grow. It's the source of all violence, injustice, social insensitivity, and hinders the human family from growing into what is truly human. Solidarity, oneness, sharing, belonging, compassion, joy in others' well-being—

all values of true happiness just don't come into focus as long as one's motivation is focused on these false programs of happiness. It can't possibly work. Most people are taking tranquilizers to get over afflicted emotions, which are gonna continue until they change their value systems. It's obvious.

It takes a little something to shake us out of our prepackaged value system and preconceived ideas. This is the purpose of the spiritual beauty. And monastic life is an environment that is designed to further that. But even there it doesn't always work because you can settle for a routine. You just have another set of problems, that's all. They are less dramatic, less obvious, but nonetheless real. There's nowhere on earth that you can escape the struggles of living in this world.

I might say here that my investment in monastic life has certainly not been disappointing, but it was totally unexpected. I mean, what I expected to happen didn't happen, and what I didn't expect to happen did happen. Well, it's just that the spiritual journey is a trip into the unknown. Whatever you think is gonna happen, you can be almost certain it won't happen. That's the only certainty on the journey. Instead of bringing me to a point that I might have anticipated, I got just the opposite. It freed me from all my expectations, and this is a kind of preliminary to a real total commitment to a journey into an unknown future.

But three projects for me have kind of emerged as convictions out of my monastic experience. One is to try to contribute something to the recovery of the contemplative dimension of the gospel and the Christian religion. As Jacob Needleman has written in *Lost Christianity*, it was pretty thoroughly lost as a practical and available tradition. And without it the Christian religion is truncated, emasculated, in pitiful degree. It becomes a set of customs or sentiments or a moralistic approach to life instead of a journey away from our self-centered, somewhat dignified selfishness.

The second thing that seems to me essential in our time is dialogue with the other world religions, not to mention the other Christian denominations. Dialogue in the sense of an immense respect and appreciation of the wisdom and truth and practices of other religions as genuine revelations of the Absolute, proper to different parts of the world, different cultures, all contributing to the religious evolution and development of the human family as a whole. It's the interreaction of the world religions that challenge each other to be sincere, genuine, and honest to their own truth that prevents human selfishness from manipulating and running off with spiritual power, which still happens in some cases, to the great disaster of well-intentioned people. One of my deepest convictions is God's will in our time for the religions of the world to come together in genuine understanding and dialogue, appreciation and support. And to remove from their teaching anything that could lead to prejudice, violence, persecution, war.

The third thing that I think is essential for someone on the spiritual path today, monk or otherwise, is a commitment to the service of the poor. No one can be indifferent to institutional injustice and poverty and claim to be on the spiritual journey. If one is in a monastery, one's life of sacrifice and prayer has to be in the service of that project. Otherwise, it seems to me, one shouldn't be there. One hasn't understood what monastic life is all about. As a corollary, it seems to me that one of the contributions of contemplative monks is to further access to contemplative practices and to provide retreat centers and encouragement to those who are working toward living the spiritual life outside the monastery; for the people who are working in these areas of dialogue or social concern so as to provide them with the kind of interior strength they need in order to persevere in some of these very difficult services they administer.

One of the practical activities that we are trying to contribute to, however modestly, is to awaken Christians in every walk of life to the fact that they are called to the transcendent potential; that is, the contemplative dimension of the gospel. And that by practicing prayer in proportions consistent with their other duties of life they also can begin to dismantle the energy centers of early childhood that are using up their strength. In this way they might free themselves for spiritual growth and therefore also prepare themselves for the globalization of humanity that is taking place, whether people like it or not, as part of the inevitable evolution of life.

Sister Sudha,
a.k.a. Dr. Sue Schrager

Ananda Ashrama, La Cresenta, California, in the foothills of the Sierra Madre. The ashram covers 120 acres of hillside and is landscaped with trees, gardens, and rock-lined pathways. The philosophy taught here is based on the teachings of Vedanta, as expounded by India's nineteenth-century philosopher Sri Ramakrishna. Vedanta literally means the end or goal of wisdom. One of India's major Hindu faiths, its principal tenets are: Truth or God is One without a second; our real nature is divine; all paths ultimately lead to the same goal; and the purpose of human life is to realize God within one's own soul.

Sister Sudha is a nun at the ashram. She's forty-four.

I remember having a wonderful Spanish teacher during my third year in high school. He gave us a sheet with Spanish poetry on it. And there were quite a few poems by Saint John of the Cross and Saint Teresa of Avila. Not having grown up Roman Catholic (my mother was a Religious Science student), I didn't know anything about either one of them. But I loved the poetry. So I went and got a book about Saint Teresa, Marcelle Auclair's book, which has stayed with me to this day. I've read it and read it. It's in shreds. I felt so close to Saint Teresa that I wanted to become a Carmelite nun. Of course I wasn't anything that was remotely Catholic; not Episcopalian, Roman Catholic, or anything. But I really was determined to be a nun. Then I saw the movie, *The Nun's Story*, with Audrey Hepburn and Dame Edith Evans. It was so moving to me. And I realized that I could become a nun, that I really had the vocation to be a nun. I had a lovely boyfriend and I had a completely happy life. It was not at all a matter of wanting to opt out of life. I had everything that a teenager could want. But it became more important than eating or sleeping or drinking or anything to give my whole life to God. Then one evening I had a vision of what I thought was Saint Teresa of Avila; I had this vision of this really remarkable face in a Carmelite habit. A very intense experience. So I became devoted to her.

I learned everything I could about nuns. And I began to live the life of a nun at home. I made an horarium for myself, I made a schedule for myself. And I got up like at 4:00 A.M. and did my meditation and said the daily offices in Latin. I mean, I hadn't taken Latin but I was fairly good in languages. And I said Mass by myself, celebrated the Mass. You know, I had a little wine, little bread. I mean, I really, I just had to live it thoroughly. I ate alone. I really was such an austere fifteen-year-old living as a nun. I couldn't want to be anything else. My father, when I told him, he said, "How can you make any money being a nun?" And I tried to explain that that wasn't the idea. (*Laughs.*) It was very hard for them. And my mother felt that somehow she had failed in being a mother.

A friend of mine was an Episcopalian. She said there are orders in the Episcopal church. Did you know that? And I began to write to different orders. Then I started taking inquiries class in the Episcopal church, still living this intense inner life. Just really living the life of a nun. And I became baptized, and my mother was baptized in the Episcopal church. Then I left for Tucson to live at the order. This was '61. I entered in January of '61. I was seventeen.

It was like that. I was so happy. I was just ready to jump in and did the Apostulant. Then I was confirmed in the Episcopal church so I could receive Communion and everything. Then I became a novice. I was sent to an Indian reservation to be a very young principal at nineteen. And I also taught fourth, fifth, sixth, seventh, and eighth grade in one room. And all Oneida Indian children. It was a wonderful year. I loved my life. I loved being a nun. I loved every part of it. I took my final solemn vows, not just simple life vows but solemn life vows.

Then a number of things happened at the order that dramatically shook my faith. I don't think I should go into the details here, because all is forgiven now, but let's just say that I learned of some highly unethical practices that were condoned by the order's leadership. And when I learned of these things it became increasingly difficult for me to do my work, especially the speeches I made on the order's behalf. It was a very difficult, emotional time for me, and I gradually came to decide that I had to leave my vows and the order. I went to confession, and the priest said, "You can't leave your vows." I said, "But I don't know how I can go on. I mean, I have to speak about the order. How can I do this?" He said, "Well, you can't do anything else."

But in April or May of '69 it all came to a head. I just couldn't go on working for the order in good conscience. So I called my father and said, "I'm gonna come home if I may." And I came home. Gee, it was a terrible adjustment. I came home in the middle of the Vietnamese antiwar demonstrations, the miniskirt, the pill. You know, I had been in a full habit sheltered from a lot that was going on, drugs and so on, a lot of the things that were happening during the sixties. And it was as if I had come from the moon, coming back into society. I went to USC to get my master's degree, because I couldn't teach in California. So just plunging out of the habit and into a miniskirt was, you know, quite a change. (Laughs.) But always I kept my spiritual practices. I had a shrine in my home and I continued to pray.

I finished my master's degree at USC and then I worked with youngsters with reading and learning disabilities in the Glendale Public School system. And I taught. And I read everything and I explored different religions. Then, in 1978, a person who was very close to me, very much like my mother in this lifetime, died suddenly. And it was as if all of my faith, all the things I believed in spiritually, had no meaning anymore. It was just a terrible thing. Because here I'd felt very deeply about inner life since I was a little girl. I always felt the companionship of God. These things were verities to me, that there's life after death and that everything happens for a reason. But somehow, with my friend's passing, all of that left me. And it was a terrible feeling. I remember one night yelling at God. I mean, it was the most revolutionary thing I could do. The most scary thing I did was say, "I hate you; I hate you, and I'll never love you again." I expected the earth would just stop for having done that. It just came from the depth of my being.

Eleven days after my friend died, my father was taken ill and was going to die. And it was like I had to be strong for him. I was still teaching school every day and then going to intensive care every night, staying till eleven and coming home and going to school. You know, it was as if something inside of me had died. I was in anguish. It was like all my props had gone away. Such a turning point.

My father had given me a gun because he felt that a woman living alone in an apartment needed one. I never shot it, I never wanted to shoot it, I didn't even want to have it. But there it was. And I thought, you know, What's the point of going on with this? I felt so awful. It was the lowest point of my life. I felt so alone, that there was no one that could really understand the pain that I was in. But I was in front of my shrine, and at this lowest nadir I remembered just this determination and I said out loud, "I will live, I will to live." And that was the bottom. Because then I came up from there. And I remember writing on my lamp, "This is the day the Lord hath made. I will rejoice and be glad in it." I would wake up with this empty feeling, but I would look at this thing I had written on my lamp and look for the joy in each day. It was as if each of my spiritual beliefs had to be really built from the ground up again. You know, that each one had to be put in place consciously. And my relationship with God put in place consciously to learn self-surrender. And I remember going into the hospital chapel and praying. And I said, "I give my life to you wholly. You know, use me for whatever you will. I just want to give my life entirely to you."

Well, my dad did eventually get better. But I backslided a bit on my commitment to God (laughs), because I was very much caught up in my career. I had an educational-consulting business. I had a Ph.D. from USC by now, been on television, was a consultant for a publishing company, went on an eleven-city tour of the United States talking about personalized books for children. I wrote books for McGraw-Hill. I mean, I really was a busy person. But then, on Palm Sunday night, 1982, Zefirelli's film *Jesus of Nazareth* was shown. And I watched it. And I was so moved, I thought, goodness, what must it be to meet your master and to be chosen to come and follow? And I thought, I would love to have that experience, to meet my teacher and drop everything and follow. What must it have been for those disciples! So I thought I really should become affiliated with some external spiritual group.

So I called up the Church of Religious Science in Glendale and I went on a Wednesday night that week. But it wasn't for me. It was very nice, but it wasn't for me. Then I had read Gayatri Devi's book, *One Life Pilgrimage.** I had picked it up at a bookstore. And I wasn't too impressed with it. It's a bunch of letters to other people. It affected me kind of neutrally. But I knew her ashram was here because I taught at Clark School, which was just a couple of blocks away from the ashram. My kids would talk about it sometimes. "There are old ladies living up there." Sometimes I'd go by the gate, but I never went in. But I knew they had meditation groups on Thursday night, so I decided to go. I sat in the front row, which I always like to do so there's not a lot of distraction. And Mataji came in the side aisle. And then she prayed at the shrine and turned. And it was the face that I had seen in my vision twenty-two years before that I thought was Saint Teresa. In other words I saw my guru's face. I just couldn't believe it. It was the culmination of my whole spiritual quest, this recognition of my teacher's face.

That was the turning, really, another major turning point in my life. From that time on I knew that I wanted to join the Vedanta order. I realized on a inner level that I would be joining the community, although I didn't want to. I wanted to stay in my apartment. I had lovely furniture and a nice, independent life. But I knew that my destiny was gonna be belonging to this community. And I really didn't want to give up my freedom.

I remember a conversation I had with my dad on Easter Sunday, that very Easter Sunday. I said, "Dad, the most wonderful thing has happened to me"—little realizing how devastating this would be in his mind. "I found my teacher and I feel just exactly as if I were meeting Christ. I mean, I was meeting her during Holy Week. I

---

* Srimata Gayatri Devi is the spiritual leader and Mother who guides the work of Vedanta in the United States and abroad. She has taught Vedanta in the United States since 1927, one of the first women to carry India's spiritual message to the West.

knew how the disciples felt to meet the teacher so that I could really be doing the Lord's work; whatever Lord, I mean the universal Lord God. God's work for the rest of my life." I was ready to give my whole life again in a religious setting. My father said, "You're looking for a mother replacement. This is a weakness for you, it's not a strength, because you should not be looking for a mother at your age." But I didn't see it in those terms. I mean, the face I had seen at fifteen was the face I had seen on the platform that Thursday night. So for me there was a connection that was so so strong.

But Mataji wouldn't let me join until I had my father's blessing, which he gave, but very reluctantly. My father said, "How can you? I mean, a religious philosophy should be just that, a philosophy. If you're on a desert island and you have a book, that should be Vedanta, the principles of Vedanta—not the teacher." I said, "Well, Christ was a teacher, who by his very persona drew the disciples. It wasn't that they were coming because they wanted more Jewishness, or coming because they wanted more Christianity. They were coming because they were attracted to him. And I think that's been the way it has been with all the great teachers."

Still, the beliefs I already held were the beliefs of Vedanta. I told my father that I already believed very strongly in reincarnation. I already deeply revered Buddha and other world teachers. I mean, that just is Vedanta. I read widely in all those and believed in the truths in all of those. So, in a way, the field was already plowed. When I met my teacher, it was the personification of that. It was like the culmination for me of that sense of Christ. So I just couldn't have imagined not joining the ashram. And I am so happy that I did.

I have always believed strongly that God is very knowable and very real. And I ask only that I can be an empty instrument, an empty vessel, to have God's love and healing and wisdom in every life that I touch and in everything that I do. And it seems to me that I help most when I'm one-to-one with people. I can work with people and they very often tell me everything about their life. You know, they feel safe. So I feel very much that that's the place where I seem to be used; working with people and helping them to feel more confidence in themselves and in the reality of God working in their own life, that nothing is happening by accident or by chance, that each thing is for us to learn from and to develop our spiritual understanding and relationship with God. Vedanta says that the reason we take bodies is to realize God, to make God real in our life, that he's not a stepmother, and that he's not some abstract principle, but that he's a real, responsive consciousness.

I remember a novice mistress, who's a very close friend of mine, saying, "How could you possibly give up Jesus Christ for that? For being a heathen or pagan?" Are we heathens or are we pagans? Both. And fundamentalist Christians will come up and say, "Do you think you're gonna be saved? How can you possibly think so?" But both Swamiji* and Mataji have such a love for Christ and such a deep appreciation for each of the world's religions—Judaism, Christianity, Islam—that I really feel that I am all of those things. You know, I can be Jewish, I can be Muslim, I feel Christian, I feel Jewish, I feel Islamic, I feel Hindu, I feel Buddhist. I mean, we study those, we worship those. I just don't feel any separation. I can feel very comfortable with many of the teachings of each of those religions and with the culture that each one of those religions comes out of. So it's very easy for me. I know there are doctrinal differences. But I feel that those are more external to the essence of it, which I think comes down to something quite the same. Which is that there is underlying everything a consciousness of a Supreme Reality of some sort that is infinite in intelligence and love and compassion.

---

* Swami Paramananda. A monk of the Ramakrishna Order and a disciple of Swami Vivekananda. He came to America in 1906 and founded the Boston Vedanta Center in 1909. He created the Ananda Ashrama in 1923 and established another ashram in Cohasset, Massachusetts, in 1929. He passed away in 1940 and was succeeded by Srimata Gayatri Devi, whom he trained and ordained.

Visiting Spirits

Becky Fischer

I come from a long line of preachers. My grandfather and my grandmother both were ordained preachers in the Assemblies of God Church and traveled for forty-five years all over the country just preaching the gospel. And I have three uncles that are born-again, spirit-filled Christians that preached in various churches around the country. So my heritage in the Church goes back two or three generations. So I'm not the typical person that got saved off of skid row, ya know.

She has lived most of her life in Bismarck, North Dakota, where we met. A sign painter by trade ("Cars, boats, small businesses—I paint all kinds of signs for all kinds of people"), the living room of her tiny, middle-class home doubles as the studio and workshop. She's thirty-seven, single, a bit pudgy, and very plainly dressed.

Fundamentalist Christians all basically believe the same thing: that Jesus was the Son of God; that he came to this earth in the form of a man; that he was God incarnate on this earth; and that he took upon himself the form of a man so that he could live out our own temptations as a human and therefore be able to overcome all temptations. So Jesus is the only sinless man that ever lived and is therefore our only savior. He didn't give us a choice. He said, "I am the Way, I am the Truth, and I am the Life." He didn't say, "I'm one of the ways," or "part of the truth," or "I can give you some life." He says, "I'm It." "No man can come to the Father but through me." You can't get there through Buddha, you can't get there through any other. So that's what a fundamentalist Christian believes. And from that point on they branch off into a thousand different directions. But approximately 33 percent of all Born-Again Christians are what's known as Pentecostal Christians. That's a statistic that George Gallup, Jr., has come up with himself. Pentecostals basically believe that there's a second experience beyond salvation that is extremely valuable, and important, to the Christian walk. I'm definitely a Pentecostal.

Jesus said, "I have to go away, and if I go away, the Comforter, or the Holy Spirit, can come to you." See, Jesus as a man could only be in one place at one time, but the Holy Spirit could be everywhere at once. And so he says it's imperative that I go away so that the Comforter can come to you. He'll give you power to witness. He'll give you power to lay hands on the sick and see 'em recover. He'll give you power to do things that in yourself you could not do. Jesus wasn't saying that it replaced him, but it was something extra to give you that extra power to be witnesses.

So Jesus said that the Holy Spirit must come. This is in the book of Acts, so Pentecostal Christians believe in that experience, and they call it the baptism of the Holy Spirit. It's just like asking Jesus to come into your heart, where you say, "Jesus, I want you to be the Lord of my life; I ask you to forgive me for my sins and just come in and be the master of my life." There is a second experience where you say, "Father, fill me with the Holy Ghost, fill me with that power. I want to have that power to live the Christian life that I can't live on my own." And so at that point he does pour out; he pours out the Holy Spirit upon you. Then you begin to speak in tongues, in unknown languages. There's no real significance to speaking in tongues other than the fact it's an outward sign of an inward experience. We believe that Jesus taught that it was a must. The reason that experience is valuable is because it does give you extra power . . . a supernatural power to live above temptation if you want to. You've still got your will, you can still choose to be a Buddhist if you want to, but God's saying, "I've made salvation available to you if you want it." And he gives us the power to lay hands on sick people and to see 'em healed instantly before our eyes. He gives us the power to stand before kings and judges without fear and to make a confession of our faith. He gives us the power to do what they did in the Old Testament. Moses parted the Red Sea, and if it was necessary that we had to do that for some reason, that power is available to us. That's the value of the baptism of the Holy Spirit.

Do you speak in tongues?

BECKY: Yes, I do—daily. Oh yes, absolutely. It's a part of my daily walk. And I think this is probably why I'm more interested in my faith now than I've ever been in my life. I grew up in it and I was taught all of my life about the truths of the Scripture, about salvation. I've been speaking in tongues since I was a young child. I just grew up being able to speak in tongues. Would you like me to pray for you? Would you mind if I spoke in tongues right here now?

Sure, go right ahead.

BECKY: All right! Praise God! Let's just pray for a couple minutes. Do you mind holdin' hands with me? Don't worry, this isn't any psychic stuff. This is all talked about in the Bible.

(She takes my hand, closes her eyes, drops her head, and begins to pray.) Father, I just thank you for this opportunity today to visit and to be an ambassador and a witness for you. Lord, I'm just a human vessel. God, there's nothin' *(tears begin to trickle down her face)* great about me, but there is something great about the person who lives in me, and the person of Jesus Christ. So Jesus, I just give myself over to you right at this moment. Father, we don't do this for a show, we don't do this for entertainment. But God, I pray that right now, that in the name of Jesus, that your power, that your presence, would be revealed in a great and a real way. Father, I thank you for bringing Phil here. I don't believe in just circumstance. I don't believe in coincidence. Father, I believe that this is a divine appointment. Holy Spirit, I just ask that you would flow through me, that if there is somethin' that you would want to say to Phil, that I would be a yielded vessel, that I would be able to speak forth the word of the living God. And Father, again I say, we don't do this for a show or entertainment. But Lord, I pray that you will do it to reveal yourself as the true and the living God, the one who is the most powerful, the God of Abraham, Isaac, and Jacob. The God who is all in all, who is the great and living one. There is no other God that can stand beside you, and Lord we give you praise and adoration this day, and we just say, Holy Spirit, whatever you want to do at this moment you do. And if there's nothin' that you want to do, there's nothin' I can do. I can only be a yielded vessel. I can't do anything in myself. So I just yield myself, Holy Spirit, to you right now, in Jesus' name.

(She begins to speak in tongues for some fifteen minutes, occasionally breaking in with a line or two of English. For the most part, however, she speaks in a strange, unrecorded dialect. What follows is a small sample of what transpired.)

Ho rabas se kora kose kodi. Ho rabas se kora se koraba se kodi. Porama dakandu debuse kodi koraba se godebus yati do kohora se kadi. Posanda a ki, posanda a ki . . . Oh Jesus we worship you. We worship you as the true and the living God. Ho rabasseco de busheku tabsantadaki. Periomaco, periomaco, periomaco! Horambaba se korabu se kanduba shedai . . .

For who do you say that I am? Who am I in your heart? Am I the living God? I say one thing, and you say another. Oh dabansada de ke shoredekabi. Badeshondi, badeshondi de kingoro babonshondo kadi . . . Have you searched my word for the truth that you seek and the hunger that you desire, the hunger for spiritual faith. Yes, it comes from Me. There is, within every man, that hunger. I have placed that hunger there, it doesn't come out of the sky . . . it comes from Me, for yes, yes, I am the true and the living God.

Badeshoko rabsa. Hetoshana high, hetoshana high. He ko! he ko! he ko! Oh dabasan dabase, korabase koba se kodi. Kobasan, kobasan. . . .

And I would, yes, I would, desire to show myself strong on your behalf. Bo, bo, bo robashan beshondo, oh sada, oh sada, oh sada. . . . The sweet things, the sweet things of the spirit, the sweet things of the spirit are available, yes, even unto you. The sweet things of the spirit that the world can't match, the world can't fabricate, the world can't come up with. No, it's from God, it's from the true and the living God. Te se korobo tosuo ko tesekadi, tesekadi. . . . Let me prove myself to you, let me prove myself to you, let me prove myself to you. Ask of me and see, ask of me and see, let me prove myself to you. Koraba se ku. . . . See, see, see if I'm not the true and the living God. Ask of me. Be bold. Be brave. I'm not afraid of your request, but be bold and be brave . . . ask of me and see, see, see, see if I won't do for you the thing that you desire. . . .

Hallelujah! Thank you, Jesus, thank you, Jesus, thank you, Jesus. Hallelujah! Hallelujah! Hallelujah! Hallelujah, Father! Praise you, Jesus! Thank you, Jesus; thank you, Jesus; thank you, Jesus; thank you, Jesus; thank you, Jesus. Hallelujah! Hallelujah! Thank you, Father; thank you, Father; thank you, Father; thank you, Father! We just receive it now, in the name of Jesus. We just receive it in the name of Jesus, Father. Hallelujah! Hallelujah! Hallelujah! Hallelujah! Thank you, Father; thank you, Father; thank you, Father! Oh hallelujah, hallelujah, hallelujah . . . thank you, Jesus, thank you, Jesus, thank you, Jesus *(whispering)*.

Ruth Norman

URIEL

People who feel themselves to be exiles in this world are mightily inclined to believe themselves citizens of another.

—*George Santayana*

At eighty-seven she's had a prolific career as a channeler of some 129 books. Some of the spirits she's channeled include Gus Grissom, John F. Kennedy, Robert Oppenheimer, Louis Pasteur, Ivan Pavlov, Dwight D. Eisenhower, Emperor Hirohito, Will Rogers, Gary Cooper, Moses, Muhammad, Mohandas K. Gandhi, Emmanuel Swedenborg, and Lao-tzu. Her books are self-published and stored at her El Cajon, California–based Unarius Academy of Sciences, a nonprofit educational foundation "dedicated to the distribution of the New World Teaching, the higher education for all truth seekers," and a "Science of Life that provides a direct pathway to infinite consciousness."

Jesus returned just as he promised he would. I met him in 1954 at a New Age convention. I knew him immediately.* He told me that he had many books to write and asked if I would like to help him. I had no immediate plans, so I said, "Yes, that would be fine, I'd love to." We immediately set out to transmit his teachings. As a matter of fact, within the very next few minutes he was transmitting a book from the minds of the higher worlds. The first three or four books were beautiful poetry. From then on he channeled. By "channel" I mean received mentally from the minds of the beings of higher worlds. He transmitted the first seventeen volumes of my library. When he changed worlds (which you Earth people call "died") the channelship energies were translated to me.

These volumes teach man how to heal himself of the problems he developed in past lives, many of which began hundreds of thousands of years ago during the war of the worlds. H. G. Wells's book talking about the "War of the Worlds" was not fiction. That was all truth. Wells had psychic memory. There were at least one hundred planets in this great war, but many of them were destroyed.

Of those who survived, there were many thousands of Unarian brothers, perfected beings who maintained not only this world but the thirty-two other worlds that were left. They are still working to build, to recombine, to make once again the single unit that once existed. These thirty-three worlds were once a unit and functioned as a unit because we traveled in spaceships from one planet to another very prolifically. It was no big deal to fly in a starship from one planet to another. The starships are very familiar to me. I remember them just like you people remember your automobiles.

I have lived on each of the thirty-three planets and have helped them to learn this higher way, this higher understanding. You could

---

* Ernest L. Norman, whom she later married. He has since died.

call it a new psychiatry. It is the Age of Reason and Logic. Many people on the earth field are aware of the New Age, but they don't know what is going to bring it about. What is bringing it about is this great organization of spiritual brothers, these Unarians. Unarius stands for Universal, Articulate, Interdimensional Understanding of Science. When the majority of the people on this world begin to use this science, they will build a better consciousness, a higher mentality.

Unarians try to teach people that life is eternal, that we have one continuous life, and that only the physical body is born repeatedly. But the spirit, the real you, the real self, lives one life, never dies, and continues on from this world to an astral world. When sufficient lessons are learned, the individual can move on to a spiritual world

. . . and on and on and on until each individual becomes an advanced being, a teacher, a brother, a supercelestial being. The ultimate for man of course is to become godlike. To me *God* has come to mean the collective infinite superconsciousness—all those who have gained true infinite intelligence. Each man has that spark, that infinite consciousness within him.

Every individual has an objective, even if he doesn't know it. His objective is to gain greater understanding while he is here and to use whatever understanding he gained in his past lives. But until man learns that he is an entity of eternity and infinity, he won't get very far. He bumps his head against the wall because he is not making any headway.

Today people are reverting in their evolution. They are not making headway. Right now all the spasmodic wars you see throughout the world are only the effects of what was set in motion eighteen million years ago. This earth is really a stupid, evil, hell world. This is a hell world. People have been sent here. It's really a prison. They've been sent here because they won't make progress, they haven't made any progress in their past lives. So they've all been dumped here, so to speak, until they begin to work out their pasts.

I have repeatedly come here to save and redeem many times. Even before my life as Mary of Bethany. I have lived fifty lives on this world, fifty other lifetimes. The earth man would not be familiar with most of the names of the people I've been, like Poseid of Atlantis or Uriel, but most people know about Queen Elizabeth I and Socrates and Buddha and Charlemagne. I plan to live in this physical body until I am two hundred, because there is so much work to do on earth. The negative forces on this earth world have been much more predominant and prevalent than the powers for good and light and truth.

In 2001 a space fleet will be landing here. All these thirty-two other worlds have been building spacecraft for the past several hundred years. Each planet has built a starship. They are very, very large structures, almost as large as this house, five thousand feet in diameter. They will come to Planet Earth and land on property that I have purchased for this purpose, about thirty miles from here. I bought that land about ten years ago. I was definitely inspired; just taken by the hand to do it.

There will be one thousand passengers on each ship. When they land, they will all be connected, one on top of another. It will be a gigantic structure, like a city, because it will be thirty-three levels tall. This is all part of the regeneration and recombining of the thirty-three worlds that were separated in the war of the worlds.

The people on the ships are coming for a twofold purpose. To help people to understand the Unarian science, and to help themselves, because they have all lived on this world before. They have created negative karma for themselves, so when they help people on this world, they will be freeing themselves from some of this karma. It will be a two-way proposition. They are planning to come to stay permanently.

Dawning of the Golden Age?

RUTH: Yes indeed. When those thirty-three ships enter this aura, it will bring about a shaking up.

Then what will you do?

RUTH: Leave this planet, I suppose. I'm not an earth person. I have long ago evolved out of this earth tie. I am not tied to the earth. Most people are tied to the earth because they don't have the energies within them to take them to another planet. But I have lived on the highest of the planets. Planet Aries is actually my home.

It takes a lot of will and volition and determination to come to a planet when you don't have the pull. I'm an alien, if you want to call it that. Yeah. I wouldn't be proud to be an Earthian. Heck no. What could one be proud about as an Earthian? How accomplished are they? Where are all your beautiful artists, sculptors, your writers, your composers? Look at the corny, crappy video and movies you have. Everything is so elemental. There is nothing beautiful or spiritual. It's a very, very low-vibration planet. Believe me, I'll be glad when I can step off of it.

Jack Pursel

JACK AND LAZARIS

Jack Pursel is a heavy, fleshy-faced, plainly dressed man whose thick glasses have chaffed his skin so much that sores have developed on the bridge of his nose. Formerly a middle manager for the State Farm Insurance Company, he is now the medium for Lazaris, one of America's most popular "channeled entities." An extremely successful New Age entrepreneur, he offers private consultations with Lazaris along with weekend workshops on Lazaris' philosophy of living. He also distributes tapes, videos, and books on Lazaris.

He operates his business, Concept Synergy, from his hilltop home in Greenbrae, California, just a few miles north of San Francisco's Golden Gate Bridge. After the electric gate swings open and you pull up the drive, it's not long before you realize that business for Jack has been good. His sprawling home boasts pyramid-shaped glass-walled rooms, a large outdoor pool, and carefully manicured canvas-covered gardens and walkways. Inside, the decor is "modern ethereal," with several airbrushed prints and New Age paintings.

I grew up in Michigan, and I had two parents and four brothers and sisters; all normal, you know. Nobody was alcoholic, nobody beat anybody up. It was a normal, all-American, apple-pie family. My father was a salesman and my mother was a schoolteacher, and all us kids strived to get straight A's to go to college so we could get a job to earn more than they did. Right out of the classic American background. As good kids we never drank, never smoked, and a date was, you know, totally on the up-and-up. And we never gave a party if our parents weren't gonna be around. So it was a very straitlaced Midwest background. Very middle-road, middle-class, very blah, really.

I'd say my life went along pretty much as planned until my wife, Peny, dragged me along to a course she'd read about in *Mademoiselle* magazine. I think this was 1972. It was called Silva Mind Control, where you learn to meditate and go to this place they call the laboratory in your mind, where you could create your reality. And they taught that you had counselors, like guardian angels, that would actually help you. So I took this two-weekend thing for a hundred and fifty bucks or somethin' like that, and that's where it hit me that I do create my own reality. It is up here *(he points to his head)* where this reality is being created. And I didn't understand it all, but I understood enough of it that it intrigued me. I started to meditate occasionally and I even started to seek advice from the counselors.

I was working in Michigan at the time, working for State Farm Insurance as a supervisor. But I wanted to move out of Michigan, 'cause we were sick and tired of Michigan winters. We wanted to go to a warm climate, so we decided on Florida. So I asked for a transfer and two State Farm offices down in Florida said they wanted to see me, but it was company policy that they wouldn't pay for any of my expenses because I initiated the transfer. Well, I didn't have the money, you know. And so I realized, I'm gonna have to drive all night and sleep in the car. And I got real angry. I don't want to travel this way. And those counselors that I had in my mind said, "Don't worry, they will pay your way . . . all expenses. Don't worry about it."

I went home from work on a Friday afternoon, thinking logically that I was gonna have to pay, even though I couldn't even afford the gas to drive. I didn't know where I was gonna get that. And yet I was given this information inside my head that it would all work out. Monday morning I go back to work, and they said, "Guess what? You know, those offices down in Florida want you to come down, they're gonna split the airfare and the rental car, and pay the hotels, etcetera, etcetera." So it's an all-expense-paid trip to Florida to interview at these two offices. And I thought, it worked! It worked! I mean, it was exactly what they said would happen! And it went that way. And that was where it really began for me, where I got the psychic input and visualized the reality I wanted—and got what I visualized. And that's really where it turned for me.

Then I went to the home office for a week-long training for supervisors. And there was a mix-up one evening as to when we were gonna go to dinner, so I had about an hour of time to do nothing. So I went back to my hotel room and, for some reason, you know, I don't know why, I thought, well, I think I'll do meditation (rather than watch TV or whatever). And this was totally out of character, because I was hardly serious at the time about meditation. Remember, I'm just a Middle American insurance guy. I mean, the meaning of life for me was a paycheck, a cost-of-living bonus, and getting a good six-month review so I could get a promotion. I wanna become a manager, you know. So I was the typical middle-class American that came home and watched TV. That's what I wanted to do when the day was done. I didn't wanna read. I'd rather watch television till eleven, and go to bed, and get up and go to work, and that was life. All that mattered. So meditation wasn't high on the agenda.

Anyway I'm in this hotel room and I sat down and really went into meditation . . . which usually meant I'd fall asleep. And what happened, instead of falling asleep, is that my meditation became spontaneous. All of a sudden I was going down this pathway in this forest with huge trees and ducking under branches, like it was very real. For the first time ever it was real. And I came to this brook, you know, and I could hear the water. I could see it splashing against the rocks. I could hear it, I could see it, and I could touch it, feel it's cold, etcetera. I mean, it was so real . . . it was thrilling, because I wasn't planning it, it just was happening. Then I turned around and I saw this cabin. It wasn't a log cabin, it was a thatched-roof kind of cabin, and the door was slightly ajar and there were lights on inside. So I went up across the porch and opened the door and went in, and there was this man there. I can't even tell you now what he looked like, because it was so long ago. But I said, "Hi." And he said, "Hi." And he talked blithely about some metaphysical concepts, basically boiling down to the message that you create your own reality, that whatever you believe is what's true. And therefore if you believe something is gonna hurt you, it will, and if you believe it won't, it won't. And, you know, you can eat what you want and you can drink what you want and you can smoke if you want to or not. Smoking is hazardous to your health if you believe it is, but not if you don't. After this discourse he basically says, "Don't call me, I'll call you" kind of thing. Well, I came out of the meditation and was just blown away. I called home to tell Peny about it: a spontaneous meditation. It was so real and this is the information I got. Then I went out to the company dinner and forgot about it. (Laughs.)

Well, a couple months later (we're living in Florida by this time) Peny read an article somewhere, and she said, "Look, this is virtually what you said, almost word for word." And I read it and, "By golly it is." And then what happened is that Peny got the feeling (Peny was very psychic naturally) that I should do a meditation and she should ask me questions. So one night, after dinner, I sat on the bed and went into my meditation. And she asked me questions, like what do you see about your job and other pretty mundane questions. And then I thought I'd fallen asleep, because from my perspective, things just went blank. And then, a few minutes later, I opened my eyes, "Oh, I'm sorry." But what had transpired in what seemed moments to me was maybe an hour, or an hour and a half, where I looked like I had fallen asleep, except that my head didn't do the usual flopping number but sat straight. So Peny waited about five minutes and then this other voice started talking through. And he explained to her that he was Lazaris and that, yes, he was the one that I had stumbled upon several months before and that this is the technique we should use so that he could come through more frequently, more regularly. He said that I should do this every day now, for two weeks, because he needed to make some final adjustments. He said that he had been working with my vibration for a number of lifetimes, nudging, suggesting, trying to kind of line me up so that I would be clear enough for him to communicate through.

So for two weeks that's what happened. And after each session, Peny would tell me, "Oh, Lazaris said this" and "Lazaris said that." But it didn't hit, it didn't hit, you know. It was like I wasn't really hearing it. But then she made a tape recording of Lazaris, and that's when it hit me like a football. I just really freaked out on it, because there on the tape I'm hearing this voice that is saying these things and they're comin' out of me when I'm not even aware of it. And I listened to it for about thirty seconds and shut it off and just had to go for a long walk, because, you know, these things don't happen to me. I just grew up in the Midwest, you know. I had normal parents, normal family, I'm not weird, I didn't fall on my head (*laughs*) when I was a kid, I didn't have any psychic experiences, I didn't have any imaginary playmates. Hey, what's going on!

It finally was through other people talking to Lazaris and benefiting from it, how accurate he was, you know, how helpful he was, how insightful he was, that I decided it was okay. Since then (it's been twelve years now) I've listened to a lot of the tapes, and people talk to me about Lazaris. And slowly I've tried to adopt his own philosophy as my own.

What does Lazaris believe? Would he be willing to talk?

JACK: Sure, he'd be more than willing to talk. (*Laughs.*) It doesn't take long, about thirty to forty-five seconds.

(*He removes his glasses, sits straight up in his chair, and takes several sharp intakes of breath. Things go silent for about thirty seconds, his eyes close, and then Lazaris begins to speak swiftly in a thick Irish accent.*)

LAZARIS: All right, fine, well, indeed a pleasure to be talking to you this afternoon. Would you for us please just state your name and your age?

My name is Phillip Berman and I am thirty-one.

LAZARIS: All right, fine. And, Phillip, the reason we ask you to mention your name and age is so as to tap into your vibration. Because in our reality there is no time, and therefore we use that point of chronology as a way of separating that which you call your past and what you call your present and future. So hopefully, in discussing with you, we can perhaps be a bit more specific and precise even though the questions you're going to be asking have, perhaps, not to do with you directly. And so let us begin with the areas or issues you'd like to discuss together.

What is your philosophy of life?

LAZARIS: Oh, all right, indeed, as concise as that can be put. First of all, life, as you know it in the physical form, is not what you consider life. Life to us has nothing to do with physicality. And therefore we see it as a continuous experience, and it does not have a beginning and nor does it have an end. Physicality and that experience that you call life we would suggest is a process of learning two things—and two things only.

Firstly, life is a process of learning how to have fun, with the emphasis on the learning; not just having fun, not just being in the right place at the right time, or knowing the right parties to go to, but learning how to have fun. It is something that you are constantly involved with. Learning how to have fun is constantly being redefined and redefined and redefined. And that, we would suggest, is the ultimate reason you are here, bottom line, not for some lofty purpose that can be described in some sort of pulpit etcetera, or that has to be dealt with in some sort of secretness of night. You've chosen to go into a physical form, you've chosen to create the reality that you've had, and your grandest opportunity is to learn to have fun.

Secondly, you are here to learn to consciously create success. Now again, the emphasis is on learning, not just being successful. A lot of people in this world are very successful, but if you ask them how they did it, they have to shrug their shoulders, "Uh, I don't know." But we would suggest here that that's not adequate enough. That's fine, but we would suggest the real power and the real sense of accomplishment in this life comes from learning how to consciously create success such that you know how you did it. At a certain point success is a financial matter. At other points success is a health matter. At other points success is a philosophical matter. But the goal is to be able to consciously create success at whatever level you're after.

Now, if that's all one does in one's life, learns how to consciously create success and learns how to have fun . . . that's it. You've done it, you've accomplished it, you've done what you're here to do, and then you have the choice, the option of either returning here to hone in those skills or moving on . . . meaning to move beyond that which is the physical, to continue life without form, to continue life without a body. And so we would suggest here that all those that want to have a very lofty and convoluted and complex physical reality, and a very complicated philosophy of that reality, they're welcome to it, most definitely. We do not criticize them, we do not put them down in any capacity whatsoever, but we would simply simplify it and put it in this form: You're here. Why are you here? What's the meaning of it all, what's the purpose of it all? All those rather lofty questions have an answer, and the answer is that you're here to learn to have fun, and to learn to consciously create success.

Men of the Cloth

Chabad Hasid

> If God lived on earth, people would break his windows.
>
> —*Yiddish Proverb*

St. Paul, Minnesota. He requested that I refer to him by the name of the group to which he belongs, the Chabad Hasid. Hasidic Jews trace their roots to the mystical Judaism of Rabbi Ba'al Shem Tov,* which flourished in Eastern Europe during the eighteenth century. Cleaving to God, or continually practicing the Presence of God, is the ideal cultivated by the Hasidim.

There's a very unusual community in Brooklyn, in Crown Heights, which is the Hasidic community, and this is where I grew up. It is centered primarily around the rabbi, who is the spiritual head. I basically grew up in that community and was raised on the Hasidic philosophy. The people who really absorb this philosophy and live by it are incredible human beings, even though they don't have any official status in the community. They're not necessarily the leaders, they're not necessarily the teachers, but they're incredible people; they have some almost superhuman virtues. Although they're not perfect, there's a certain selflessness and innocence that makes them really very, very special.

At the age of thirteen I remember davening one day and seeing the rabbi bow, and it was a very divine moment for me. Because the thought that he bows to something . . . or someone . . . was awesome. And his bowing was so simple, so unassuming, so innocent, so natural that it wasn't like he was being religious when he bowed or that he was being pious. It was like he was transparent, and whatever he was bowing to suddenly became very important. He went through eleven years of Russian labor camps, survived, not only physically but mentally, emotionally, religiously, and comes to New York and he's just full of life and fun and enthusiasm and faith and no scars . . . no scars. His legs are crippled, his body's broken, but no scars. He would tell us stories about all those years in labor camps and so on, and every

---

* Ba'al Shem means a person who performs wonders using the name of God.

one of the stories was entertaining, some of them were funny, and every one of them had a moral. Not a single one had anything to do with violence or with anger against his captors, oppressors . . . nothing, ever. The man who taught us Hasidic philosophy, our teacher, was an unbelievable human being. Superman. A genius of the first order and the most gentle person in the world. Any criticism from him was devastating. He never raised his voice . . . didn't have to. It's a very, very precious thing when a kid has someone he can admire that much. He saw us roughhousing just once and he was stunned . . . he was genuinely stunned . . . and he says, "Using your hands? You're using your hands?" And that's it . . . after that we couldn't do it again. Things of that nature.

The point of the whole thing is that the Jewish people are basically the representatives of God on earth; that every Jew is a little investment of God into creation; that the Jew is somehow not really organic to creation, as human beings are. The Jew is a messenger, a priest that stands apart. We represent Creator rather than creation, and therefore carry this incredible mission of 613 commandments, or 613 ways to reveal God to the world. And this has been our mission for 3,300 years. And this is why we have been scattered all over the world, so that this godliness reaches every corner of the world. He prefers earth to heaven and intends to have earth become his main dwelling place, and in order for that to come about, he needs earth to become more hospitable to him. So our mission in life . . . the reason we were created . . . is to make this world a dwelling place for God. That's how we understand the idea of "servant."

Serving implies more than just doing good stuff. Serving implies that you're not here for yourself—you're here for somebody else. You don't exist for you, you exist for somebody else. And you're here to serve means your function, or your place in this service, is to be invisible, is to be transparent. So you're trying to bring together God and the world, and you gotta make sure you don't get in between and block it. Like being a good arbitrator . . . you don't wanta become a third party, you just wanta bring the two parties together. So serving is very self-effacing; you don't count, it's not about you—it's about him. Serving means that every act counts because it's what's important to him, not what's important to me, and after all that, we're fulfilling a divine function, and there's nothing greater than that. So, superficially, it might be a paradox there: We are totally insignificant, we don't exist for ourselves, our place is to be transparent, and yet we're fulfilling a most important, cosmic mission.

It's not true that the Ten Commandments are good for us, that they were given for our benefit, that God in his concern and love for us wanted to protect us from our own wildness or from our own evil and therefore he gave us rules to protect us from ourselves. It's not true. God gave commandments because he needs them. When he communicated on Mount Sinai, he was communicating his needs; or, in different words, he was expressing himself, baring his soul. He was saying: "Look, I am God, I'm the creator, I made everything, I can destroy everything, I can do whatever I want, but I need you. I need you to do this for me." And since this is not a book about theology or religion, we won't get into how could God need and still be God.

We can if you want.

CHABAD HASID: Yeah, but we don't need to, because the very question is immoral. If somebody tells you he needs something, to ask him why he needs it is immoral. Either do it or don't do it, but don't ask him why. If your wife says she needs something, it's inappropriate to ask why. If your wife offers an opinion, you can ask why, and you can have a nice conversation. But if she expresses a need and you say, "Why?" you've destroyed the relationship because you've invalidated her. By saying, "Why?" you're saying, "The fact that you want it is not important. Give me a reason. If you can give me a reason, then maybe I'll agree and I'll take it seriously. If you can't give me a reason, then forget it." In any, any intimate relationship, you don't do that. It's an inappropriate response. If we want to ask, "What did God say?" that's a good question. "What does it mean?" is a good question. "How 'bout the contradictions?"—that's a good question. But when God says, "I need," there are no questions. So the question, "How can God need?" is a good question if you're studying theology, but if you're responding to God's need, then that question doesn't exist.

So, this idea that the commandments, morality, goodness, piety, is God's need, not ours, is basically at the heart of the whole thing and the uniqueness of this particular approach to Judaism, to the Ten Commandments. As a result of it, you have people who are very devoted, very disciplined, sometimes self-sacrificing, and yet without any self-consciousness. They're very special, doing very special things, and they don't know it. They're very ingenuous about it. And that's because the focus is not on you. The focus is not on whether you are religious. In fact we don't want to be religious, we don't like being religious, we're not even the type to be religious. Jews in general are not the religious type; we don't like religion; we don't need religion. Our response to God is a relationship based on his needs, not ours. Not even our spiritual needs. It's really him. And once we know what he needs, everything else just pales into insignificance.

So the person who needs to be religious or needs to be spiritual or has a thirst for spiritual things, that's all beside the point. It may even be a distraction. So religious impulses, spiritual needs, spiritual hunger, spiritual desires, that's all interference—it's all about "me." God did not come down to Mount Sinai to satisfy my needs, not even my most spiritual needs. I came to Mount Sinai to see if I could satisfy one of God's needs. I didn't bargain for 613, though. *(Laughs)*

See, that ties into this whole thing as well. What is belief in God? What if I don't believe in my wife? What does that mean? Either you have a wife or you don't have a wife. What do you mean, you believe or you don't believe? See, belief, again, is a spiritual talent. Some people have more of a talent, some people have less of a talent. But everybody has some amount of belief or of faith. So what is this issue with whether I believe or not? So I believe in God or I don't believe in God. But he's still my Father, whether I believe him or not. Belief does not create God. My disbelief is not gonna undo him. So my belief in him or my doubts of him . . . these are my issues. I can either be strong and clear-minded and firm in my belief, or I can be weak and doubtful and hesitant—and what's the difference? If I was working at perfecting myself, it would be a big issue. I would start with this. If I was working on making society a better society, I would start with this. But we're starting off with God, not with our reaction to him, not our perception of him, not our capacity for him, but with him. So we're starting off with the assumption God needs something from his creation, otherwise he wouldn't have created it. That's the beginning. His existence transcends what we feel or what we think of him.

When people say, "How can God allow cruelty? How can God allow suffering?" the problem they have is that they already have a belief and a commitment and a devotion to goodness. Now, if you're going to believe in God, he'd better be as good as you, otherwise you don't accept him. So really your devotion to goodness is your God, and then God has to match that. God has to obey the dictates of goodness, and for a spiritual person God has to obey the dictates of spirituality. Otherwise he's not acceptable. So it's like we're creating God in our own image, or we have an ideal that is greater than our God, and God is acceptable only because he reaches the same ideal that I already have. The ironic thing is, God created those ideals, and now we're making him suffer for it. See, God comes along and says, "I want you to be good," and we turn around and tell God to be good. So we take his commandment, turn it into God, and then turn him into a worshiper. And he has to worship at the altar of his commandments.

So what is God? God is that reality which existed before any of your reality existed. He's the creator. He created everything out of nothing. So before you had your ideology, before you had your virtues and your principles and your values, before you had your religion, there was God. And he created all that. He created goodness, he created spirituality, he created heaven, he created all that. And therefore none of those things can be God. They're all creations. And I personally feel that if we ever are going to get together, if there's ever going to be peace, and if people are going to be able to live and get along with each other, the only way that it's going to happen is by getting past the religion, back to God. Which is where Judaism is. Judaism is not a religion. You see, when you become religious, you focus on what your obedience to God has done for you. God says run down the street. So you run down street, and you ask, "Do I feel any different now? Am I different now? Look at me, do I look any different? Do you see the glow? *(Laughs.)* I feel different." But that's all childish . . . that's all childish. God asked you to do something, and you did it. What does that make you? Nothing. It doesn't make you anything.

The truth is that we are nothing. We all run around, in our entire life, trying to make believe that we don't realize that we're nothing. *(Laughs)* Psychologists call it ego. But basically what that is is a denial of our mortality. So we spend our entire life denying our nothingness. Sometimes we convince ourselves that we are something, and sometimes we don't convince ourselves. But either way that's what we're struggling with all the time. Every moment of our life we struggle to avoid becoming a zero, because we're on the verge of zero at all times. And the fact that God comes along and gives us commandments and books and homework is used as a reassurance . . . do you see that? You see that you really are significant, you really are something . . . God loves you and God wants you and God cares about you and God gets angry—that's religion. And religion is actually turning it inside out. It's proving our significance from God, rather than acting on God's significance.

The truth is, God gives us commandments and wants us to do certain things and cares very deeply what we do in spite of our insignificance, not because of it. So religion actually inverts the whole thing. Religion is really like, you speak to God for ten minutes and then you run to the mirror to see if you look any different or you take your pulse to see if your heartbeat is any different. So, you were focused on God for a minute and then immediately you focus on yourself, and that's religion.

But if God tells you to do something and you do it, that's not religion. He comes to us and he says, "Listen . . . can you stay calm for a minute? I want to talk to you, and don't freak out on me." But if we start getting religious, then we're not listening again. And what he's saying might not be awesome, and it might not be holy, and it might not be cosmic. He's saying, "I want you to wear strings on your garments." So what's so awesome about that? I mean, if there is something awesome about it, I'm missing it. *(Laughs)* In fact, religious people, spiritual people, don't like the commandments. They don't like God's commandments . . . they're disappointed in them cause they're so mundane. God says, "On Sabbath, eat three meals," "On Hanukkah eat latkes." Religious people look at that, they say, "What is this? What's all this food? What's with all this eating? We're supposed to be holy. We're supposed to be fasting, not eating." God says, "Do your business at honest scales." Business! What kind of God is this anyway? We're supposed to be holy, we're supposed to be spiritual, what kind of business? The commandment should be "Thou shalt have no business. Thou shalt engage in no materialistic pursuits." But God comes along and says, "Have an honest scale, lend money to each other to help your businesses." Money? The root of all evil. What kind of commandments . . . what kind of God is this anyway? So religion actually interferes with God.

So when God comes down to Mount Sinai, the one thing he needs of us is, "Please, don't get religious on me. I'm tryin' to talk to you. Can I talk to you? Will you listen?" But when we have these preconceived notions of spirituality, of godliness, of holiness, of awesomeness, this is the early idolators. The early idolators, before God gave the commandments, were into spiritual things, they were into mystical things and religious things. And when God came and wanted to talk to us, the first think he had to say was, "Cut that out. Stop it with this religion already and listen to me."

F. Forrester Church

THE CATHEDRAL OF THE WORLD

I was raised a Presbyterian, sort of an ice-cream-social Presbyterian. High holidays and nice clothes, but not serious. As a matter of fact one of the keys to success for being a Presbyterian Sundayschooler in those days was being able to color Jesus in a meaningful way. And I wasn't very good at art, so I had a hard time keeping the sky out of his face. And I think if my religion would have ended there, I would have failed.

He's the eldest son of the late U.S. senator Frank Church. We met by accident in Aspen, Colorado, where I had come to interview physicists at the Aspen Institute. On a sunny summer day, with a light breeze blowing, we sit outside on one of the Institute's carefully manicured lawns and begin to talk. Boyish, warm, eloquent, he's easy to imagine booming out Sunday inspiration to a packed house at New York City's All Souls Unitarian Church, where he serves as pastor.

The key experience or transforming moment for me was when my father, Frank Church, was elected to the Senate. He was given a Bible, and the Bible was Jefferson's Bible. Thomas Jefferson, during his time in the White House, took the Gospels and excerpted from them those passages that he found most worthy, most compelling, and most enduring . . . and cut out the rest. He cut out the Virgin Birth. It ends with the rolling of the stone against the tomb. It was the first Bible I'd ever really read . . . all words, no pictures. And I found myself gripped by the human Jesus. My father said to me after I read that Bible that for him religion could best be summed up in Jefferson's own words, that "it is in our lives and not in our words that our religion must be read." In other words deeds, not creeds.

Jesus, as represented in Jefferson's Bible, had no miraculous birth or miraculous death. He lived through force of example and the power of his teachings—in a way, a miraculous life. As I grew older, I began to realize that we couldn't emulate Jesus in his birth because our births were natural. And we couldn't emulate him in our deaths because our deaths will be natural. But we could, if we were to study his teachings and be transformed by them, to a small degree anyway, emulate his life. And our challenge somehow is, in the same way that he did, to live our lives in such a way that they would be worth dying for.

That stuck with me, and through my time at Harvard—master of divinity and also my Ph.D. work—I gradually gravitated toward Unitarianism, then only discovering that Jefferson himself had been a Unitarian. So there was a sense that there was a kind of coherence in my own developing religious orientation, grounded back in that early experience of reading Jefferson's Bible and having religion for the first time really make sense to me. And that finally prompted me to go into the Unitarian ministry. I don't think, however, that I truly became a grounded and thoughtful religious person until I left academia and began working in a church. And I'm not sure I became a minister until I presided over my first funeral.

My own definition of religion comes out of those experiences, with people who are dying, with families who are struggling. My own definition of religion is that it's our human response to the dual reality of being alive and having to die. And following that definition, I believe each of us is a religious being. We probably are the religious animal. We are the one animal who knows that we are going to die and therefore has to make some sense of who we are, why we live, what the purpose of our life is, where we come from, and where we are going. Birth and death are the two hinges upon which life turns. Life would not exist without death as that hinge.

I was asked by a little girl in my congregation, "Where was I before I was born?" And it is interesting, because that's a question we don't think of very often. But for a little three-year-old girl it's a much more meaningful question, much more existentially immediate than the question, "What happens to me after I die?" When she asked that question, I thought, Gee, that's about the same question. Where was I before I was born? It's about the same question as, What happens to us after we die? I thought about it for a while, and I'm not sure this answer satisfied the little girl, but it began to help me a little bit. I told her that before we were born, we were with God, we were part of the body of God, part of the mind of God, we were potential life in our present individual form, but only in a potential state, and a part of the whole great body of potential life, the meaning of which we cannot finally understand. And then we enter into life as God carriers. We bring that part of us which was in God when we come into this world; it's within us, it's a part of us. But we also have a mortal existence as a unique individual, really quite wondrous. Then when we die, we leave that unique individual, wondrous but also mortal carrier, and that part of us which once was a part of God returns to God—to the undifferentiated life force. And beyond that I would not want to be too specific, because I can't know what the nature of that mystery life force–miracle is.

But I do fear dying, although I don't fear death. The great blessing of the ministry is that one is invited as a participant into the lives of people who are facing death and dying, and that does a couple of things. First of all it helps to put one's own little petty problems, envies, jealousies, bitterness, anger, strivings into perspective. These things are so unimportant compared to that ultimate passage. It blows all the dust off of one's psychological desk. And then one is invited in fully to participate in the sacrament of death with others. And I have seen enough people die to know that there is a potential in that passage for peace, for beauty, and for completion.

I live according to a few simple principles. One of them I call nostalgia for the present; looking forward to each day as it passes rather than ruing it after it's gone. Another way you might put that is "looking forward to the present." Expecting that which you have and enjoying it in anticipation *and* in fruition rather than always looking longfully for that which very likely will not be. By focusing one's energy, to the extent that it is possible, upon the present, one is liberated from fears of the future and also liberated from regrets about the past. And the way this fits in to the whole question of death is that I have seen people in the last weeks of their lives living every minute more fully than they ever have before, because they recognize what most of us don't in our daily living. That is that each moment is precious. Soon it will be gone. It is ours fully to enjoy only once, while we're there. And that is a tremendously religious approach to life. So I have seen people, as they were dying, wish that they had taken better care of themselves while they were alive, or while they were in the prime of their life wish they'd spent more time with their family, wish all of these things.

The opposite of wishful thinking (wishing for something you haven't) is thoughtful wishing—thinking to wish for what you've got right now. And what you have right now is this day with the wind blowing and the light motley on the mountains in this beautiful place carrying on a conversation with another human being who is also going to die, and it's very precious. It's a miracle we're even able to converse. We tend, I think, to take our lives for granted rather than receiving them daily as a gift. And I would hope that each day I live I might, through some encounter, be born again to an awareness and appreciation for the gift of life, the mystery of being, and the wonder and the miracle. Not the miracle *out there*, but the miracle in here.

I think our lives find their meaning in the extent to which we empty ourselves and are filled, lose ourselves and are found, give ourselves away to others and find ourselves in the encounter with them, without which there is nothing but isolation and self-absorption and ultimately estrangement and emptiness.

I find myself guided more and more in my own thinking by paradox. My definition of the devil, for instance, is evil disguised as good. My definition of angels, apart from their being messengers of the divine, little epiphanies of the divine, is goodness disguised. So the one thing that I try to do is be most suspicious of my finest actions, to be most wary of my most compelling thoughts, to try to find something redemptive in the thoughts or actions of others that

I either don't understand or don't admire. Righteousness and self-righteousness are completely opposite things. Righteousness is always spontaneous and never self-conscious. Self-righteousness is highly self-conscious, highly patterned, and terribly dangerous. Really it also goes, in another sense, with my theology. I'm only dogmatic upon one point, and that is that there is no single truth.

To give you another metaphor, I see us living in something that might be called the cathedral of the world. And this cathedral is vast of course, and there are literally hundreds and thousands of windows, some of which have been fashioned over centuries. Some of which are abstract. Some representational. Some opaque. Some translucent. Some have crosses. Some have figures of Jesus on the cross. Others have yin-yang symbols. You have every possible kind and variation of these windows. And through each of these windows shines the light. We are either raised to be particularly appreciative of the special nuances and meanings of a given window or perhaps we walk in the darkness with our heads down, looking at the floor, mopping up, trying to find some nugget of gold. And suddenly the light comes through one of those windows, refracts through one of those windows and splashes on the floor right in front of us, and we look up and say, "There's the light." And we go to that window and we see something as we've never seen before and we worship and we are changed; in fact we're saved. Now, the only danger is that once that's happened to us, we say, "This is the window through which the light shines." Then there's a tremendous temptation to go and either urge other people to come to your window and worship the light there or to gather your group of co-worshipers and go out and throw stones through other people's windows.

Now, these windows each to a certain degree reflect the truth. But what we do is end up confusing the window for the light, confusing the images of Truth refracted through that window for the Absolute Life that shines through all of them. And in this way Universalism becomes, for me, the only possible theology, only possible uniting theology for our time. Universalism takes away no specificity. It simply posits that though I don't understand the way the light comes through that window, there is no way in which I am competent to tell the person who's worshiping there that the light comes through my window more clearly, more brightly, more profoundly. The only rule is the rule that each group can worship the light through its window so long as it doesn't block out the light coming through the other groups' windows.

So you have particularism, because different truths shine through these different configurations. But you also have Universalism, because the light out there, which is the mystery and the miracle, is God. God's our name. But it doesn't matter. "That which is greater than all yet present in each." That which is shining through all windows is not ever going to be finally comprehended or contained by any given faith, group, race, or creed.

Now, that being the case, is there greater good? Well, I would say there's ever-deepening good and understanding and truth for each group shining through each window as we better understand it, reflect upon it more seriously, take what we gain from it, and go back into the cathedral and help other people muck about with a little bit more joy and a little bit more purpose and a little bit more meaning. But when it comes to the final Truth, that is absolutely veiled from us. There's no way we can ever know. The only dangerous people in this world are the people who know that they know. They are the fundamentalists of the left who know that there is no God and know that this is an utterly mechanistic universe and that all religion is hokum. They are the fundamentalists of the right—Islamic, Jewish, Christian—who know that there's only one way to salvation and divide the world into those who are saved and those who are damned. Both groups, both kinds of dogmatists, are truly terrifying to me for the simple reason that they hold it in their power to destroy others. I don't doubt that they have been saved. But that kind of salvation can be very destructive indeed.

We are truly blasphemous when we demand from the Creator or any of the Creator's children ultimate answers which will explain for our satisfaction—our petty, silly little satisfaction—the meaning of our being. This whole quest, which is inevitable, somehow has to be transcended. And I think the only way it can be transcended is by giving ourselves away to others. That's why, going back to the Jeffersonian quote, it's in our deeds or our lives and not in our words that our religion must be read. That's so true to me. I couldn't care less finally what a person's beliefs were. I care a great deal about how he or she treats her family, his or her neighbors, and me in fact, and the extent to which his or her life in the world is a redemptive one. Redemption. Redemption.

The two things, I think, to remember in terms of any kind of religious search are humility and openness. The humility says no matter how much we learn, how much we grow, how much we give, how much we receive, we never really are going to get close to understanding who we are, where we've come from, or where we're going.

The openness principle posits that there is absolutely no limit to how much we can grow, love, serve, redeem, or be redeemed. So you've got these two things, humility and openness. Some people will take a look at how little they can finally know and either give up or make a leap of faith that answers all of these questions so they don't have to think anymore. Other people will sense that openness and be scared and batten themselves down at some point. But if you work the two principles together, always remaining humble about how little we possibly can know and always remaining open to how the sky is the limit in terms of our growth, then there is a dynamic of life that is wondrous, and one doesn't have to worry too much again about having not gotten there, because one knows one won't; but neither does one become dangerous by having assumed that he or she has gotten there.

As I say to my congregants, "If you believe in God, the best thing you can do for yourself is to suspend your belief for a while, because undoubtedly your God is too small and you must grow beyond that God. On the other hand if you don't believe in God, your very disbelief is a stumbling block. Kick it away and take a leap of faith and believe in something, something more than disbelief."

Once one can get to this point, then there is no end to the openings for growth. And the only way we really finally can grow is by changing. This is one of the reasons why I think that we learn more from people who are radically different from ourselves than we do from people who are like ourselves. However, as human beings, the tendency is to group, according to prejudice, in tribes and then to close the other out. The tendency is to take gays, AIDS victims, or prostitutes, for example, and close them out. Quarantine them. Try to get them in such a situation that we don't have any contact, 'cause we're frightened. We're not only frightened of disease, we're frightened of difference. We're frightened of having our pet prejudices challenged. And again, you know, the moment that one becomes too sure of one's beliefs, one really ought to spill them out, tip them over, mess them around, throw some new things in so as not to become a victim of one's own prejudices.

Beliefs are self-ratifying and disbelief is self-ratifying. We tend to see what we look for, whereas, as Jesus points out, the kingdom of God is not where you're going to be looking. The kingdom of God is in a mustard seed, the least portentous of all seeds. The kingdom of God is not revealed by the good son but by the prodigal son. It's revealed by prostitutes and tax collectors. Depending upon your prejudices, the parable of the good Samaritan is the parable of the good homosexual or the good redneck. The kingdom of God is revealed where you least expect to find it.

So it's pretty simple for me: Love the person you're with. Do the work that is yours to do. Be the person that is yours to be at any given time. Think to wish for what is yours at this very moment. To love. To serve. To touch. To know. Think of what it is that is yours. Think to wish for what it is that is yours to do. And think to wish that you might be who it is that you, at that time, might most fully be. Avoid wishful thinking. Avoid the traps and pitfalls of nostalgia for the past. And savor every moment as it passes. And enlist yourself in the work of saving that which can be saved at that very moment so that it, too, may endure for others to enjoy.

<hr>

Ed Nelson

ONLY TOO GLAD TO PRAY FOR YOU

I'm not a very smart man, and I don't know much. I really don't. But I do have a book, I do have this Bible. And I honestly stand on this one primary conviction: This IS the word of God, and I believe it. I stand on it. I'm not proud of that fact, it's just a fact. I know that book's true. I'm a sinner, but I'm under God's grace.

Denver, Colorado. He's pastor of the South Sheridan Baptist Church and a powerful Republican precinctman. A strapping blue-eyed, white-haired, six-foot-four Swede, his knuckle-breaking handshake hardly takes you by surprise. "I've been pastor here for twenty-six years. I've got five children, eight grandchildren, and been married for thirty-eight years." Wherever he goes, he carries a copy of the Bible. He's sixty-three.

When I grew up, I wanted to be a soldier. Oh, there was a patriotism in America that you don't have today. I loved America and I wanted to fight for America. And when World War II came around, I wanted to fight terribly. I had a hatred for Japs. But I had all these problems with my heart from a terrible wagon accident I'd had on our farm. So I wasn't sure that I'd pass the physical to get into the army. When the draft board finally called, I was really scared I wouldn't pass the physical. So I called my doctor and said, "If my heart's still acting up, what can I do?" He said, "Go to bed three days and stay there. Then get out of bed, just get up and go." I did that for three days and I managed to pass the physical. I thought I was home free.

Then they said there's one more thing you gotta do. You gotta pass a psychological evaluation. So they sent me in to meet with this psychologist. He looked at me and said, "What do you do for a good time?" I said, "I go to church." He said, "You go to church for a good time" (laughs). Oh, he couldn't believe it. What in the world. "Did you hear God talkin' to you?" he says. And I said, "No." He said, "You must." I said, "I don't know what you're talkin' about. I've never heard God talk." He said, "You have anything to do with girls? Do you date?" I said, "Yes." He said, "What do you do on a date?" I said, "Well, do I need to answer that?" He said, "Yes, you do. Tell me what you do on a date." I said, "I'll tell you. I don't commit adultery and I don't have sex with an unmarried girl." He said, "You've never had relations with a girl?" I said, "Never." He said, "Why not?" I said, "I believe in the Bible and I was taught the idea that you don't sleep with a girl until you marry her." Well, this guy went crazy and he sent in this other guy to examine me. So this other guy comes in and says, "They tell me you're a religious fanatic." I said, "No, I'm not, I'm not a fanatic." And he said, "Well, do you read your Bible?" I said, "Yes, I do read my Bible every day. I accepted the Lord."

So they dismissed me and then said I'm not gonna be admitted into the service. I asked why. They said I'm a paranoid schizophrenic. Well, that bothered me for a while, I really wanted to fight for America, but I finally got over it. I realized that a lot of people are opposed to the Lord and that a Christian had better get used to criticism. Out of that experience I gave my life to the ministry and went to Bob Jones University. And I switched entirely from what I did. I was a churchgoer where the Bible was not preached at all. But after I became a Christian, I decided this Bible had become my book. And my whole attitude changed. The book became my life.

So what are my strong beliefs? My very, very strong belief is that this Bible is the word of God, that here's all we need. I am a man of the book. It's all right here. All Scriptures are given by inspiration of God for correction, for instruction. So my primary belief is the Bible, is the word of God. I accept the Bible as my law in every area of life. The more you study the word of God, the more it fits into every life situation.

Because I'm a Bible believer, I believe that Jesus Christ is the Son of God. I believe that he is the Virgin-born Son of God, that Mary was a virgin, and that salvation is only by the atonement that Jesus accomplished at the cross. I believe that he literally rose from the dead. I believe that he's literally going to come again. And he will return and set up a reign in Jerusalem. And there will be a thousand-year period of peace. I believe there's a heaven. I believe there's a hell. I believe that each person needs to personally accept Jesus.

In the social area I believe that the Bible teaches that life begins at conception. In Psalm 139, verse 16, God makes it very clear.* So I believe life begins at conception. Of course you've got a lot of medical evidence of that now. Our surgeon general of the United States has written an article on it. And the president has written an article on it. So I believe abortion is a sin. I believe the biggest crime Americans do today is kill four thousand babies a day. I believe God is going to judge this nation because of abortion. And unless we do something about it, I believe there's going to be a judgment from almighty God on this nation.

In the area of homosexuality, lesbian and gay rights, I am totally opposed to that. I believe that homosexuality is a sin. Leviticus, chapter 27, says, "Whenever a nation gets into homosexuality, the earth vomits that nation out." And every nation that has been plagued with homosexuality has gone down as a national power. I believe the homosexuality in this nation is going to destroy us unless we do something about it.

ERA, equal rights, I don't believe it's necessary. Equal pay for equal work, I'm not opposed to that. But I don't think a secretary ought to be getting as much pay as a truck driver or as a doctor. I'm glad ERA was defeated. I believe ERA would open a can of worms in this country. The lesbians, the gay-rights people, the ultraliberal facet are all for it. And I'm convinced that it will open up new avenues of gay and lesbian rights that would be very serious, and so I am deadly opposed to it on scriptural grounds.

I believe this book gives us a work ethic, that if a man would not work, he should not eat. This book also teaches the principles of capitalism without greed. I wish President Reagan would not have given any apology when he said that Russians are evil. I believe that communism is atheistic, anti-God, anti-Bible. And I feel that we just must fortify ourselves. I'm for national defense. Doing everything we can. All we can do is trust them to lie. That's about all we can trust them to do. Communism believes the end justifies the means. If they think taking a life will help communism, well, they've got

---

* "Thy eyes beheld my unformed substance; in thy book were written, every one of them, the days that were formed for me, when as yet there was none of them." (Oxford Annotated Bible, RSV, 1977)

a right to do it. Mikhail Gorbachev is a Communist and he's a thorough-born Communist. He didn't get into that position by being a compromiser. And I believe the fact that we've drawn so much concern from him is a good indication that our president's done the right thing. I feel very strongly that we must stand for freedom in the free world.

On capital punishment, the Bible teaches in Genesis 9:6, "He that sheds man's blood by man shall his blood be shed." Jesus said, "They that live by the sword shall die by the sword." So I believe wholeheartedly in capital punishment.

I personally believe that Jews or Gentiles need to accept Jesus Christ. So my recommendation to you, since you're not a Christian, is that you accept the Lord. We have a man running for United States Senate right now here in the state of Colorado, Ken Kramer.* Ken's a Jew. And he and I met the other day for lunch. I talked to him. Again I said, "Ken, I'm praying that you'll come to know the Lord and I want to help you." And he's reading his Bible. He said, "Look, I've read the Bible all the way through and I've come to the place where I'm willing to accept Jesus as the Messiah, but I'm not willing to accept him as God." And I said, "Well, Ken, the two go together. You can't really believe in his messiahship if you do not accept his deity."

So I believe that you, like anybody else, without Christ you're a lost soul and you need that. Your only hope for redemption is that your Messiah's already come, already died on the cross for you. All you've got to do is accept him. I'd be only too glad to pray for you.

Rabbi Joseph Weizenbaum

There is a spiritual hunger among our people today. I'm talking about Jews in particular, but I could probably talk about the world. But I wanna talk about Jews, 'cause I'm a rabbi.

He is the first Jewish leader in America to actively support the Sanctuary movement, and rabbi of Temple Emmanuel, a reform synagogue

---

* A conservative Republican, he was narrowly defeated by Democrat Tim Wirth in 1986.

in Tucson, Arizona. "I feel very strongly the plight of the refugee. . . .
My father was an undocumented alien; he came to this country as a
stowaway. 'Know the heart of a stranger; you were strangers.' That's a
very central part of Judaism, and our rituals don't make a lot sense if
you forget that one."

I was involved in a counseling situation a few years back with a
husband and a wife and their twenty-eight-year-old daughter, who
had been in the Moonies for seven years. Her father was a well-
known attorney in his town, a liberal, and was involved in secular
Jewish causes, but never involved in a synagogue. At one point his
daughter turns to him and says, "You never taught us" (the brothers
and sisters) "you never taught us to believe in God." Her father (and
this is not a joke) very seriously looked at his daughter and said,
"But dear, we've been to Israel four times." So I make the point
frequently that, in Jewish arithmetic, one should learn that four trips
to Israel equals not one God. "We've been to Israel." Israel is one
of the idols that we use, and Israel's a foreign country. I have nothing
against Israel, except I like to point out that the Israelis have enough
time minding their own business; they don't have time to carry us
on their backs through life, see. The American Jew says, "I don't
pray and I don't study, but I do pay."

You can give water to a crying child when it wants milk, and for
the moment it will be quiet—but it will not be satisfied. So what is
our mistake? We Jews confuse identity with religion. We give water
when we should be giving milk. It has become so important for us
to be able to say, "I'm a Jew," that we have made a religion of it.
And the spiritual problems that plague all humankind are such that
for a Jew to turn to that identity search is to turn to water instead
of milk.

The average American Jew has as his first article of faith: "I never
denied I was a Jew." Well, that's very nice. My response is, "Did
you ever affirm it?" And they reply, "I'm proud I'm a Jew." My
response is, "That's nice, but are you thankful you're a Jew?" Both
questions usually give me an uncomprehending stare, because not
one Jew in a thousand has ever thought about whether he's thankful
he's a Jew, or whether he has affirmed it. They say, "I never denied
it." And therefore I'd like to point out to people that to go into the
delicatessen and eat a corned beef sandwich does not require that
you be a Jew. They don't stand at the door checking, see? I always
like the great line from the vaudeville days: "Everybody gotta be
somewhere." So you were born a Jew. Wonderful. So what! So what!

I find in my own life (this is a personal statement) that as I grow older, I have less and less in common with more and more Jews. They're my family, and I love them as my family. I'm one of them, could be nothing but that, but because of that I grow more unhappy with what I see. I so often feel about Jewish life like the old story of the emperor's clothes: I see nakedness, and everybody's raving about how beautiful the outfit is. Am I looking at the same thing they're looking at? Maybe I'm nuts. But I know I'm not. This is one of the reasons I'm so fond of Buber and his writing,* because Buber deals with the milk, with the substance of what it is to be a Jew, not with the trappings.

The Bible knows little or nothing about atheism, but it knows a lot about idolatry. So it is not that we're missing God. The problem is that we've got too many of the wrong ones! We have all kinds of idols, some of which have Mogen Davids on them. Israel is an idol for most Jews. After all, most Jews in America have never been to Israel, will never go to Israel; more people are leaving Israel than going there. But Israel has become our football team, see. We like to sit in the stands and watch the gladiators clobber each other, and we cheer for the ones from our city. Well, Israel, in the world of geopolitics, is right in there doing our work for us. But that's idolatry, ethnicity.

People like to say, "Well, I'm an ethnic Jew." And I say, "What is your ethnicity? Are you from Poland?" But no Jew from Poland was ever a Pole. No Jew from Lithuania was ever a Lithuanian. "What's your ethnicity?" Do all Jews have the same ethnicity? Of course not. And so what? What does ethnicity have to do with anything? Everybody gotta be somewhere, no one was born in a vacuum. What is the meaning of it? So what? And that's what Judaism is about—the so what. So I try, when I deal with Jews, as I do every day, to bring to them as best I can the stuff of Jewishness. What does it mean to be a Jew? And I speak of Judaism in the same way I would of Christianity: "If you take it seriously, it will blow your mind." So I like to say, "Be very careful about what I'm telling you, see. Because it will blow you away and cause you to think things you don't want to think about and maybe even to do things you don't want to do."

I'm a great believer in the Isaiah view of mission, of bringing light up to the nations. We have a purpose, we are here to teach. Which doesn't mean God doesn't love the other children, but rather that the firstborn's supposed to know better 'cause he came first. "Israel, thou art my firstborn," he says. That's obligation, see. I think

---

* Martin Buber (1878–1965), Jewish philosopher, Zionist, and scholar of Hasidism.

being one of the chosen people is not being given, as so many people think, a star on your forehead 'cause you're a good boy. It's more somebody offering you a pin and saying, "Have a seat and make yourself comfortable." *(Laughs.)* You must act it out, and it has nothing to do with whether you choose. If you're a Jew, things happen to you, situations are thrust on you whether you choose them or not, see. I know Jews whom I describe in the following way: "I would if I could, but I can't, so I won't." *(Laughs.)* I know Jews who are so angry at being thrust in that situation that it colors everything they think about. They know they're Jews, and that's why they're angry. See, if they could assimilate and become something else, they wouldn't have to be angry. They're angry because they know that's what they are. I don't have that anger. Whatever causes that was not put into me. I have come to feel nothing but thankful I'm a Jew and challenged by the fact that I'm a Jew. When I go as a Jew into the Christian world, as I do frequently, I go as a Jew. In fact I tell people (maybe you have the same reaction), "I never feel more Jewish than when I'm sitting in a church."

I don't speak for the Jews. I'm not their elected representative to quote whatever it is the consensus of Jews are thinking. No, I'd rather walk in the shadow of the prophets and speak to the Jews. See, most Jews are not descendants of the prophets. They're descendants of the people who heard the prophets and turned against them. That's who most Jews are, the ones who turned away from the prophets. I can't say who is a prophet and who isn't, but I can talk about the shadow of the prophets. Are we gonna stand in the shadow, or stand outside of it, in our dealings? There is, for example, a sense of compulsion evident in the Sanctuary movement. These people (Christians, Jews, what have you) are putting it on the line for others. I think this is what the Jew is to do.

In other religions the ultimate instrument of God, whether it be the Christ, the Buddha, is a perfect instrument. In Judaism it is not. It is the people of Israel, who are an imperfect instrument. We are the prophets' people, which means that our ears must hear our mouths. That is why the worst things ever said about Jews were said in Scripture by Jews. If you read the diatribes of the prophets against Israel, if you read that stuff today, the Anti-Defamation League's gonna come after you, see? *(Laughs.)* They'll accuse you of terrible things. But you'll find it in Jeremiah and Isaiah . . . the ear has to hear the mouth.

I'm tempted (I haven't done it yet), but in the entrance of the temple I'm tempted to have two barrels in which people put food. On one barrel it's going to be written, "For the Ethiopian Jews" (since that was the most recent drive), and over the barrel it'll say, "If I'm Not for Myself, Who Is for Me?" And on the other side of the entrance I'm gonna have another barrel. It's gonna be for my Salvadoran and Guatemalan refugee children, and it's gonna say over that barrel, "But If I'm for Myself Only, What Am I?" And then, overarching the whole thing, it's gonna say, "And If Not Now, When?" I'd like every Jew that walks into this place to walk under that arch every time. That's the Jewish experience, see? It's to walk that line and not fall off either way.

When I see the refugee children, as I do, I see Jews. That's part of the pitch I give. I speak all over the country now for the Sanctuary movement. And I say to people, "If you crossed the Atlantic in 1913, or the Rio Grande in 1986, what's the difference? The same people." I remember the first freedom seder we held here for those Central Americans and for Russian Jews. I had a special seder; threw them all together with translators and all, and it was great. At dinner I'm walking from table to table, and a Jewish lady stops me. She'd been talking to this Chinese woman who was a Cambodian boat person. And she said in Yiddish to me, "Rabbi, we're the same people, we're the same . . . the same stories." You know, this was a great revelation to her.

I agree with the astronaut who looked out of his spaceship and all he saw was this ball floating through space. He couldn't see boundaries and he couldn't see that good guys live here, bad guys live there. All he could see was a ball floating through space. That's all we are. It's one ball (laughs), one object. So the universal is not a denial of Jewishness. Rather, it's my Jewishness that impels me into the world. I don't run to the world to get away from my Jewishness. That won't work.

I'm a great believer in messianism. Doesn't mean next Tuesday, but that's what it's about . . . you work toward it. I'll tell you one of my favorite stories that illustrates it, came out of Israel years ago. Kissinger needed a job (that shows you how old the story is), he was out of work, so he goes to the Israelis and says, "You've always been nice to me, and, after all, I was always nice to you, so you've gotta be nice to me. I need a job." So they look in the card catalog. The only job available: curator of the Tel Aviv zoo. He says, "I'll take any job." So he took the job; they forgot about him. Six months went by, and they thought, "Hey, we'd better look in on him." They go down to the zoo, and every blade of grass is perfect, very Germanic; achtung, clean, nice. And a crowd of people are standing in front of a cage. In the cage is a lion next to a lamb. They're sitting there together. Henry's in the front. And they said, "Henry, you have achieved the messianic dream: the lion and the lamb. How'd you do that?" Henry says, "Very simple. Every morning a fresh lamb."

Now that's the definition of an unredeemed world. *(Laughs.)* A premessianic world is a world in which you need a fresh lamb every day. When you don't need a fresh lamb, that's the messianic age, and that's what we're working toward.

Steve Wickson

KINGDOM MENTALITY

We met in 1980 at the Harvard Divinity School, where I had come to study comparative religions and he to study the Bible. A brilliant but often troubled student, he had dropped out of medical school two years earlier because: "I hated the values, hated that I was asked to renounce my own spiritual values to become a doctor." After graduating Harvard he joined the Boston Jesuit Novitiate, where he served as a chaplain in a psychiatric hospital, spent six months ministering in Guyana, and worked as a campus minister. In 1985, a year before we met for this interview, he left the novitiate. "I felt a growing need for increased physical intimacy and also came to reject the traditional Church teaching that the authentic word of God and the only legitimate teaching authority comes from the hierarchical church. That's poppycock."

He presently works in Boston as a pastoral counselor for those whom he calls marginalized people: "Gays and lesbians, the poor, women, blacks, or whomever."

Asking me about what I believe is like asking me where I think God is in our world. So where is God in our world? He's right in the hearts and in the minds and in the hands and the sufferings of the people who are poor and people who are oppressed. So God right now is with the gay people and with people with AIDS and with people in the Third World and with people of color and with women.

The hardest challenge to me is to find God in North America. He's here, I guess; he/she/God is here. But it's hard for me to see that, because I think we are a sinful, decadent people. Profoundly so. I'm a product of that too. I live in this culture and I think we constantly have to bring ourselves back to asking what did we do with all of the fruits of what we've been given? We've been given so much. An awesome responsibility goes with that, that we use our advantage on behalf of the least advantaged. And I don't think we all do that. I know I don't do that all the time. I constantly struggle with that, you know, saying, "Where do I belong? Do I belong in the Third World? Do I belong with the gay people? I know I belong with people in need and I know I don't belong amid personal affluence and decadence. That's not where I belong nor where I want to live."

I used to think one had to belong in the Third World. That's where need was. That's where people were really suffering and really hungry and really oppressed by governments—totalitarian ones—like in Guyana. But I've found the response of a lot of people there is that they don't necessarily want us to do that. They want Americans to be American and come back and raise the consciousness of American people. They don't need me to liberate Central America. In fact they probably don't even want me. They don't need me to make the world better in Guyana . . . I can't. It's far greater and far more oppressive than I can handle. What they do need me to do is to be a person of faith and an American and to come back and take that as a mission to other people. Be present to people in need. Be present to their experience, but be a source of God's love for them. That's ministry; to somehow be a mouthpiece for God's love in the world in concrete action with people who are hurting. And I think, for right now anyway, that's where I seem to belong.

To me God is a source of overflowing love. I've gone beyond the God with the beard and tried to reject all my infantile personalized notions. My God is an imageless God, but a God who is in his purest form all love, all forgiveness, all compassion, all mercy, all availability, all accessibility. And that love is so awesome that it can't be contained. Hence the incarnation. God loved the world so much that he sent his only begotten son. Another way to say that is that God's love overflowed into the world in the person of Christ. And that becomes the model of how we're supposed to love in the world. We're supposed to love in the same way that Christ did, with this perfect, self-donating kind of love. You love until you can't love anymore. You love until you can't live anymore. You love until you empty yourself, giving of yourself completely, trusting that in doing so God will fill up that emptiness with his own love.

So the irony of my faith is that in communicating love to other people, in emptying myself, I get filled up and overflow. Then it becomes easy to be a source of God's love in the world. That's when kingdom mentality becomes crucial to me. I think the central message of Christ was about the kingdom of God, the reign of God. It's here. It's in our midst. It's right here, right in this world right now. It's a radical simultaneity, present and future. It's not in heaven. It's not a life to come. It's right here. Right now. With God's people. Right in our very midst. God intends for us the fullness of life. And for that to happen all we need to do is surrender to God, to allow God's will to take over. And God's will is that we have abundant life and that love dominate the world and not hatred and not bigotry and not discrimination and not prejudice.

Me at my best is when I can hold on to that kingdom mentality. And the kingdom mentality doesn't care about numbers. I had to learn that in campus ministry. You know, you work for months preparing a program, maybe a wonderful program on sexuality, on peace and justice or civil disobedience, on economic justice, on Third World politics, and you might get five people to show up. And there's a part of you by every calculus of the world that says that's stupid. What a waste of your effort. But by kingdom mentality, all God cares about is did you love? Did you love fully? Did you use your talents on behalf of trying to be more loving in the world? Numbers don't matter. Strategy doesn't matter. Results don't matter. What matters is the lovingness . . . as with Christ. He didn't care about numbers. He didn't care about converting the world. He didn't care about how many converts he had, how many baptisms he did. He didn't care about that. What he cared about was the overflowing of his love, allowing himself to become an instrument so that God the Father's love could overflow in the world.

I believe in kingdom mentality. And it's wonderful. It's very free. Because then it makes just as much sense to spend an afternoon with a chronic schizophrenic who's never going to get better as to be in a university studying or teaching. Or it makes just as much sense to spend two hours with one person in therapy as being in a university structure where you might be teaching fifteen, or in Congress where you might be making a bill that's going to affect 230 million. You know, it's given me a real sense of inner peace. All those other kinds of things are about the calculus of the world, about numbers and results and consequences. That's not what Christ is about. Christ is about creating a space where love can overflow . . . doesn't care about numbers. So for me the central challenge of my faith right now is to ask what can I do to be more loving at every minute—and ask myself that every night. Was I loving? What did I do to be loving? How was I loving? And all that I believe God asks of us is that we be loving to those people who come into our lives. It's very simple.

None of the sense of grand ministry and mission that I used to ag-onize over; you know, what shall I do with my life and what does it all mean? But simply can you love those people that you care about? Whoever they are. So you can be doing anything. You can be a waiter. You can be cleaning toilets, you know; you can be a university pro-fessor. It doesn't matter. Wherever you are, there will be people present in your life who need your love and compassion. Were you able to be loving to them?

It's all rather simple. We just make it complicated. Churches would rather be complicated. They add this whole layer of guilt on it and all these moral codes, all these things that have very little to do with a living, dynamic faith. But that is all that Christ did. So I put my trust in the revelation of Christ, Christ's words. I came here to have life and have it abundantly. I trust that. I trust that. That's really the voice of a living God. It gets validated, I guess, with per-sonal experience. I think we all know when we're being compas-sionate. I think we all know when we're being loving. I think we all know when we're helping someone. I think we also all know when we're exploiting someone, when we're ripping someone off, and when we're taking advantage of the system. We know that internally. This internal validation of God is there for all of us. It might be buried under layers and layers and layers of all kinds of stuff, but it's there. That to me is the voice of a living God alive in us. In my traditional Catholic categories that's our soul—if you want to use that language, you know. And that's the part of the living God that I try to pay attention to.

There's a wonderful quote in the Old Testament that summarizes my faith right now, a quote from Micah. "What does Yahweh ask of you? Only this: That you act justly, that you love tenderly, and that you walk humbly with your God."

Life would be pretty absurd for me without this faith. It's rather silly, when you think about it. Life is just, "Oh, whoever gets the most toys wins." You know, the American ethos. "Hurray for me and to hell with everybody else. Me and my family and I'm going to make the world right for me and my family and to hell with the rest of the world." Those are the kinds of American beliefs that other people seem to live by who don't want to live by an act of faith. This doesn't make a lot of sense to me.

So I think I do need faith. I need it in order to make sense out of the world, in order to make sense out of my own existence, in order to feel good about being alive.

Alternative Altars

Ma Bodhitara, a.k.a. Diane Searles

THE JEWEL INSIDE

Boulder, Colorado. She's casually dressed in black sweatpants and a baggy orange flannel top. Resting at the bottom of her wood-beaded necklace is a pendant containing a picture of Bhagwan Shree Rajneesh. Formerly a resident of the guru's Oregon desert religious community, Rajneeshpuram, she's studying for her bachelor's degree at Naropa Institute, an accredited Buddhist college. She's twenty-eight.

I was born in Brooklyn, New York. Jewish. Family of three girls. I'm the youngest. I was very much born into a situation where I got a lot of support. I was the prosperity child. A lot of things were offered to me—music, dance, the creative arts, education.

I was always very precocious, very rebellious, very much a leader as a kid. I was able to articulate well and get people to understand what I was talking about. I was a very good rhetorician. I could make someone believe anything that I wanted to. I was a good manipulator of energy, because I was so intelligent. I had a very quick mind and I was very talkative.

My first spiritual inclinations started arising very early. In Hebrew school, when I would ask questions, there seemed always to be teachers around that picked up on the fact that I was probing more than the usual. I remember coming into school and asking questions like "Is God in everything?" And I had one particular teacher who was an ex-concentration-camp victim. She pulled me aside and took care of me and just said, "It's really possible that what was written in the Bible is not really the whole story."

I remember at nine, ten, eleven, in those years, my eyes being really opened. I also had a very big sensation of all the pain that was going on. I remember being deeply disturbed by people abusing the life force. I saw it most clearly in the animal kingdom—with the seals, with the extinction of animals. Just a nonrespect for the life force. I think that theme has always moved through me, more than anything. It led me into going premed. I've worked in hospitals for years.

I remember a very significant experience once while working in a hospital, walking down a hallway, and being really open, really joyous. A smile beaming on my face. One of the big doctors stopped me and said, "Let me tell you one thing right now. This is not a place to have that sort of energy; this is not the sort of place where you can be smiling all the time." It really threw me back, because I thought, Where else do you need loving energy more than in a hospital? Should everybody walk around with this sort of dismal, dismal, dismal attitude. It really threw me back. I remember feeling, Oh my God, it's not okay to wear my heart out on my sleeve, on my chest, on my face, because somehow it offends people.

That sort of feeling, again I can say, I brought with me into my education. I went to Bryn Mawr College in Pennsylvania. I was a philosophy major and a biology major. Biology was the thing I would just love. And philosophy was getting me into these other realms. By my second year I realized that these things that I was learning about had to be real, that somehow this ivory-tower nurturing was not nurturing me at all, that something was being destroyed, that in this education process something was not being taken care of. The realness, my vitality, my lust for life was not being taken care of.

I was always in this state of sort of philosophical angst at Bryn Mawr. My third year in school I quit. I just went into the dean's office and basically said, "I can't continue." I left school, I left home. I never went back home. And I went out to California. The typical New York–to–California route. 1979.

I ended up staying in a Stanford fraternity for about two months because I had a friend who was at Stanford. I ended up getting into Krishnamurti.* It was the first time I had come across a philosophy that was no longer like a textbook. It was somebody saying that these beckonings of the beyond are something that you can feel, just as I'm sitting here talking to you. I was just blown open.

Finally one day I left Stanford and I went to the ocean. I said, "I need to be near the ocean." So I went to Pacific Grove, Monterey, that area. I ended up baking in a natural food store and living in a house with a very eclectic group of people. One woman was a prac-

---

* J. Krishnamurti, an Indian-born religious philosopher who toured the world regularly speaking and leading Socratic-like discussions. His many books were translated into nearly every language. He died at the Krishnamurti Foundation, Ojai, California, on February 17, 1986.

ticing witch, very into tarot, belly dancing, psychic reading, the whole thing. Her boyfriend was into New Age Christianity. There was also a Rastafarian living in the house,* and a preacher's son who had been a rebel during the sixties. I was with one character after another.

I started dabbling in all different kinds of things—psychic stuff, tarot. Then one day I went to a bookstore. It was a rainy day, and I had about $6 in my pocket. The woman who was running the bookstore was a *sannyasin.*** I started reading a book by Bhagwan and it was just a beautiful, beautiful book. I looked down at the price, but it was too much. I didn't have enough money. So I ended up taking another Bhagwan book.

I went home and I read this book and I just burst out in tears. It was this real recognition in myself of something I had been searching for. Whether it was just a pinpoint of light that said, "You can trust this," or "You can trust that very deep feeling inside," something caught me. I just was overwhelmed. Leading up to this time, I had definitely been very near suicidal. As much as I was expanding, there was also a lot of depression . . . finding a real meaninglessness in everything. Somehow in reading this Bhagwan book, something in me got exposed. Sort of like a disease that came to the surface was finally able to begin to yield. I began to realize that the responsibility for my life lay in my own hands and that I had been very unnourished. I had not nourished myself. I had not opened myself up to a real affinity with the things that I loved. I just was keeping myself from it somehow. So that started a real process for me of inward growth.

I got pulled deeper and deeper into wanting to go to India to see Bhagwan. This was probably in '82, close to '82, or it was '81. Then I went up to the Rajneeshpuram and visited. And I had a sense of arriving home. I just loved it. I wanted to be there. So I moved up there in '82. And I stayed there until the end.***

Now that the community has been broken up, what's happening

---

* Member of a Jamaican messianic movement dating back to the 1930s. Rastafarians believe that the only true God is the late Ethiopian emperor Haile Selassie (originally known as Ras Tafari) and that the only true Zion is Ethiopia. They also believe that white Christian missionaries concealed the fact that Adam and Jesus were actually black. Rastafarians use marijuana as a sacrament, and the popular music of the movement is reggae.

** A sannyasi (Sanskrit, *sannyasin*) is a Hindu ascetic who has taken a vow of overt renunciation. In this instance, however, the term is used more loosely to mean a person who has taken a vow to follow the practices of Bhagwan Shree Rajneesh.

*** Rajneesh was deported from the United States in November 1985. Shortly thereafter the city's status was declared illegal. The land and holdings of the guru were sold to an insurance company in 1988.

for me is meditation, the culturation of my inner world. What I trusted the first time I connected with Bhagwan was the silence, something that just went through me. That's the space I am cultivating within myself with meditation.

I'm really coming home to the fact that the world can be changed if my energy is clear. Sort of like a drop in the water and it ripples out from that. I'm not a social activist. I can't get out there and rally up social support. For me it's very much the personal journey that's going to create change in the world.

I suppose I'd like to restore ourselves almost to the state of being mystics. That for me is the vision that I have. Because I feel like in that state of mind there is such a deep respect for living beings, for the connection that living beings have with one another—in that state of mind most of the social problems we have would disappear. I feel like if that happens on an individual level, then socially we take care of ourselves. We no longer will be at war with one another. It's like if a certain peace happens inside of ourselves, then that will take care of itself.

For me there's been no answers, ever. I mean, every day in my meditation I sit and question deeply, "Who am I?" And there's no answer. And any answer that I get I realize is an effort from inside of myself to produce something. But if I let go of that, then I can just live in the mystery somehow and take care of it. It's so fabulous to be taking care of something that's a mystery. That gives me so much juice; it's capable of giving me so much joy.

Bhaghwan's biggest message is that belief systems are like concentration camps. I have a set of belief systems and all I can do is live inside of them. And if something else comes, I can't even let it in. I see that most people are so stuck in their belief systems that they can't possibly see what Bhagwan's doing. He drove those Rolls-Royces to push people's buttons because most people believe that wealth and spirituality do not go hand in hand. Bhagwan's whole message is that there is no rule of thumb when it comes to belief. His teaching is about getting out of the concentration camp. The point of his dialectic is that space is nothingness. Behind his words is nothingness. And that's what I have to be at peace with ultimately. It's the emptiness. He's saying nothing.

I think my concentration camp gets bigger and bigger. I've gone from one to the next to the next. And I don't know if there's a way out. I don't know. There is this thing out there that says that enlightenment is possible. But even that is a concentration camp in itself. It's very much the story of, you know, if you meet the Buddha on the road, kill him. To be locked inside a system that says that enlightenment is the only way is the same thing as saying that if you die, you go to heaven. It's no different. But I feel like the only way for me to discover if enlightenment is possible is to exist outside the concentration camp, exist without the lenses of my glasses on; to be shrewdly experimental and to experiment with everything. And for me the best way to do this now is to go inside, to meditate . . . I can see what is outside. I can see what's inside a microscope. I can study energy theories. But I haven't gone as deeply as I know I can inside. I haven't talked to everything inside. I haven't made friends with everything inside of me yet.

There's a beautiful story that I one time heard about a man that's given a magnificent carved box. Just magnificent. In fact the most beautiful thing that he could ever, ever imagine. And he receives this box as a gift. And he takes it home. And he walks from room to room in this house. And he can't decide where would this box be appropriate to put, you know. "Where should I put it?" He walks into one room, and somehow the environment is not perfect for it. So he has to fix up the room for that box to be in there. So he fixes up this room with this box in it. And he realizes that this room now wasn't appropriate for the rest of the house, so he had to fix up the whole house. Then he realized that the house wasn't appropriate for the garden around it, so he had to fix up the garden. Then his field where he plowed his food for his family, he had to fix up.

It's the same thing that I feel in myself. It's like cultivating this essence, and that spreads out. Then I take care of my body, then I take care of my soul, then I take care of my emotions, then I take care of the people around me who I love. And they in turn take care of what they love in their environment. But very much the feeling of I have to acknowledge this jewel inside of me. And the mystery.

Postscript: Bhagwan Shree Rajneesh died January 19, 1990.

Burtrand

THE GOOD WITCH OF THE WEST

I grew up in a small community, and a very Lutheran community, north of here in Minnesota. And, coming from a quite religious family, I'd gotten the standard upbringing, none of which made particular sense to me. I'd already started to question much of the supposed tenets of the Christian religion by the time I was ten, including the one that bothered me the most, which was the idea that a loving God should frighten people into belief. I saw a lot of the hypocrisy of the religion up there, and so by the time I got down to the University of Minnesota, I was not particularly interested in religion at all. But then I did some work in parapsychology and drifted, with the help of my wife, toward witchcraft. Now my wife and I are members of the Church of Wicca, which is a church of witchcraft.

Minneapolis, Minnesota. He's a short, heavyset man with a football player's neck. Dressed conservatively, much in the style of a small-town insurance salesman, you'd never suspect him for a witch.

Witchcraft is a religion like any other religion. So a spell for me is nothing more than a formalized version of prayer. It's an attempt to use my abilities, and the abilities of the god-force that I'm dealing with, to produce a certain end. And magic does work. It's not the sort of thing like the old "Samantha" idea, where you wiggle your nose and something happens. It's far more statistical. You have to say that if you're trying to do something, it may or may not work. But if you have a fifty-fifty chance, and you're putting magical effort into it, and all of a sudden you're getting 90 percent results, you know you're creating a result.

I remember well when I came to believe in the power of magic. It was fifteen years ago. I'd had to go downtown for some reason, and I was fairly broke, and I didn't have any change to put in the parking meter. So consequently I tried to cast a spell to make my car invisible to the meter monitors. Not to other drivers, but just specifically to the meter monitors. I didn't get a ticket that day, but I thought, That's pure coincidence. It took me almost a year before I realized, I'm not getting tickets anymore. And I started looking at this, and at least a half dozen times I watched meter monitors ticket cars in front of me and after me and leave my car, also sitting at an expired meter, all alone. Now, this has held true for close to fifteen years, through several different cars, and I'm not messing with it. *(Laughs.)*

I'm not a miracle worker in the sense that everything will go my way, by any means. I have to work within certain rules and regulations, but it can work. And anything that I do, whether it be in the form of a spell or anything else, will have some form of negative impact on somebody else. So the craft is a religion of responsibility. You are responsible for your actions. If you do something wrong, there's no way of going and saying, "I'm sorry I sinned. I didn't mean to do that." You have to be responsible for whatever you do. And the one thing that is absolutely forbidden to people working in the craft is to interfere unnecessarily with somebody's rights.

Of course if I feel I am justified in casting an evil spell, even to the point of death, there's nothing within the religion that says, No, I cannot do this. But I have to be responsible within this life, and in future lives, for whatever I do. So I have to be very sincerely angry enough at somebody over a long enough period of time to truly wish them dead. Because it can work. You do not wish bad luck upon someone lightly. But, you know, there're times when there is no other way. There're times when the mundane laws of man cannot balance the situation out, and so you might have to do something. Normally if I am really mad at someone, I do what is called a tanglefoot, which means simply that everything that person is going to try to do is going to go slightly wrong, that his own actions will cause him harm, rather than anything that I do. It'll cause him a lot of hassle, but it isn't going to necessarily do him any major harm. But it's something that you do very seldom.

So I'm not Satan, I'm not the devil, and contrary to what many Christians think, I'll be happy to let them be if they just let me be.

Geoffrey and Wendy Walker

A week before we met they were married in an elaborate Indian ceremony at the Hare Krishna Temple in Denver. Wendy has been a Hare Krishna since 1968. She's thirty-four, the mother of a twelve-year-old son, and runs the Temple's vegetarian restaurant, Govinda's. Geoff has been a Hare Krishna since 1975. He's in charge of supervising the temple.

Across the street from the temple Geoff and Wendy live in a small, immaculately clean home. After treating me to a dinner of Indian food, we relax on floral-patterned couches in the living room. To my right a glass-enclosed bookshelf contains several volumes of sacred Indian texts; on the wall behind me is a gold-framed oil painting of Prabhupada, founder of the movement; to my left a picture of dancing Indian gods painted in bright primary colors.

GEOFF: When I was in high school, I was in a couple of music classes. I liked to sing a lot. And I had a teacher, one of these rare teachers that everybody loves, and we used to have parties at her house on Christmas Eve and everybody'd go out chanting Christmas carols. After having her for a teacher for four years in a row, I can very clearly remember the last day of class. I had this very heavy feeling that I always knew it was gonna come to a point when I was gonna be in her class for the last time; you know, this realization of how time works. And I just started realizing that today I'm a senior, tomorrow I'm a graduate. (Snaps fingers.) I can't do anything to get it back. It's gone. Then college will come and go. Then I'm gonna be married, and that's gonna come and go. My youth is gonna come and go. And I realized then that one day I'm gonna be thinking: What day is it? It's today. I'm gonna die. I was thinking, It's like a train. You hear it way off in the distance, choo, choo, choo. Then, all of a sudden, choooooooo . . . and whoosh it's gone. I was realizin' that, you know, I don't have an unlimited amount of time. And I want to know what I should do with this time. And I didn't feel comfortable at all.

Later on, when I came across different religious philosophies, I realized that the reason I felt uncomfortable was my soul. The soul just isn't meant to experience these temporary things coming and going. It's totally unnatural, because the soul is really eternal. It all really made sense. It really made a lot of sense.

WENDY: In the Bhagavad Gita there's a verse: "Earth, water, fire, air, ether, mind, intelligence, and false ego." Krishna says these eight comprise my separated material energy. So there's material energy, gross and subtle, and then there's spiritual energy. The gross material energy is earth, water, fire, air, ether, just like the Greeks divided it. But the subtle material energy would be mind, intelligence, and false ego. False ego is the sort of linking point between matter and spirit. But real ego is spirit—I am spirit-soul. That means eternal; the soul is full of bliss, full of knowledge, and eternal. It can't be wet by water, it can't be burned by fire, it can't be cut, can't be dried, can't be blown away.

So the soul is the real "I am"; I'm not the body. When the body dies, I remain. I am spirit, but I'm also a servant of God. God is very great. And I am tiny. I have the same quality as God. But he is infinite and I'm infinitesimal. Prabhupada would say that if you taste a drop of ocean water, you get a taste of the essence of the ocean or the quality of the ocean. But the ocean is vast. That one drop is tiny. But still you can taste the taste of the ocean by that one drop. In the same way the individual soul is tiny, yet has the same quality as

God. As the Bible says, man is made in the image of God. So just as I want to love, so God is loving. Whatever emotions I have, whatever range of emotions I have, those emotions are there in God. And it's all meant to be uncovered by awakening the spiritual essence, by the spiritual practice, spiritual discipline.

I realize who I am and I can function in this world right now as a spiritual being. The Sanskrit term for that is *jivan-mukta*, which means you don't have to die and go to heaven. You can be a liberated person right here in this life. A liberated person already realizes that he's not the body, that the body is, as Saint Francis put it, Brother Ass. In other words the body is a tool for my use. I can use it as I like, but it's not me. So in that way, I'm the soul, I'm part of God.

GEOFF: The journey of the soul for us is like the Judeo-Christian idea that there's the Garden of Eden and the soul disobeyed God and ate the apple and was banished. We don't accept that literally. But it's a nice figurative story. It has limitations, but it's a figurative description of how the soul is an eternal person and God is the eternal Supreme Person. And we're eternal associates of his, meant to help him enjoy. And by helping him enjoy, we automatically enjoy a relationship of love and service.

We have our free will. And the journey is that the soul chooses to try to exist independently from God, tries to be happy separately from God. So Krishna creates the material world to fulfill the desire of his wayward sons and daughters. This, as I understand it, is the purpose of this material creation. It's like a big playground for us to come and try to satisfy ourselves. But in the same way it's designed in such a way that we'll get our knuckles rapped. And we'll come to understand that something's wrong here. It seems like such a nice wonderful place, but there's a lot of problems. And when I try to solve the problems, they just get deeper. And after a certain period of time I realize I was much happier in my Father's home. So this is the soul's journey. We're meant to be in this world, especially in this human form of life, to realize we'd be much happier if we were just back with our Father, with God in the kingdom of heaven. The perfection of our lives is to return to him. And as long as we don't learn the lesson, as long as we continue to be rebellious, we have to stay in this material world.

WENDY: It's sort of like that option is always there, to love or not to love. But love can never be forced. It's just like, you're a guest here today, so if we say, "Well, Phil, are you comfortable? Did you have enough to eat? Do you need another pillow? Are you comfortable here?" And you say, "Oh yeah, I'm fine." And then we say, "Well, great, because you can never leave. The door is eternally closed to you, and we're glad you're happy here because you no longer have the option to leave." Then all of a sudden you'd be completely uncomfortable. *(Laughs.)* As comfortable as you were, you'd be completely uncomfortable because it wasn't your choice. So the kingdom of God is like that. According to all religious books the kingdom of God is meant for the people who want to love God. And those who want to try their hand at being God themselves come down to this world and get their little independence to try to do that. But actually their real independence and real freedom is by exercising their real nature—which is their God nature.

This ties in with our understanding of why there's so many different religions and why they often appear to be in conflict. Religions

serve dual purposes. One purpose is to direct people in the satisfaction of their materialistic tendencies, to do so in a regulated, moralistic way so that their consciousness is gradually elevated. The other
purpose is to teach people the principle of renunciation, so that gradually they understand that the whole thing isn't sufficient to satisfy
themselves anyway. So you have these different purposes. And because there's so many great religious systems that were taught in
different times and places and circumstances, they had to teach according to the particulars of a given culture. So sometimes people
find conflicts: "Our religion says this." "Our religion says this." What
is the purpose of it? If you were taking college-level calculus and I
was taking some remedial math at the freshman level to get my grades
up, our professors would teach us different rules and regulations.
But the purpose is ultimately the same. It's just a question of where
we're at and how much of the truth we can assimilate. Therefore
there's different messages and different teachings.

We're Hare Krishna devotees, so we find a lot of knowledge in
the Bhagavad Gita. But if you walk into a Christian church, you can
find one person who's sitting there because he knows if he appears
there every Sunday, more people will buy insurance from him. But
then there's a woman sitting right next to him who is actually, in her
heart, crying out to God in a pure, devotional way. So she would be
a devotee of God. In other words it's not just the framework, it's
the actual emotion from the heart. It's not where you took your birth
or the family you were born in or what tradition you're in.

GEOFF: That's our philosophy, that the individual soul with the
help of the guru and the Scriptures and fellow devotees can move
closer toward God realization. But we have to individually choose
to try to develop our love for God. And at that point he judges us,
you know. And when he thinks our hearts are pure, then he takes
us back to him.

WENDY: What is the last thing that you give another? I mean,
what is your most cherished thing? You might give a bum a quarter.
Or you might have some intellectual talk with someone. You might
give someone some money, or you might give someone a little knowledge. But your love, that's your most cherished thing. So when we
talk about devotion, we are talking about the very, very most cherished thing. Devotion encompasses everything. If I love someone,
then I want to give them everything.

GEOFF: This is one of the things that attracted me to Krishna
consciousness. I was understanding from biblical readings that we're
supposed to give everything to God. And I was going and asking

ministers and different people, "Well, how do you do that, what's that mean?"

There's this book, *The Way of the Pilgrim*. He was always wondering, "What does it mean, incessant prayer?" That was his whole search. He read that he should have incessant prayer and kept trying to find spiritual teachers. So I was feelin' the same thing. If you're supposed to serve God twenty-four hours a day, love God with all your heart, what's that mean? You know, how do I eat for God? What's God want me to eat? And I have to sleep, so what time of day am I supposed to get up? And I have to work, so what kind of work am I supposed to do? And what kind of clothes should I wear? So, in Krishna consciousness we understand that we should aspire for God twenty-four hours a day. The most important thing for us to do is train our mind to always remember God and think of God and remember what he wants us to do as we build on the Scriptures and things like that. That's why our morning meditation is very important. We get up no later than four o'clock in the morning, while most everybody else is still sleeping, practicing our prayer or our meditation. And our prayer, a translation of the Hare Krishna mantra, is, "O my Lord, O energy of the Lord, please engage me in your service." Because we understand theologically that we're all servants.

So that's the beginning of our days. We get up very early and we do our meditation. Then we have classes very early in the morning, so we can intellectually, philosophically enliven our conviction. Then during the day different devotees have different types of activities. For the last two months I've been in charge of supervising the temple. This temple is also very active in trying to publish Vedic literatures and Bhagavad Gita. And we actively distribute them, mainly at Stapleton Airport. I want to do everything for Krishna.

I spent the first seven years of my Krishna consciousness mainly in the airport. I still go. I try to go every Friday, because that's kind of like the front lines of our attempts to help society. We feel that the knowledge we have is our most valuable contribution. Sometimes people accuse us of being beggars, you know. Not a lot, but we hear it. "You're beggars. What are you contributing to society? Why don't you get a job?" But we feel there's plenty of people digging ditches and hanging telephone wires and a lot of computer operators. What is lacking in this society is spiritual knowledge and a viable process for people to live in a peaceful way with God. So we feel this is our contribution. We feel this is the most valuable thing. So the most practical way for us to do that is to share the wisdom of this ancient religion. Prabhupada's books are actually not just his writings; they're his translations and elaborations on the oldest writings and spiritual texts in the world—like five thousand years old. What we're presenting is a philosophy, and some very nice literature, and books that Thoreau and Emerson appreciated. And this is a very important pillar of our religion, to approach people regardless of their background, financial, educational, social, and to share with them our understanding of God and how you can find God. And we take a lot of flack for this. You'll be distributing and talking to someone and then someone else will come up to criticize you, blaspheme the book, tell you you're brainwashed, tell you you're worshiping the devil, and so many horrible, horrible things. You know, "All the money's goin' to some big shot on top." Just everything you could ever think of to say that's nasty. And you kind of stand there, like, phew, geez. It really forces you to become very transcendental. To become very undisturbed by praise or blame and happiness and success and stress and failure. It very much focuses you on meditating. And I'm doing this for God. God wants these people to be given knowledge about him. This is the best thing I can do for Krishna, try to help his sons and daughters get back to him. Whether I'm a success or whether I'm a failure, it's what he wants. And this is what I have to do.

A lot of times people have this idea we're makin' money out there. But we're losin' money left and right. (Laughs.) Especially like at the airport, where we're passing out these big hardcover books. We're losin' tons of money; it's not a profit-making venture. Our profit is to see the literature distributed. I mean, we're giving a book that in a bookstore would sell for $25 to $30. It's got at least six to ten color plates, some of them sixty color plates. And the average donation is $1.75. So is that a profit-making venture? No. The only profit is bringing a few more people closer to God.

Kamal Ibrahim

THE EXAMINATION HALL

When I was twelve or thirteen, I used to get in one room, close myself in, and study religious books. I studied a little bit of Bible, then Koran with translation. That was the first time I studied

Koran with translation, because when I was younger, we used to study just in Arabic, and we didn't know what was going on; I mean, it didn't affect us, because we didn't know what the meaning of it was. I had a book which had side-by-side columns. First was the Arabic original (how it was revealed), and then second was the English, and the third was in my local language, Urdu. So I studied Koran little by little, and after about a few months it caught me. I'm eating, I'm thinking of it; I'm playing, I'm thinking of it. It so trapped me that every time I used to do something, something out of the Koran used to come to my mind. And it was as if the great power, you know, the God, was trying to show me something. It really got me thinking. Is there any God, really? I mean, is it the truth? Do I really believe? And then I took time and said, Okay, let's first decide if I want to really believe. Either I will be this way (*laughs*), or this way.

He was born in northern Pakistan in the city of Lahore and came west to open up Oriental rug businesses after graduating from college. We met by accident at his Denver rug shop, Ibrahim's, while I was out shopping for a wedding present. Although sweet and somewhat shy by nature, he's an extremely effective salesman—I walked out not only with the one rug I wanted but with another I couldn't afford.

After a lot of thinking and questioning, the thing which really made me convinced that there is certainly a power was looking at my own body. I was about fourteen or so, and I looked at my hands and face, eyes and legs and arms. This couldn't be without being made by somebody? That was the real thought which really convinced me. We cannot have eyes without being given them by some power. There are teeth inside the mouth . . . why? So that we can eat, you know. Hands with fingers so that we can pick something up . . . grapes and things. By just looking at me, that made me a hundred percent convinced that definitely there is some power. That was a big change which happened inside me. That made me a little bit more religious than other surrounding people, you know.

But then I got involved in this rug business (*laughs*) and I started to travel all over the world. It fascinated me. And I wanted to raise my standard of living, so I focused my life on making money more than God. This was kind of a curious period. I came to North America and I established businesses, and only casually and periodically was I involved in the religion. But I had it in my mind that I'm gonna allocate my life to the religion. And the time factor I had in my mind was about forty years; when I would get to about forty, I would devote myself more to the matter of relating to God.

In one year I will be forty. (*Laughs.*) And I have been feeling a change in myself, like I want now to be prepared, really, for the reality that I'm gonna die. That is the main point in front of me, because I know everybody's dying. Nobody can stop it, so the feeling I had developed long before, that when I get near the age forty, I would devote more toward religion, that is coming out more strongly. Like right now, what I'm doing is waking up 'round about three A.M. I wake when everybody's sleeping, and it's getting kind of normal to me. I just wake up, leave the bed, and I clean myself. I just remember God and pray. I repeat the same wordings. I say, "God, I want to have a refuge in you. This I am doing to seek refuge in you. My only desire for waking up and cleaning and standing and remembering you is to seek refuge in you." That is the first thing I say. Then I say, "I want to be healthy. That's my desire. But you can do whatever you want to me, but this is my own desire. I don't know if it's good or bad. You know the best." Then I say, "Keep me away from obligations with other people. I don't want to involve myself in borrowing and owing." That I say. And then the fourth thing I say is, "God, I love you. If you choose me to serve you and die in your faith, that is fine. Whatever you feel is best." That's the four things I say. We call it the "Prayer for Desire." It's exclusively for desire, so that God may fulfill it if I am deserving. It's like putting in an application to somebody when seeking a job. *(Laughs).* Simple as that. If I don't apply somewhere, how can I get the job? So, that's the practice I am doing right now. That lasts for about an hour. Then I again go to bed.

Here in this world, I feel, we are like in an examination hall. The whole purpose is to seek the pleasure of the master of the universe, because he's the boss of the world . . . boss of the universe. And if he's happy, that's it! What else we need? Nothing. But that has to be real, sincere desire, exclusive, without any other involvement—not a single percentage of any other desire. Just this simple desire. That's what I'm going after. So I have decided, after studying the world religions, that, yes, I want to stick to the teachings of Koran. That is the basic whole point. It's like a central point for my life now. I cannot leave. There is a hundred percent feeling inside me that Koran is from God, and I have really developed a kind of faith on it. So in that way you can say that I am Muslim.

Everything in the Koran is basically related to the Supreme Being and how we should live our lives for him. What is the purpose of your life? Why are you here? What's gonna happen when you die? The Koran tells you that you are here as a guest, and only as a guest. And after you die, you will be judged. When you die, the paper is finished; you cannot touch the paper after that. The examination is over. And angels will come to question you. The first question we will be asked is, "What do you believe in? Who is your God? Was your God some statue in the world? Or was your God the boss of the world, the boss of the universe, who is controlling all this?" And you cannot give different answers other than what you believed in when you were alive. You cannot change yourself, because the control of your life has gone. You cannot lie, because the time for that is over. And if you damaged your soul in the world by living wrongly, God will punish you accordingly. If you didn't believe in God, you will wake up blind.

So the deepest intention of my life is to please the Lord. I should never have anything in my mind except just seeking his exclusive pleasure. Not the world, not my own desire—there shouldn't be any of it. The moment my own desire takes over, then I cannot get his pleasure. I should one hundred percent submit to seek knowledge of God and one hundred percent sincerely devote myself, exclusively, to seek his pleasure. We have a prayer that says that, "God, every praise is for you. Every praise is for you. We know we are here for the test. And you are the best, and you are Lord of the worlds, you are Lord of the Day of the Judgment." The Day of the Judgment is very important for us, because that's the whole purpose of being created. I mean, what else are we here for? Just to come here and die and that's it? That doesn't make any sense. We have been given eyes, ears, and hands to act, and the minds to believe. And millions and millions of people have died and they are finished. We don't know after seven generations who our forefathers were. It doesn't make any sense that they were created for nothing. In a few generations nobody will know who we were, you know. I mean, the maximum I know is seven generations of my own. But before that, who we were we don't know. And that time is nothing. Seven generations, what is it? Nothing. So it doesn't make any sense for me that we have been here just for nothing. No, it doesn't make any sense. Everything here is for the test. We are in the examination hall.

Kanya Okamoto

I was born in Gila Bend, Arizona, on October 29, 1943. Gila Bend was one of the many concentration camps, or "relocation centers," that the United States had created to intern Japanese and Japanese Americans during World War II. I was born behind barbed wire and machine gun towers on U.S. government property, so I'm more American than most Americans. I was born on government property.

His small, windowless office at the Denver Buddhist Temple, where he serves as priest, is crammed with books and files. Pinned to the wall above the doorway is "Civilian Exclusion Order No. 5," dated April 1, 1942, providing "Instructions to All Persons of Japanese Ancestry" on the details of their evacuation and internment.

The emperor of Japan died this month, as I'm sure you know. I had many phone calls from people in the press asking me, basically, "How do you feel about the emperor's death?" And I thought about it and, you know, I'm an American. I was born here; I went to school here. A lot of my values are American. And I remember my feelings when President Kennedy died. I was in the United States Navy, a thousand miles out to sea, when I heard this. I was shocked. And my feelings were more intense then than when I heard that the emperor of Japan had died.

I'm not American like apple pie. But I'm not Japanese like Japan. Back in '74, when I was studying in Japan, I remember when a Japanese soldier was found on Guam. Since the end of the war he hid out in a cave, continuing to do his reconnaissance or whatever. And, you know, he came back to Japan a hero. I asked my fellow students (they were all born and raised in Japan), I said, "What d'you think about this guy?" And they said, "Oh, that's really great . . . never giving up." And what I flashed on was, "This guy is crazy!" *(Laughs.)* I woulda given up a long time ago. So I knew I wasn't Japanese like my fellow students.

Here in America I'm always asked, "What are you? Are you Chinese or Japanese?" And when I meet a person who's white, I don't ask them, "Are you French or German?" I don't worry about that. If I meet a person who's black, I don't ask them, "Are you from Ethiopia or South Africa?" I don't ask them that. But I'm always asked, "Are you Japanese or Chinese." So I am fully aware this is a racist society. And racism is the oldest tradition known to human beings. Racism is taught from father to son, mother to daughter. Wars are fought because of racism, you know. And that's why understanding the evacuation of Japanese Americans is really important, because as a Japanese American born in the camp, I don't want to see it happen again to any other minority.

I was just two years old when we left the camp. My family moved to northern California, and my mother took me to a Methodist church five miles away from where we lived. There was a Buddhist temple in Stockton, California, but it was fifty miles away. So my mom, being very practical, said you're gonna go to the Methodist church because it's only five miles away. I enjoyed going there. But

I had questions. And every time I asked a question, the minister said, "You have to have faith." But I said, "I have questions."

When I was nine, my family moved to Los Angeles, and at that time my mother said, "Well, there's a Buddhist temple there, the Methodists are there, the Protestants over there." And she said, "Choose." So I went to three or four different places and I ended up at the Buddhist temple. The reason was, all the cute Japanese girls were at the temple. (Laughs.) When I was at the Buddhist temple, I was very fortunate that I had an English-speaking priest. And every time that I asked a question, he would say, "Very interesting question." And he would explain his own answer to my question and then ask me a question. Which made me ask another question. So one thing that was very interesting about the Buddhist temple was questions were allowed.

You know, the Buddhist approach to life is horizontal. The Christian approach is vertical. In terms of architecture, for example, when you come into a Buddhist temple, you enter from the so-called side, not the peaked, or front part of the building. A Christian church has a peaked roof, and you enter at the base of the peak, so you get a more vertical feeling. And there's a cross on top, or a steeple, which makes you look up. So this is all vertically oriented. Whereas the Buddhist temple, you enter from the side, so you get the horizontal feeling from the roof lines; you're looking right-to-left across what would be the side of the roof. Another thing is music. The Christian Gregorian chants (very beautiful) have a melody . . . up and down. But Buddhist chanting is monotone, very flat. And in terms of concepts, in Christianity heaven is symbolically up and hell is symbolically down. But the Buddhist nirvana is symbolically located in the west. The historical Buddha, when he died, died lying down. His head was pointed north and he was facing the west. Jesus died vertically . . . he died on the cross. So young Christian children are reared with an emphasis on the vertical, whereas Buddhist children are reared with an emphasis on the horizontal. One approach isn't better, it's just how the environment has influenced the individual. And I have been influenced emotionally, spiritually, and psychologically by Buddhism. That's definite.

The Buddhist way of thinking is generally called the middle path. Don't dwell on the negative, but don't dwell on the positive either. Dwelling on the positive leads to egomania, and dwelling on the negative leads to negativism. The most important concept in Buddhism is called the Three Characteristics of Life. One is *duhkha*, or suffering. The other is *anitya*, or impermanence. And the other is *anatma*, or nonself or nonsoul. And the way we see it, all suffering arises because we are unable to accept impermanence. Because of impermanence, everything changes. So there is nothing in me that stays the same. No "immortal soul" that doesn't change. And if there's something in me, it's changing, because everything is changing. If I cannot accept that idea of myself, then I'll suffer some more because I'm living a life of illusion or delusion, thinking that I am permanent.

Here in America people don't wanna change. Men are dying their hair, women are buying all sorts of cosmetics to stay young, and people are going to health spas. America has geared itself to youth. To be young is what's happening—the Pepsi Generation. But Japan has been influenced by the great sage K'ung Fu-tzu, also known as Confucius. He said old age is to be revered, old age is to be respected. So the Asian tradition stresses old age, and the Western tradition stresses youth. The reason why old age is respected and revered in Asia is because the older you get, the closer you come to the reality of your own death. And in the realization of your own death, life becomes beautiful, meaningful, precious.

Well, all I'm saying is that life is about change, and if you can't accept that, you're bound to suffer. But there is a way out—or at least our tradition says there is. *(Laughs.)* And the way out is to follow the Four Noble Truths. Basically the first Noble Truth is that "Life is *duhkha*." As I just said, *duhkha* has been translated as "suffering." The way it's translated in the Sanskrit dictionary is that it's like having an axle with a wheel that's not sitting exactly in the center, but off to the side. So it's wobbling, there's friction . . . off-balance, disharmony. So life is basically this. And the Buddha said there's four major sufferings we go through—birth, old age, illness, and death—and four minor ones—not getting what you want, getting something you don't want, being separated from loved ones, and being with people you don't like.

The second of the Four Noble Truths is that suffering comes from selfishness, from craving, or from what we call *tanha*. Because of my selfishness, my self-centered ego, I become attached to things. And therefore I continually suffer when I lose the things I'm attached to. So the goal here is to get rid of this ego-centered self . . . this craving. And that takes us to another step.

The Third Noble Truth says there is enlightenment; there's a way out, okay? And the fourth of the Four Noble Truths is called the Eightfold Path, which shows you how to get rid of your ego-centeredness. And the Eightfold Path is: Right view, right thought, right speech, right action, right livelihood, right meditation, right concentration, and right effort. The problem is, what's right? What's right livelihood? Depending upon what country you live in, that determines a lot of what's right; you know, the laws of your country, the norms and values. So, as Buddhism enters a country, it doesn't change a country; it accepts a country's customs into Buddhism. So Japanese Buddhism is uniquely Japanese, Vietnamese Buddhism is uniquely Vietnamese; Thai Buddhism uniquely Thai. They have their own language, their own customs.

Our school of Buddhism is uniquely Japanese. It's called Jodo Shinshu. And we talk a lot about the three poisons. The three poisons are greed, anger, and stupidity. It's called gas. *(Laughs.)* I'm fulla gas, man. *(Laughs.)* So if what I say is based on greed, anger, or stupidity, it's best for me to remain silent. If what I'm going to do is based on greed, anger, or stupidity, I better not do it. Greed, anger, and stupidity are controlled by my ego. But my ego won't let go of them. So there's a problem there, because it's impossible to use my ego to become egoless. *(Laughs.)* The ego will not allow that to happen, okay? Other schools of Buddhism say you can do it. Zen, for instance, says you can do it through meditation. But our school says that the only way is to not give up, but give in. So we give in to the compassionate beauty of Amitabha Buddha. Amitabha Buddha is a Buddha of immeasurable light and life, and his compassionate beauty surrounds you and me.

So my goal, and the goal of this temple, is to become aware of this compassion . . . to feel the compassion. And with the feeling of the compassion of the Buddha comes a deep sense of *arigatai*, or gratefulness; gratefulness for the many things that support and sustain my life. Realizing this, you come to fully appreciate all manifestations of life and live in harmony.

True enlightenment means to be aware of complete wisdom, and we don't experience that in our human life. When I die, the ultimate enlightenment, or *nirvana*, will come. *Nirvana* means "extinguished through lack of fuel." It's not the same connotation as *heaven*, you know, "extinguished through lack of fuel." The gas is gone. *(Laughs.)* When the wax is gone, the flame goes out. Where does it go? Energy cannot be created or destroyed. It changes form. Within me there's an energy level, a spark, a flame. I consume fuel to keep it going. But this fuel is gonna run out. This flame's gonna go out. Where does it go? Well, it changes form. It returns to the oneness from where I came. Just like the wave of an ocean returns to the ocean.

Motherhood

PART I: PERFORMANCE ANXIETY

Catherine Hale

I come from a family of three boys and myself. And we were brought up as strict Mormons, so my folks instilled in us, from the time we were little, a deep sense of honesty, family unity, things like that. I remember when I was little my mother telling me a story of how, when she was a girl, she came home from a friend's house with a straight pin and how her mother sent her back to the house to return that straight pin because you don't take things that don't belong to you—even something as small as a straight pin. So that's the way that we were raised. And to this day if I'm overchanged in a store, I'll go out of my way to return it. I find it funny that people are amazed at that. I remember going clear to the other end of the mall when I was given a nickel too much, and the guy in the store looked at me with great amazement. "Why are you returning this nickel?" He couldn't believe that someone would be that honest, but that's been an important thing in our family and something I want to instill in my kids.

Sandy, Utah, a bedroom community on the outskirts of Salt Lake City. Her sparsely decorated, spotlessly clean suburban home sits in the foothills of the towering Wasatch Range. Of the few books about, all are religious in nature and presented in multivolume sets, including Illustrated Stories from Church History, The Illustrated Story of the New Testament, *and* Stories from the Book of Mormon. *She's thirty-seven and the mother of five girls, ages nine, eleven, thirteen, fifteen, and seventeen.*

I remember always, from the time I was a little tiny girl, my mom and I would go to sacrament meetings together. And in those meetings there would usually be guest speakers, and most of them were missionaries. And Mom and I would look at each other and say, "That's the kind of man you ought to marry. You want one of those when you grow up." So that was always instilled in me, that I would want to marry a returned missionary and marry in the Temple. It's very important to Mormon girls that we live our lives trying to keep ourselves worthy to go to the Temple and be married. And we believe that when we're married, it is not until death do we part, for time and eternity, that we'll be families forever. And that's all there is. I mean, everything that we do, you know, really centers around the family unit. That is the basic unit of the LDS Church; it's more important than any organization in the Church. The family is it. There's a saying that one of our former Church presidents said that kind of sums up our attitude: "No success can compensate for failure in the home." And that goes for men and women. It doesn't matter how successful a man is, how high on the corporate ladder, if he fails with his children and his wife and his home.

We Mormons are taught to live our religion more on a day-to-day basis rather than a once-a-week-type thing. I know that in this area Mormons are looked at very closely, and, boy, if one doesn't keep the standard, all fingers point. And it's difficult, because there're Protestants in the valley, and Methodists, and Lutherans. But, you know, people aren't really aware if they're not keeping their standard, because people aren't as aware of what that standard is. You know, you wouldn't say, "Oh! you're a Presbyterian and you did this and this and this, but you're not supposed to." Because it's not generally known what Presbyterians are not supposed to do. But everyone in the area knows that Mormons are not supposed to drink coffee, tea, or alcohol. They're not supposed to smoke, take any drugs, things like this. If people see a Mormon with a cigarette, everybody goes, "Ahhhhhh!" So I think the big difference is that we're really out in the spotlight, and people really know when we're not living up to the standard, whereas the other religions don't have it quite so hard.

There're a lot of people that say, "Oh, yeah, you're Mormons. You're the ones that don't smoke or drink." But I would rather have them say, "You're the Mormons, you're the ones that believe in strong families, you're the ones that believe in being honest and fair with your fellow man, you're the ones that believe in living a Christlike life and doing good to your fellow man."

So I admit that the Mormon church is a difficult one; it's a hard religion to live; it's not easy. And there're times when I think, Boy, maybe it's just too hard. The peer pressure is hard. In the women's meeting that we go to, called Relief Society, you're supposed to be uplifted, but many times I come home very depressed, thinking I'm not this perfect woman. I mean, I don't bake eighty loaves of bread a week, and I don't make all my husband's suits, and I don't grow a garden. So sometimes when you're sitting there, you think everybody's perfect but me. But you know that that's really ridiculous. They are teaching the conglomerate perfect women and they don't expect us to be that. You get talking individually with the sisters around you, and you know that we're all having struggles. You know, we all have our struggles, we're kind of expected to be full of hope and good cheer. The definition of *the gospel* is "good news," and we're supposed to be happy and full of hope and cheer and stuff. And, you know, financial pressures come along and it's hard to try and be up all the time, and a lot of Mormon women experience depression over the fact that we want our children to be like we want them to be. And, you know, kids are kids, and sometimes they deviate from that, and it's really devastating to us, but I think it's probably that way with any other people.

(She pauses and then laughs.) There's a cartoon in a Mormon cartoon book that we have, which is just hilarious. It's got this girl standing at a pulpit at BYU, it has a big *Y* on it, you know, and she says, "I came to this school not to get a career but to teach nuclear physics to my children in the home." You know . . . sure! You know? *(Laughs.)* Nuclear physics in the home! And, you know, there are Mormon girls all over the place getting really terrific careers, but the thing that the Church teaches is that you don't let that career supersede your real mission on the earth, which is to be a mother.

PART II: TUNNELS OF LOVE

Lois Erdmann

I grew up in a very conservative Lutheran family. And I've always attended church and I've always believed in God. But it wasn't until I was forty, until I had my out-of-body experience, that I understood the meaning of my faith.

She's a housewife, part-time secretary, and a member of the Good Shepherd Lutheran Church in Bismarck, North Dakota. Although much of her fifty-six-year life has been plagued by poor health, she's an amazingly attractive and radiant woman—just the sort you expect to find on a TV commercial sipping a piña colada on the deck of a Caribbean cruise ship.

Although I had three beautiful babies born to me, I had numerous problems having children, including several miscarriages. After my last miscarriage I had a lot of medical problems and was in and out of the hospital a great deal of the time. So it was determined that after my fortieth birthday I would have surgery to stop me from having any more kids. The night before I was ready to go to the hospital, I went to bed with a euphoric feeling of anticipation. At first I just assumed it was because I figured I'm finally going to be well; I'm going to have energy and I'll be able to do all the things I want with my family. The next morning when I awoke, I still had this wonderful feeling. I really don't have words to describe it, but I awoke in the wee hours of the morning and realized I was going to die, that I would not survive the surgery. *(She begins to cry softly.)* And this made absolutely no sense to me; I mean, how could I feel so good knowing that I was about to die and knowing that I had three young children that needed me, a husband that needed my support, and a widowed mother who was very dependent upon me? It just made no sense to me that I should feel so good about dying. I knew that heaven was supposed to be a wonderful place, but I couldn't conceive of leaving my family. So I just kind of pushed it out of my mind.

Well, I checked into the hospital later that day, and the next morning I went into surgery. And something went wrong. I remember seeing doctors and nurses talking to each other, saying that something had gone sour and that without another surgery to check the internal bleeding (my lungs had collapsed) there was absolutely no hope. They kept trying to put the second surgery off, because they felt I was too weak, but then, I guess, the final hour came and it was either do it or don't do it. It was during that second surgery that I went into a coma for ten days.

During the coma I had my first out-of-body experience, which I remember vividly. This was when a young nurse came to check my vital signs and couldn't find any. And I remember observing this, watching her as if I were watching a movie of a nurse coming into a hospital and checking a patient's vital signs. I was looking down on the scene, like a spirit. As I was observing this young nurse, she panicked . . . so she kept taking my vital signs over and over again. I knew I couldn't communicate with her, but I wanted to reassure her that it was okay, that everything would be fine. Then she called for some assistance, and a team came in with the paddles to revive my heart. I remember them getting set up for that, but then I blanked out.

The next experience, which followed very quickly upon that one, was my husband and my teenage daughter sitting at my bedside. I saw their positions, the clothing they had on, and I knew their thoughts. And their thoughts were that I was going to die. My daughter was wondering (*softly weeping*) how she was going to finish her life without her mother. She was a teenager, she had her whole life ahead of her, with dating, getting married someday, and all her thoughts were about how does one do this without a mother? How will I cope with these things without my mother? And yet she was not articulating these things in her own mind, but this was the emotion that was just charged through all her being. She was grieving for me, she was grieving for herself and her situation, and that's what was in her mind. My husband was experiencing somewhat the same thing, although he had a feeling of regret that he had not devoted more time to us, because he was so busy making a living for us, spending long hours at work. So he was feeling regret that he hadn't done more, and now it was too late. He was offering prayers . . . "God, if only it wouldn't be too late." But it was too late, and it was a conviction he had. So these were the emotions that were going on with them, and as I looked down on them, I wanted to communicate with them, I wanted to let them know that it was all right, that they should not have regret.

In my mind at the time was the phrase that Christ spoke to his disciples when they were in the boat during a storm. The disciples asked for help to get through, they wanted supernatural help to get through, and Christ said, "O ye of little faith." I had always read that as a rebuke, but then I saw that it wasn't a rebuke at all. It was Christ's expression of compassion and his understanding of their humanness: "If only you had more faith, you wouldn't be experiencing all this fear and anguish." So when Christ said, "O ye of little faith," those were the words that came to me, and that's what I felt for my husband and daughter. I wanted them to have more faith so they wouldn't be sad. And yet I understood and had compassion as to why they were experiencing this. I was very much aware of their humanness . . . that that was the way it was. So I had a compassion; I really hurt for them, but there was a perfect peace within me, a peace like I'd never felt before. And I haven't experienced it since.

The next thing I remember was my son Scott arriving. I followed him walking down a lit corridor coming to my room. He did not like hospitals, and still does' not like hospitals, but he knew that if he wanted to see me, he had to come. On the way to the hospital he stopped in the produce department of a market and bought some flowers for me. And Scott is always the clown; when he's in an uncomfortable situation, he clowns. So he walked in the room talking about the flowers because he was very uncomfortable. He was chattering about the flowers, and then when he saw my lifeless body lying in that hospital bed, he panicked and ran out of the room and down the corridor. A nurse saw him and asked if she could help him, and he thrust the flowers at the nurse and said, "Here, I brought these flowers for my mother, but I don't have a vase. Maybe you could get a vase and put them in water." Then the elevator arrived, he got on the elevator, and ran out of the hospital. And I remember thinking, If only Scott would understand. But I knew he would grow and understand someday, and I was only sad that he would have to learn that through a great deal of pain.

In her books Elisabeth Kübler-Ross writes about others who have experienced life after death. (But I didn't know about her work until a year after I got out of the hospital.) She talks about the sensation of being in a tunnel, a very dark tunnel, and approaching light. And I felt that I entered and traveled down that tunnel, and it was the last and most powerful experience I had. It was interesting, because I had a feeling of peace and anticipation, but also a bit of discomfort, because there was this very uncomfortable sound. The closest thing I can relate it to is when my automatic washer is on spin. It was kind of that sort of hum. But the farther I moved toward the light (the more I got inside the tunnel), the quieter the sound became. And I was glad to be leaving it behind. I did not see friends in the tunnel; I did not see people; and my life did not flash before me, which is different than some experiences I've heard of. All I remember is that I was getting closer and closer to the light. The light was pure and white, and yet it didn't blind me. It was not like trying to look at the sun on a beautiful hot day: It was comfort, and it was fine, and it was beautiful. I knew that the closer I came to the light, that at some point the light would envelop me and I would be on the other side. There was another side of that light, and I was sure of that, and I knew I was going to be there. I was anticipating it. It was warm, but there was discomfort with it. And just as I was about to be enveloped (in a blinking of the eye I'd be across, and I could see that it was going to be perfection and wonder), I was sent back.

No words were spoken. I did not hear my Lord's voice. But I

knew that I would be sent back. And I can't say that I regretted going back. Death was nothing to fear any longer, and I knew life wasn't permanent, so I came back without a regret. All I knew was that there was something left undone before I began my journey, so I had to come home and finish that. At the time, I believed that I was to come back and help my son Scott through the growth of his religious conviction, to explain to him death and dying and trust and faith. I knew I would do that, and I would be a part of Scott's Christian growth. It was a feeling of peace that when the right time presented itself, words would flow. A greater power, which I believe is my Lord, or the Holy Spirit, would give me the words to say to Scott. There was no urgency to this, but I knew that I would not be returning until this was done.

That was sixteen years ago, and it wasn't until this past Christmas that I became convinced that Scott had found his own deep Christian conviction. So maybe my mission is complete, but I can't be sure.

All I know is that I am here to glorify my Lord; the only reason I am here on earth is to glorify my Lord. I can do that in heaven, but the reason I'm here on earth is to allow myself to be used when he wants to use Lois. He uses many people to see that his will is done, that they live out their purpose in life. And each of us has a different way of fulfilling that potential. I believe that he wants me to live my life just as I am, adoring him, praising him, glorifying him, and then having that within me, that conviction in me, to reach out and touch others.

So now I'm doing all of the right things for the right reasons. When I was young, I did many good things, but they were done for the wrong reasons. Now I'm doing things to glorify my Lord, and *(her voice is filled with warmth and excitement)* it's a wonderful thing because before I do something now, I ask myself, Lois, why are you going to be involved in this? Is it to build your own popularity? Is that why you're doing it? Are you doing it for your own ego? Are you doing it because you want people to like you? Are you doing it because you don't want people not to like you? Why are you doing these things? If I become involved in this, is that going to glorify my Lord? Is it going to be using the gifts that he has given me in a very unique way? So you see, I believe that each individual on earth, no matter what your religious convictions are, is given gifts. And it's our choice whether or not we use them in a way that would give glory and honor to our Creator. How our Lord has honored me, and how he honors others, by giving us these opportunities . . . my God shares these things with me.

Cecilia A. Walen

One Hundred Eighth Street, Harlem, New York. The Franklin Plaza
Cooperative Apartments, a low-income housing complex.

I was born in Central America, a place called Belize, and was raised there as a Wesleyan Christian, went to a Wesleyan school. But I was troubled by the cultural aspect of religion, even at five or six, and the hypocrisy of it. I saw that the minister said one thing and did another, so I became very rebellious. By the time I was twelve, I didn't want to go to church anymore, and I told the other kids not to put any money in the collection plate, because the church was beautiful enough already. You know, all the money was just going to the minister. I was really angry, because I felt very spiritual, but I didn't see any spirituality in the Church. I used to say to God, "Why do you put me down here around people who don't do right? They don't show me who and what you are. How could you do this to me?" God just said to me, "In time, in time." So I never despised the idea of worshiping God. What I was concerned about was *how* I did it, okay?

On my fourteenth birthday we had a terrible, terrible hurricane. And it was devastating. It was the first time I really recognized death. I'll never forget when the man on the radio said, "Ladies and gentlemen, Hurricane Hattie is approaching Belize, and there is no way that it can be stopped." And they sang the national anthem. They said the Lord's Prayer. And the man said, "Ladies and gentlemen, may God bless us all," and all we heard was like "ch-h-h-h-." And the rain was unreal; I mean, the water was like boiling. And we were in a shelter, and people were just screaming and going all over the place. And the water was just coming in. And people were praying to God; I mean, prayers appeared from every corner of the place! Eventually the water started coming in, and the man said if it rose any higher, there's nothing we could do. And that was the closest I had ever come to feeling death. And I remember my sister and I, we sat there and we just prayed. We just said, "Well, if this is the way God want us to go, we gonna have to go."

But then it was over. Just that quick, you know. Twenty-four hours later the wind died down. And there's five feet of mud and a lot of dead bodies under there, and then the whole epidemic process started. And I remember we went back to our house. The only thing that happened to it was that it had fallen off its stilts. But the house was fine. It was filled with mud. But some of my friends got killed. Some of them lost everything. And I remember that I just wanted to know why God wanted to do this. How could he do this to me? I thought, What did I do wrong? Because, you know, they always told you that if you do something wrong, God will punish you. And to me this was a serious punishment. And then, to make things worse, the American government offered refugee status to anyone who had any family in America, so my sister and myself moved up here to America. I'm still trying to search that out with God, being stuck in the middle of a hurricane and then taken from my country and brought here. It was in winter. And of course there was a whole new ritual of learning, because we'd never seen snow. We'd never seen this many lights. It was just overwhelming. It was awesome. And my whole struggle with God and spirituality intensified here; I just became more questioning.

I managed to get through college, got married, and had three children. I got a good job at Young and Rubicam advertising agency. I was a traffic coordinator, you know. I did all the billing and purchasing and everything for ads. Things were going along okay for several years until, you know, my husband left me. And I just sat there one day and realized that here I was, I had three children and I had to take care of them. And I have to take care of myself. Somehow I didn't know how to do either. And then I really began to get into God, really began to get into what it is that God really means to me. If I was gonna raise these children and if I was gonna raise myself and take care of myself, I felt God had to be a part of this, you know. So I went to a Moravian church on Staten Island. And I said, "I'm gonna really deal with God. Forget the minister, forget the people. God is what I want." And at that time I was reading the Bible. And I would sit down with the Bible and I would try to read it and find God in it. And sometimes it was like, "God, I can't see, I can't hear you. Where are you?"

Then I became ill. The doctor called it meningitis, but I actually had MS. He said the infection had gone into the spine, so they put me into a room, isolated me. The doctor said that they couldn't do anything to help me. And I went through this death process where I was laying there, and I heard them say, "She's dying." I was saying, "No, I'm in here. I'm not dying. They can't hear me." Then I realized that who me was, was not what they thought me was. And I said, "They don't know me. They've never known me. I'm not dying, I'm right in here." It's like when you have a dream and feel like you're falling off a cliff, and you're dreaming you're screaming for help, and nothing is coming out; nobody's seeing you, but you're screaming at the top of your lungs. That's how I was. I was screaming, "I'm in here. I'm not dying, I'm alive, I'm in here." Because I could hear they were giving up on me.

Then all of a sudden I began to get very tired. I had a tiredness that I'd never felt before. I mean, real tired. But I wasn't tired physically. It was like darkness was coming over me. Then I saw my daughter and I saw my son. And I saw my daughter as just concerned about her physical beauty, because she had grown to be lovely. Men had just given in to her every whim, and she had just totally become an outrageous little whore. You know, seriously. She was just all over the place. And that hurt me. I said, "Look, they're dealing with her physically. They're not dealing with the soul of this girl. And look at what is happening to her." And then I looked at my son and I saw the same thing; because of his physical beauty the same thing was happening. Everybody was just giving in to him; whatever he wants, he was just getting it.

I said, "No, I can't die. I've got to save these children. Because nobody understands them. Look at what they're doing to them. They're not dealing with the soul of the child." And while I'm going through all of this, this darkness is coming closer and closer. This darkness is descending over me. And then the darkness engulfed me. And it stayed for like a split second. Then I came back again. And I felt like there was an inner me, an inner person inside of me, and that the head of that inner person was here, right here, at my forehead. That's weird, the head of the inner person was at my forehead. And I said, "No, I don't want to die. I don't want to die. Please, I don't want to die." And then the darkness engulfed me again. This time it stayed a little longer, because when I did come to, my head was like by my neck. And I said, "Something is slipping out, it's like my whole body was sliding right out of me." And it was by my neck. And I said, "Please, I don't want to die. Please, I don't want to die. Please, I've got to come back to save the children. I can't die." By that time the darkness had gotten me; it must have held me a little longer, because when I did come to, my head was down to my waist. And then it hit me again, and by the time I woke up from it, it was by my knees; my head had slid down by my knees. And I saw this body just sliding right out, till eventually every time I got engulfed by the darkness, it slid out a little bit more. Eventually my head was to the tip of my toe and this body floated right out.

I said, "I don't want to die, I don't want to die." And I knew it was not this body saying it didn't want to die. It was whatever that body was that had just come out. Then my body began to vibrate, and it was like I saw, instead of a body, trillions of cells. My whole body was just little, little, little things, little circles. And then all of a sudden my foot began to shrink and the cells began to reduce. And it just kept reducing, reducing, reducing, reducing. And ten became eight, and eight became six, and six became four, just like that. Until eventually it was only two. And then they came together and there was only one. And then, all of a sudden, I was going back. It was like a narrow canal, and I was just swimming back up it. Then I got to the other side, and there was total and complete darkness.

The next thing I remember, I saw this light. And I was still saying, "I don't want to die." The light was coming toward me, and I said, "I don't want to die. I don't want to die." When I approached the light, it said, "What do you want?" I said, "I don't want to die. I want to go back. I want to save the children." And it says to me, "You want to return." I said yes. And the light says, "What do you want to do?" I said, "I want to save the children." And it said to me, "As long as you take care of the children, you're always going to be taken care of. But if you don't take care of the children, you're going to suffer." And I said, "Yes, I understand." And it said, "Okay, fine." From that moment on I don't know what happened to me. But the doctor said to me that he was sitting in the nursing center in the hospital and he said something just told him to take 1 cc of a certain antibiotic and put cortisone in it. He said he felt that this was what he had to do. And then the nurses said to him that I was already dead, what was the use. And he said, "Well, we have nothing to lose."

So I came back, but I came back knowing God. I came back having a real sense of who God was in me and that I had made a covenant with God. I said I wanted to do something, and I had to do it. I wanted to save the children. This was my whole thrust in life from that point on, that I was gonna save the children. And that's what I've done.

I realized after the illness that my belief in God was what made me overcome the illness, my belief that God never inflicts any harm on you. You are the one who, in terms of how you interpret what is happening to you, create harm or imbalance or disharmony. But if you look at everything as a lesson, something good and valuable for you, you can overcome anything. I believe that.

Note: Cecilia Walen later converted to Islam and changed her name to Sayiddah Ahmed. She then went on the hajj, or pilgrimage to Mecca, nearly blind and in a wheelchair. "Before I embraced Islam, I remember saying very clearly to myself, my children, and all my friends, 'I want to know who God is.' Two months later I met someone who was a Muslim, gave me a Koran, and I've been on the path of knowing God ever since. Making the hajj cleared a lot of things out for me. And I feel that the Koran is the book, the only book I can go to, where I can find all the answers that I am looking for in life. I no longer want to know God. Now all I want to do is live in a godlike manner."

Epilogue

John Schneeweis, Jr.

THE DISTANT VIEW

We must all become familiar with the thought of
death if we want to grow into really good people. We
need not think of it every day or every hour. But
when the path of life leads us to some vantage point
where the scene around us fades away and we contemplate the distant view right to the end, let us not
close our eyes. Let us pause for a moment, look at
the distant view, and then carry on.

Thinking about death in this way produces true
love for life. When we are familiar with death, we
accept each week, each day, as a gift. Only if we are
able thus to accept life—bit by bit—does it become
precious.

—Albert Schweitzer

*Saint Paul, Minnesota. It's a sweltering 104 degrees outside, I don't
have an air conditioner in my car, and by the time I arrive at his modest
home I'm soaking in sweat. He greets me at the door with a kindly smile
and offers me some juice. "I'm not used to sharing my story, so if we
can be conversational, that might be more helpful."*

*Last February he was diagnosed as having adenocarcinoma, a glan-
dular cancer of unknown origin. It's estimated he has a year or less to
live. In 1979, while he was completing his Ph.D. in psychology, his wife,
Sally, contracted lymphoma cancer. "She's had radiation treatment, a
bone marrow transplant, and has three or four times been within a breath
of death."*

*Prior to his illness he worked as an academic adviser at the University
of Minnesota and as a facilitator of group seminars at the university's
Hubert Humphrey Reflective Leadership Center. He's forty-four and the
father of two children.*

I think I've sort of entered this period of cancer, and confronting
death, with a notion that when I die, that will be it. People will
remember me (hopefully), but I don't give much thought about there

being something that comes after. I've already received enough, and that's having had the opportunity to be sort of sentient, to be conscious and alive; to have this consciousness born. And that is gift enough. I see nothing that suggests that there should be an afterlife for me, that it needs to be.

What has made the last eight months interesting is confronting that notion and sort of coming up against my wife, Sally's, very different conception that there is some consciousness after death. And what has made this most interesting for us (oh, I don't know if it made it interesting, but at least made it something that's tangible and something that has brought about deep reflection) is that she had cancer too. And having gone through that experience with her, my feelings about that, and her feelings about that, and now going through it myself, having those feelings reversed, she's now seeing me as the one that may die and now I see myself as the person that may die. So we each have very different notions of what it means to die, and what happens to consciousness, and how that reflects how we live right now.

So it's posed an interesting problem for me. One that I haven't resolved. I'm not sure, though, whether it's made a difference in terms of how I've chosen to live my life. My sense, I suppose, is that if there is some form of consciousness that is in a sense born again when I die, or continues, or whatever, I'm not sure that that reality (if I can use that term), but if that reality exists, whether it makes any difference how I live. I would see it as, I think, a pure gift. So, I think, I still see living my life as though it is simply contained in this existence, and no more. So what really matters to me is what I do now, and the experiences that I have now. And, you know, there is an intensity about and around these days, a specialness about them, even a wonder about them, even amid the pain, or whatever, that wasn't present before. There is a sense that this life that we have is a gift, and this is very present to me now.

Someone once mentioned to me that our time with others and our good-byes to others should be based on—in some ideal sense— the fact that you will never see them again. If this was the last time I were ever to see you, what would we do together, how would we say good-bye? There's sort of an intensity about that connection that should be there all the time, and it isn't. It wasn't when I was healthy, and it's not there when I'm sick. But there are days when I approach some of that, and it really generates a kind of intensity about relationships that is not present when you aren't confronted with death. I think people can see it. Sally had the same feeling. There was a friend of ours who came over at a point where Sally was getting well again (this was a miracle, because no one expected her to live), and Sally was just in a horseshit mood. She was angry, and just kind of pissy about life in general, and this friend came over and got really angry at her because she'd sort of become normal again. She wasn't taking every day as this wonderful gift that we're given, and how wonderful it is to be alive. So her friend chastised her for what she saw as sort of falling into the normality trap.

Still, confronting the reality of an imminent death is somewhat paradoxical. On the one hand I'm doing this self-hypnosis, doing visualization, doing relaxation and meditation, going through chemotherapy, trying to stay healthy by exercising, all of these kinds of things to say, you know, regardless of what those physicians say, "I'm going to beat this. I'm not ready to give up this gift yet." On the other hand I'm preparing myself for the very real chance that in six months I'll die. There are many days that the sense of life that I have within me is heightened beyond any other period in my life. The awareness of being alive, and being conscious what a treasure that is, whether there's some afterlife or not. For all its suffering and tragedy it still is wonderful. In fact sometimes, when I'm in public, it takes everything I have to keep from just whooping out loud at the wonderfulness of being alive. Sure, you know its tears and its passion, its poverty and its hate. And I know there were periods of time when I went through the Job kind of sense that "How can you do this?" and "This must be evidence that there is no God," that there is no personality or consciousness, no "ground of being," or whatever theologians use to describe that presence. But in this balance of trying to keep this tension alive, I've just held on to the sense of the wonderfulness of life and the love that's in it.

I think evil in the world is still problematic. You know, how can you love a world that has so much evil in it? But, you know, in some sense there's a connection that might almost even be necessary: Without evil, without suffering, however we may term it, I'm not sure we would ever have a conception of love. I think in some respects it's sort of the nonperfection or the imperfection in lives that makes love possible. There is some connection that I don't understand. I don't think you or I would be a very interesting person, or would even have much of a capacity to generate love in each other or in others, if we were capable of perfection, if we didn't almost kind of present some of the faults that we condemn and say, "I'm going to work to get rid of these." You know, it continues to baffle me and to confuse me intellectually as to how that can be the case. How I can say that about a world that basically did nothing to avert the Cambodian holocaust, or the Jewish holocaust. How do you love a world, and love people that do that . . . permit that to occur? And all the other kinds of small violences that we allow. And yet, in some way, I really feel that it's those kinds of things, writ large and writ small, that even allow us to love. And I'm not sure how I get there intellectually, but it's something that I feel very strongly.

The suffering that my wife and I have experienced together has drawn out a real sense of care between us. In a book he wrote Henri Nouwen makes a distinction between curing and caring. And what he's suggesting is that much of modern culture has oriented itself around curing but not caring. Caring involves, for me, a sense of letting go, of not being in control. In some of the work that I have done, some of the consulting I have done with hospital chaplains, I have tried to ask the question, What does it mean to be a caring person in a culture that is curing oriented? And that, in a sense, is to be with someone as they die, and not necessarily to keep them from dying. I remember, for example, one of the episodes that my wife had when, as a result of her immunosuppression, she got shingles (we were out in California). And because of her immunosuppression she got them very, very bad: blisters about the size of grapefruits. And we had to fly back to the Twin Cities, had to pack her in ice because her whole metabolic system went haywire. And because of the drugs she took for pain control she became paranoid. I was with her that evening till about 2:00 A.M. and I physically couldn't stay with her anymore. I had to go home and get some sleep. And when I told her that, that I couldn't stay with her, she sort of accused me of being a very mean person. And it's funny, but in reflecting back on that, she was conscious enough to remember that she didn't want to say, "You're a mean man," but instead said, "You're a mean person for leaving me." She didn't want to be sexist. (*Smiles.*) So I went home. And on the drive home, which was about three o'clock in the morning, I sort of let go of curing her. I was so convinced that my energy could save her. And it was in the context of that evening that I realized I couldn't. And that I had to let go of that, but I still had to be with her, to be present to her. And that's a very very different stance, for me, than to be with her as a curer, trying to make her well. To be in control of that.

I've thought that this tension between curing and caring is akin to the realization that some Eastern religions have, whether it be Hinduism or Buddhism, that suggest that you work at the world with that tension. You work like the dickens to cure this person, but you also have the stance that it is not connected to whether you succeed or not. So there is a real sense of being able to let go of whether or not you are successful in the activity that you're engaged in. Like I

said before, I work like the dickens to stay alive. But I also work at letting go of that, and saying it's not important whether I live or die. What's important is what I'm doing right now. How am I present to others? You know, how am I caring? What does it mean to be a caring parent and not a curing parent? You know, a lot of people, when they've heard I have cancer, really want to do something to help me. It's very human. But what helps me most is not what someone does, whether it be cooks a meal or rubs my back, or whatever it might be to make me feel better ... sometimes it's just their presence, their willingness just to sit with me. And to be there. And I might not need to ask them to do a darn thing. You know, it may just be to be there to hold my hand. It's a very special kind of thing, I think, to be able to approach others and, in a more general sense, to be able to be a caring rather than a curing person.

You know, in suggesting that we talk about my spiritual and intellectual journey, you've generated a metaphor within which to talk about these kinds of things. We all have images of journey. You know, you start someplace and you're going to someplace, and it carries certain images with it. It's a very powerful metaphor, that my life is a journey. And what do you do on that journey? How do you get there? How do you overcome the obstacles that present themselves on your way to wherever it is that you're going? There are times I see that metaphor as a very important one, and it can circumscribe my experience. I can talk about my life in that context of this journey, and from a very early age I've been concerned about right and wrong, about what does it mean to die, and working around all those kinds of issues. The eventual journey taking me to death and what leads beyond that. There are times, however, that I think the metaphor of a journey is too linear as a way of talking about my life and the lives that we live. That in some context it's maybe too future oriented, maybe too past oriented, and not enough with the present, you know, just kind of being. I have a friend who says, "If you don't know where you're goin', any road will lead you there." So there are times that I say, "Right, I gotta know where I'm going so I'll be on the right road." And that's journey talk. But, very honestly, there are times in which I have absolutely no idea where I'm going. And if I had to kind of circumscribe my life in those contexts, uffta, I have nothing. Sometimes I'm on this road, and I'm not sure very much why, and I don't know where it's going. And sometimes where it's going isn't as important as what's just happening where I am. I mean, "journey" and "where you're going" and "overcoming obstacles" and whatever—I think that indicates a certain kind of control over where we go. Or that it's important that we get control of where we go. I'm not sure that's accurate. Most of us end up on roads that weren't connected to where that journey was going at all.

Some people have asked me, "John, the doctors are saying, right or wrong, that you've got six months to a year. What are you going to do with that time? Are there things that you want to sort of put together, that you didn't get done?" And yeah, sure. All kinds of things. Am I going to live my life in such a way over the next twelve months that I'm going to just work like hell to finish those things, just to up my score, so that my success or failure rating on this journey is greater or less? I've thought about how do I want to spend the next six months of my life. Some of that is just doing what I'm doing, being who I am. A really important part of that is being around people that I care about. Having lunch with them, working with them. And having time to myself. The only thing that I hope for myself over that period of time is the physical strength to be able to do that. That might not be, because it hasn't been so far. The last six months the pain of the tumors and the reaction to chemotherapy has meant that I haven't had the physical strength to do those kinds of things. I haven't worked since April.

My daughter, from a song that she heard somewhere, put together a little saying that I have: "Your life is not your work, and your work is not your job." I haven't been able to do my job, and I haven't been able to do my work, but I'm doing pretty well doing my life. Part of that is that I've had to work on how I care for myself, that I don't get angry at myself when I'm not able to cure myself. I think, ultimately, this business that we're about, this being-alive stuff, has a lot to do with what Joseph Campbell calls "following your bliss." What do you do with life, what is the meaning of life? He says the main concern is not what life means but what kind of experience it is . . . sort of going after what you feel good about.

Postscript: John Schneeweis, Jr., died on November 20, 1988.

About the Author

Phillip L. Berman was educated in philosophy and religion at the University of California and at Harvard. He is the author of more than twelve non-fiction books, among them *The Courage of Conviction* (nominated for the Kennedy Book Award) and, with Connie Goldman, *The Ageless Spirit*. He is founder and past-president of The Center for the Study of Contemporary Belief and a leading lecturer and writer on spiritual development over the course of the human life cycle. He lives in Boulder, Colorado, with his wife, journalist Anne Gordon, and three year old son, Aaron.

For information on Phillip Berman's lectures, seminars, or spiritual enrichment retreats, please write to:

Phillip L. Berman
5295 Centennial Trail
Boulder, CO 80303.